MCSE Guide to

Microsoft® Windows® 2000 Networking

MCSE Guide to

Microsoft® Windows® 2000 Networking

Kelly Caudle

Walter J. Glenn

COURSE
TECHNOLOGY

THOMSON LEARNING

Australia • Canada • Mexico • Singapore • Spain • United Kingdom • United States

COURSE TECHNOLOGY
™
THOMSON LEARNING

MCSE Guide to Microsoft Windows 2000 Networking

by Kelly Caudle and Walter J. Glenn

Managing Editor:
Stephen Solomon

Senior Product Manager:
Dave George

Marketing Manager:
Toby Shelton

Production Editor:
Elena Montillo

Associate Product Manager:
Elizabeth Wessen

Editorial Assistant:
Janet Aras

Quality Assurance Manager:
John Bosco

Manufacturing Coordinator:
Denise Sandler

Cover Design:
Joseph Lee, Black Fish Design

Text Design:
GEX Publishing Services

Composition House:
GEX Publishing Services

BRIEF
Contents

TABLE OF
Contents

CHAPTER TEN
Configuring Certificate Services   **317**

APPENDIX
Exam Objectives for MCSE Certification Exam # 70-216:
Implementing and Administering a Microsoft Windows 2000 Network
Infrastructure   **343**

GLOSSARY   **349**

INDEX   **361**

Preface

Hello and welcome to the *MCSE Guide to Microsoft Windows 2000 Networking*. This book prepares you for Microsoft Exam 70-216: *Implementing and Administering a Microsoft® Windows® 2000 Network Infrastructure*. Throughout this book, skills needed to deploy and manage Windows 2000 networking components are constantly reinforced. It is assumed that readers of this book either already have certification in Windows 2000 Professional and Server or that training has been completed in both products.

This book offers training in the skills needed to install, configure, manage, monitor, and troubleshoot Windows 2000 networking. In particular, topics covered include proper use of networking protocols and networking services such as Dynamic Host Configuration Protocol, Domain Name Service, Windows Internet Name Service, Routing and Remote Access, IP routing, IP security, Internet Connection Sharing, Network Address Translation, and Certificate Services. In each chapter, the text is reinforced with relevant end-of-chapter review questions, hands-on exercises, and case studies. After completing this text, you should be able to manage daily operations of a Windows 2000 networking infrastructure.

The Intended Audience

This book is intended for individuals and networking professionals who must implement and support Windows 2000 networking on a day-to-day basis. In addition, this text is for individuals who wish to obtain Microsoft certification on this topic. The materials contained in this book are designed to provide readers with the information needed to prepare for the certification exam.

Chapter 1, "Windows 2000 Networking Overview," introduces the major new features in Windows 2000 and describes the four Windows 2000 product family members, Windows 2000 Professional, Windows 2000 Server, Windows 2000 Advanced Server, and Windows 2000 Datacenter Server. Also, it explains the Windows 2000 networking architecture and defines the major networking protocols supported by Windows 2000. Finally, it introduces many of the networking services that are the basis for later chapters.

Chapter 2, "Implementing, Configuring, and Troubleshooting Networking Protocols," discusses the TCP/IP protocol stack. In particular, it explores TCP/IP addressing, subnetting, and packet filtering. It also describes when and how to use static and dynamic TCP/IP addressing. Another important topic presented in Chapter 2 is troubleshooting TCP/IP using command line tools such as ping and tracert. The chapter also presents the theory, installation, and configuration of NWLink IPX/SPX. Finally, it details optimizing network bindings.

Chapter 3, "Dynamic Host Configuration Protocol," introduces the concept of dynamically leasing IP addresses and configuring clients to obtain IP addresses dynamically. It also describes how to install, configure, manage, monitor and troubleshoot the DHCP server service. Finally, it discusses integration of DHCP with Active Directory and DNS.

Chapter 4, "Domain Name System," provides an overview of the Domain Name System and describes the features of DNS in Windows 2000. In addition, it details how to install and configure DNS in Windows 2000, both for the server and for clients. The chapter also provides the steps necessary to create resource records manually. Finally, it discusses the proper tools to manage, monitor, and troubleshoot DNS.

Chapter 5, "Windows Internet Name Service," defines NetBIOS names and NetBIOS name resolution. It also details how to install and configure WINS in Windows 2000. In particular, the chapter describes how to configure NetBIOS name resolution and WINS replication. Finally, the chapter relates the proper steps to manage and monitor WINS.

Chapter 6, "Remote Access in Windows 2000," details the correct methods for creating inbound RAS connections using remote access policies and profiles. It continues the discussion of remote access technologies with an in-depth discussion of authentication protocols, encryption protocols, and the methods used to manage and monitor remote access. Finally, the chapter also shows how to configure virtual private network connections.

Chapter 7, "IP Routing in Windows 2000," focuses on using Windows 2000 server as a router within a network consisting of multiple network segments. It details the proper methods to view and create static routes, install dynamic routing protocols such as RIP and OSPF, and manage and monitor IP routing. Throughout the chapter, internal and border routing protocols are discussed at length.

Chapter 8, "IP Security," describes how to enable IPSec to increase security on Windows 2000 networks. It details how to configure IPSec for transport and tunnel mode. It also enumerates how to customize policies and rules within IPSec. Finally, it covers management and monitoring of IPSec.

Chapter 9, "Network Address Translation in Windows 2000," explains the differences between Internet Connection Sharing (ICS) and Network Address Translation (NAT). It describes the address translation process. It also presents the proper technique to install and configure both ICS and NAT on Windows 2000. Finally, it details how to manage and monitor NAT.

The final chapter, **Chapter 10**, "Configuring Certificate Services," describes the components of a public key infrastructure and the public/private key encryption process. It provides a definition of certificates and their uses. It also teaches how to install and configure the Microsoft Certificate Server to allow for issuing, managing, and revoking certificates. Finally, it delivers the proper steps to remove Encrypting Files System (EFS) recovery keys.

Features

To aid you in fully understanding Windows 2000 concepts, there are many features in this book designed to match the ways in which you learn.

- **Chapter Objectives.** Each chapter in this book begins with a detailed list of the concepts to be mastered within that chapter. This list provides you with a quick reference to the contents of that chapter, as well as a useful study aid.

- **Illustrations and Tables.** Numerous illustrations of server screens and components aid you in the visualization of common setup steps, theories, and concepts. In addition, many tables provide details and comparisons of both practical and theoretical information and can be used for a quick review of topics.

- **Chapter Summaries.** Each chapter's text is followed by a summary of the concepts it has introduced. These summaries provide a helpful way to recap and revisit the ideas covered in each chapter.

- **Review Questions.** The end-of-chapter assessments begin with a set of review questions that reinforce the ideas introduced in each chapter. These questions not only ensure that you have mastered the concepts, but are written like the test questions to help you become familiar with the types of questions used in Microsoft certification examinations.

- **Hands-on Projects.** Although it is important to understand the theory behind server and networking technology, nothing can improve upon real-world experience. To this end, along with theoretical explanations, each chapter provides numerous hands-on projects aimed at providing you with real-world implementation experience.

- **Case Project.** Located at the end of each chapter is a multi-part case project. In these real-world scenarios, you implement the skills and knowledge gained in the chapter through implementation and administration of a Windows 2000 network.

Text and Graphic Conventions

Wherever appropriate, additional information and exercises have been added to this book to help you better understand what is being discussed in the chapter. Icons throughout the text alert you to additional materials. The icons used in this textbook are as follows.

Tips are included from the authors' experience that provide extra information about how to attack a problem, how to set up Windows 2000 Server for a particular need, or what to do to in certain real-world situations.

The Note icon is used to present additional helpful material related to the subject being described.

The cautions are included to help you anticipate potential mistakes or problems so you can prevent them from happening.

Each Hands-on Project in this book is preceded by the Hands-on icon and a description of the exercise that follows.

Case project icons mark the case project. These are more involved, scenario-based assignments. In this extensive case example, you are asked to implement independently what you have learned.

About your CertPack

The CertPack envelope bound into this book contains additional training tools designed to prepare you for MCSE certification. On the CD-ROM you will find CoursePrep exam preparation software, which provides 50 sample MCSE exam questions mirroring the look and feel of the MCSE exams, and CourseSim simulation software, which allows you to perform tasks in a simulated Windows 2000 environment. Accompanying the CD-ROM is a coupon for a discount on your MCSE exam at any Prometric testing center.

Instructor's Materials

The following supplemental materials are available when this book is used in a classroom setting. All of the supplements available with this book are provided to the instructor on a single CD-ROM.

Electronic Instructor's Manual. The Instructor's Manual that accompanies this textbook includes:

- Additional instructional material to assist in class preparation, including suggestions for lecture topics, suggested lab activities, tips on setting up a lab for the hands-on assignments, and alternative lab setup ideas in situations where lab resources are limited.

- Solutions to all end-of-chapter materials, including the Review Questions, Hands-on Projects, Case and Optional Team Case assignments.

ExamView®

This textbook is accompanied by ExamView, a powerful testing software package that allows instructors to create and administer printed, computer (LAN-based), and Internet exams. ExamView includes hundreds of questions that correspond to the topics covered in this text, enabling students to generate detailed study guides that include page references for further review. The computer-based and Internet testing components allow students to take exams at their computers, and also save the instructor time by grading each exam automatically.

PowerPoint presentations. This book comes with Microsoft PowerPoint slides for each chapter. These are included as a teaching aid for classroom presentation, to make available to students on the network for chapter review, or to be printed for classroom distribution. Instructors, please feel at liberty to add your own slides for additional topics you introduce to the class.

Acknowledgements

Once again, first and foremost, I want to thank the Lord for giving me the opportunity to write another book for Course Technology. I would also like to thank Stephen Solomon, managing editor, for considering me as an author for a book in the MCSE 2000 series. In addition, I must thank Dave George, product manager, for showing patience and understanding well beyond the call of duty when this author missed a deadline (Okay, maybe it was more than one, but that is just between us, right?). I also want to pay special thanks to Walter Glenn, my co-author. Walter, thank you for stepping in to help with the completion of this project.

As with my first book project, I cannot forget to thank the wonderful team I work with at Stanly Community College. As usual, everyone was willing to lend a hand when I needed it most. In short, you are the best team I've ever worked with. I also want to thank my former co-worker Bill Frey. Bill, your unique blend of wit, intelligence, and inspiration are second to none. —Kelly Caudle

Dedication

I must thank my wonderful wife Susan for putting up with me over the course of this project. Susan, you are the best wife a man could have.—Kelly Caudle

For my wife, Susan —Walter Glenn

Read This Before You Begin

TO THE STUDENT

This book provides you with the information you need to install and manage network services on a Windows 2000 network. Each chapter presents a different networking service or concept that is an integral part of every modern day network. Every chapter also ends with review questions, hands-on projects, and case project assignments that are written to provide you with real-world questions. Your instructor will provide you with answers to the review questions and additional information about the hands-on projects. Although this book is designed for use in a classroom environment, the hands-on labs can be easily modified to work within the confines of your own home network. Please ask your instructor for more information on what may be necessary to perform the labs in a test environment at home.

TO THE INSTRUCTOR

Each pair of students will require two computers configured as shown in the setup figure. One machine should be configured to dual boot Windows 2000 Server (Advanced Server may also be used, but it is not required for the exercises) and Windows 2000 Professional.

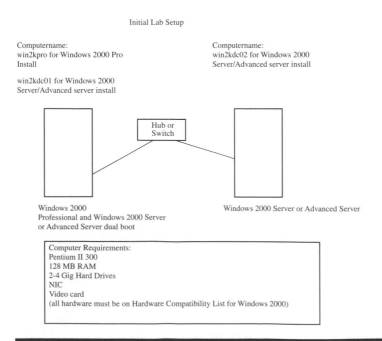

Initial Lab Setup

Computername:
win2kpro for Windows 2000 Pro Install

win2kdc01 for Windows 2000 Server/Advanced server install

Computername:
win2kdc02 for Windows 2000 Server/Advanced server install

Hub or Switch

Windows 2000 Professional and Windows 2000 Server or Advanced Server dual boot

Windows 2000 Server or Advanced Server

Computer Requirements:
Pentium II 300
128 MB RAM
2-4 Gig Hard Drives
NIC
Video card
(all hardware must be on Hardware Compatibility List for Windows 2000)

Throughout the hands-on exercises, this computer uses the computer name of win2kpro for the Windows 2000 Professional install and win2kdc01for the Server install. The second computer in the pair should have Windows 2000 Server installed with win2kdc02 as the computer name. Although the naming schemes hold consistent throughout the hands-on exercises, you should feel free to change names based on your classroom environment. In a classroom environment, you will be required to issue students computer names that are unique. It is suggested that you start with the base names above and then change the ending number. For instance, in a classroom of four students, the dual boot machine in the second pair would be named win2kpro2 in Windows 2000 Professional and win2kdc03 in Windows 2000 Server. The other machine would then be named win2kdc04. You could then continue to extend the scheme to meet your classroom needs.

Each machine used for the hands-on labs must meet the following minimum requirements:

Windows 2000 Professional

- All hardware listed on Windows 2000 Hardware Compatibility List
- Pentium 133 MHZ or higher
- 32 MB of RAM
- VGA or better resolution monitor
- Mouse or pointing device
- High density 3.5 inch floppy disk drive
- 12X or faster CD-ROM drive
- One or more hard disks with at least 2 GB free space

Windows 2000 Server

- All hardware listed on Windows 2000 Hardware Compatibility List
- Pentium 133 MHZ or higher
- 128 MB of RAM (Microsoft recommends 64 MB of RAM, but the networking services in this book require more RAM)
- VGA or better resolution monitor
- Mouse or pointing device
- High density 3.5 inch floppy disk drive
- 12X or faster CD-ROM drive
- One or more hard disks with at least 2 GB free space

1

WINDOWS 2000 NETWORKING
OVERVIEW

After reading this chapter and completing the exercises you will be able to:

♦ Describe many of the new features in Windows 2000

♦ Detail differences between the four main Windows 2000 product family members

♦ Explain the Windows 2000 networking architecture

♦ Define the major networking protocols supported by Windows 2000

♦ Recognize many of the networking services available in Windows 2000

New features and services in Windows 2000 raise the bar for the modern **network operating system (NOS)**. This chapter introduces you to several of these new features. It also describes the four products found in the Windows 2000 product family. In addition, this entire book focuses on networking, protocols, and networking services. This chapter introduces you to each of these topics, in particular, the Windows 2000 network architecture, networking protocols, and networking services.

NEW FEATURES IN WINDOWS 2000

Windows 2000 includes most features found in Windows NT 4.0 and expands those features to include many new and useful items. The people at Microsoft listened to what customers needed in order to expand their networks and used many of their suggestions in Windows 2000. The list that follows enumerates many of the new features in the operating system. The list is not comprehensive. Instead, it focuses on the most important new features and two features that were once part of either the Enterprise version of NT or available only via add-on software: clustering and terminal services, respectively. The most notable new features are:

- *Active Directory (AD) services*: Active Directory is an enterprise-level directory service used to simplify administration and management of Windows 2000 networks. AD extends the Windows NT 4.0 domain model by building a framework for combining many domains into a single AD tree or forest. Within this overall directory, objects represent all networking resources, such as users, computers, and printers. **Objects** are components within the AD structure that can have **attributes** defined for them. For example, user accounts are objects about which attributes such as First and Last name can be defined. AD operates in two different modes: **native mode** and **mixed mode**. Native mode is used on networks where only Windows 2000 domain controllers reside, on a network either fully migrated to Windows 2000 or on a network with Windows 2000 newly installed. Mixed mode allows Windows NT 4.0 domain controllers and Windows 2000 domain controllers to function and reside in the same domain. This design allows for coexistence until all Windows NT 4.0 domain controllers can be migrated to Windows 2000. This book discusses Active Directory as it relates to networking services. For more information on Active Directory, refer to *MCSE Guide to Microsoft Windows 2000 Active Directory* (ISBN 0-619-01600-0, copyright 2001).

- *Enhanced security*: Windows 2000 uses **Kerberos version 5** security to provide client-to-server or user-to-Active Directory authentication. Kerberos replaces the weak security found in the Windows NT 4.0 NT LAN Manager security with a shared secret key authentication system. Unfortunately, in a mixed mode configuration, Windows 2000 can and does allow authentication using Windows NT LAN manager methods. Therefore, you should upgrade all domain controllers to native mode to take full advantage of Kerberos security.

- *Encrypting file system (EFS)*: Windows 2000 extends existing Windows NT 4.0 attributes allowed for files and folders with the encrypting file system or EFS. EFS, like the compression attribute, requires that a drive be formatted with NTFS. EFS allows file and folder encryption on a per user basis.

- *IP security (IPSec) protocol*: This set of predominately network layer protocols provides data integrity, end-to-end confidentiality, and network authentication. IPSec allows encryption of data packets within a local area network (LAN) or across a wide area network (WAN). Windows 2000 implements IPSec below the Transport layer of the **Open System Interconnection (OSI)** model. This makes IPSec policies transparent to normal network users.

■ *Plug and play support*: Windows 2000 fully supports plug and play devices. Network administrators finally have the ease of installation and use of devices associated with the Windows 9x product family. This feature automatically detects most installed or connected hardware devices. Plug and play support also allows for the hot insertion of devices such as PC cards. (Microsoft recommends stopping PC cards before ejecting.) Figure 1-1 shows the Unplug or Eject Hardware dialog box where you can stop PC cards.

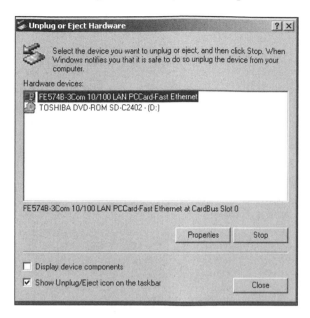

Figure 1-1   Unplug or Eject Hardware dialog box

■ *Universal Serial Bus (USB)*: Windows 2000 supports the connection of USB devices via an external connector. USB devices can be connected "hot," while the machine is running.

■ *File allocation table (FAT) 32 support*: Windows 2000 offers fully implemented support for the FAT 32 file system. FAT 32 can be used on any partition within the operating system, but many new features such as the encrypting file system require NTFS.

■ *Clustering support*: Windows 2000 Advanced Server and Windows 2000 DataCenter Server support for server clusters allows the creation of highly fault-tolerant server configurations. Previously, only the Enterprise version of Windows NT 4.0 made this functionality available.

■ *Terminal services*: All versions of Windows 2000 Server include and support terminal services. With this service, you can take previously underpowered client computers and serve applications off of a high-powered applications terminal server. Terminal service also allows highly controlled deployment of specific applications to thin clients such as Windows terminals.

WINDOWS 2000 PRODUCT FAMILY

With the release of Windows 2000, Microsoft continues to provide a fully scalable client/server operating system. Like Windows NT 4.0, Microsoft provides Windows 2000 in four versions to provide specific functions within a network: Windows 2000 Professional, Windows 2000 Server, Windows 2000 Advanced Server, and Windows 2000 DataCenter. This book focuses on the networking services available in the server versions of Windows 2000. It describes the use of Windows 2000 Professional only as a client for these networking services.

Windows 2000 Professional is the client version of the Windows 2000 product family. Its design provides a stable, reliable, 32-bit multitasking operating system for the desktop. In a corporate environment, Windows 2000 Professional gives everyday users a stable platform to run business applications ranging from Microsoft Office to database applications. Support professionals benefit because they can administer Windows 2000 Professional centrally via Active Directory policies. Figure 1-2 shows the minimum and maximum hardware requirements for Windows 2000 Professional.

Minimum requirements:
- Pentium 133
- 32 MB of RAM
- 650 MB of free hard drive space

Maximum hardware:
- Supports 2 processors
- Up to 4 GB of RAM

Figure 1-2   Minimum and maximum hardware specifications: Windows 2000 Professional

Windows 2000 Server is a network operating system designed to provide file, print, application, and Web services to small companies or workgroups within larger corporations. Businesses that currently use Windows NT 4.0 server are likely to upgrade to Windows 2000 Server. Most businesses never need to upgrade to the two more sophisticated versions of Windows 2000 because Windows 2000 Server meets their needs. Figure 1-3 shows the minimum and maximum hardware requirements for Windows 2000 Server.

Minimum requirements:
- Pentium 133
- 128 MB of RAM
- 671 MB of free hard drive space

Maximum hardware:
- Supports 4 processors
- Up to 4 GB of RAM

Figure 1-3   Minimum and maximum hardware specifications: Windows 2000 Server

Windows 2000 Advanced Server replaces the Windows NT 4.0 Enterprise Edition. It is designed to provide file, print, Web, application, and clustering services to large departments or entire enterprise networks. Windows 2000 Advanced Server scales the operating system to support large numbers of processors and huge amounts of RAM. Figure 1-4 shows how well Windows 2000 Advanced Server scales.

Maximum hardware:
- Supports 8 processors
- Up to 8 GB of RAM (if the server supports Intel's Page Address Extension specification)

Figure 1-4   Maximum hardware specifications: Windows 2000 Advanced Server

Windows 2000 DataCenter Server is a new Microsoft offering. No version of Windows NT 4.0 provides the functionality associated with Windows 2000 DataCenter Server. Microsoft designed Windows 2000 DataCenter Server to provide services for massively processor-intensive applications such as large data warehouses or large-scale simulation tasks. Figure 1-5 describes the extent to which DataCenter Server can scale.

Maximum hardware:
- Supports 16 processors out of the box
- Supports 32 processors in special original equipment manufacturer (OEM) versions
- Up to 64 GB of RAM (if the server supports Intel's Page Address Extension specification)

Figure 1-5   Maximum hardware specifications: Windows 2000 DataCenter Server

WINDOWS 2000 NETWORKING ARCHITECTURE

The networking architecture in Windows 2000 borrows heavily from the Windows NT 4.0 model. Overall, the Windows 2000 model is an updated version of the Windows NT 4.0 model, enhanced to provide more services. Like the Windows NT 4.0 model, Windows 2000's networking architecture model is modular, allowing networking components within the model to be changed without requiring a complete rewrite of all networking components. Windows 2000 does this via **boundary layers**, which create standardized interfaces between the different layers of the Windows 2000 networking architecture.

Services found above the **transport device interface (TDI) boundary layer** reside in the upper layers of **OSI model**. Items between the TDI layer and the **network driver interface specification (NDIS) boundary layer** are normally associated with the Network layer of the OSI model. Finally, components below the NDIS layer work at the Data Link or Physical layer of the OSI model. To understand fully the networking architecture of Windows 2000, you must know the functions of the two major boundary layers: TDI and NDIS.

Transport Device Interface

The TDI boundary layer falls between upper-layer services and layer 3 networking protocols. Its main function is to "translate" between the protocols such as TCP/IP and upper-layer services such as redirectors and server services. TDI keeps developers from the unenviable task of rewriting each upper-layer service for each networking protocol. Instead, developers can write to the TDI specification and ensure that upper-layer services work with all current and future networking protocols.

Network Driver Interface Specification

NDIS version 5.0 is the version currently available in Windows 2000. NDIS specifies the boundary layer between network interface card drivers and networking protocols above the NDIS layer. NDIS version 5.0 includes many new features. Two are wake-on-LAN capabilities, the ability to "wake" computers via special network signals; and media sense, the ability to "sense" when a network interface card is actually connected to a network cable. An icon in the information area of the taskbar represents the media sense feature. Figure 1-6 shows the icon (a red X) that signifies that the network interface card is not connected to a "live" network cable.

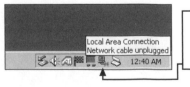

Red X signifies that your NIC is not connected to the network. Placing the mouse cursor over the icon displays a message stating that the computer is not attached to an active network jack

Figure 1-6   Media sense example

Binding is another important function of the NDIS boundary layer. **Binding** is the process of associating or connecting a layer 3 protocol with a specific network interface card. NDIS allows a single protocol to bind to multiple NICs or multiple protocols to bind to a single NIC. Figure 1-7 shows a single protocol bound to multiple NICs.

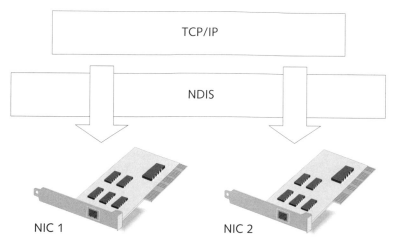

Figure 1-7   Binding single protocol to multiple NICs

Figure 1-7 shows TCP/IP bound to two separate NICs using NDIS services. This process also requires an NDIS-compatible driver for the NIC. All NICs on the hardware compatiability list (HCL) have an NDIS-compatible driver. Figure 1-8 displays multiple protocols bound to a single NIC.

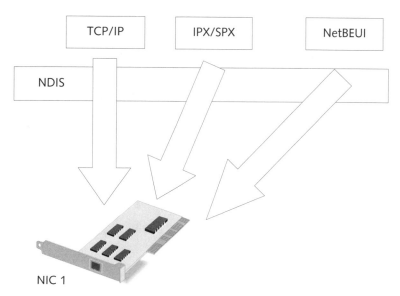

Figure 1-8   Binding multiple protocols to single NIC

The ability to bind multiple protocols to a single NIC is extremely important in any multi-protocol network. These networks, which usually consist of networks running Novell Netware, Unix, and Windows 2000, are very common in today's enterprise networks.

NETWORKING PROTOCOLS OVERVIEW

Windows 2000 supports nearly all the major networking protocols. In addition, the modular nature of Windows 2000 networking architecture allows the easy addition of new and future protocols—**Internet Protocol version 6 (IPv6)**, for instance. Windows 2000 supports the following networking protocols:

- *Transmission Control Protocol/Internet Protocol (TCP/IP)*: By default, Windows 2000 includes (and installs) TCP/IP, a routable, layer 3, enterprise-ready protocol stack. TCP/IP, the protocol of the Internet, is the protocol of choice for most networks today. Windows 2000 fully supports a standards-based implementation of TCP/IP. TCP/IP and the services built upon it form the basis for nearly every aspect of this book. Windows 2000 uses TCP/IP for locating servers for domain login and many other functions. Therefore, all Windows 2000 networks must run the TCP/IP protocol stack.

 Although Windows 2000 supports many protocols, Microsoft clearly specifies TCP/IP as the protocol of choice. In short, Windows 2000 cannot function without TCP/IP.

- *Internetwork Packet eXchange/Sequenced Packet eXchange (IPX/SPX)*: Novell developed this routable, layer 3, protocol stack to provide network connectivity between clients and Novell servers. The Microsoft version of IPX/SPX is NWLink IPX/SPX. Windows 2000 includes this 32-bit version of the protocol stack used by the Novell operating system to allow both operating systems to coexist on a network. NWLink IPX/SPX is discussed in Chapter 2.

- *NetBIOS Enhanced User Interface (NetBEUI)*: NetBEUI is a nonroutable protocol originally used to connect computers in small workgroups. Very small, very fast, and very efficient, this protocol's nonroutable nature makes it useless in most modern networks. A nonroutable protocol cannot be routed through layer 3 devices such as routers. In short, you cannot have multiple networks if you use a nonroutable protocol.

- *Data Link Control (DLC)*: DLC is a nonroutable protocol originally developed to connect IBM mainframes. Today's networks use DLC to connect to network-enabled printers such as Hewlett-Packard printers with Jet Direct cards.

- *Asynchronous Transfer Mode (ATM)*: Windows 2000 now provides native support for ATM via Local Area Network Emulation or LANE.

NETWORKING SERVICES OVERVIEW

Windows 2000 Server includes a wide variety of standard networking services. The operating system can provide everything from dynamic assignment of IP address via **Dynamic Host Configuration Protocol (DHCP)** to dial-up server services via its **Routing and Remote Access Server (RRAS)** components. This book focuses on the installation and administration of these network services, in particular, Dynamic Host Configuration Protocol, Domain Name System, Windows Internet Name Service, Routing and Remote Access, IP Security (described earlier), certificate services and Network Address Translation. The following list briefly describes each of these networking services.

- *Dynamic Host Configuration Protocol*: The DHCP service allows clients to obtain TCP/IP addresses automatically, thus freeing the administrator from manually visiting each workstation. DHCP lets an administrator provide options to clients via option fields. Options can include, but are not limited to, a Domain Name System server TCP/IP address, a Windows Internet Naming Service server address, or a default gateway TCP/IP address.

- *Domain Name System (DNS)*: DNS resolves host names to TCP/IP addresses. Its hierarchical nature creates a **Fully Qualified Domain Name (FQDN)** for each host. DNS is critical to the operation of Windows 2000; it is the naming service clients use to find network resources such as domain controllers. **Dynamic DNS (DDNS)**, an extension of the normal DNS service, is available in Windows 2000. DDNS clients can automatically register themselves with the DNS server.

- *Windows Internet Naming Service (WINS)*: Mixed mode environments— networks consisting of clients that are aware of the Active Directory and clients that are not—must continue to provide NetBIOS name resolution. WINS resolves NetBIOS names to TCP/IP addresses. This book discusses both NetBIOS names and WINS in detail later in Chapter 5.

- *Routing and Remote Access Server*: Providing a multitude of services to Windows 2000 networks, RRAS handles everything from dial-up connections to portions of TCP/IP routing. Due to its many components, RRAS features prominently in many chapters of this book.

- *Network Address Translation (NAT)*: NAT is a new networking service formerly part of the Proxy Server product family. NAT allows companies to use the private address space defined by Request for Comment 1918 to shield their inner network from the outside world. Using two NICs and the private address space, a Windows 2000 machine using NAT can act as a router between the private internal numbers and a public external number.

- *Certificate services*: In Windows 2000, certificate services serve as the bases for a public key infrastructure. Certificate services allow certificates to be issued for digitally signing messages and encrypting e-mail and Web sessions.

CHAPTER SUMMARY

❑ Windows 2000 takes the modern operating system to new levels of reliability and stability. New features such as Active Directory, plug and play support, Kerberos security, and IP Security help administrators configure and support modern networks. Most of these new features are built into all four versions of the Windows 2000 product family. The client version of the operating system is Windows 2000 Professional. Windows 2000 Server, the workgroup or small business version of the operating system, provides file, print, and Web services. The two other products, Windows 2000 Advanced Server and Windows 2000 DataCenter Server, scale the operating system to the upper end of current hardware and software capabilities.

❑ The modular Windows 2000 networking architecture enables the operating system to be updated quickly with new protocols or services. Its two main boundary layers, TDI and NDIS, serve as intermediaries within the different components in the architectural model. Also, NDIS allows a single protocol to bind to multiple network interface cards or multiple protocols to bind to a single network interface card.

❑ Windows 2000 gives a network administrator choice of a wide range of networking protocols. For your network, you can choose to use just TCP/IP (the required protocol for Windows 2000) or you can use any combination of TCP/IP and NWLink IPX/SPX, DLC, NetBEUI, or others.

❑ Finally, this book focuses on the multitude of networking services available in Windows 2000. The server version of the operating system supports the Domain Name Service, Dynamic Host Configuration Protocol, Windows Internet Name Service, Routing and Remote Access Service, Network Address Translation, and certificate services. These services are the backbone of nearly all modern networks.

KEY TERMS

Active Directory (AD) services — Enterprise-level directory service designed to combine domain structures into a manageable, extensible, network structure.

Asynchronous Transfer Mode (ATM) — Cell-based LAN/WAN networking technology that can handle voice, video, and data traffic; Windows 2000 provides native ATM support.

attributes — Specific values associated with an object; an example is the attribute of First or Last name for the User object.

binding — Associating or connecting a network layer protocol (or even a network service) to a specific network interface card.

boundary layers — Layers in the Windows 2000 networking architecture that act as intermediaries between upper layers, the network protocols, and lower layers of the model.

certificate services — Networking service in Windows 2000 that creates and manages a public key infrastructure within an organization.

1

clustering support — Ability of an operating system to connect multiple servers in a fault-tolerant group. If one server in the cluster fails, all processing continues on another server. Clusters ensure high availability and reliable performance.

Data Link Control (DLC) — Nonroutable protocol used mainly to connect to Hewlett-Packard printers using Jet Direct network cards.

Domain Name System (DNS) — Network service that provides host name to TCP/IP address resolution.

Dynamic Domain Name System (DDNS) — DNS version that allows clients to register their host names automatically with a DNS server.

Dynamic Host Configuration Protocol (DHCP) — Networking service that can distribute TCP/IP addresses to clients configured to obtain dynamic addresses.

encrypting file system (EFS) — New file and folder attribute provided by NTFS version 5.0; allows file and folder encryption on a per-user basis.

enhanced security — Increased security measures available in Windows 2000 via the inclusion of Kerberos version 5 security and IP security.

Fat allocation table (FAT) 32 support — Ability of an operating system to read, write, and otherwise fully support the new version of the file allocation table file system introduced in the Win9x product family.

Fully Qualified Domain Name (FQDN) — Entire name of a host that includes the host name and the domain name; for example, host1.win2k.org signifies the computer host1 in the win2k.org DNS domain.

IP Security (IPSec) protocol — Set of security protocols used to provide data integrity, end-to-end confidentiality, and secure network authentication.

Internetwork Packet eXchange/Sequenced Packet eXchange (IPX/SPX) — Routable protocol stack designed by Novell to provide networking services for the Netware network operating system.

Internet Protocol version 6 (IPv6) — Advanced version of the Internet Protocol that uses 128-bit addresses in hexadecimal format.

Kerberos version 5 — Shared secret key encryption mechanism used to provide security for authentication sessions in a Windows 2000 network.

mixed mode — Mode that Windows 2000 domain controllers use when the network consists of Windows 2000 servers and Windows NT servers (or machines not Active Directory-aware). All Windows 2000 servers run in mixed mode by default. You must manually change them to native mode.

native mode — Mode used by Windows 2000 domain controllers when the entire network consists of only Windows 2000 servers and Active Directory-aware clients.

NetBIOS Enhanced User Interface (NetBEUI) — Small, fast, efficient, nonroutable protocol stack used in small networks only.

Network Address Translation (NAT) — Network service used to "translate" between public TCP/IP addresses and private internal addresses specified in Request for Comments 1918.

network driver interface specification (NDIS) — Boundary layer in the Windows 2000 networking architecture that serves as an intermediary between the networking protocols and the Data Link layer drivers and network interface cards.

network operating system (NOS) — Computer software designed to provide network services to clients.

objects — Components found within the Active Directory structure; an object represents each network resource in the Active Directory structure

Open System Interconnection model (OSI model) — Seven-layer conceptual model designed to help standardize and simplify learning, implementing, and creating network communication between two network hosts.

plug and play support — Ability of an operating system to automatically detect and install drivers for devices that conform to plug and play standards; simplifies hardware device management and installation.

Routing and Remote Access Server (RRAS) — Windows 2000 networking service responsible for dial-up connectivity and some portions of TCP/IP routing.

terminal services — Services that allow a server to host applications for clients; with terminal services, clients no longer used to run applications can act as dumb terminals for applications on a terminal server.

Transmission Control Protocol/Internet Protocol (TCP/IP) — Enterprise-ready protocol stack designed to work in heterogeneous networks, that is, networks with many different types of network operating systems.

transport device interface (TDI) — Boundary layer in the Windows 2000 networking architecture between networking protocols and the upper-layer services.

Universal Serial Bus (USB) — Hardware specification that allows for hot insertion and removal of hardware devices.

Windows 2000 Professional — Client version of the Windows 2000 product family; designed to provide a stable, reliable, and fast platform for end users to run their applications.

Windows 2000 Advanced Server — Enterprise or large department version of Windows 2000; supports clustering and eight-way multiprocessor systems with up to 8 GB of RAM.

Windows 2000 DataCenter Server — Data warehouse or extremely large-scale version of Windows 2000; designed for processor intensive simulations or massive processing tasks; supports up to 32 processors with 64 GB of RAM in special original equipment manufacturer versions.

Windows 2000 Server — Small department or workgroup version of Windows 2000; supports four-way multiprocessor systems with up to 4 GB of RAM.

Windows Internet Naming Service (WINS) — Network service that provides NetBIOS name to TCP/IP address resolution.

REVIEW QUESTIONS

1. Which one of the following network services provides dynamic assignment of TCP/IP addresses to clients?

   a. DNS

   b. DHCP

   c. RRAS

   d. NAT

2. Bill needs to replace 100 Windows 98 client machines with a stable, reliable, client operating system. Which one of the following should he install?

   a. Windows 2000 Server

   b. Windows 2000 DataCenter Server

   c. Windows 2000 Advanced Server

   d. Windows 2000 Professional

3. If you have both Windows 2000 and Window NT 4.0 servers on the same network, for which mode must the Windows 2000 servers be configured?

   a. Mixed mode

   b. Fixed mode

   c. Native mode

   d. Broadcast mode

4. Which one of the following network services provides NetBIOS name to TCP/IP address resolution?

   a. DDNS

   b. WINS

   c. DHCP

   d. RRAS

5. What new Windows 2000 feature eases the task of installing and configuring hardware devices?

   a. Plug and play support

   b. Kerberos security

   c. Active Directory services

   d. Encrypting file system

6. Which one of the following versions of Windows 2000 would provide network services to support a small business with approximately 200 users?

   a. Windows 2000 Advanced Server

   b. Windows 2000 Server

   c. Windows 2000 Professional

   d. Windows 2000 DataCenter Server

7. What portion of the Windows 2000 networking architecture provides a boundary layer between upper-layer services and network-layer protocols such as TCP/IP?

   a. TDI

   b. NDIS

   c. IDIS

   d. TNDIS

8. Which of the following networking protocols are routable? (Choose all that apply.)

   a. TCP/IP

   b. DLC

   c. NetBEUI

   d. NWLink IPX/SPX

9. Network Address Translation provides which one of the following services?

   a. Dynamic assignment of TCP/IP address

   b. NetBIOS name to TCP/IP address resolution

   c. Host name to TCP/IP address resolution

   d. Translation between private internal TCP/IP addresses and public addresses

10. What process associates a protocol with a particular network interface card?

    a. NDIS

    b. Boundary layers

    c. Binding

    d. Network associating protocol

11. Which new Windows 2000 Server feature provides enhanced manageability, simplified administration, and increased security through the use of network policies?

    a. Active Directory

    b. Kerberos v5

    c. IP Security

    d. Plug and play support

1

12. The _____ allows users to encrypt files and folders on drives formatted with NTFS version 5.0.

13. Which versions of Windows 2000 provide clustering services? (Choose all that apply.)

   a. Windows 2000 Server

   b. Windows 2000 Professional

   c. Windows 2000 Advanced Server

   d. Windows 2000 DataCenter Server

14. You would like to dual boot Windows 98 and Windows 2000. You should format the first active primary partition with the _____ file system.

15. NDIS allows which of the following? (Choose all that apply.)

   a. Binding multiple protocols to a single NIC

   b. Binding certificate services to multiple NICs

   c. Binding a single protocol to multiple NICs

   d. None of the above

16. What protocol can you use to connect to HP printers using JetDirect cards?

   a. NetBEUI

   b. DLC

   c. NDIS

   d. IPX/SPX

17. Which version of Windows 2000 would you use to replace the network operating system on servers in an organization with 100 servers and approximately 25,000 users?

   a. Windows 2000 Advanced Server

   b. Windows 2000 Server

   c. Windows 2000 DataCenter Server

   d. Windows 2000 Professional

18. Your network consists of only Windows 2000 machines and Active Directory-enabled clients. Which one of the following modes should your domain controllers use?

   a. Asynchronous mode

   b. Native mode

   c. Mixed mode

   d. Multi mode

19. Which Windows 2000 networking service allows older client machines to be served applications off of powerful server machines?

   a. Universal Serial Bus

   b. Clustering support

   c. Active Directory services

   d. Terminal services

20. Windows 2000 Server supports up to _____ processors and _____ GB of RAM.

CASE PROJECTS

Case 1

You are hired to design a new network installation for a small engineering firm. The firm, Freytech Inc., currently has Windows NT 4.0 workstations configured in several peer-to-peer workgroups and 75 clients currently in the office. The company owners want to make the best use of existing hardware, but they do understand that they must purchase some new machines. Create a plan to implement a server-based network using Windows 2000 servers. First and foremost, you must justify your decision to choose Windows 2000 by relating the benefits that the operating system's new features would bring to the company. Then you must determine how to configure the servers. Finally, describe what networking protocol or protocols you would configure on the network and what networking services would be appropriate for network use.

Case 2

Your CIO recently read an article concerning the modularization of the Windows 2000 networking architecture. He worries that this limits the operating system's effectiveness for your organization. Create a one-page report detailing why modularization of the Windows 2000 networking architecture actually offers great benefit to your organization.

Case 3

Your network currently consists of Unix workstations, and Windows 3.11, Windows 98, and Windows NT workstations. Also, four Novell Netware servers are running a mission-critical application on the network. As part of a pilot project, you are drafted to provide a PowerPoint presentation detailing how Windows 2000 can be integrated into your network. Create a short presentation detailing the networking protocols supported by Windows 2000 and how they can help Windows 2000 work in your environment.

2

IMPLEMENTING, CONFIGURING, AND TROUBLESHOOTING NETWORKING PROTOCOLS

After reading this chapter and completing the exercises, you will be able to:

♦ Describe the history of the TCP/IP protocol stack

♦ Identify TCP/IP addresses, classes, and subnet masks

♦ Create a subnetting scheme for a given TCP/IP network address

♦ Define and assign static and dynamic TCP/IP addresses to Windows 2000 machines

♦ Establish TCP/IP packet filtering

♦ Troubleshoot TCP/IP using command-line tools

♦ Describe the IPX/SPX protocol stack and frame types

♦ Install and configure NWLink IPX/SPX

♦ Optimize networking protocol bindings

Before you can begin installing any networking services, you must first install, configure, and sometimes troubleshoot a **protocol stack**. In this chapter, you explore the two most common protocol stacks: TCP/IP and IPX/SPX (implemented in Windows 2000 as NWLink IPX/SPX). In particular, you learn about TCP/IP addresses, from the basics of addressing up to the creation of complex subnetting scenarios. You also discover the NWLink IPX/SPX protocol stack. This chapter introduces you to installation, configuration, and troubleshooting tasks for both of these protocol stacks. Finally, you learn how to optimize networking protocol bindings properly.

TRANSMISSION CONTROL PROTOCOL/INTERNET PROTOCOL

TCP/IP runs the majority of all major networks today. The ubiquitous nature of the Internet in everyday life brought TCP/IP to the forefront of the information systems world. Created before the **OSI model**, the TCP/IP protocol stack does not follow the seven-layer model. TCP/IP does use a four-layer model that relates to the OSI model. Figure 2-1 shows how the four layers of TCP/IP map to the OSI model.

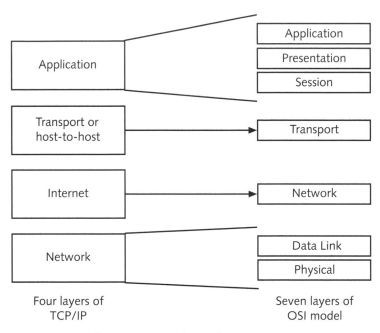

Figure 2-1   TCP/IP versus OSI model

The Application layer of the TCP/IP model corresponds roughly to the first three layers of the OSI model or its Application, Presentation, and Session layers. The Transport layer or Host-to-Host layer of the TCP/IP model maps one-to-one with the Transport layer of the OSI model. The Internet layer maps to layer 3 or the Network layer of the OSI model. Finally, the Network layer of the TCP/IP model maps to the Data Link and Physical layers of the OSI model. You can easily remember the four layers of the TCP/IP model by using the mnemonic **AT IN** or **A TIN**: **A**pplication, **T**ransport (or host-to-host), **I**nternet, **N**etwork.

Figure 2-2 displays the generic architectural model of TCP/IP with some of the standard protocols supported by Windows 2000 listed. Each protocol within the model performs a specific function for the protocol stack.

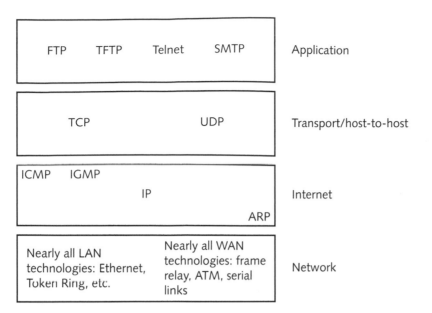

Figure 2-2   TCP/IP architecture

 The model in Figure 2-2 is not Microsoft's exact implementation of TCP/IP. Microsoft does, however, support every protocol shown in the figure.

The following list describes the function of each protocol in Figure 2-2.

- *File Transfer Protocol (FTP)*: This protocol allows TCP/IP hosts to exchange files between one another. FTP uses TCP as its transport protocol and is therefore connection-oriented and reliable.

- *Trivial File Transfer Protocol (TFTP)*: Like FTP, TFTP allows hosts to exchange files between one another. However, TFTP uses UDP as its transport protocol and is therefore connectionless and unreliable (unless Application layer processes guarantee delivery).

- *Telnet*: This application allows a host to log into a remote system and run applications and processes on the remote system.

- *Simple Mail Transfer Protocol (SMTP)*: The basis for all Internet mail, SMTP provides mail delivery services for the TCP/IP protocol stack.

- *Transmission Control Protocol (TCP)*: A connection-oriented, reliable transport protocol. TCP sacrifices speed to ensure reliable, error-free transmission of data.

- *User Datagram Protocol (UDP)*: This connectionless, unreliable transport protocol stresses speed over reliability.

- *Internet Control Message Protocol (ICMP)*: Providing messaging and communication for protocols within the TCP/IP stack, ICMP handles many communication error messages. PING uses ICMP echo requests and ICMP echo replies to verify that a host is functioning on a TCP/IP network.

- *Internet Group Management Protocol (IGMP)*: TCP/IP uses IGMP to provide functionality for multicasting. **Multicasting** allows broadcasting of information to specific computers within a multicasting group. IGMP defines group memberships and provides that information to routers.

- *Internet Protocol (IP)*: This connectionless, layer three protocol determines proper routing within multiple networks.

- *Address Resolution Protocol (ARP)*: ARP maps a known IP address to a Media Access Control (MAC) layer address.

- *Local area network (LAN) and Wide area network (WAN) technologies*: TCP/IP does not officially define network layer (OSI Physical layer) technologies. Because of this open approach, nearly all LAN and WAN technologies work with TCP/IP.

- **Connection-oriented protocols**: These protocols guarantee that packets arrive intact, in sequence, and without errors. Connection-oriented protocols sacrifice speed for reliability.

- **Connectionless protocols**: These protocols send packets without regard for guaranteed delivery. A connectionless protocol sacrifices reliability for speed.

TCP/IP ADDRESSING

TCP/IP addresses, also simply referred to as **IP addresses**, consist of 32 bits normally expressed either as four binary octets separated by periods or as four sets of decimal numbers separated by periods. Therefore each of the following is an example of a valid IP address:

- 192.168.12.8

- 11000000.10101000.00001100.00001000

In fact, each of the examples represents the same IP address. One displays the address as dotted decimal, while the other represents the same address in binary format. You must be able to convert between decimal and binary in order to understand the intricacies of subnetting and IP routing.

The easiest way to convert from binary to decimal or vice-versa involves looking at each octet separately. In each octet, you have the possibility of seven binary bit positions or a maximum of 2^7. The following example shows the possible values of each bit position within the octet.

128	64	32	16	8	4	2	1
2^7	2^6	2^5	2^4	2^3	2^2	2^1	2^0

You can convert the binary IP address 11010000.00110010.11110100.00000111 to decimal by taking each octet and adding together the value of each bit turned on (set to 1). The following example converts the first octet of the binary address above to decimal.

128	64	32	16	8	4	2	1
2^7	2^6	2^5	2^4	2^3	2^2	2^1	2^0
1	1	0	1	0	0	0	0
128 +	64 +	0 +	16 +	0 +	0 +	0 +	0 = 208

Using this technique, you can convert each octet of the IP address above to a decimal number. The end result is the dotted decimal IP address 208.50.244.7.

Using a slight variation of the first technique, you can also convert from decimal to binary. If you have the IP address, 192.168.24.5, you convert each octet by subtracting each bit position until you are left with a zero remainder. For each bit position you can subtract, you must turn on that bit position (set it to 1). The correct technique for this conversion is shown next:

192 − 128= 64 means the 2^7 bit position should be turned on (set to a 1).

64 − 64= 0 means the 2^7 bit position should be turned on (set to 1).

Since the remainder is 0, all other bit positions should be set to off (set to 0). The result is:

128	64	32	16	8	4	2	1
2^7	2^6	2^5	2^4	2^3	2^2	2^1	2^0
1	1	0	0	0	0	0	0 = 192

To convert a decimal to binary correctly, you must subtract the decimal number from the values of each bit position. When the remainder is zero, the conversion is complete and you have your binary number. The following shows the conversion of the second octet, 168, to binary.

- 168 − 128 = 40 means the 2^7 bit position should be turned on (set to 1).
- 40 − 64 = ??? because you cannot subtract 64 from 40. Therefore, the 2^6 bit position should be turned off (set to 0).
- 40 − 32 = 8 means the 2^5-bit position should be turned on (set to 1).
- 8 − 16 = ??? because you cannot subtract 16 from 8. Therefore, the 2^4 bit position should be turned off (set to 0).
- 8 − 8 = 0 means the 2^3 bit position should be turned on (set to 1).

Since the remainder is 0, all other bit positions should be set to off (set to 0). The result is:

128	64	32	16	8	4	2	1
2^7	2^6	2^5	2^4	2^3	2^2	2^1	2^0
1	0	1	0	1	0	0	0 = 168

Now that you can convert between binary and decimal IP addresses (and vice versa), it is imperative that you learn more about the makeup of an IP address. Every IP address contains a **network ID** and a **host ID**. In other words, a portion of each IP address represents the network a particular host is on and a portion signifies the actual host number. This is most easily represented through the use of classes of IP addresses.

TCP/IP CLASSES

IP addresses are broken into five different classes. The first three classes reserve a certain portion of the 32 bits available for the network ID and the host ID. The last two classes are used in special situations only. Table 2-1 shows the classes of addresses and several properties of each.

Table 2-1   TCP/IP classes

Class of Address	Decimal Range	Leading Bit Values	Number of Networks	Number of Hosts
A	1–126	0	126	16,777,214
B	128–191	10	16,384	65,534
C	192–223	110	2,097,152	254
D	224–239	1110	N/A	N/A
E	240–254	11110	N/A	N/A

You can see from Table 2-1 that Class A addresses provide a small number of networks consisting of a very large number of hosts. Class B addresses are more balanced. They can accommodate a fairly large number of networks and hosts on each network. Class C addresses provide the largest number of networks, but each individual network can support only 254 possible hosts. You can use the Leading Bit Values column in Table 2-1 to quickly identify a binary number. If, for instance, you encounter an IP address with the first octet shown as 01100010, you know that this entire address is a Class A address. Likewise, if the first octet of an IP addresses consists of 11011010, you can ascertain that the IP address is a Class C address. You can also easily determine the class of address by converting the binary number to a decimal number and using the ranges found in the Decimal Range column of Table 2-1.

Table 2-2 shows what portions of Class A, B, and C networks represent host bits or network bits. The table does not include Class D addresses because they are used for multicasting, nor does it include Class E addresses, which are not currently used in production networks. They are reserved for experimentation.

Table 2-2   Network ID and host ID

Class of Address	Network ID	Host ID
A	First octet	Final three octets
B	First two octets	Final two octets
C	First three octets	Final octet

The network ID and host ID in Table 2-2 assume that no subnetting, borrowing of host bits to increase the number of available network bits, is occurring on a network address. Therefore, using the tables you can tell that the address 34.12.4.76 is a Class A address. Also, again assuming no subnetting is occurring, the network ID is 34.0.0.0 and the host ID is .12.4.76.

Again, you know that the number 198.23.54.213 is a Class C address with 198.23.54.0 as the network ID and .213 as the host ID. In short, Class A addresses, by default, have eight bits for the network ID and 24 bits for the host ID. Class B addresses have 16 bits for the network ID and 16 bits for the host ID. Finally, Class C addresses reserve 24 bits for the network ID and eight bits for the host ID.

SUBNET MASKS

Subnet masks are the final general component of IP addressing that you must understand to configure TCP/IP. **Subnet masks** are 32-bit numbers that allow hosts on a network to determine which bits in an IP address are network ID bits and which are host ID bits. Subnet masks place a 1 in bit positions that correspond to network ID bits and a zero in bits that represent host ID bits. This allows the host to perform a logical AND function to determine if a destination IP address is on a local network or a remote network. **ANDing** is the process of combining the binary bits in a function very similar to multiplying. If you AND a 1 and a 1, you are left with a 1. ANDing together any other combination (a 1 and 0, or a 0 and 0) gives you a zero. Hosts use subnet masks and the ANDing process to check if destination IP addresses are local or remote. The easiest way to understand this process is with an example.

Host A has an IP address of 192.168.12.4, and Host B has an IP address of 192.168.12.12. If Host A wants to send data to Host B, Host A must determine if the destination IP address is on the same network. Host A first ANDs its IP address with its configured subnet mask. The process works as follows:

11000000.10101000.00001100.00000100 or 192.168.12.4	Host A's IP address
11111111.11111111.11111111.00000000 or 255.255.255.0	Host A's subnet mask
11000000.10101000.00001100.00000000 or 192.168.12.0	the network ID after ANDing

Host A then ANDs the destination IP address, 192.168.12.12, with its configured subnet mask. The result is:

11000000.10101000.00001100.00001100 or 192.168.12.12	Host B's IP address
11111111.11111111.11111111.00000000 or 255.255.255.0	Host A's subnet mask
11000000.10101000.00001100.00000000 or 192.168.12.0	the network ID after ANDing

Since the results of the ANDing procedures are the same, Host A knows that Host B is on the exact same network and can attempt to send data directly to Host B. If the two networks IDs are not the same after ANDing, Host A attempts to send data to Host B through its **default gateway**, the IP address of a router port leading to other networks.

Each class of address has a default subnet mask that corresponds to the number of bits assigned as network bits and the number assigned to host bits. (Again, this assumes no additional subnetting is occurring.) Table 2-3 shows the default subnet masks for Class A, B, and C addresses.

Table 2-3   Default subnet masks

Class of Address	Default Subnet Mask in Decimal	Default Subnet Mask in Binary
A	255.0.0.0	11111111.00000000.00000000.00000000
B	255.255.0.0	11111111.11111111.00000000.00000000
C	255.255.255.0	11111111.11111111.11111111.00000000

Not all networks use the default subnet masks. Instead, many administrators borrow bits from the host portion of a Class A, B, or C address to create more bits for the network ID. This is called subnetting. Subnetting forces networks to use subnet masks greater than the defaults in Table 2-3.

SUBNETTING

Subnetting allows administrators to better utilize IP networks that are either assigned to them from the **Internet Assigned Numbers Authority (IANA)** or that they decide to use from the public address space defined by **Request for Comments** (RFC) 1918.

 RFC 1918 sets the following addresses aside for use on internal private networks: 10.0.0.0, 172.16.0.0 through 172.31.0.0, and 192.168.0.0 (or 254 possible Class C networks). Marked for use on private networks, these numbers can never be used on the public Internet. In fact, these numbers cannot be routed through the Internet.

The following sections walk you through the process of working with a Class C subnetting scheme and a Class B subnetting scheme.

Creating Class C Subnetting Scheme

Basic subnetting is very easy when performed in seven steps. This example uses the Class C address 211.212.10.0. Using the seven steps provided here, you can create a subnetting scheme that allows you to use this address on your network.

Step 1: Determining Number of Subnets Needed

Determining the number of subnets you need is the very first step in subnetting. The number really depends upon your particular network. In Figure 2-3, the network consists of three routers connected via serial links. Each router also has a single Ethernet network attached.

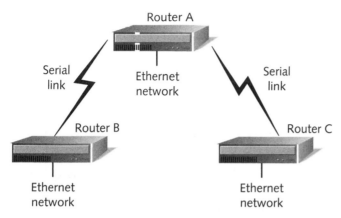

Router A

Serial link   Ethernet network   Serial link

Router B   Router C

Ethernet network   Ethernet network

Figure 2-3   Example of network with three routers

Each shared serial link requires one subnet. Therefore, you need two subnets for the serial links between Router A and Routers B and C. You must also have one subnet per Ethernet interface on each router. Since you have three Ethernet networks, you need three subnets. Using this very simple counting method, you find that you need a total of five subnets. Unfortunately, you have been assigned a Class C address. The network address 211.212.10.0 allows for a single network of 254 hosts. You must borrow host ID bits to make this address work for you.

Step 2: Determining Number of Bits You Can Borrow

In Step 2, you must determine the number of bits that you can borrow. This number changes depending on the type of network address you start with. For Class A addresses, you have 24 host ID bits, but you can only borrow up to 22. For Class B addresses, you have 16 host ID bits, but, you must leave a minimum of two host bits; therefore, you can borrow 14 bits. Your Class C address (211.212.10.0) has eight total host ID bits, but you can only borrow a maximum of six. The easiest way to determine the number of bits you can borrow is to write the number of octets that contain host ID bits in binary. In the Class C example network 211.212.10.0, you have the following bits to "play" with:

00000000

Step 3: Determining Number of Bits You Must Borrow to Get Needed Number of Subnets

After you determine the number of subnets you need and the number of bits you can borrow, you must calculate the number of host ID bits you must borrow to get the needed number of subnets. The formula for determining the number of bits you must borrow is: $2^n - 2$ = # of subnets. The n represents the number of bits you borrow. In other words, raise two to the power of the number of bits you borrow and subtract two from that number. The result is the number of usable subnets created when you borrow that number of bits.

 For nearly all subnetting, it is helpful to place a chart on your page that lists two raised to the powers of 0, 1, 2, up to 2^{13}. With this chart, you can quickly figure the number of bits you must borrow to get a certain number of subnets.

For the example network, you need five subnets. If you borrow three bits, the formula's result is six usable subnets: $2^3 = 8 - 2 = 6$.

Step 4: Turning On Borrowed Bits and Determining Decimal Value

In Step 4, using the bits you determined were available in Step 2, you turn on (set to 1) the number of bits you determined you must borrow in Step 3. You must always begin with the high-order bits (the bits starting on the left of a binary number). Using the number of bits you can work with and the number of bits you must borrow (from Step 3), your result is the following: 11100000. In other words, from the eight total bits from Step 2 (six of which you could borrow), you borrow three host ID bits. In Step 4, you also need to determine the decimal value of the octets from which you borrow host ID bits. In this example, 11100000 equals 224.

Step 5: Determining New Subnet Mask

Step 5 calculates the new subnet mask after you borrow the host ID bits in Step 4. You must add the decimal value from Step 4 to the default subnet mask for the class of address you are subnetting. This example is a Class C address, so the default mask is 255.255.255.0. The new mask after borrowing three bits becomes 255.255.255.224.

Step 6: Finding Host/Subnet Variable

In Step 6, you must find the lowest of the high-order bits (bits starting from the left) turned "on." Step 6 takes you all the way back to earlier in the chapter to the values found in each bit position within the octet. Our example defines the octets from which we borrow as 11100000. The highest order bit turned on represents 2^5, which equals 32. Since 2^5 is the last high-order bit turned on, the Host/Subnet variable you use in Step 7 is 32.

Step 7: Determining Range of Addresses

The final step allows you to take the Host/Subnet variable from Step 6 (32) and create your subnet ranges. Using the Class C network above, the range of subnets when you borrow three bits are:

211.212.10.0	to	211.212.10.31
211.212.10.32	to	211.212.10.63
211.212.10.64	to	211.212.10.95

211.212.10.96	to	211.212.10.127
211.212.10.128	to	211.212.10.159
211.212.10.160	to	211.212.10.191
211.212.10.192	to	211.212.10.223
211.212.10.224	to	211.212.10.255

IP addresses cannot be all ones or all zeros; therefore, in most cases the first range of addresses and the last range of addresses are unusable. (In some special circumstances, you can use the first range of addresses, or subnet 0. Only certain manufacturers' equipment, such as Cisco Systems, fully supports the use of subnet zero.) In each subnet, the first IP address is unusable because it represents the subnet ID. The final address is also unusable because it is the broadcast address for the subnet. Due to these two restrictions, in subnet one, 211.212.10.33 is the first usable host ID and 211.212.10.62 is the last usable host ID.

Tailoring a Class B Address

This example takes a Class B address and tries to fit it within the needs of a network containing 1000 subnets. You are assigned the Class B address 131.107.0.0. Using the following seven steps, you are going to subnet the Class B address to meet your needs.

Step 1: Determining Number of Subnets Needed

Examine your network and determine your needs based on current network configuration and future growth (in this case, 1000 subnets).

Step 2: Determining Number of Bits You Can Borrow

With this Class B network address, you have 16 total bits to work with. You can only borrow up to 14 of these. On your sheet of paper, you should write the number of bits you have in the host ID portion of the address:

00000000.00000000

Step 3: Determining Number of Bits You Must Borrow to Get Number of Subnets Needed

Using the formula $2^n-2 = $ # of usable subnets, you can easily see that you need to borrow 10 bits. When you plug in 10 borrowed bits, you get the following result:

$2^{10} = 1024 - 2 = 1022$ usable subnets.

Step 4: Turning on Borrowed Bits and Determining Decimal Value

If you turn on 10 bits, you get the following:

11111111.11000000.

The decimal values for the octets are 255.192.

Step 5: Determining New Subnet Mask

Your example is a Class B address. In Class B addresses, the default subnet mask is 255.255.0.0. To get your new mask, you add the default mask to the decimal values found in Step 4. The new mask becomes:

255.255.255.192

Step 6: Finding Host/Subnet Variable

In the next-to-last step, you must find the value of the lowest high-order bit turned on in each octet, from which you borrowed host bits. Since this example is a Class B network and you must borrow a great number of bits to get the proper number of subnets, the borrowing crosses an octet boundary. As a result, you have two Host/Subnet variables. In this example, the variable in the third octet is 1, and the variable for the fourth octet is 64. You get these values by looking at the binary numbers in Step 4. The third octet has the final bit position, or the 2^0 bit position, turned on. Since $2^0 = 1$, your variable is 1 in the third octet. In the fourth octet, the second high-order bit or 2^6 is turned on. The variable in this octet is 64.

Step 7: Determining Range of Addresses

Figuring the range of addresses for Class B networks is much harder than for Class C. This is especially true in cases like this scenario in which you must borrow a large number of bits. Using 1 as the variable in the third octet and 64 as the variable in the fourth octet, the range of the first 9 subnets would be:

131.107.0.0	to	131.107.0.63
131.107.0.64	to	131.107.0.127
131.107.0.128	to	131.107.0.191
131.107.0.192	to	131.107.0.255
131.107.1.0	to	131.107.1.63
131.107.1.64	to	131.107.1.127
131.107.1.128	to	131.107.1.191
131.107.1.192	to	131.107.1.255
131.107.2.0	to	131.107.2.63

STATIC AND DYNAMIC TCP/IP ADDRESSES

You can assign IP addresses to Windows 2000 machines via two main methods: static assignment or dynamic assignment. Each method has certain advantages and disadvantages. In this section, you learn how to use each method to assign an IP address to Windows 2000 machines.

Static IP Addresses

Static assignment is the most work-intensive method for assigning IP addresses, but it also allows the greatest control over address assignment. In order to assign static addresses, you must visit each machine and manually configure the IP address, subnet mask, and, if you have a network with multiple subnets or networks, the default gateway address. Also, in the Windows 2000 environment, you need to configure the DNS settings manually for each machine with a static address.

 With static IP addresses, it is imperative that you maintain accurate records on what address has been assigned to each machine. If you do not maintain an accurate database, you can end up having two machines with the same IP address. Since this causes a multitude of communication problems, you must ensure that your static IP list is accurate and up-to-date. Certain machines, such as domain controllers, Web servers, and most application servers, require that the machine have a static IP address. Later in this book, you learn that nearly every networking service requires the server to have a static IP address.

To begin the process of assigning static IP addresses, you need to access the properties for your local area connections. You open the Local Area Connection Status dialog box by clicking Start, Settings, Network and Dial-up Connections, Local Area Connection.

 You can also access Local Area Connection and open the Local Area Connection status box by right-clicking the **My Network Places** icon on the desktop and then double-clicking Local Area Connection. Regardless of the method used, you need to click the Properties button in the Local Area Connection Status dialog box to access the network settings.

Figure 2-4 shows the **Local Area Connection Properties** dialog box where you actually configure your TCP/IP settings with a static address.

You must click Internet Protocol (TCP/IP) and click the Properties button to assign a static IP address. Figure 2-5 shows the Internet Protocol (TCP/IP) Properties dialog box.

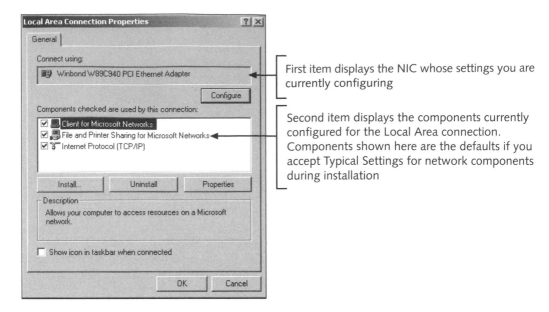

First item displays the NIC whose settings you are currently configuring

Second item displays the components currently configured for the Local Area connection. Components shown here are the defaults if you accept Typical Settings for network components during installation

Figure 2-4   Local Area Connection Properties

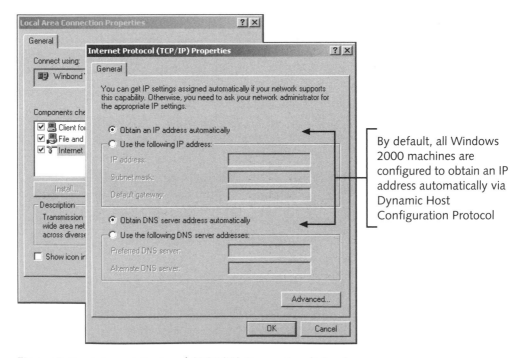

By default, all Windows 2000 machines are configured to obtain an IP address automatically via Dynamic Host Configuration Protocol

Figure 2-5   Internet Protocol (TCP/IP) Properties dialog box

Once you obtain a unique static IP address, you can assign it by clicking the Use the following IP address radio button. Figure 2-6 shows the configuration of the static IP address, 192.168.0.200.

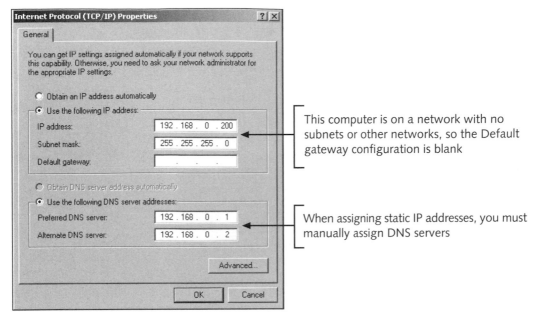

This computer is on a network with no subnets or other networks, so the Default gateway configuration is blank

When assigning static IP addresses, you must manually assign DNS servers

Figure 2-6   Configuring a static IP address

Once you click **OK**, your address is configured. Unlike Windows NT 4.0, which requires you to restart your machine, your static IP address is immediately configured and usable on the Windows 2000 machine. In Figure 2-6, the Advanced button is in the lower-right corner of the Internet Protocol (TCP/IP) Properties dialog box. If you click the Advanced button, the Advanced TCP/IP settings dialog box opens, as shown in Figure 2-7.

You can assign multiple static IP addresses to a single NIC and assign multiple default gateways in the Advanced TCP/IP Settings dialog box. Windows 2000 supports automatic Dead Gateway Detection: if a Windows 2000 machine determines that its primary default gateway is unreachable, it switches to a secondary gateway if one has been configured.

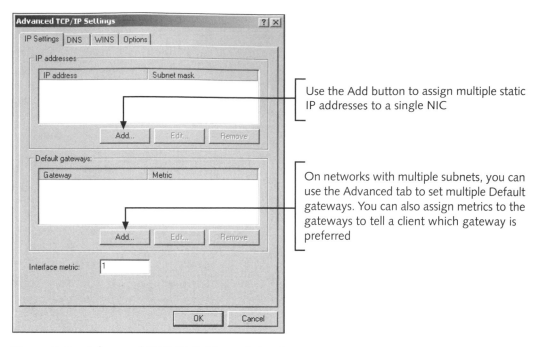

Figure 2-7   Advanced TCP/IP Settings dialog box

Dynamic IP Addresses

Dynamic assignment is much less labor intensive than static assignment. The fact that you can easily configure clients with IP addresses without visiting each machine is a huge advantage of dynamic IP addresses. Since you can also assign options such as DNS servers, default gateways, and WINS servers via dynamic addressing, you can save an enormous amount of time. The downside of dynamic addresses involves the use of a **Dynamic Host Configuration Protocol** or DHCP server to hand out addresses. Chapter 3 discusses in detail DHCP servers and the actual process a client goes through to obtain a dynamic address. For now, you just need to know that dynamic IP address assignment requires an installed and properly configured DHCP server on your network.

Configuring a Windows 2000 machine for a dynamic IP address is very easy. You must navigate to the Internet Protocols (TCP/IP) Properties dialog box. Once there, you simply click the Obtain an IP address automatically and Obtain DNS server address automatically buttons. (You are not required to obtain DNS information automatically, but most clients using a dynamic IP address also get their DNS information dynamically.) Figure 2-8 shows the correct settings for a client configured to obtain a dynamic IP address.

Although dynamic IP addressing is by far the easiest method of IP address assignment, it is not appropriate for all Windows 2000 machines. As mentioned in the "Static IP Addresses" section, some machines, such as the server running the DHCP server service, must use a static address. Still, to lessen the administrative overhead of IP addressing, you should use dynamic IP addresses on as many machines on your network as possible.

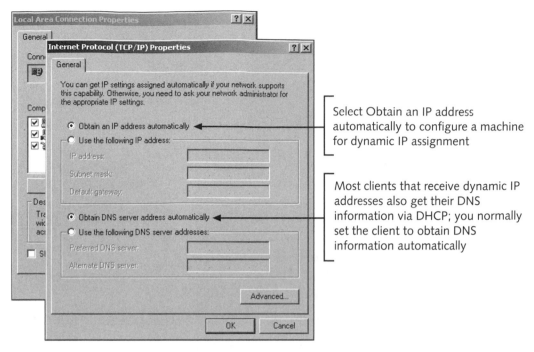

Figure 2-8   Configuring a dynamic IP address

TCP/IP PACKET FILTERING

Windows 2000 provides support for TCP/IP packet filtering. TCP/IP packet filtering allows you to control the types of incoming IP traffic that all network interface cards in a machine will process. TCP/IP in Windows 2000 provides very rudimentary packet filtering that is usually only implemented if no other type of packet filtering is utilized.

You must access the Advanced TCP/IP setting dialog box to enable TCP/IP packet filtering. Then click the Options tab, and double-click TCP/IP filtering to work with the filtering options. Figures 2-9 displays the TCP/IP Filtering dialog box.

Since you can filter by TCP port, UDP port, or IP protocols, you must carefully plan exactly what incoming traffic you wish to filter. Suppose, for example, that you want to block all incoming TCP traffic to a particular machine, except for Web traffic. Allowing TCP port 80, the hypertext transport protocol port, is the easiest way to accomplish this task. Figure 2-10 shows TCP/IP filtering configured to allow only Web traffic.

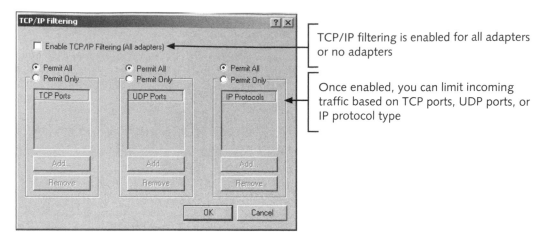

Figure 2-9   TCP/IP Filtering dialog box

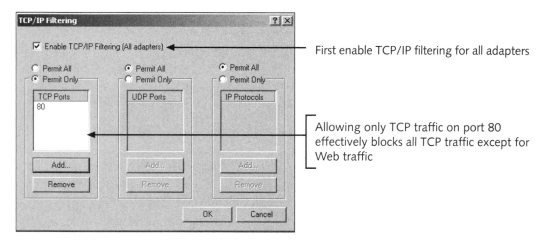

Figure 2-10   Allowing Web traffic with TCP/IP filtering

Using careful planning, you can allow only incoming traffic that is absolutely necessary for a particular machine. You must use caution, however. Once you decide to permit only certain TCP ports, UDP ports, or IP protocols, all ports or protocols not explicitly defined are not allowed. You can very easily block necessary ports or protocols by mistake.

TROUBLESHOOTING TCP/IP

Windows 2000 includes a variety of command-line tools that you can use to test and troubleshoot TCP/IP. These tools allow you to do everything from verifying IP configuration on the local machine to testing connectivity with a remote host. This section discusses the command-line tools ipconfig, ping, tracert, netstat, nbtstat, netdiag, and pathping.

Troubleshooting TCP/IP is a five-step process. Other utilities, like nslookup, hostname, and route, are "*real world*" tools that you can use in addition to the five steps. They are discussed later in this book.

2

In most cases, it takes a combination of command-line tools to test a machine fully. The following five steps are recommended to troubleshoot TCP/IP related problems:

1. Run ipconfig/all.

2. Ping the loopback. This tells you if TCP/IP has been loaded.

3. Ping the local IP address.

4. Ping a host on the same network.

5. Ping a remote host.

If you start all troubleshooting with the ipconfig /all command, you can verify that a machine with a static address has been configured with the correct IP address, subnet mask, and default gateway information. The ipconfig /all command also allows you to determine if clients configured to get dynamic IP addresses have actually received addresses. Step 2, pinging the loopback, is a bit redundant because the ipconfig /all command tells you if TCP/IP has been loaded, but pinging the loopback guarantees that the machine has TCP/IP loaded and initialized. Step 3 helps you determine if you did indeed load the correct address on a statically assigned machine or that you do have a dynamically assigned address. Step 4 tells you that the machine is connected with your local LAN and that the correct network and subnet mask is configured in its IP address. Finally Step 5, ping a remote host, ensures that the default gateway is configured correctly and that routing is active between your network and other networks.

Ipconfig Commands

One of the first troubleshooting tasks is to verify that the TCP/IP configuration has been entered correctly. This is especially important for machines configured with static IP addresses. Mistyping an address is very easy when you must manually enter each IP address. Ipconfig is a command-line tool that, among other things, displays the current IP configuration on a Windows 2000 machine. All command-line utilities run from the **command prompt**, a command-line interface to Windows 2000. You can find the command prompt by clicking Start, Programs, Accessories, Command Prompt. Once you open the command prompt, you can issue the ipconfig /? command to see all the switches available. You get the following output from the ipconfig /? command:

```
Windows 2000 IP Configuration

USAGE:
    ipconfig [/? | /all | /release [adapter] | /renew
[adapter]
            | /flushdns | /registerdns
```

```
                     | /showclassid adapter
                     | /setclassid adapter [classidtoset] ]

        adapter      Full name or pattern with '*' and '?' to 'match',
                       * matches any character, ? matches one
    character.
       Options
          /?                      Display this help message.
          /all                    Display full configuration
                                  information.
          /release                Release the IP address for the
                                  specified adapter.
          /renew                  Renew the IP address for the
                                  specified adapter.
          /flushdns               Purges the DNS Resolver cache.
          /registerdns            Refreshes all DHCP leases and re-
                                  registers DNS names
          /displaydns             Displays the contents of the DNS
                                  Resolver Cache.
          /showclassid            Displays all the dhcp class IDs
                                  allowed for adapter.
          /setclassid             Modifies the dhcp class id.

    The default is to display only the IP address, subnet mask
    and default gateway for each adapter bound to TCP/IP.

    For Release and Renew, if no adapter name is specified, then
    the IP address leases for all adapters bound to TCP/IP will
    be released or renewed.

    For SetClassID, if no class id is specified, then the
    classid is removed.

    Examples:
        > ipconfig               ... Show information.
        > ipconfig /all          ... Show detailed information
        > ipconfig /renew        ... renew all adapters
        > ipconfig /renew EL*    ... renew adapters named EL..
..
        > ipconfig /release *ELINK?21* ... release all matching
    adapters,e.g.ELINK-21, myELELINKi21adapter.
```

This output shows the wide variety of switches available to change the functionality of the ipconfig command. The most used switches are /all, /release, /renew, and /registerdns.

ipconfig /all

If you start all troubleshooting with the ipconfig /all command, you can verify that machines with static addresses are configured with the correct IP address, subnet mask, and default gateway information. The ipconfig /all command also allows you to determine if clients configured to get dynamic IP addresses actually received addresses. The correct command syntax and output received from the ipconfig /all command are:

```
H:\>ipconfig /all

Windows 2000 IP Configuration

        Host Name . . . . . . . . . . . . : win2kpro
        Primary DNS Suffix  . . . . . . . :
        Node Type . . . . . . . . . . . . : Hybrid
        IP Routing Enabled. . . . . . . . : No
        WINS Proxy Enabled. . . . . . . . : No

Ethernet adapter Local Area Connection:

        Connection-specific DNS Suffix  . :
Description . . . . . . . . . . . : Winbond W89C940 PCI
Ethernet Adapter

        Physical Address. . . . . . . . . : 00-20-78-11-4A-62
        DHCP Enabled. . . . . . . . . . . : Yes
        Autoconfiguration Enabled . . . . : Yes
        IP Address. . . . . . . . . . . . : 192.168.0.26
        Subnet Mask . . . . . . . . . . . : 255.255.255.0
        Default Gateway . . . . . . . . . : 192.168.0.1
        DHCP Server . . . . . . . . . . . : 192.168.0.1
        DNS Servers . . . . . . . . . . . : 192.168.0.1
        Primary WINS Server . . . . . . . : 192.168.0.1
        Lease Obtained. . . . . . . . . . : Saturday, May 27,
        2000 1:58:21 PM
        Lease Expires . . . . . . . . . . : Tuesday, May 30,
        2000 1:58:21 PM
```

This command provides a large amount of information about the IP configuration of the machine. In the lower portion of the output, you can see the Media Access Control address of the machine, IP address, subnet mask, default gateway, DHCP server, DNS server, and WINS server. Using this information, you can see that this particular machine is configured for dynamic addresses via DHCP. Once you know that, you can run the ipconfig /release command to release the currently configured IP address.

ipconfig /release

The ipconfig /release command produces the following output:

```
H:\>ipconfig /release

Windows 2000 IP Configuration

IP address successfully released for adapter "Local Area
Connection"
```

At this point you can run the ipconfig /all command to verify that the IP address has actually been released. The following results show that the machine is indeed no longer configured with a dynamically assigned IP address.

```
        Windows 2000 IP Configuration

            Host Name . . . . . . . . . . . . : win2kpro
            Primary DNS Suffix  . . . . . . . :
            Node Type . . . . . . . . . . . . : Hybrid
            IP Routing Enabled. . . . . . . . : No
            WINS Proxy Enabled. . . . . . . . : No

        Ethernet adapter Local Area Connection:
            Connection-specific DNS Suffix  . :
            Description . . . . . . . . . . . : Winbond W89C9
            40 PCI Ethernet Adapter
            Physical Address. . . . . . . . . : 00-20-78-11-
            4A-62
    DHCP Enabled. . . . . . . . . . . : Yes
    Autoconfiguration Enabled . . . . : Yes
    IP Address. . . . . . . . . . . . : 0.0.0.0
    Subnet Mask . . . . . . . . . . . : 0.0.0.0
    Default Gateway . . . . . . . . . :
    DHCP Server . . . . . . . . . . . : 255.255.255.255
    DNS Servers . . . . . . . . . . . :
            Primary WINS Server . . . . . . . : 192.168.0.1
```

ipconfig /renew

To obtain a dynamically assigned IP address after you release all addresses, run the ipconfig /renew command. This command forces the machine to acquire a new IP address. (Of course, if the old address is still available, the client may end up configured with the old address.) Acquisition of DHCP addresses is discussed in more detail later.

ipconfig /registerdns

New to the ipconfig command is the /registerdns switch. This switch provides the functionality described in the /release and /renew switches, but it also refreshes dynamic DNS name registrations. Since Windows 2000 uses DDNS as its primary naming tool, this command is very useful.

2

 If you wish to save a copy of the information provided by the output of any command discussed in this section, you can use the > character to redirect output from the command to a text file. For instance, if you want the information provided by ipconfig in a text file, you type ipconfig /all >d:\ipconfig.txt. The item after the > is the complete path to the file you wish to contain the information.

ping

The **Packet Internet Groper**, or ping, command is the second important troubleshooting command you need to understand. The ping command verifies connectivity with remote hosts. It does this via ICMP echo requests and ICMP echo replies. Whenever you issue the ping command, you send a series of four ICMP echo requests to the designated host. If connectivity is possible, the host returns an ICMP echo reply for each request. The following command output displays the ping command and the responses you get from a successful reply.

```
C:\>ping 192.168.12.2

Pinging 192.168.12.2 with 32 bytes of data:

Reply from 192.168.12.2: bytes=32 time<10ms TTL=128
Reply from 192.168.12.2: bytes=32 time<10ms TTL=128
Reply from 192.168.12.2: bytes=32 time<10ms TTL=128
Reply from 192.168.12.2: bytes=32 time<10ms TTL=128

Ping statistics for 192.168.12.2:
    Packets: Sent = 4, Received = 4, Lost = 0 (0% loss),
Approximate round trip times in milli-seconds:
    Minimum = 0ms, Maximum =  0ms, Average =  0ms

C:\>
```

If you issue the ping command and the ICMP echo replies are not returned, you get the following output:

```
C:\>ping 192.168.12.1

Pinging 192.168.12.1 with 32 bytes of data:

Request timed out.
Request timed out.
Request timed out.
Request timed out.

Ping statistics for 192.168.12.1:
    Packets: Sent = 4, Received = 0, Lost = 4 (100% loss),
Approximate round trip times in milli-seconds:
    Minimum = 0ms, Maximum =  0ms, Average =  0ms

C:\>
```

If the ping command fails, it is important to begin troubleshooting both the basic network configuration of the host (and remote host) and the IP configuration. Begin with simple troubleshooting. Check to see if the host has a network cable patched into a network jack. Also use the ipconfig command to verify IP settings.

The ping command, like the ipconfig command, has a large number of command line switches. When you type ping /?, you receive the following list of switches:

```
                        H:\>ping /?

  Usage: ping [-t] [-a] [-n count] [-l size] [-f] [-i TTL]
  [-v TOS]
                 [-r count] [-s count] [[-j host-list] |
  [-k host-list]]
                 [-w timeout] destination-list

  Options:
      -t              Ping the specified host until stopped.
                      To see statistics and continue -
                      type Control-Bre
                      To stop - type Control-C.
      -a              Resolve addresses to hostnames.
      -n count        Number of echo requests to send.
      -l size         Send buffer size.
      -f              Set Don't Fragment flag in packet.
      -i TTL          Time To Live.
      -v TOS          Type Of Service.
      -r count        Record route for count hops.
      -s count        Timestamp for count hops.
      -j host-list    Loose source route along host-list.
      -k host-list    Strict source route along host-list.
      -w timeout      Timeout in milliseconds to wait for each
                      reply.
```

You can use these switches in a variety of ways. The ping –t command starts a continuous string of ICMP echo requests. This can be useful if you wish to monitor connectivity for a short time period. The –l switch allows you to specify the size of the ICMP packet sent. Each switch follows the syntax ping –[*switch*] *destination IP address*. Ping should be the first command you use to verify connectivity with a remote host.

tracert

The tracert (or trace route) command traces the route a packet takes to a remote system with the use of ICMP echo requests and an incremental Time To Live (TTL) counter. Tracert first sends an ICMP echo request packet with a TTL of 1. Once this packet crosses the first router, it times out and returns. Tracert then sends an ICMP packet with a TTL of 2, 3, and so on. Tracert, by default, allows a maximum TTL of 30. (Using the –h *# of hops* command line switch, you can increase the number of hops to above 30). If a destination host is more than

30 routers or "hops" away, it is considered unreachable. The syntax for the tracert command is simply tracert *w.x.y.z*, where *w.x.y.z* is the IP address of the destination host, the host whose path you wish to learn. Figure 2-11 shows the output from the tracert command and the path to a particular host.

The tracert command displays the path to a particular host plus information on round trip times. The round trip time information can be used to find out if a slow link is causing communication problems. Also, the tracert may reveal that a path to the remote host stops after a particular hop. In this example, if the host had not been found after the series of time-outs (signified by three*) on hop 15, the administrators would know to contact the administrator for the router found in hop 14 to see if there are any known problems

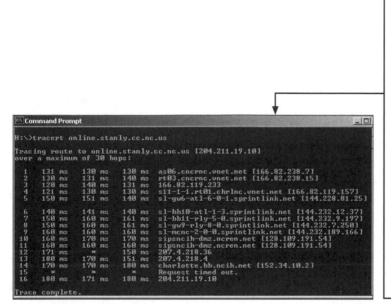

Figure 2-11   Output from tracert command

Tracert allows local administrators to determine if problems with communication are on the local area network, the wide area network, or the Internet service provider's network. If the tracert command returns successful values for all paths on the internal LAN but has time-outs on the way to a particular host, administrators know that the problems are not on their networks. Instead, in this case, congestion on wide area links provided by ISPs is probably causing the problem.

netstat

Netstat displays information about a host's established TCP/IP connections. The following output shows a TCP/IP host that used a Web browser to access Course Technology's Web site at *www.course.com*.

```
H:\>netstat

Active Connections
Proto  Local Address    Foreign Address      State
TCP    win2kpro:1113    199.95.72.8:http     ESTABLISHED
TCP    win2kpro:1114    199.95.72.8:http     ESTABLISHED
TCP    win2kpro:1044    HOMEPDC:netbios-ssn  ESTABLISHED
```

The workstation, win2kpro, accessed the Web site at 199.95.72.8 via TCP using http. In other words, the user of this station is browsing Course Technology's Web page. Netstat also has a series of switches that you can use to customize it. You can view the switches using the netstat /? switch.

If you only want to see TCP connections to a machine, you could issue the netstat –p tcp command. Likewise, you can view only UDP connections with the netstat –p udp command. Netstat allows you to quickly view what resources are either accessing a workstation or being accessed by a workstation.

nbtstat

Since NetBIOS naming is still an integral part of Windows 2000 networks, Microsoft continues to provide the nbtstat command-line tool for viewing NetBIOS over TCP/IP connection information.

Nbtstat allows you to view the currently open NetBIOS connections on a machine. You must run the nbtstat command with either the –a switch, which requires you to specify the NetBIOS name of the machine you want NetBIOS information on, or with the –A switch, which lets you specify the IP address of the machine you want information about. Output from the nbtstat command is similar to the following output.

```
H:\>nbtstat -a win2kpro

Local Area Connection:
Node IpAddress: [192.168.0.26] Scope Id: []

        NetBIOS Remote Machine Name Table
    Name              Type          Status
    ---------------------------------------------------
    WIN2KPRO          <00>  UNIQUE  Registered
    WORKGROUP         <00>  GROUP   Registered
    WORKGROUP         <1E>  GROUP   Registered
    WIN2KPRO          <20>  UNIQUE  Registered
    WORKGROUP         <1D>  UNIQUE  Registered
    .._MSBROUSE__.    <01>  GROUP   Registered
    WIN2KPRO          <03>  UNIQUE  Registered
    ADMINISTRATOR     <03>  UNIQUE  Registered

    MAC Address = 00-20-78-11-4A-62
```

Using the NetBIOS codes and the information the nbtstat command (along with many of its switches presented), you can troubleshoot NetBIOS naming problems. The WINS section of this book discusses in greater detail the nbtstat command as well as NetBIOS naming.

netdiag

 Netdiag is only available on a Windows 2000 machine if the Windows 2000 Support Tools are loaded from the \support\tools folder on the Windows 2000 CD-ROM.

A new troubleshooting command in Windows 2000 is netdiag. This command performs a series of tests on the networking components of a system. The tests check many parts of the networking configuration including such items as all configured protocols. In fact, netdiag tests items such as NDIS, WINS, DNS, trusts, modems, and even the IPX/SPX protocol stack. Although switches and information on them are available using the netdiag /? command, one of the best ways to run the command is with the netdiag >*d:\filename.txt*. (*d* is the name of the local drive where you want to save the information.) Output from this command follows.

```
Computer Name: WIN2KPRO
DNS Host Name: win2kpro
System info : Windows 2000 Professional (Build 2195)
Processor : x86 Family 6 Model 5 Stepping 2, GenuineIntel
List of installed hotfixes :
    Q147222

Netcard queries test . . . . . . . : Passed
[WARNING] The net card 'RAS Async Adapter' may not be work-
ing because it has not received any packets.


Per interface results:

    Adapter : Local Area Connection

        Netcard queries test . . . : Passed

        Host Name. . . . . . . . . : win2kpro
        IP Address . . . . . . . . : 192.168.0.26
        Subnet Mask. . . . . . . . : 255.255.255.0
        Default Gateway. . . . . . : 192.168.0.1
        Primary WINS Server. . . . : 192.168.0.1
        Dns Servers. . . . . . . . : 192.168.0.1

        AutoConfiguration results. . . . . . : Passed
```

```
            Default gateway test . . . : Passed

            NetBT name test. . . . . . : Passed
                 No remote names have been found.

            WINS service test. . . . . : Passed

        Adapter : {4DDF24E5-6F69-4B69-95AB-ABACD6BD9D8E}

            Netcard queries test . . . : Passed

            Host Name. . . . . . . . . : win2kpro
            IP Address . . . . . . . . : 166.82.50.90
            Subnet Mask. . . . . . . . : 255.255.255.255
            Default Gateway. . . . . . : 166.82.50.90
            NetBIOS over Tcpip . . . . : Disabled
            Dns Servers. . . . . . . . : 166.82.1.3
                                         166.82.1.8


            AutoConfiguration results. . . . . . : Passed

            Default gateway test . . . : Passed

            NetBT name test. . . . . . : Skipped
                 NetBT is disabled on this interface. [Test
        skipped]

            WINS service test. . . . . : Skipped
                 NetBT is disable on this interface. [Test
        skipped].


        Global results:


        Domain membership test . . . . . . : Passed
            Dns domain name is not specified.
            Dns forest name is not specified.

        NetBT transports test. . . . . . . : Passed
            List of NetBt transports currently configured:
                NetBT_Tcpip_{85507B45-378F-45FA-BF7C-58C97784ED5A}
            1 NetBt transport currently configured.


        Autonet address test . . . . . . . : Passed
```

```
IP loopback ping test. . . . . . . : Passed


Default gateway test . . . . . . . : Passed


NetBT name test. . . . . . . . . . : Passed


Winsock test . . . . . . . . . . . : Passed


DNS test . . . . . . . . . . . . . : Passed


Redir and Browser test . . . . . . : Passed
    List of NetBt transports currently bound to the Redir
        NetBT_Tcpip_{85507B45-378F-45FA-BF7C-58C97784ED5A}
    The redir is bound to 1 NetBt transport.

    List of NetBt transports currently bound to the browser
        NetBT_Tcpip_{85507B45-378F-45FA-BF7C-58C97784ED5A}
    The browser is bound to 1 NetBt transport.


DC discovery test. . . . . . . . . : Skipped


DC list test . . . . . . . . . . . : Skipped


Trust relationship test. . . . . . : Skipped


Kerberos test. . . . . . . . . . . : Skipped


LDAP test. . . . . . . . . . . . . : Skipped


Bindings test. . . . . . . . . . . : Passed


WAN configuration test . . . . . . : Passed
Entry Name: Vnet
Device Type: Framing protocol :  PPP
LCP Extensions :  Disabled
Software Compression :  Enabled
```

```
Network protocols :
    NetBEUI
    IPX
    TCP/IP
IP Address :  Specified
Name Server: Specified
IP Header compression :  Enabled
Use default gateway on remote network : Enabled

    Connection Statistics:
    Bytes Transmitted       : 497371
    Bytes Received          : 1124089
    Frames Transmitted      : 4956
    Frames Received         : 4486
    CRC     Errors          : 4486
    Timeout Errors          : 0
    Alignment Errors        : 1
    H/W Overrun Errors      : 0
    Framing Errors          : 0
    Buffer Overrun Errors   : 0
    Compression Ratio In    : 2
    Compression Ratio Out   : 5
    Baud Rate ( Bps )       : 31200
    Connection Duration     : 4779162


Modem diagnostics test . . . . . . : Passed

IP Security test . . . . . . . . . : Passed
    IPSec policy service is active, but no policy is assigned.


The command completed successfully
```

Netdiag actually performs many of the same functions already offered by other troubleshooting tools such as nbtstat, netstat, and the ipconfig /all command. Its /fix switch can also solve some trivial DNS problems. In fact, many switches associated with netdiag prove invaluable troubleshooting tools. The following output lists all netdiag switches.

```
H:\>netdiag /?

Usage: netdiag [/Options]>
    /q - Quiet output (errors only)
    /v - Verbose output
    /l - Log output to NetDiag.log
    /debug - Even more verbose.
    /d:<DomainName> - Find a DC in the specified domain.
    /fix - fix trivial problems.
```

2

```
/DcAccountEnum - Enumerate DC machine accounts.
/test:<test name>  - tests only this test. Non -
skippable tests will still be run
Valid tests are :-
      Ndis - Netcard queries Test
      IpConfig - IP config Test
      Member - Domain membership Test
      NetBTTransports - NetBT transports Test
      Autonet - Autonet address Test
      IpLoopBk - IP loopback ping Test
      DefGw - Default gateway Test
      NbtNm - NetBT name Test
      WINS - WINS service Test
      Winsock - Winsock Test
      DNS - DNS Test
      Browser - Redir and Browser Test
      DsGetDc - DC discovery Test
      DcList - DC list Test
      Trust - Trust relationship Test
      Kerberos - Kerberos Test
      Ldap - LDAP Test
      Route - Routing table Test
      Netstat - Netstat information Test
      Bindings - Bindings Test
      WAN - WAN configuration Test
      Modem - Modem diagnostics Test
      Netware - Netware Test
      IPX - IPX Test
      IPSec - IP Security Test
/skip:<TestName> - skip the named test.  Valid tests are:
      IpConfig - IP config Test
      Autonet - Autonet address Test
      IpLoopBk - IP loopback ping Test
      DefGw - Default gateway Test
      NbtNm - NetBT name Test
      WINS - WINS service Test
      Winsock - Winsock Test
      DNS - DNS Test
      Browser - Redir and Browser Test
      DsGetDc - DC discovery Test
      DcList - DC list Test
      Trust - Trust relationship Test
      Kerberos - Kerberos Test
      Ldap - LDAP Test
      Route - Routing table Test
      Netstat - Netstat information Test
      Bindings - Bindings Test
      WAN - WAN configuration Test
      Modem - Modem diagnostics Test
```

```
Netware - Netware Test
IPX - IPX Test
IPSec - IP Security Test
```

The netdiag /v /l command provides you, as an administrator, with a huge amount of information concerning network configuration and status. This command creates verbose output and saves it in a file called NetDiag.log in the root directory of the active drive (the drive on which the system files reside).

pathping

The last command-line tool discussed in this section is a new tool called pathping. This command combines functions of the ping command and the tracert command. You can display its command syntax with the pathping /? command. When you run the command, its output is similar to the following.

```
H:\>pathping 192.168.0.1

Tracing route to HOMEPDC [192.168.0.1]
over a maximum of 30 hops:
  0   win2kpro [192.168.0.26]
  1   HOMEPDC [192.168.0.1]

Computing statistics for 25 seconds...
              Source to Here    This Node/Link
Hop   RTT     Lost/Sent = Pct   Lost/Sent = Pct   Address
  0
win2kpro [192.168.0.26]
          0/ 100 =   0%
            1    0ms     0/ 100 =   0%            0/ 100 =   0%
HOMEPDC [192.168.0.1]

Trace complete.
```

The | item in statistics displays the packet loss during the round trip from source to destination. In this example (pathping between two computers on the same network), both the round trip time (RTT) and packet loss rate are extremely good. Over the Internet or on a busy LAN, RTT and packet loss may be considerably worse. The pathping command allows you to run the same test available with the ping or trace command, but with only a single command.

INTERNETWORK PACKET EXCHANGE/SEQUENCED PACKET EXCHANGE

On many networks today, TCP/IP is not the only protocol stack running. In fact, most networks consist of heterogeneous components from many different manufacturers. One of the most common network configurations today is one with Windows NT 4.0 servers and Novell Netware servers running concurrently. Another common configuration is Netware servers and Windows NT 4.0 workstation clients. The people at Microsoft knew that these configurations would continue to be used, so they built into Windows 2000 the same support available now for the Netware/NT/Windows 2000 hybrid networks. *The MCSE Guide to Microsoft Windows 2000 Server*, ISBN: 0-619-01517-9 from Course Technology discusses in detail such items as Client Services for Netware and Gateway Services for Netware. This book focuses on what IPX/SPX is and how Windows 2000 implements it as NWLink IPX/SPX.

Novell developed IPX/SPX from a protocol stack created by Xerox. Novell needed a protocol stack to run its newly developed Netware network operating system. IPX/SPX uses an 80-bit address format consisting of a network.node format. The first 32 bits form the network portion of the address. The last 48 bits are the node (or host) portion of the address. In fact, the node portion of the address is made up of the media access control address of the node. The following is an example of an IPX/SPX address:

> 200.0020.7811.4a62

In the address, 200 is the network id, while the last 12 hexadecimal digits (48 bits) represent the node or MAC address of the client. Note that the network address does not occupy the entire 32-bit range. While the network id can be up to 32 bits, it does not need to be a full 32 bits in length.

When you begin to configure NWLink IPX/SPX (the Microsoft 32-bit implementation of IPX/SPX), you need to know the frame type used by other IPX/SPX clients on your network. IPX/SPX and NWLink IPX/SPX support the four frame types listed in Table 2-4.

Table 2-4   Novell supported frame types

Novell IPX/SPX Frame Types	Used by:
802.3	Networks running NetWare 3.11 or lower
802.2	Networks running NetWare 3.12 or higher
Ethernet_II	Networks running both IPX/SPX and TCP/IP
Ethernet_snap	Networks running IPX/SPX, TCP/IP, and AppleTalk

Later, in the section, "Installing and Configuring NWLink IPX/SPX," you learn that you can set a Windows 2000 machine to use either Auto Frame Type detection or you can manually set the frame type. A common problem with Windows 2000 machines occurs when a network running IPX/SPX uses multiple frame types. If you set a Windows 2000 machine to Auto Frame Type detection on a network with multiple frame types, it only configures and uses the 802.2 frame type. This causes the machine to be unable to "see" any machines running other frame types. In this scenario, you should manually configure each frame type.

The architecture of IPX/SPX, like the TCP/IP protocol stack, does not follow the OSI model exactly. Instead, as Figure 2-12 shows, it maps very loosely to the OSI model.

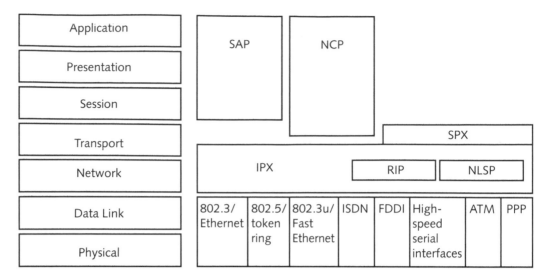

Figure 2-12   IPX/SPX protocol stack architecture

The following list describes the main protocols of the IPX/SPX protocol stack.

- **Internetwork Packet eXchange (IPX)**: IPX is a connectionless, predominately layer 3 protocol, although as you can see in Figure 2-12, it does assume some layer 4 functions. It is responsible for finding the best path through a multipath IPX network. IPX is similar in function to the IP protocol found in the TCP/IP protocol stack. It can use RIP and NLSP to determine the best path among multiple paths through the internetwork.

- **Sequenced Packet eXchange (SPX)**: SPX, a connection-oriented, layer 4 protocol, provides guaranteed delivery services for the connectionless IPX protocol. SPX is similar in function to TCP in the TCP/IP protocol stack.

- **Service Advertisement Protocol (SAP)**: SAP, an upper-layer protocol (layers 5, 6, and 7), advertises services running on IPX/SPX servers and helps clients locate network services.

- **NetWare Core Protocol (NCP)**: NCP facilitates client/server interaction on a NetWare network. NCP handles basic file and print sharing, authentication services, and directory services. NCP functions at layers 4, 5, 6, and 7 of the OSI model.

- **Routing Information Protocol (RIP)**: RIP is an integrated, distance-vector, routing protocol that uses ticks (1/18 of a second time counts) and hop count as metrics to determine the best path within an IPX/SPX internetwork. In IPX/SPX, RIP sends routing table updates every 60 seconds. RIP functions at layer 3 of the OSI model.

- *NetWare Link State Protocol (NLSP)*: Novell designed NLSP, a link state routing protocol, as the successor to RIP. Like RIP, NLSP functions at layer 3 of the OSI model.

Now that you have a basic understanding of the IPX/SPX protocol stack, you must learn how to configure NWLink IPX/SPX on Windows 2000 machines. The next section covers installing and configuring this protocol.

INSTALLING AND CONFIGURING NWLINK IPX/SPX

If you choose the typical network settings during installation, Windows 2000 only installs the Client for Microsoft Networks, File and Printer Sharing for Microsoft Networks, and TCP/IP. To install other protocol stacks such as NWLink IPX/SPX, you must access the Local Area Connection Properties. First access the Local Area Connection icon by right-clicking My Network Places and clicking Properties. Then, right-click the Local Area Connection icon and click Properties to access the Install icon. Figure 2-13 shows how to access the dialog box for the Local Area Connection properties.

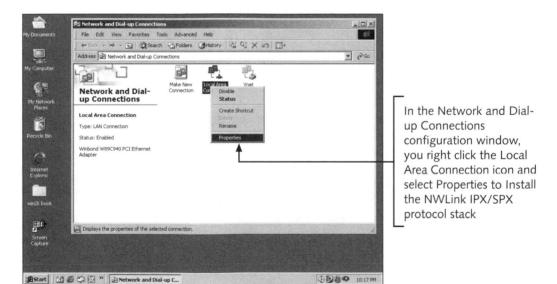

In the Network and Dial-up Connections configuration window, you right click the Local Area Connection icon and select Properties to Install the NWLink IPX/SPX protocol stack

Figure 2-13   Accessing Local Area Connection properties

After clicking Properties, you see the Local Area Connection Properties dialog box shown in Figure 2-14.

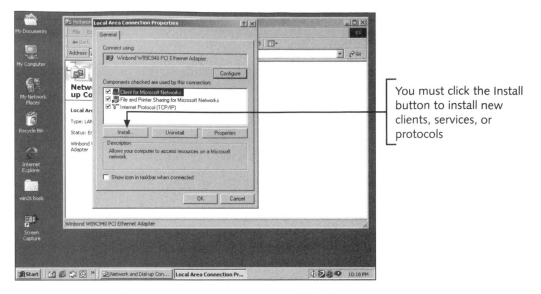

Figure 2-14 Local Area Connection Properties dialog box

To install the NWLink IPX/SPX (or any other client, service, or protocol, for that matter), you must click Install to access the Select Network Component Type dialog box. You can either select Protocol and click the Add button, or double-click Protocol to open the Select Network Protocol dialog box shown in Figure 2-15.

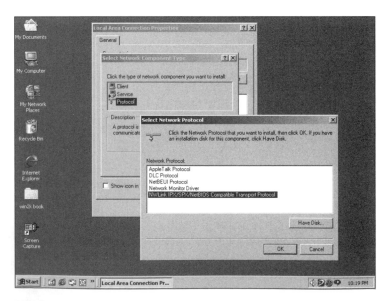

Figure 2-15 Select Network Protocol dialog box

At this point, NWLink IPX/SPX is installed with Frame type set to Auto Detect. If your environment requires the use of multiple frame types, you must manually assign the frame types and network number. You accomplish this task by accessing the properties for the NWLink IPX/SPX/NetBIOS Compatible Transport Protocol Configuration dialog box. Figure 2-16 shows this box.

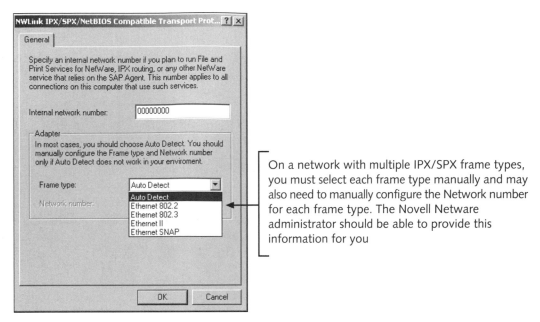

On a network with multiple IPX/SPX frame types, you must select each frame type manually and may also need to manually configure the Network number for each frame type. The Novell Netware administrator should be able to provide this information for you

Figure 2-16   NWLink IPX/SPX/NetBIOS Compatible Transport Protocol Configuration dialog box

NWLink IPX/SPX is now installed and configured on your Windows 2000 machine, but if you need to connect to Netware servers, you still need to install either one or both of the additional services provided for Netware: Client Services for Netware or Gateway Services for Netware.

NETWORK PROTOCOL BINDINGS

Binding is the process of associating or connecting a particular protocol or service to a network adapter card. Each networking protocol on a Windows 2000 machine must be bound to at least one NIC. The rules for optimizing protocol bindings are very simple. First, you should move your most used protocols up in the protocol binding order. To do this, you must access the Advanced Settings from the Advanced command in Network and Dial-up Connections, as shown in Figure 2-17.

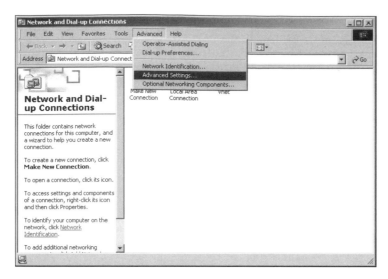

Figure 2-17   Using Advanced Settings for network and dial-up connections

Once you click the Advanced Settings, you open the Advanced Settings dialog box shown in Figure 2-18.

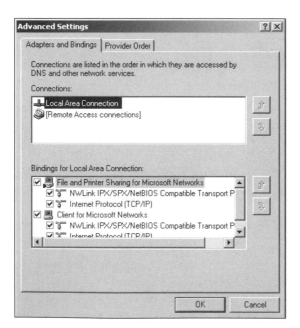

Figure 2-18   Advanced Settings dialog box

In Figure 2-18 NWLink IPX/SPX is above the Internet Protocol (TCP/IP) in the binding order. If NWLink IPX/SPX is the protocol predominantly used by all servers and clients on the network, then the binding order is set correctly. On most Windows 2000 networks, the Internet Protocol (TCP/IP) is the most used protocol. To correct the binding order, you click Internet Protocol (TCP/IP) and click the right most up arrow to move TCP/IP up in the binding order. Figure 2-19 shows the same Advanced Settings dialog box after you move TCP/IP up in the binding order.

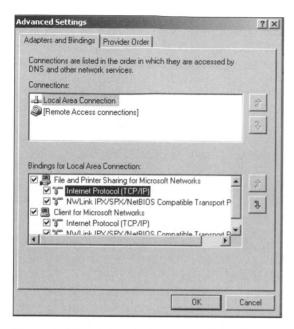

Figure 2-19   Advanced Settings dialog box after moving up Internet Protocol (TCP/IP) in the binding order

Removing unused bindings is the second rule for optimizing network binding. If you are not going to use a protocol for a particular service, you should remove it by deselecting it in the Adapters and Bindings area of the Advanced Settings dialog box. Refer to Figures 2-17 through 2-19 and assume that you have decided that you do not need to use NWLink IPX/SPX for either File and Printer Sharing for Microsoft Networks or the Client for Microsoft Networks components. You can disable NWLink IPX/SPX by removing the check mark from the check box next to the protocol's name.

CHAPTER SUMMARY

❏ Implementing, configuring, and troubleshooting networking protocols is an essential task in preparing a Windows 2000 Professional or Windows 2000 server machine for participation in a network. Windows 2000 supports a multitude of networking protocols, but two of the most important are TCP/IP and IPX/SPX.

❏ TCP/IP is a robust, scalable, mature internetworking protocol developed originally by the ARPANet project. It is designed to allow dissimilar systems to "talk" to one another. IP addresses are the 32-bit logical addresses that, along with subnet masks, must be installed on all clients on a TCP/IP network to allow communication to occur. These addresses can be set either as static addresses or dynamic addresses. The choice between the two depends mainly on the desired function of the Windows 2000 machine. (Most clients use dynamic; most servers use static.) During IP address assignment, you can set optional components such as DNS servers and default gateways. In addition, using advanced features such as TCP/IP packet filtering, network administrators can control what types of incoming packets access various machines.

❏ Windows 2000 includes numerous command-line tools to help troubleshoot TCP/IP once it is installed. Ipconfig can verify IP settings while ping can test connectivity with remote hosts. Tracert, or trace route, tests and displays the path between two TCP/IP hosts on the same network or different networks. Netstat displays a list of current TCP/IP connections. Nbtstat can check NetBIOS over TCP/IP configurations and settings. Netdiag, a new command, gives administrators access to a wealth of information about the current network configuration of a machine. Pathping combines the best of tracert with ping, providing detailed statistics about the connection between two hosts.

❏ TCP/IP is not the only protocol supported by Windows 2000. NWLink IPX/SPX allows Windows 2000 machines to communicate on networks running the IPX/SPX protocol stack. NWLink IPX/SPX supports all four major frame types found in IPX/SPX: 802.3, 802.2, Ethernet_II, and Ethernet_SNAP. Installing NWLink is easy, but you must be careful when setting the frame type to Auto. On networks with multiple IPX/SPX frame types configured, this causes communication problems. In these cases, you must set the frame type and network number manually.

❏ Finally, administrators must carefully manage protocol bindings to ensure optimal performance by network components. The most used protocols should be moved up in the binding order and any unnecessary binding should be removed.

Key Terms

Address Resolution Protocol (ARP) — Lower-layer protocol that resolves a known IP address to a MAC address.

Advanced Research Projects Agency Network (ARPANet) — Original name for the Internet; ARPA was the government agency responsible for sponsoring the research that lead to the TCP/IP protocol stack and the modern-day Internet.

ANDing — Logically combining binary numbers; the results are similar to multiplying binary numbers; ANDing a 1 and a 1 gives a 1. All other combinations (1 and 0, and 0 and 0) result in 0.

binary format — IP address displayed as four sets of eight binary numbers separated by periods.

binding — Process of associating a protocol with a NIC or a network service.

2

dead gateway detection — Feature of Windows 2000 that allows a machine to detect when a default gateway is unreachable and then switch to a configured back-up default gateway.

default gateway — IP address of the router port to networks outside the local network.

dotted decimal — IP addresses displayed as a series of four decimal numbers separated by periods, for example, 192.168.12.2.

dynamic assignment — Configuring a host to obtain an IP address automatically using DHCP.

Dynamic Host Configuration Protocol (DHCP) — Protocol used by clients to obtain IP addresses dynamically from a DHCP server.

Ethernet — Most widely used networking architecture; contention-based architecture that uses carrier sense multiple access/collision detection as its access method.

File Transfer Protocol (FTP) — Provides for file transfer between two TCP/IP hosts; uses TCP as its transport protocol.

host ID — Portion of an IP address that represents the bits used for host identification.

Internet Assigned Numbers Authority (IANA) — Group responsible for controlling allocation of IP addresses to the Internet community.

Internet Control Message Protocol (ICMP) — Handles the communication of errors and status messages within the TCP/IP protocol stack.

Internet Group Management Protocol (IGMP) — TCP/IP protocol used to establish and maintain multicasting groups.

Internet Protocol (IP) — Connectionless, best-effort delivery protocol in the TCP/IP protocol stack that handles routing of data and logical addressing with IP addresses.

Internetwork Packet eXchange (IPX) — Connectionless, layer three protocol that provides routing function for the IPX/SPX protocol stack.

IP address — 32-bit logical addresses that must be assigned to every host on a TCP/IP network.

ipconfig — Command-line tool used to verify IP settings; can also be used to renew or release dynamically assigned IP addresses and DNS information.

local area network (LAN) — Network confined within a small area such as a single building or a small campus.

Media Access Control (MAC) address — Physical address burned into the EPROM on a network interface card.

multicasting — Broadcasting packets to only certain hosts on a TCP/IP network.

nbtstat — Command-line tool that displays NetBIOS over TCP/IP information.

netdiag — New command-line tool in Windows 2000 that tests a large portion of the networking components on a machine. Provides much of the same information as other command-line tools such as netstat, nbtstat, and ipconfig.

netstat — Command-line tool that provides information about current TCP/IP connections.

Netware Core Protocol (NCP) — Primary upper-layer protocol in IPX/SPX that facilitates client/server interaction.

Netware Link State Protocol (NLSP) — More advanced link state routing protocol in the IPX/SPX protocol stack Designed to replace the RIP protocol.

network ID — Portion of an IP address that represents the bits reserved for the network number.

OSI model — Open Systems Interconnection model, a theoretical model for the process two machines go through when communicating with one another over a network.

Packet Internet Groper (ping) — Command-line tool used to test connectivity between two IP hosts.

pathping — Command-line tool that combines ping and tracert functions with new statistics reporting functions.

protocol stack — Group of protocols working together to complete the network communication process.

Request for Comments (RFC) — Proposals presented to the Internet community describing everything from possible TCP/IP standards to simple informative tracts.

Routing Information Protocol (RIP) — Routing protocol provided with the IPX/SPX protocol stack.

Sequenced Packet eXchange (SPX) — Layer four protocol that provides guaranteed delivery; similar in function to TCP.

serial links — Generally slow-speed connections used for wide area network connectivity.

Service Advertisement Protocol (SAP) — Protocol used on IPX/SPX networks by clients to find network services and by servers to advertise network services.

Simple Mail Transfer Protocol (SMTP) — Application layer TCP/IP protocol that provides mail delivery services.

static assignment — Manually assigning an IP address to a host.

subnet mask — 32-bit number used to determine the portion of an IP address that represents the network ID and the host ID.

subnetting — The process of borrowing host bits to increase the number of network bits.

telnet — Application layer protocol in TCP/IP that allows a user to log on to a remote host and execute programs remotely.

tracert — Trace route command-line tool that allows testing of the entire path between two hosts.

Transmission Control Protocol (TCP) — Transport layer protocol in the TCP/IP protocol stack that is connection-oriented and reliable; provides guaranteed delivery.

Trivial File Transfer Protocol (TFTP) — Like FTP, provides file transfer between two TCP/IP hosts; TFTP uses UDP as its transport protocol and is faster, but more unreliable than FTP.

User Datagram Protocol (UDP) — Connectionless, best-effort delivery transport layer protocol in the TCP/IP stack.

wide area network (WAN) — Network or collection of networks spread across a large geographical area.

REVIEW QUESTIONS

1. Which one of the following command-line tools can you use to release and renew dynamically assigned IP addresses?

   a. ping

   b. ipconfig

   c. netdiag

   d. pathping

2. What class of address is the IP address 135.12.5.4?

   a. A

   b. B

   c. C

   d. None of the above

3. Which of the following does assigning a static IP address require? (Choose all that apply.)

   a. A properly configured DHCP server

   b. Manually visiting the machine to be configured

   c. An IP address, subnet mask, and optional default gateway

   d. The ipconfig /release command

4. What is the default subnet mask for a Class B network?

   a. 255.255.255.0

   b. 0.0.0.0

   c. 255.255.0.0

   d. 255.0.0.0

5. Which of the following are possible frame types on an IPX/SPX network? (Choose all that apply.)

   a. NCP

   b. 802.2

   c. Ethernet_II

   d. 802.3

6. Which TCP/IP protocol provides connection-oriented, guaranteed delivery, transport layer services?

   a. TCP

   b. UDP

   c. IP

   d. FTP

7. Which of the following decimal numbers represents the binary number 11011001?

   a. 213

   b. 217

   c. 205

   d. None of the above

8. Which command-line tool displays information concerning nearly every networking component on a system?

   a. ipconfig

   b. netstat

   c. nbtstat

   d. netdiag

9. The four layers of the TCP/IP protocol stack model are _____, _____, _____, and _____.

10. You can use the ping command to verify network connectivity between two TCP/IP hosts. True or false?

11. Which of the following should be done to optimize network bindings? (Choose all that apply.)

   a. Move most used protocols up in the binding order.

   b. Add as many protocols as possible, more is better.

   c. Remove or deselect protocols from any unnecessary networking component.

   d. Do nothing, Windows 2000 auto configures protocol binding with optimal settings.

12. If you borrow 10 bits from the host portion of the IP network 10.0.0.0, what is the new default subnet mask?

   a. 255.0.0.0

   b. 255.255.255.0

   c. 255.255.224.0

   d. 255.255.192.0

13. You added NWLink IPX/SPX to your system, but it cannot communicate with some IPX/SPX hosts on your network. Other IPX/SPX clients can see the hosts in question. Which one of the following is the most likely cause of the problem on your Windows 2000 machine?

   a. The binding for IPX/SPX has been removed.

   b. NWLink IPX/SPX is set to Auto Frame type detection.

   c. TCP/IP is interfering with the NWLink IPX/SPX protocol stack.

   d. The hosts on the network are configured incorrectly.

14. You need three subnets and you have the private address space 192.168.12.0. What is the range of the first usable subnet?

    a. 192.168.12.0 to 192.168.12.31

    b. 192.168.12.10 to 192.168.12.15

    c. 192.168.12.32 to 192.168.12.63

    d. 192.168.12.64 to 192.168.12.95

15. What are advantages of dynamically assigned IP addresses? (Choose all that apply.)

    a. Excessive administrative overhead

    b. Easy configuration of options

    c. Need for a DHCP server

    d. Easy client configuration

16. Which one of the following shows the correct allocation of network ID bits and host ID bits in a Class A network?

    a. Network.network.host.host

    b. Network.host.host.host

    c. Network.network.network.host

    d. None of the above

17. Which of the following must be configured on machines with static addresses if they are on a network that is not connected to any other subnets or networks? (Choose all that apply.)

    a. Subnet mask

    b. Unique IP address

    c. Default gateway

    d. DNS server information

18. Which protocol communicates error and informational messages within the TCP/IP protocol stack?

    a. IGMP

    b. TCP

    c. ARP

    d. ICMP

19. The first octet of an IP address is 01110110. What class of address is this IP address?

20. List the three private address spaces provided for in RFC 1918.

HANDS-ON PROJECTS

All Hands-on Projects in this chapter require two computers set up as described in the lab set-up section in the front of this book. For these exercises, you use the PCs named win2kpro1 and win2kdc02.

Project 2-1

To install a static address on the Windows 2000 machine named win2kdc02:

1. Right-click **My Network Places** and choose **Properties**, as shown in Figure 2-20.

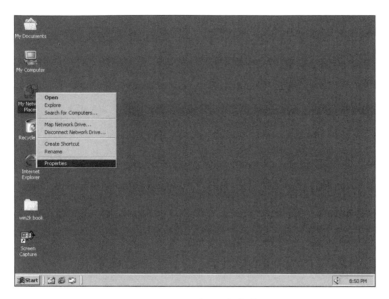

Figure 2-20   Accessing network and dial-up properties via My Network Places

2. Right-click **Local Area Connection** and choose **Properties**.

3. Click **Internet Protocol (TCP/IP)** and then choose **Properties**.

4. In the General section of the Internet Protocol (TCP/IP) Properties dialog box (shown in Figure 2-21), select the **Use the following IP Address**.

5. In the IP address: field, enter **192.168.12.2**, and press **Tab**.

   Windows 2000 automatically fills the subnet mask with 255.255.255.0.

6. Click **OK** to close the Internet Protocol (TCP/IP) Properties dialog box.

7. Click **OK** to close the Local Area Connection Properties box.

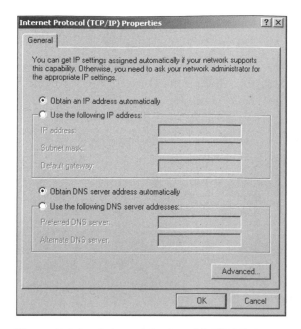

Figure 2-21   Internet Protocol (TCP/IP) Properties dialog box

8. Close the Networking and Dialup Connections dialog box by clicking the **Close** button in its upper-right corner.

Repeat the steps in Hands-on Project 2-1 on the machine named win2kpro1. In Step 5, use the IP address 192.168.12.10.

Project 2-2

To verify that the static address in Project 2-1 is configured correctly:

1. Click **Start** and choose **Programs**, **Accessories**, **Command Prompt**.

   The command prompt in Figure 2-22 should appear.

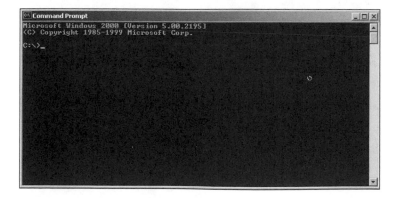

Figure 2-22   Command prompt

2. After the Command Prompt, type **ipconfig /all** and press **Enter**.

3. Verify on win2kdc02 that the IP address is **192.168.12.2** and the subnet mask is **255.255.255.0**.

Repeat the steps in Hands-on Project 2-2 on the machine named win2kpro1. In Step 3 verify that the IP address is 192.168.12.10 and the subnet mask is 255.255.255.0.

Project 2-3

This Hands-on Project requires completion of Hands-on Projects 2-1 and 2-2.

To test connectivity between hosts win2kdc02 and win2kpro:

1. From win2kdc01, click **Start** and choose **Programs**, **Accessories**, **Command Prompt**.

2. After the command prompt, type **ping 192.168.12.10** and press **Enter**.

   If you correctly configured the IP addresses in Hands-on Project 2-1 and verified them in Hands-on Project 2-2, you should receive successful replies to the ping command. Figure 2-23 displays successful ping replies.

```
Command Prompt                                              _|□|x|
Microsoft Windows 2000 [Version 5.00.2195]
(C) Copyright 1985-1999 Microsoft Corp.

C:\>ping 192.168.12.10

Pinging 192.168.12.10 with 32 bytes of data:

Reply from 192.168.12.10: bytes=32 time<10ms TTL=128
Reply from 192.168.12.10: bytes=32 time<10ms TTL=128
Reply from 192.168.12.10: bytes=32 time<10ms TTL=128
Reply from 192.168.12.10: bytes=32 time<10ms TTL=128

Ping statistics for 192.168.12.10:
    Packets: Sent = 4, Received = 4, Lost = 0 (0% loss),
Approximate round trip times in milli-seconds:
    Minimum = 0ms, Maximum = 0ms, Average = 0ms

C:\>_
```

Figure 2-23   Successful ping replies

Project 2-4

To reset win2kpro1 to obtain an IP address dynamically via DHCP:

1. Right-click **My Network Places** and choose **Properties**.

2. Right-click **Local Area Connection** and choose **Properties**.

3. Click **Internet Protocol (TCP/IP)** and then click the **Properties** button.

4. In the Internet Protocol (TCP/IP) Properties dialog box (shown in Figure 2-21), select **Obtain an IP address automatically**.

5. Click **OK** to close the Internet Protocol (TCP/IP) Properties dialog box.

6. Click **OK** to close the Local Area Connection Properties box.

7. Close the Networking and Dialup Connections dialog box by clicking the **Close** button in its upper-right corner.

Project 2-5

To install the NWLink IPX/SPX protocol stack:

1. Right-click **My Network Places** and choose **Properties**.

   See Figure 2-20.

2. Right-click **Local Area Connection** and choose **Properties**.

3. Click **Install** button to open the Select Network Component Type dialog box shown in Figure 2-24.

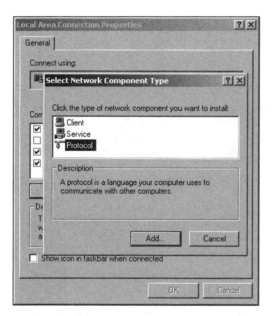

Figure 2-24   Select Network Component Type dialog box

4. Select **Protocol** and then click **Add**.

   After a short pause, the Select Network Protocol dialog box shown in Figure 2-25 opens.

5. Select **NWLink IPX/SPX/NetBIOS Compatible Transport Protocol**, and then click **OK**.

6. Click **Close** to close the Local Area Connection Properties dialog box.

7. Close Networking and Dialup Connections by clicking the **Close** button in its upper-right corner.

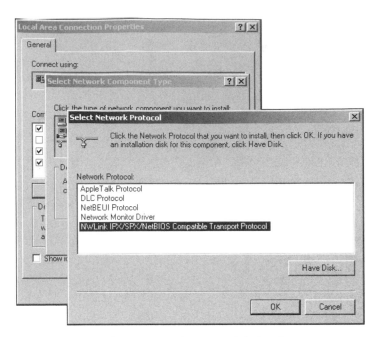

Figure 2-25   Select Network Protocol dialog box

Project 2-6

Although TCP/IP is installed by default with the Typical Network settings during a Windows 2000 installation, you must still know how to install the protocol in case someone accidentally removes it.

To install the TCP/IP protocol stack:

1. Right-click **My Network Places** and choose **Properties**.

   See Figure 2-20.

2. Right-click **Local Area Connection** and choose **Properties**.

3. Click **Install** to open the Select Network Component Type dialog box shown in Figure 2-24.

4. Select **Protocol** and then click **Add**.

   After a short pause, the Select Network Protocol dialog box shown in Figure 2-25 opens.

5. Select **Internet Protocol (TCP/IP)** and then click **OK**.

6. Click **Close** to close the Local Area Connection Properties dialog box.

7. Close the Networking and Dialup Connections dialog box by clicking the **Close** button in its upper-right corner.

Project 2-7

To configure TCP/IP packet filtering to allow only incoming http over TCP:

1. Right-click **My Network Places** and choose **Properties**.
2. Right-click **Local Area Connection** and choose **Properties**.
3. Click **Internet Protocol (TCP/IP)** and then click the **Properties** button.
4. Click the **Advanced** button.

    You should see the Advanced TCP/IP Settings, Options tab illustrated in Figure 2-26.

5. Click the **Options** tab.

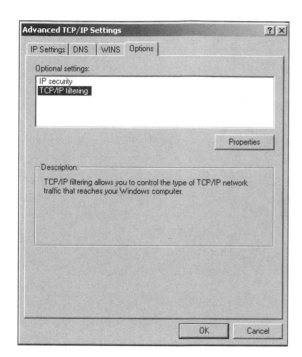

Figure 2-26   Advanced TCP/IP Settings, Options tab

6. Click **TCP/IP Filtering** to select it, and then click the **Properties** button.

    You should see the TCP/IP Filtering dialog box shown in Figure 2-27.

7. Click the **Enable TCP/IP Filtering (All adapters)** check box.
8. Select the **Permit Only** radio button over **TCP Ports**.
9. Click the **Add** button.

    The Add Filter box shown in Figure 2-28 appears.

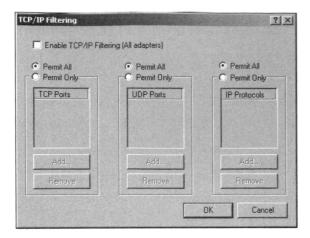

Figure 2-27   TCP/IP Filtering dialog box

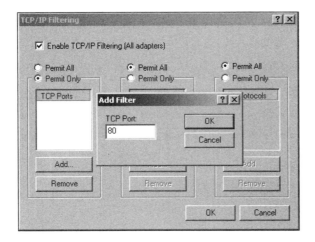

Figure 2-28   Add Filter entry box

10. Type **80** for the TCP Port.

11. Click **OK** to close the Add Filter dialog box.

12. Click **OK** to close the TCP/IP Filtering dialog box.

13. Click **OK** to close the Advanced TCP/IP Settings dialog box.

14. Click **OK** to close the Internet Protocol (TCP/IP) Properties dialog box.

15. Click **OK** to close the **Local Area Connection Properties** dialog box.

    You see a warning box with the text: "You must shut down and restart your computer before the new settings will take effect. Do you want to restart your computer now?"

16. Click **Yes** to restart your computer.

Project 2-8

To change the binding order of multiple protocols:

1. Right-click **My Network Places** and choose **Properties**.
2. Click the **Advanced** command shown in Figure 2-29.

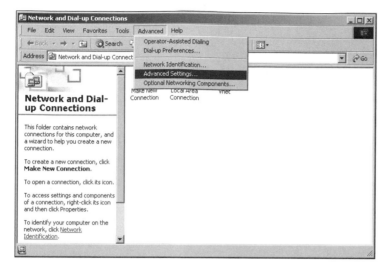

Figure 2-29   Advanced menu

3. Click **Advanced Settings**.

   This opens the Advanced Settings dialog box with the Adapters and Bindings tab shown in Figure 2-30.

4. Under Client for Microsoft Networks, click **Internet Protocol (TCP/IP)** and then click the rightmost **up arrow** to move TCP/IP up in the binding order.

5. Click **OK** to close the Advanced Settings dialog box.

6. Close the Networking and Dialup Connections dialog box by clicking the **Close** button in its upper-right corner.

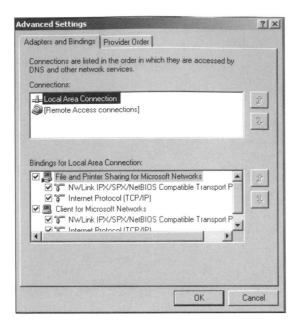

Figure 2-30   Advanced Settings, Adapters and Bindings tab

CASE PROJECTS

Case 1

Your network administrator decides to use the private class B address 172.16.0.0 for a network redesign. The network currently has 30 subnets, and its size is expected to double in the next two years. Using the seven steps of subnetting, design a subnetting scheme that meets the company's present situation while allowing for future growth.

Case 2

A fairly large corporation hired you to develop a plan for IP address allocation. During a meeting, the CIO states that every machine on the network should use dynamic address assignment. Prepare a short summary about both dynamic and static IP address assignment. In the summary, clarify any problems the CIO's plan may cause.

Case 3

At Freytech Inc., the IS department needs simple tools to monitor and manage its Windows 2000 machines. Prepare a list of the tools currently available in Windows 2000, and describe the function of each.

3

DYNAMIC HOST CONFIGURATION PROTOCOL

After reading this chapter and completing the exercises, you will be able to:

♦ Describe the dynamic host configuration protocol (DHCP)

♦ Describe the dynamic IP leasing process

♦ Configure a client to use DHCP

♦ Install the DHCP server service

♦ Configure scopes within the DHCP server service

♦ Define and create scope options

♦ Authorize a DHCP server in Active Directory

♦ Configure DHCP for integration with DNS

♦ Manage, monitor, and troubleshoot DHCP

Chapter 2 introduced the concept of dynamic IP address assignment. The hands-on exercises showed how to configure a client to obtain an IP address from a Dynamic Host Configuration Protocol (DHCP) server. The entire section on dynamic IP addressing referred to DHCP as the network service responsible for dynamically assigning IP addresses. Unfortunately, the DHCP server does not magically appear on your network. You must install, configure, manage, and monitor it to ensure that clients can obtain dynamic IP addresses.

This chapter explains the process used by clients to obtain dynamic IP addresses from a DHCP server. It also describes how to properly install and configure a Windows 2000 server as a DHCP server. In addition, it tells how to integrate a Windows 2000 DHCP server with WINS and DNS. Finally, you learn some basic monitoring, troubleshooting, and management procedures for Windows 2000 DHCP servers.

OVERVIEW OF DYNAMIC HOST CONFIGURATION PROTOCOL

Network administrators constantly try to ease their overloaded workday. As a result, any network service that reduces manual administration of network clients is a welcome addition to most administrators' toolboxes. DHCP allows client machines that are configured to obtain IP addresses automatically to lease an IP address (and a subnet mask) for a configured amount of time. Clients can also receive much more than just an IP address and subnet mask. With a DHCP server, you can assign options that include everything from the default gateway address to a DNS and a WINS server address. The automatic assignment of IP addresses also reduces the work associated with moving clients between subnets or even between complete networks. For instance, workers who travel constantly from site to site within a company can connect to any network jack, receive correct IP addressing, and begin working, if they have laptops configured to obtain IP addresses via DHCP.

The DHCP server with Windows 2000 supports several important new features:

- *Rogue DHCP server detection*: DHCP servers in an environment with Active Directory fully implemented are required to register their IP address with the DHCP Active Directory object. If an unregistered Windows 2000 DHCP server comes online, its DHCP server service shuts down, and it cannot respond to client DHCPDiscover packets. This prevents unauthorized DHCP servers from providing incorrect information to network clients.

- *Integration with DNS*: The DHCP service in Windows 2000 can use the dynamic DNS protocol to dynamically register **A records** or host records and **pointer (PTR) resource records** for clients that do not support **Dynamic DNS (DDNS)**. This configuration actually requires setting parameters on your DNS servers. The section, "Integrating DHCP and DNS," discusses DNS Intergration in detail.

- *Support for superscopes*: The Windows 2000 DHCP server supports superscopes, which group several IP address scopes into a single administrative unit. The section, "**Configuring Scopes**," provides more information on superscopes.

- *Support for multicast scopes*: You can now give multicast addressing information to clients. This feature allows clients to participate in multicast groups.

- *Increased monitoring and management tools*: The DHCP server in Windows 2000 provides new performance counters for System Monitor. These counters allow you to monitor nearly every aspect of DHCP server performance. Windows 2000 also includes the DHCP snap-in for easy management of IP addresses within the **Microsoft Management Console (MMC)** framework.

DHCP Lease Process

A successful DHCP lease process consists of four steps between a client and a server: discover, offer, request, and acknowledgment. Figure 3-1 illustrates the four steps, showing whether the client or server initiates each step.

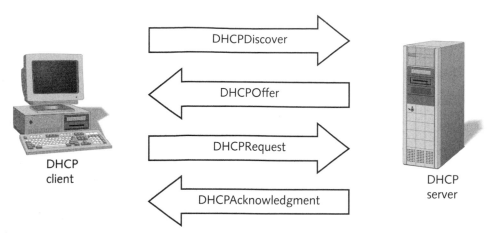

Figure 3-1   Four steps in successful DHCP lease

As shown in Figure 3-1, the client is responsible for starting the process of IP address leasing. Clients broadcast a **DHCPDiscover** packet when they are first turned on or when their current dynamic lease expires and they must obtain a new IP address. In essence, you can think of leasing an IP address as borrowing an address for a set amount of time, the lease duration.

All DHCP servers on the same **network segment** as the client return a **DHCPOffer** that includes a possible IP address that the client may use. The client accepts the first returned offer by requesting it from the DHCP server with a **DHCPRequest** packet. Finally, the DHCP server marks the address as "leased" in its database of addresses (commonly known as scopes) and verifies that the client can use the address with a **DHCPAcknowledgment** (DHCPAck). **Scopes** are continuous ranges of IP addresses that a DHCP server can give to clients. The scopes configured on a server contain the addresses leased to clients.

If for some reason the DHCP server does not verify the address of a client, it issues a **DCHPNack** or negative acknowledgment. This can occur when a client with a dynamic IP address moves to a different network and tries to obtain its previous IP address. Since the old address is not valid for the new network, the DHCP server issues a DHCPNack to force the client to restart the leasing process.

You can easily remember the four steps in the DHCP leasing process using a simple sentence: Aunt **DORA** helps with DHCP addressing. In other words, Aunt **D**iscover, **O**ffer, **R**equest, **A**cknowledgment helps with DHCP addressing.

To understand the DHCP process fully, you need a detailed understanding of exactly what happens in each of the four phases. In the next four sections, you learn exactly what happens.

Step 1: DHCPDiscover

The DHCP client initiates the first step in the DHCP process. When a client is first turned on, its lease expires or it receives a DHCPNack from a DHCP server, it must find a DHCP server on its local segment. All four steps in the DHCP leasing process are broadcast based. In other words, the process sends the DHCP packets to the broadcast MAC address of FFFFFFFFFFFF and the broadcast IP address of 255.255.255.255. Therefore, a DHCP server must be located on the same **broadcast domain** as the client, or the client cannot lease an IP address. Figure 3-2 shows a Network Monitor capture of the DHCP Discover process.

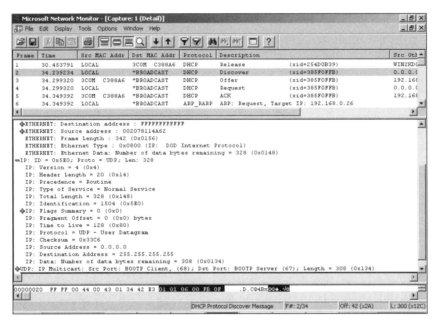

Figure 3-2   DHCPDiscover packet capture in Network Monitor

As shown in Figure 3-2, the ETHERNET: Destination Address of the DHCPDiscover packet is the broadcast **MAC address** of FFFFFFFFFFFF. The ETHERNET: Source Address is the MAC address of the client initiating the DHCPDiscover packet. The IP: Source Address for the packet is 0.0.0.0 because the client does not have an IP address configured yet. The IP: Destination Address is the broadcast address 255.255.255.255. In short, the DHCPDiscover packet is a broadcast packet at both the MAC layer (layer 2 of the OSI model) and the IP addressing layer (layer 3 of the OSI model). All clients on the local segment can see and examine the DHCPDiscover packet. However, only DHCP servers respond with a DHCPOffer packet.

Step 2: DHCPOffer

All DHCP servers that see the DHCPDiscover packet respond to the client with a DHCPOffer packet. Figure 3-3 shows a DHCPOffer packet.

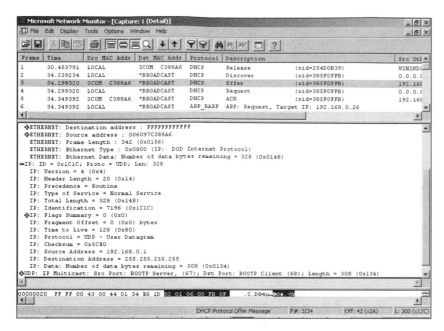

Figure 3-3   DHCPOffer packet capture in Network Monitor

The DHCPOffer packet has an ETHERNET: Destination address of FFFFFFFFFFFF, the broadcast MAC address. The ETHERNET: Source Address is the MAC address of the DHCP server. The IP: Source Address field displays the IP address of the DHCP server. The DHCP server uses this and upper layer information to determine if a client is requesting an IP address from that particular server. The IP: Destination Address is still the broadcast address of 255.255.255.255. The broadcast IP address must be used as the destination because at this point the DHCP client has no IP address.

The client accepts the first DHCPOffer packet it receives from a valid DHCP server and responds with a DHCPRequest packet to obtain the IP address from the DHCP Server.

Step 3: DHCPRequest

The DHCPRequest packet, like every packet in the DHCP process, has an ETHERNET: Destination Address of FFFFFFFFFFFF. The ETHERNET: Source Address is the MAC address of the DHCP client. The IP: Source Address is 0.0.0.0 because the client, although halfway through the lease process, still has no IP address. The IP: Destination Address must remain 255.255.255.255 for this very same reason. Figure 3-4 shows the information discussed about the DHCPRequest packet.

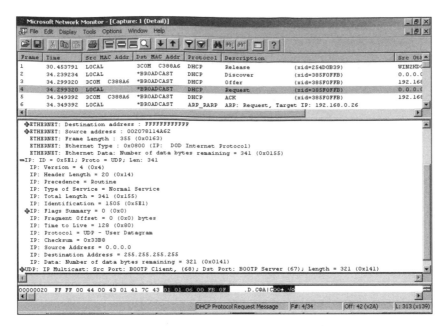

Figure 3-4   DHCPRequest packet capture in Network Monitor

At this point, using information in the DHCP options field of the DHCPRequest packet, shown in Figure 3-5, the DHCP client requests a single IP address, DHCP: Requested Address = 192.168.0.26, for the DHCP: Host Name = win2kdc02 (the DHCP client's name). You can also see that the DHCP options field displays the IP address of the DHCP server as DHCP: Server Identifier.

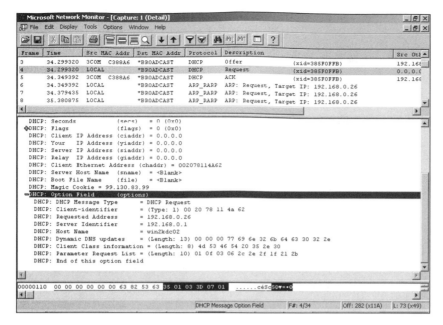

Figure 3-5   DHCP options in the DHCPRequest packet

Step 4: DHCPAcknowledgment

The final step in the four-step DHCP process finds the DHCP server actually leasing the IP address to the client. Figure 3-6 shows the DHCPAck packet.

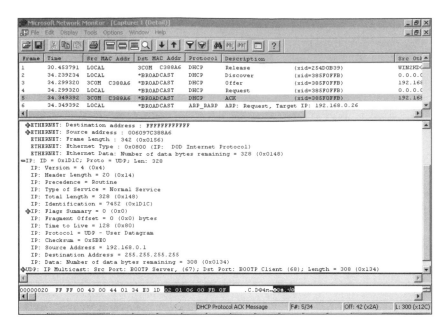

Figure 3-6   DHCPAcknowledgment packet capture in Network Monitor

The ETHERNET: Destination address is still the broadcast MAC Address. The ETHERNET: Source address is the MAC address of the DHCP Server. Also, because the client does not load and initialize TCP/IP until after it receives the DHCPAck, the IP: Destination Address remains the broadcast address 255.255.255.255. The IP: Source Address is the IP address of the DHCP Server. The client uses the IP: Source Address information to renew its lease after a certain time interval.

DHCP Renewal Process

DHCP clients use the entire four-step DHCP process to obtain their initial IP addresses or to renew an expired address. However, renewing an IP lease does not require all four steps. By default, halfway through their lease interval, all DHCP clients attempt to contact the DHCP server at the IP address specified in the DHCP options field for the DHCP: Server Identifier. For instance, eight days is the default lease for Windows 2000 DHCP servers. If this default lease is not changed, clients attempt to renew their IP addresses four days into the lease interval. If they cannot renew their leases, clients attempt again when 87.5% of the lease expires. Clients that cannot renew their leases with the original DHCP server (the one specified in the DHCP: Server Identifier) at the 87.5% interval, attempt to contact any DHCP server to renew their current lease. If their leases expire before they can renew their addresses, clients must complete the entire four-step process to get a new address. Administrators can manually renew a client's lease with the ipconfig /renew command.

Clients who successfully renew their leases halfway through the lease interval use a shorter, two-step process. They send a directed DHCP request to the DHCP server and the server responds with a DHCPAck. Figure 3-7 shows the DHCPRequest from a renewing client.

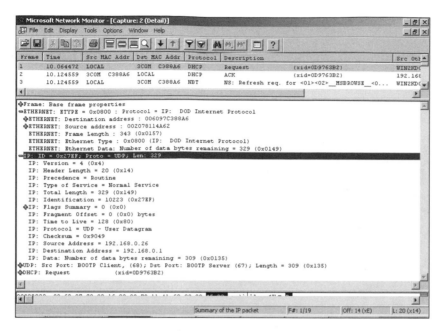

Figure 3-7   DHCPRequest for a renewing client

Unlike the initial DHCPRequest packet, the DHCPRequest renewal packet has the client MAC address as the ETHERNET: Source Address and the DHCP server address as the ETHERNET: Destination Address. Also, the IP: Source Address is the IP address of the client. The IP: Destination Address is the IP address of the DHCP server. In short, instead of a broadcast, the DHPCRequest packet is now a directed message asking the DHCP server to renew the IP lease.

The server returns a DHCPAck if the client can continue to use the leased IP address. This packet is a directed message just like the DHCPRequest. It is possible that the DHCP server may issue a DHCPNack to the client. A DHCPNack occurs when the client has moved to another subnet, the range of addresses on the local subnet has changed, or the client's previous address has expired and was subsequently leased to another client.

CLIENT CONFIGURATION FOR DHCP

Any client that supports a standard implementation of DHCP can obtain an IP address from a Windows 2000 DHCP server. As long as a client follows the standards outlined in RFCs for a DHCP client, a Windows 2000 DHCP server can provide the client with a dynamic IP address.

Configuring Windows 2000 clients for use with DHCP was covered earlier in Chapter 2 in the section on TCP/IP.

To configure Windows clients, you must specify that they obtain an IP address automatically. In Windows 2000 you must access the Internet Protocols (TCP/IP) properties found under Local Area Connections properties. Figure 3–8 displays the internet protocols (TCP/IP) settings for a Windows 2000 machine configured as a DHCP client.

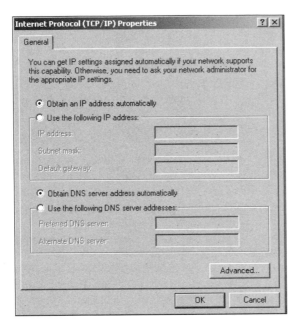

Figure 3-8   Windows 2000 machine configured as a DHCP client

Once configured, the client uses the four-phase DHCP process to obtain an IP address and the two-step renewal process to keep an IP address. On occasion, you may want to force a client to release a currently leased IP address or force it to renew its current IP lease. The ipconfig /release command issued after the command prompt forces a client to release its current dynamic IP address. The ipconfig /renew command forces the client either to renew the current lease, or if no lease is active, to start the lease process with a DHCPDiscover packet.

Sometimes a client cannot find a DHCP server when it issues a DHCPDiscover packet. This can occur because the DHCP server service on the DHCP server has stopped, the scope on the DHCP server has leased all available addresses, or the client is on a different broadcast domain than the DHCP server. When this happens to clients that had no previous lease, Window 2000 clients (and Windows 98 clients) implement **Automatic Private IP Addressing (APIPA)**. With APIPA, the client selects an address from the Class B network 169.254.0.0 with the default subnet mask 255.255.0.0. (Microsoft has reserved the

169.254.0.0 address as a private set of addresses with Internic, the organization that controls public IP addresses.) The client selects an address on the network 169.254.0.0 and then pings to see if any other device is using that address. If a client receives a successful ping reply, the client selects a different address. Each client tries up to 10 private addresses before it stops attempting to load IP. The client continues its attempts to contact a DHCP server every five minutes even though it has an APIPA. If it finds a DHCP server, the client accepts configuration information from the server and abandons the autoconfiguration information.

Windows 2000 clients that still have active leases at system start, but cannot find the DHCP server to renew their IP addresses, ping their default gateway. If the default gateway responds, the client assumes its current IP lease information is correct and continues to use it until it expires or the DHCP server renews it. If the default gateway does not respond, the client assumes it has been moved to another subnet and, because it cannot find a DHCP server, it performs APIPA as just described.

INSTALLING THE DHCP SERVER SERVICE

Installation of most networking services in Windows 2000 Server is not difficult. You must, however, make sure that your server meets the minimum requirements for each service. The DHCP server service requires the following:

- A Windows 2000 server machine configured with a static IP address, subnet mask, and, on networks with multiple subnets or networks, a default gateway

- A range of addresses that can be used to create scopes

- Active Directory installed and configured to allow DHCP servers to be authorized in AD

Although there are many ways to install DHCP, one of the easiest involves accessing Network and Dial-up Connections via the Start menu or by right-clicking on My Network Places and selecting Properties. Once in Network and Dial-up Connections on the server you wish to install DHCP, you must select the Advanced, Optional Networking Components item. This brings up the Windows Optional Networking Components Wizard shown in Figure 3-9.

You must select Networking Services and then click the Details button to open the Networking Services dialog box. To install the DHCP server service on your server, select Dynamic Host Configuration Protocol (DHCP), click the OK button, then click Next after you return to the Windows Optional Networking Components Wizard. You can manage the installed DHCP server service from the DHCP manager snap-in that is added to the Administrative Tools folder after installation. Figure 3-10 shows the DHCP manager snap-in.

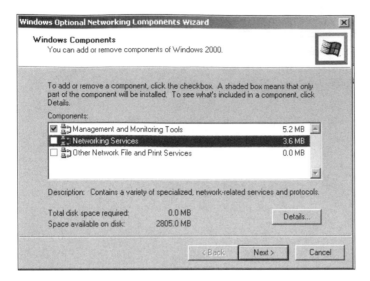

Figure 3-9   Windows Optional Networking Components Wizard

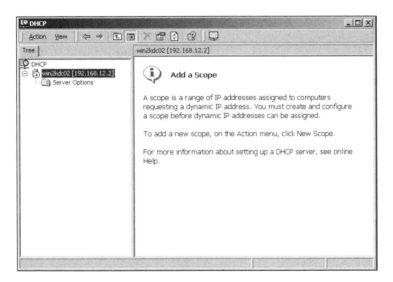

Figure 3-10   DHCP Manager snap-in

The green up arrow next to the small server icon signifies that the DHCP server service is installed and currently running. You can also verify that the service is running by selecting Services under Administrative Tools. If the DHCP Server service Status is Started and its Startup Type is Automatic, you installed the service correctly. Installing the service is only part of the configuration necessary to plan successful DHCP services. As an administrator, you must also plan where to place your DHCP servers. Since all four phases of the initial DHCP lease process are broadcast-based, you must carefully plan placement of DHCP servers or implement **DHCP relay agents** or routers capable of forwarding DHCP broadcasts.

Figure 3-11 portrays a common problem on most networks attempting to implement DHCP. The problem occurs when a network consists of two Ethernet segments (or broadcast domains) connected by Router A. By default, routers do not pass broadcasts, so Router A discards any DHCPDiscover packets broadcast by the DHCP client. The client cannot contact a DHCP server; it uses APIPA to obtain an IP address. Unfortunately, that means that the client cannot use the services of Router A to access either the Internet or any other servers or machines out Router A's Ethernet0 (E0) interface.

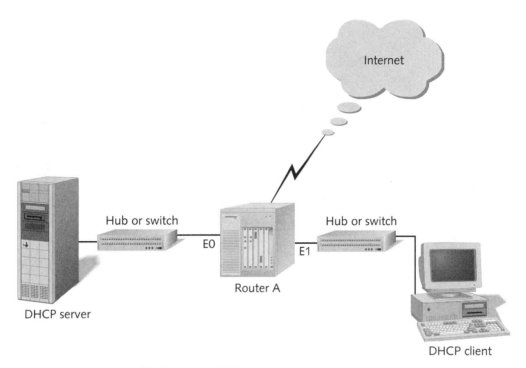

Figure 3-11   Router blocking DHCPDiscover packets

Configuring a Router to Pass DHCP Traffic

There are three ways to solve this problem. If the router supports it, it can be configured to allow DHCP traffic to pass. Most routers support the forwarding of DHCP broadcast traffic. Depending on the software installed on the router, Cisco routers allow DHCP traffic via the ip helper-address [*ip address of DHCP server*] command. Therefore, if the DHCP server in Figure 3-11 has the IP address 192.168.12.12, you use the ip helper-address 192.168.12.12 command to allow DHCP packets from the client to pass to the DHCP server. With this configuration, you would need only a single DHCP server configured with multiple scopes to support your DHCP clients. Unfortunately, the configuration also has a single point of failure—the single DHCP server. Regardless, many networks use this configuration to save server resources and to simplify management.

Configuring a DHCP Server per Physical Segment

Placing a second DHCP server on the same segment as the client is another way of solving this problem. While this method may seem extreme, it does limit the amount of traffic associated with DHCP that needs to pass through the router. Figure 3-12 shows a network with a DHCP server on each side of the router. The clients on each side can receive dynamic IP addresses from the DHCP server on the local segment. This solves the problem of broadcast traffic's inability to pass through the router.

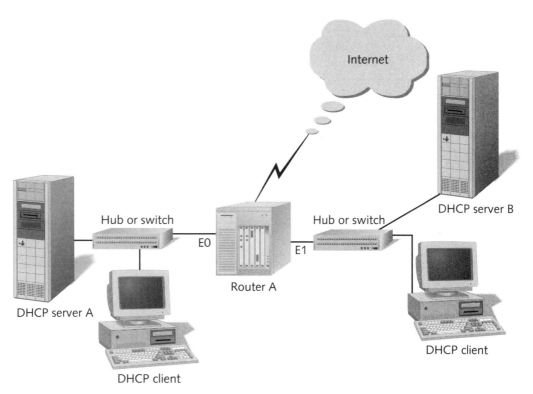

Figure 3-12   Multiple DHCP servers

You can use the same basic setup to create a fault-tolerant configuration for your DHCP servers. You can increase fault tolerance by creating two scopes on DHCP Server A. The first scope holds 75% of the available addresses for the local segment. The second scope holds 25% of the available addresses for the segment served primarily by DHCP Server B. Server B has a scope with 75% of its local available addresses and 25% of the addresses available on Server A's segment. Once you enable the router to pass DHCP traffic with the ip helper-address command on Cisco routers (or with similar commands on other manufacturers' routers), the two DHCP servers can provide addresses for their local clients, and, in the event one server fails, the remaining server provides addressing for the clients on the remote segment.

DHCP Relay Agents

The final way to solve the problem presented in Figure 3-11 is with a DHCP relay agent. A DHCP relay agent acts as a proxy for a DHCP server. If the DHCP relay agent sees a packet destined for a DHCP server, it grabs that packet and uses a directed message to the DHCP server that has been configured in its relay agent properties. It also receives packets sent back from the DHCP server and broadcasts those onto the local segment, so the DHCP clients can receive the DHCPOffer and DHCPAck packets. You must enable Routing and Remote Access services to configure a Windows 2000 machine as a DHCP relay agent. Once you do this, go to the local computer name listed in the Routing and Remote Access snap-in, expand the IP Routing item, right-click General, and then select New Routing Protocol. In the New Routing Protocol dialog box, select DHCP Relay Agent and click OK. This loads the DHCP Relay Agent. Figure 3-13 shows the New Routing Protocol item you must select to open the New Routing Protocol dialog box. Once configured, the relay agent begins forwarding DHCP packets.

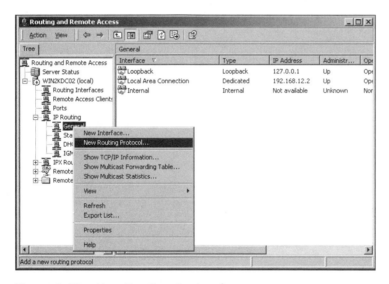

Figure 3-13   New Routing Protocol

 You cannot configure a Windows 2000 machine to run both the DHCP server service and the DHCP relay agent. Doing so results in erratic behavior by both networking components.

CONFIGURING SCOPES

After you correctly install the DHCP server service, you must create a scope of addresses for the server to dole out to clients.

For instance, if you have the Class C private network address of 192.168.12.0 with the default mask of 255.255.255.0, then you can configure a scope that consists of the entire usable range of addresses, 192.162.12.1 to 192.168.12.254, or any portion of these usable addresses. Normally, network administrators reserve some portion of usable addresses for machines that require static IP addresses. In a Class C network, you will probably want to create scopes that do not include the first twenty or so usable IP addresses. Then you can use these addresses for static clients. Although the exclusion feature lets you exclude certain IP addresses from scopes, it is much easier to simply remove a portion of your IP addresses from the scope before creating it.

To begin creating a scope, you must open the DHCP manager snap-in found in the Administrative Tools folder on the Start menu, right-click the server name, and then select New Scope. Figure 3-14 shows the New Scope Wizard that appears when you select New Scope.

Figure 3-14   Creating a new scope in the DHCP manager snap-in

The New Scope Wizard then walks you through the steps of creating a new scope. Specifically, the wizard prompts you for the following items:

- *Name and Description*: The name of the scope as it will appear in the DHCP Manager and a short description of the scope

- *IP Address range*: The range of addresses to be leased to clients

- *Subnet mask*: The subnet mask information for the scope. The recommendation for Windows 2000 is a subnet mask based on the class of the addresses placed in the IP address range. If you have custom subnet masks (that is, you are subnetting), then you can specify the subnet mask in bits or with a decimal equivalent.

- *Add Exclusions:* At this point, you can exclude any addresses in the IP address range that you do not want dynamically leased to clients. However, it is better to place only the IP addresses that you want leased in the IP address range. That way, you do not need to add any exclusions.

- *Lease duration:* You can either accept the default lease duration of eight days or change it to a value more suitable for your network. If you constantly move computers from one subnet to another or if you are in danger of running out of IP addresses, you may want to shorten the lease for a scope to three days (the old Windows NT DHCP default lease duration) or less. If your network clients rarely change subnets and you have abundant IP addresses, increasing the DHCP lease duration lessens the network traffic created by DHCP renewals.

- *Configure DHCP Options:* The final question the New Scope Wizard asks is if you want to configure scope options. **Options** are extra configuration information such as default gateway, DNS server, and WINS server addresses that you can give to a DHCP client when clients lease an IP address. The section, "Scope Options," later in this chapter, provides greater detail.

The Windows 2000 DHCP server service also supports providing multicast addresses to clients via DHCP. The process of creating a multicast scope is very similar to creating a normal scope. To create a multicast scope, you right-click on the server name in DHCP manager snap-in and select New Multicast Scope. The New Multicast Scope Wizard then walks you through the process of creating a multicast scope.

Finally, superscopes are available to allow grouping and management of multiple scopes as one unit. This allows administrators to assign multiple IP ranges to a single physical subnet or to group scopes together for easier management. Superscopes allow administrators to expand a physical segment beyond its initial limit of one range of addresses. For instance, an administrator may assign a single Class C address range for a physical segment. That segment may grow beyond the 254 hosts allowed for a single Class C range of addresses. With superscopes, the administrator can group two Class C ranges together to serve a single physical segment.

Another common use of superscopes involves the process of migrating to a new range of dynamic IP addresses. You can use superscopes to configure and manage both ranges during the transition process. Combining multiple member scopes together creates superscopes. **Member scopes** are just normal scopes placed within a superscope. To create a superscope, you create the scopes you want to include in the superscope, then you right-click the server name in DHCP Manager and select New Superscope. The New Superscope Wizard allows you to group multiple scopes into a superscope.

On occasion, you may want to reserve a specific IP address for a specific client. In effect, **reservations** allow you to assign one particular IP address in the scope to a single client. You configure reservations in the Reservations folder under a particular scope. Right-click the Reservations folder and select New Reservation to open the New Reservation dialog box shown in Figure 3-15.

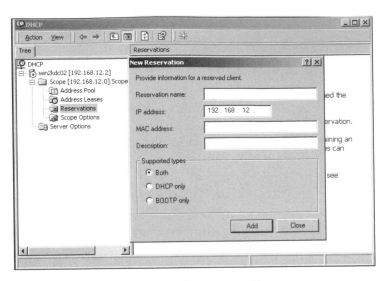

Figure 3-15   Configuring a client reservation

You must specify a Reservation name, an IP address in the scope, and the MAC address of the client for which you want a reservation. You may include an optional description. You can also select if this reservation is for DHCP, BootP, or both.

 BootP is the method that diskless workstations originally used to obtain IP addresses from BootP servers. The specifications for DHCP borrowed from the old BootP methods. Windows 2000 supports BootP clients to provide backward compatibility.

If you do not know the MAC address of the client, obtain it by running the ipconfig /all command from the command prompt.

SCOPE OPTIONS

Once you install the DHCP server service and create your scopes, it is time to specify options. Options are additional parameters that you can configure for clients using dynamic IP addresses. You can configure options globally for all scopes (for such items as DNS servers or WINS servers), for a single scope (for such items as default gateways), for a vendor-defined or user-defined class, or on a reserved client basis. You configure most options at the **scope options** or **server options** level. **Vendor-defined option classes** and **user-defined option classes** are available for clients that need special configuration parameters. Use them only if no other means are available for assigning an option. **Reserved client options** allow you to give a specific configuration to a client with a reservation. Again, whenever possible, try to use server and scope options. Table 3-1 describes the main options used with DHCP.

Table 3-1 DHCP options

Option	Parameter	Function
003 Router	IP address of default gateway	Provides clients with IP address of default gateway on their local network segment
006 DNS servers	IP addresses of DNS servers on network	Provides clients with IP address of DNS servers on their network
015 DNS Domain Name	Domain name for network; for example, course.com or microsoft.com	Provides clients with DNS domain name of their network
044 WINS/NBNS server	IP address of WINS server(s) on network	Provides clients with IP address of WINS servers on their network; setting this option automatically adds the 046 WINS/NBT Node Type option to your scope options
046 WINS/NBT Node Type	0x1: broadcast node 0x2: point-to-point node 0x4: mixed-node 0x8: hybrid mode (the section on WINS discusses each of these in detail)	Provides clients with a NetBIOS Node Type; although four settings are possible you should always set 046 to 0x8.

Configuring options is a very simple procedure. To configure global options, you navigate to Administrative Tools on the Start menu and select DHCP to start the DHCP manager snap-in. Once it loads, you right-click the Server Options folder and select Configure Options. All options created under the Server Options folder are server and apply to all scopes on the DHCP server. You use server options for items such as DNS servers and WINS servers, items that are the same for all clients in all scopes.

You must right-click the Scope Options folder for a particular scope in order to set scope options. Once you select Configure Options, you can configure options for a particular scope. Also, under the Advanced tab in scope options or server options, you can select and define vendor-defined option classes and user-defined option classes.

Configuring reserved client options requires that you first create a client reservation. Then you can right-click the reservation and select Configure Options to set the required options.

DHCP AND ACTIVE DIRECTORY

Rogue DHCP server detection is one of the most important new features of the Windows 2000 DHCP server service. If Active Directory is installed and configured correctly on your network, you can create a DHCP object within AD to validate DHCP servers. When a DHCP server comes online and registers with Active Directory, its IP address is checked against the authorized DHCP servers. If its IP address is not one of the authorized servers, the DHCP service stops and the server cannot answer the client request. Integrating DHCP server with Active Directory requires that all DHCP servers run Windows 2000 (Windows NT DHCP servers cannot be authorized in the AD) and that the first DHCP server in your network is installed as either a domain controller or member server. To authorize a Windows 2000 DHCP server, you must first login as an Enterprise Administrator or with a user account that has the right to add DHCP servers to your Active Directory. Then follow these steps:

1. Open the **DHCP manager snap-in** under Administrative Tools

2. Click the **Action** menu and select **Manage Authorized Servers**

3. Click the **Authorize** button and type the **IP address of the Windows 2000 DHCP server** you want to authorize

4. Click **OK** to close the dialog box

If Active Directory is not loaded, an error message appears, stating that the Active Directory cannot be found. Without Active Directory properly loaded, you cannot authorize DHCP servers, and rogue DHCP server detection is not available.

INTEGRATING DHCP AND DNS

The Domain Name System server that ships with Windows 2000 supports dynamic updates of both A records and pointer (PTR), also known as **reverse lookup records**. In fact, the DHCP server service that ships with Windows 2000 can act as a proxy for clients that do not support dynamic DNS updates. Using this feature of DHCP ensures that clients receiving dynamic IP addresses have the correct information stored in the DNS database. Before DHCP can act as a proxy, you must enable DNS to allow updates for non-dynamic DNS aware clients. You accomplish this task in the DNS snap-in with the Properties command on the Action menu. If you select Enable Updates for DNS Clients that Do Not Support Dynamic Update, the DHCP server can dynamically register non-DDNS aware clients with the DNS service.

Of course, you must also configure your DHCP server to act as a proxy. Figure 3-16 displays the DNS tab that you see when you right-click the DHCP server in the DHCP snap-in and select Properties.

To enable the DHCP server to dynamically register all clients, select the Always update DNS radio button and check the item, Enable updates for DNS clients that do not support dynamic update. These two options force the DHCP server to register both A records (host name to IP address mappings) and pointer (PTR) or reverse lookup (PTR) records (IP address to host name mappings) with the DNS server.

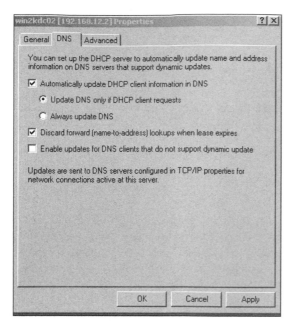

Figure 3-16   DHCP DNS configuration tab

   Windows 2000 clients support registering their own A records via dynamic DNS updates. They do, however, rely on the DHCP server to register their PTR records with the DNS server.

MANAGING, MONITORING, AND TROUBLESHOOTING DHCP

Many tools are available for managing, monitoring, and troubleshooting DHCP. In this section you explore some of these tools and learn how to perform basic troubleshooting.

Managing DHCP

Throughout this chapter on DHCP, the DHCP snap-in has been your main tool for managing DHCP. During real-world, day-to-day administration, this is the tool you use to create scopes, manage options, and configure most DHCP settings. There are, however, other tools for managing DHCP.

One management task you may need to perform is to stop the DHCP service. You can accomplish this task in several ways. First, you can open the DHCP snap-in, then click Action, All Tasks, Stop. From the command prompt, you can stop the DHCP server service with the net stop dhcpserver command. Likewise, you can restart the DHCP server service from the command prompt with the net start dhcpserver command. It is also possible to start and stop the DHCP server using the Services snap-in found under Administrative Tools. You must locate the DHCP server service and then click the Stop button to shut down the service.

Compacting the DHCP database with the jetpack command is a fairly uncommon but essential administrative task in certain circumstances. The DHCP database resides in the systemroot\winnt\system32\dhcp directory in a file named dhcp.mdb. If the file dhcp.mdb is 30 MB or larger in size, you probably need to run the jetpack utility on the database. Running the utility requires three steps:

1. Stop the **DHCP server service** from either the DHCP snap-in or the command line with the net stop dhcpserver command.

2. From the command prompt, navigate to the systemroot\winnt\system32\dhcp directory, and run the following command: jetpack dhcp.mdb temp.mdb. (The second database name can be anything; .mdb is a temporary database used only during the jetpack process.)

3. Restart the **DHCP server service**.

Managing DHCP also means managing DHCP clients. The easiest way to retrieve configuration information from a client is the ipconfig /all command issued at the command prompt. This command displays all information concerning a client's DHCP configuration. You can use the ipconfig /release and ipconfig /renew commands to force a client to release its lease and renew its lease. This is useful if you change the scope of addresses on a network and want all clients to obtain IP addresses in the new range.

Moving the DHCP database to a different DHCP server, dhcp.mdb, is one task you may need to perform if you upgrade to a newer machine or if you need to remove a DHCP server from the network for maintenance. The steps for moving a DHCP database are very simple. First, you must stop the DHCP server service on both computers using one of the methods described earlier in this section. The easiest method is the net stop dhcpserver command issued after the command prompt. You must then copy the entire contents of the systemroot\winnt\system32\dhcp folder to exactly the same path on the new computer. It is possible to move the database to a new directory, but you should not copy the .log or .chk files to the new directory. Finally, you should restart the DHCP service on the new computer. On both computers you should also click on the server, select Action, and then select Reconcile All Scopes.

Monitoring DHCP

DHCP monitoring is like DHCP management: you can perform it with many different tools. Basic monitoring is available within the DHCP snap-in by clicking on a particular server and then selecting Action, Display Statistics. Figure 3-17 displays the statistics available within the DHCP snap-in.

These basic statistics allow you to quickly view server uptime, numbers of available addresses, and the number of leased addresses.

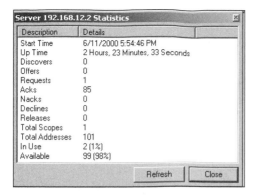

Figure 3-17   DHCP statistics within DHCP snap-in

In addition to these basic statistics, the Windows 2000 DHCP server service can write a daily log of DHCP activity. This log is stored in the systemroot\winnt\system32\dhcp folder. This is a daily log saved as DhcpSrvLog.sun. The extension corresponds to the day of the log. For example, a Saturday log has the same name, DhcpSrvLog, but a different extension, .sat. You can configure some aspects of this logging activity within the DHCP snap-in. If you select a server in the snap-in, click Action, and then select Properties, you see the Properties dialog box for that particular server. On the General tab shown in Figure 3-18, you can enable or disable the DHCP audit log. It is enabled by default. On the Advanced tab shown in Figure 3-19, you can set the path to the audit logs.

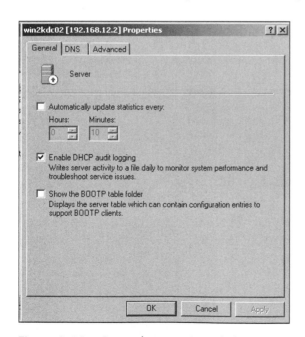

Figure 3-18   General properties tab for a DHCP Server

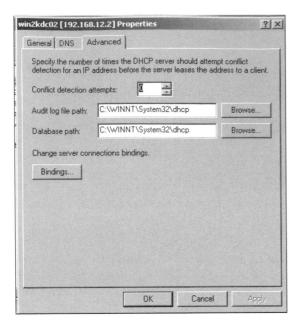

Figure 3-19   Advanced properties tab for a DHCP Server

Using System Monitor is probably the most powerful and effective way to monitor DHCP server performance. Once you install the DHCP server service on a Windows 2000 server, new counters are added to System Monitor to allow detailed monitoring. You can access System Monitor from the Performance snap-in located in Administrative Tools. Once started, selecting the System Monitor and right-clicking in the chart area on the right allows you to select from the multitude of DHCP performance counters shown in Figure 3-20.

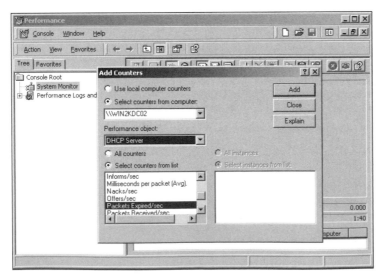

Figure 3-20   System Monitor counters for DHCP

3

The DHCP Server Performance Object under System Monitor provides multiple counters that you can use to monitor your DHCP server performance. Discovers/sec, Offers/sec, Requests/sec and Acks/sec are all counters that allow you to see exactly how much DHCP traffic your server must handle. If the workload becomes excessive, you may need to add additional DHCP servers.

Troubleshooting DHCP

Most problems with DHCP involve misconfigured scopes or options, a stopped DHCP server service, a scope that has run out of addresses, or an improperly configured network.

Misconfigured scopes and options normally result from simple typos by the network administrator. If you suspect that a client is receiving incorrect option information, use the ipconfig /all command to verify client settings and information. Many times the incorrectly configured option is readily apparent in the DHCP client configuration information. Once you know what has been incorrectly set, you can change the options within the DHCP snap-in.

If a DHCP server does not respond to client requests and clients use APIPA to obtain IP addresses, you may have a stopped DHCP server service. As mentioned previously, the net start dhcpserver command should fix this problem quickly.

Sometimes, a scope runs out of addresses to lease. When this occurs, Windows 2000 clients use APIPA to complete their IP configurations. This can cause a multitude of network communication problems. Fixing this problem is not as simple or straightforward as solving other problems discussed in this section. Decreasing the length of lease for the scope is one possible solution to this problem. If more addresses are available, you may be able to increase the range of addresses in the scope. Final possible answers are renumbering the entire scope with a new and larger range of addresses or removing some clients from the overcrowded network segment.

Other problems with DHCP have nothing to do with the configuration of the client or the server. Instead, they may result from poor network design. As mentioned earlier, all four steps of the DHCP process use broadcast extensively. If any network device that blocks broadcast separates the DHCP clients and DHCP servers, the DHCP process fails.

If a DHCP client cannot send UDP broadcast to the DHCP server, it cannot obtain an IP address. To fix this problem, you must either place a DHCP server on each subnet or implement DHCP relay agents on subnets without DHCP servers.

CHAPTER SUMMARY

- ❏ The dynamic host configuration protocol provides an easy way for network administrators to provide IP addressing information for network clients. Instead of visiting each client to configure a static IP address, network administrators can use the Windows 2000 DHCP server service to create a pool of IP addresses known as scopes that can be dynamically assigned to clients.

❐ Clients use a four-step process when initially leasing an IP address via DHCP. You can easily remember the four steps, **D**iscover, **O**ffer, **R**equest, **A**cknowledgment, by thinking of the sentence. "Aunt **DORA** helps with IP addressing."

❐ Configuring a Windows 2000 server with the DHCP server service includes the following steps:

1. Configuring a static IP address, subnet mask, and default gateway on the server
2. Installing the DHCP server service
3. Creating scopes and, if needed, multicast scopes and superscopes
4. Creating and specifying options on a server, scope, vendor-defined, user-defined, or reserved client basis (most options are server and scope)
5. Authorizing the DHCP server in Active Directory

❐ DHCP in Windows 2000 is tightly integrated with the new Dynamic DNS features. You can configure DHCP to create DDNS entries for clients that do not support DDNS. This feature helps with support of legacy, non-DDNS aware clients. Windows 2000 clients can register their own A records, but they still rely on the DHCP server to create reverse lookup records.

❐ Finally, myriad tools are available for managing, monitoring, and troubleshooting DHCP. The final section of this chapter discusses many of these tools.

KEY TERMS

Automatic Private IP Addressing (APIPA) — New feature in Windows 98 and Windows 2000 that allows DHCP clients to select an IP address from the private range 169.254.0.0/16 whenever they cannot find a DHCP server on the local segment.

A records — Host name to IP address mappings in the DNS database that are used in host name resolution.

BootP — Older alternative to DHCP that diskless workstations used to obtain IP addresses.

broadcast domain — That portion of a network where broadcasts are propagated; normally broadcast domains are created by router placement in a network.

DHCPAcknowledgment — Packet broadcast by a DHCP server to a DHCP client that grants the client a lease for a particular IP address; fourth step of four-step DHCP lease process.

DHCPDiscover — Packet broadcast by DHCP clients to find DHCP servers on the local segment; first step of four-step DHCP lease process.

DHCPNack — Negative acknowledgment that a DHCP server broadcasts if it must decline a client's request for a particular IP address.

DHCPOffer — Packet broadcast by a DHCP server to a DHCP client that contains a possible IP address for lease; second step of four-step DHCP lease process.

DHCP relay agent — Software component loaded via Routing and Remote Access Service to a Windows 2000 machine; allows a machine to act as a proxy for DHCP clients on a segment.

DHCPRequest — Packet broadcast by a DHCP client requesting the IP address offered in a DHCPOffer packet; third step of four-step DHCP lease process.

Dynamic Domain Name System (DDNS) — Extension to the DNS systems that allows dynamic updates to the DNS database. The Windows 2000 DHCP server service can integrate with DDNS to allow dynamic DNS registration for clients that receive dynamic IP addresses.

Media Access Control (MAC) address — Physical address burned in the EPROM on a network card when it is manufactured.

member scopes — Scopes joined together in superscopes.

Microsoft Management Console (MMC) — Extensible framework within which Windows 2000 management snap-ins such as the DHCP snap-in reside.

multicast scopes — Ranges of multicast addresses configured to be dynamically assigned to host via DHCP.

options — Extra IP configuration parameters that can be given to DHCP clients when they lease an IP address.

pointer (PTR) resource records — Map an IP address to a fully qualified domain name (FQDN). *See also* reverse lookup records.

Reserved client options — Scope options created for a single client that has been given a DHCP reservation.

reverse lookup records — Another name for PTR records. These records resolve a host name from a known IP address.

reservations — Using the MAC address of the client to ensure that a particular IP address is always leased to that client.

scope options — Options that apply to all clients in one scope only.

scopes — Ranges of IP addresses configured for lease to clients via DHCP.

server options — Options that apply to all clients in all scopes configured on a DHCP server.

superscopes — Multiple scopes grouped together to allow centralized management; also allow for more than one range of IP addresses on a single physical subnet.

user-defined option classes — Allow expansion of DHCP options to include parameters determined by the network administrator for a particular client.

vendor-defined option classes — Expanded DHCP options created for one particular vendor's computers or network hardware.

REVIEW QUESTIONS

1. Which of the following steps does a DHCP client perform in the DHCP lease process? (Choose all that apply.)

    a. DHCPOffer

    b. DHCPDiscover

    c. DHCPNack

    d. DHCPRequest

2. What scope option allows you to define the default gateway for DHCP clients?

   a. 044

   b. 003

   c. 006

   d. 015

3. Which of the following are advantages of using DHCP on your network? (Choose all that apply.)

   a. Easier IP address management

   b. Elimination of all static IP addresses

   c. Reduction in server load due to less network services being needed

   d. Leasing of options such as DNS server, WINS server, and Domain Name

4. A _____ is a range of IP addresses that DHCP clients can lease.

5. All four steps in the DHCP lease process are sent to the broadcast IP address 255.255.255.255. True or false?

6. What does combining multiple scopes together for administrative purposes create?

   a. Multicast scopes

   b. Superscopes

   c. Big area scopes

   d. DHCP relay agents

7. A DHCP server requires a static IP address, subnet mask, and default gateway. True or false?

8. At what interval do clients attempt to initially renew their lease?

   a. Once every 24 hours

   b. Every 5 minutes

   c. 87.5 percent of the lease interval

   d. One-half the lease interval

9. Which one of the following can forward DHCP packets to a DHCP server on a different network segment?

   a. DHCP Server Agent

   b. DHCP Relay Agent

   c. DHCP DNS Agent

   d. DHCP Broadcast Agent

10. When you install DHCP, counters are added to facilitate monitoring in which one of the following?

    a. Performance Monitor

    b. DHCP snap-in

    c. System Monitor

    d. Active Directory

11. You can configure the DHCP server to create _____ records and pointer (PTR) records for hosts that do not support DDNS.

12. Which of the following commands stops the DHCP server service?

    a. net start dhcpserver

    b. net stop dhcp

    c. net stop dhcp snap-in

    d. net stop dhcpserver

13. Which one of the following new features of the Windows 2000 DHCP server service stops inappropriate leasing of IP addresses from unauthorized DHCP servers?

    a. Rogue DHCP server detection

    b. DHCP validation and reconfiguration via DDNS

    c. Superscopes

    d. DHCP and DNS integration

14. If you configure the 044 WINS/NBNS server option for a scope, which one of the following options **must** you configure?

    a. 003

    b. 046

    c. 005

    d. 006

15. Your DHCP database is over 30 MB, and clients have trouble getting fast response from the DHCP server. Which one of the following commands should you run to fix the problem?

    a. ipconfig /renew

    b. jetpack

    c. ipconfig /release

    d. None, just reinstall DHCP

16. A DHCP client has problems attaching to network resources. You run the ipconfig command and find that the client's IP address is 169.254.12.4. What is the most likely reason your client has this Class B address?

    a. The client was unable to find a DHCP server and used APIPA to configure TCP/IP.

    b. The DHCP server is configured to give out addresses in the 169.254.0.0 range.

    c. The client has been assigned 169.254.12.4 as a static address.

    d. Because of an address conflict between this client and another client, the client used APIPA to configure TCP/IP.

17. A DHCP server performs which of the following steps in the DHCP lease process? (Choose all that apply.)

    a. DHCPOffer

    b. DHCPDiscover

    c. DHCPNack

    d. DHCPRequest

18. If they support DHCP broadcast forwarding, routers can be used instead of DHCP relay agents on networks with a single DHCP server and multiple physical network segments. True or false?

19. To authorize a DHCP server in Active Directory, what must you log in as? (Choose all that apply.)

    a. Enterprise Administrator

    b. Server Operator

    c. Local Administrator

    d. An account that has the right to authorize DHCP servers

20. Which one of the following creates and stores a daily log of DHCP activity?

    a. DHCP snap-in

    b. DHCP activity log

    c. System Monitor

    d. Active Directory

HANDS-ON PROJECTS

All Hands-on Projects in this chapter require two computers set up, as described in the lab set-up section in the front of this book. For these exercises, you use the PCs named win2kpro1 and win2kdc02. To complete these exercises, you must have completed Hands-on Projects 2-1 and 2-2 on the machine named win2kdc02.

Project 3-1

To install Active Directory so the DHCP server can be authorized in AD:

1. Click **Start** and then select **Run**.

2. In the Run dialog box, type **dcpromo**.

3. In the Active Directory Installation Wizard dialog box, click **Next**.

4. Select the **Domain controller for a new domain** radio button, and then click **Next** to continue.

5. Select the **Create a new domain tree** radio button, and then click **Next** to continue.

6. Select **Create new forest of domain trees**, and then click **Next** to continue.

7. In the Full DNS name for new domain: box, type **win2kclass02.org**, and click **Next**.

8. Click **Next** to accept the default NetBIOS Domain Name.

9. Click **Next** to accept the default Database and Log locations.

10. Click **Next** to accept the default Shared System Volume location.

11. Click **OK** to close the Active Directory Installation Wizard concerning DNS.

12. Select the **Yes, install and configure DNS on this computer (recommended)** radio button, and then click **Next** to continue.

13. Click **Next** to accept the default Permissions settings.

14. Type **password** in the Password and Confirm password boxes for the Directory Services Restore Mode Administrators Password, and click **Next**.

15. Click **Next** on the Summary page to continue.

16. Click **Finish** to close the Active Directory Installation Wizard.

17. Click **Restart Now** to restart the system and load Active Directory.

Project 3-2

To install the DHCP server service on the domain controller win2kdc02:

1. Click **Start**, **Settings**, **Network and Dial-up Connections**.

2. In Network and Dial-up Connections, click **Advanced** and then click **Optional Networking Components**.

3. Double-click **Networking Services** to see a list of networking services you can install.

4. Click in the box beside **Dynamic Host Configuration Protocol (DHCP)** to select the DHCP server service.

5. Click **OK** to close the Networking Services dialog box.

6. Click **Next** to complete installation of the DHCP server service.

3

Project 3-3

This project requires you to log in as Administrator. (This account is a member of the Enterprise Administrator's group by default.)

To authorize a DHCP server in Active Directory:

1. Click **Start**, **Programs**, **Administrative Tools**, **DHCP**.

2. In the DHCP snap-in, click **Action** and then click **Manage Authorized Servers**. The Manage Authorized Servers dialog box shown in Figure 3-21 appears.

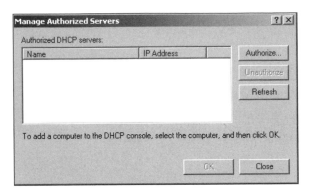

Figure 3-21   Manage Authorized Servers dialog box

3. Click the **Authorize** button and type the **IP address** of your server. (From the command prompt, use the ipconfig /all command to determine your server IP address.) Click **OK**.

4. Click **Yes** in the informational dialog box concerning adding the server to the authorized list.

5. Click **Close** to close the Manage Authorized Servers dialog box.

   You authorized your server as a DHCP Server within Active Directory.

Project 3-4

This project requires the use of the machine configured as win2kdc02 and the second machine running Windows 2000 professional and installed as win2kpro01.

To create a scope of IP addresses and add a client reservation:

1. Click **Start**, **Programs**, **Administrative Tools**, **DHCP on win2kdc02**.

2. Right-click your **servername** (win2kdc02), and select **New Scope**.

3. Click **Next** in the New Scope Wizard dialog box.

4. Type **Partner's Scope** in the Name field, leave the Description field blank, and click **Next** to continue.

3

5. In the Start IP address field, type **192.168.12.100** (or the number assigned by your instructor), and then in the End IP address field, type the same number you placed in the Start IP address field. You are creating a scope of one.

6. In the Subnet Mask field, type **255.255.255.0**.

7. Click **Next** to continue.

8. Click **Next** to skip the Add Exclusions part of the wizard.

9. Click **Next** to accept the default lease duration of 8 days.

10. Select the **No, I will configure these options later** radio button, and click **Next** to continue.

11. Click **Finish** to complete the New Scope Wizard.

12. On the client computer (win2kpro01), issue the ipconfig /all command at the command prompt. Note the physical address here _____. (It should be a 12-digit hexadecimal address.)

13. Click **+** to expand the scope.

14. Right-click **Reservations** and select **New Reservation**.

15. Enter **Partner's Computer** in the Reservation name: field.

16. Type the address from Step 5 in the IP address field.

17. Type the physical address from Step 12 (minus the hyphens) in the MAC address: field.

18. Leave the Description blank and leave Supported types set to **Both**.

19. Click **Add** to add the reservation, then click **Close** to close the New Reservation dialog box.

To create a superscope, select **New Superscope** in Step 2 and follow the New Superscope Wizard directions. To create a multicast scope, select **New Multicast Scope** and follow the New Multicast Scope Wizard directions.

Project 3-5

To test the scope and reservation:

1. On the DHCP server, right-click your configured scope and select **Activate**.

2. On the DHCP client machine, win2kpro01, right-click **My Network Places** and select **Properties**.

3. Right-click **Local Area Connection**, and select **Properties**.

4. Double-click **Internet Protocol (TCP/IP)** and verify on the General tab that the client is configured to Obtain an IP address automatically. (If the client has a static address, select the **Obtain an IP address automatically** radio button, and then click **OK**.)

5. Click **OK** to close the Local Area Connections Dialog Box.

6. Click **Start**, **Programs**, **Accessories**, **Command Prompt**.

7. After the command prompt, type the **ipconfig /release** command.

   This releases any previous dynamic IP addresses that may be on the client.

8. After the command prompt, type the **ipconfig /renew** command to obtain a new IP address lease.

9. The client should receive the IP address you reserved in Step 16 of Hands-on Project 3-4.

10. After the command prompt, type **ipconfig /all |more** to verify that the client did indeed receive the reserved IP address.

Project 3-6

To configure DHCP for DNS integration and allow the DHCP Server to register with DNS those clients that do not support dynamic DNS updates:

1. Click **Start**, **Programs**, **Administrative Tools**, **DHCP**.

2. Right-click your **servername** and select **Properties**.

3. Click on the **DNS tab** in the Properties Dialog box.

4. Click to select **Enable updates for DNS clients that do not support dynamic update**. Click **OK**.

   You configured your DHCP server to register clients such as Windows 95, Windows 98, and Windows NT that do not support dynamic DNS updates.

Hands-on Project 3-6 sets the DNS properties for all scopes on the server because you set the property at the server level. You can also set the DNS properties on a per scope basis.

Project 3-7

To view statistics available in the DHCP snap-in:

1. Click **Start**, **Programs**, **Administrative Tools**, **DHCP**.

2. Click your **servername** to select the DHCP server.

3. Click **Action** and then select **Display Statistics**.

4. Click **Refresh** to update the statistics. Click **Close** to return to the DHCP snap-in.

Project 3-8

To stop the DHCP service, compact the DHCP server database, and restart the service:

1. Click **Start**, **Programs**, **Accessories**, **Command Prompt**.

2. Type **net stop dhcpserver** after the command prompt.

   This command stops the DHCP server service.

3. Type **cd systemroot drive letter\winnt\system32\dhcp**, and press **Enter**.

4. After the command prompt, type **jetpack dhcp.mdb temp.mdb** to compact the DHCP database. A message similar to the following appears:

   Compacted database dhcp.mdb in 1.432 seconds.
   moving temp.mdb => dhcp.mdb
   jetpack completed successfully.

5. Type **net start dhcpserver** to restart the DHCP server service.

6. Type **exit** to close the Command prompt.

Project 3-9

To configure System Monitor to examine the DHCP server service:

1. Click **Start**, **Programs**, **Administrative Tools**, **Performance**.

2. Right-click in the chart area of the right pane, and select **Add Counters**.

3. In the Performance Object box, scroll up and select **DHCP Server**.

4. Add **Discovers/sec**, **Offers/sec**, **Requests/sec**, and **Acks/sec**.

5. Click **Close** to shut the Add Counters dialog box.

6. On your Windows 2000 client machine configured for DHCP in earlier projects in this chapter, issue the **ipconfig /release** and **ipconfig /renew** commands several times, and watch DHCP activity on System Monitor.

CASE PROJECTS

Case 1

Your network is configured as shown in Figure 3-22. Your boss wants you to design a DHCP implementation that uses as few servers as possible. Create two possible plans for supporting DHCP on this network.

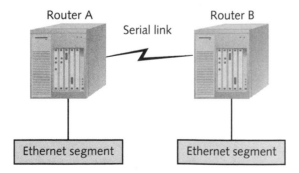

Figure 3-22   Example Network

Case 2

Hillier, Inc. has hired you to install DHCP services. For the initial meeting, prepare a short summary of new features in the Windows 2000 DHCP server service. For the summary, prepare a preliminary design for scopes and option assignments. (Determine how many scopes are needed, how many servers, what options must be specified.)

Case 3

After your meeting at Hillier, Inc., the chief information officer, Merlin, sends you an e-mail questioning the need for Active Directory in the design of DHCP services. Draft a quick e-mail to the CIO detailing the benefits Active Directory brings to a DHCP implementation.

4

DOMAIN NAME SYSTEM

After reading this chapter and completing the exercises, you will be able to:

♦ Provide an overview of the Domain Name System (DNS)

♦ Describe the features of DNS in Windows 2000

♦ Install the DNS service

♦ Configure a DNS server

♦ Create resource records manually

♦ Configure a client to use DNS

♦ Manage, monitor, and troubleshoot DNS

In order to communicate on TCP/IP networks, clients must resolve host names to IP addresses. On very small networks, static hosts files may be used to map the host name to an IP address. Most networks, however, need Active Directory installed, which must use DNS servers to handle host name to IP address resolution. This chapter introduces you to the DNS service as a prelude to actually installing and configuring a DNS server on a Windows 2000 network. In this chapter, you also learn to manage, monitor, and troubleshoot the DNS service.

DOMAIN NAME SYSTEM OVERVIEW

Host names are simple names used as aliases for IP addresses. Early in the development of TCP/IP, researchers realized that humans are much more adept at remembering names than numbers.

As a result, the TCP/IP protocol stack developed with the idea that computers on a network would have host names that could be used to access resources such as files and printers. Unfortunately, computers are much better at numbers than names. Host files and DNS perform the task of translating from names (host names) to IP addresses.

The **hostname** command entered after the command prompt returns the currently configured host name on the computer.

Hosts Files

The ability to perform host name to IP address resolution is an extremely important task on a TCP/IP network. Without host name resolution, users cannot access Internet or intranet resources via Fully Qualified Domain Names (FQDN). For example. *www.course.com* is the Fully Qualified Domain Name for the Web server for Course Technology: *www* represents the host name, while *course.com* is the domain name. FQDN makes Internet resources accessible with easy-to-remember names used instead of IP addresses.

Windows 2000 provides a variety of methods to perform host name to IP resolution, but, in the end, the **Domain Name System (DNS)** is the resolution method of choice on all Windows 2000 networks.

Originally on TCP/IP networks, hosts used a text file called a **host file** to perform host name to IP address resolution. When the Internet consisted of 30 or 40 computers, manually editing the host file was not a labor-intensive task. Host files have a specific format. The following example is the host file available in Windows 2000 in the systemroot\system32\drivers\etc folder.

```
# Copyright (c) 1993-1999 Microsoft Corp.
#
# This is a sample HOSTS file used by Microsoft TCP/IP for
#Windows.
#
# This file contains the mappings of IP addresses to host
#names. Each entry should be kept on an individual line. The
#IP address should be placed in the first column followed by the
#corresponding host name.
# The IP address and the host name should be separated by at
#least one space.
#
```

```
# Additionally, comments (such as these) may be inserted on
#individual lines or following the machine name denoted by a
'#' symbol.
#
# For example:
#
#        102.54.94.97       rhino.acme.com          # source server
#        38.25.63.10        x.acme.com              # x client host

127.0.0.1 localhost
```

4

In the sample host file, the # symbol is used to mark and allow for comment lines within the host file. To add an entry to the host file, you must type the IP address of the host and then the host name or Fully Qualified Domain Name of the host. For example, to add and to comment on an entry for the host 192.168.1.21, you place the following in the host file:

```
192.168.1.21 example.win2kbook.org #sample entry for a host
```

Host files in Windows 2000 must be stored in the \%systemroot%\system32\drivers\etc directory. (\winnt is the default path for the systemroot directory.) Because entries need to be added manually to the host file, it is not a practical method for host name resolution on anything but the smallest of networks. However, if your network is very small and you do not want to spend the money or take the trouble to install and configure DNS, a host file is a viable alternative for host name to IP address resolution.

Windows 2000 provides six different ways to perform host name to IP address resolution. Figure 4-1 displays the six support methods for host name resolution in Windows 2000.

The local host name is the first item a Windows 2000 machine checks when trying to resolve an IP address to a host name. If the local host name is the same as the host name being resolved, resolution occurs very quickly and efficiently. If, however, the local host name and the host name to be resolved are not the same, the Windows 2000 machine attempts to locate a host name to IP address mapping in the locally defined host file. If no resolution occurs using the host file, the Windows 2000 machine contacts the DNS server specified in its static IP address settings or in the DNS entry it receives from a DHCP server. If no resolution occurs via contacting the DNS server, the Windows 2000 machine tries a fourth method: it falls back on NetBIOS naming resolution methods by contacting a **Windows Internet Name Service (WINS)** server to attempt to find a mapping between the host name and an IP address. Using the final two methods, the client attempts to resolve the host name via either a broadcast or the **LMHOSTS** file, a text file that maps NetBIOS names to IP addresses. (Chapter 5 discusses NetBIOS names and name resolution.)

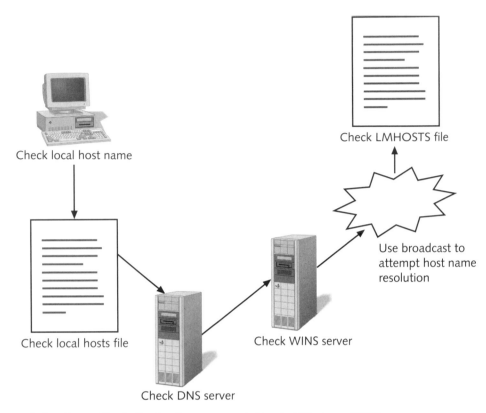

Figure 4-1   Six methods for host name resolution in Windows 2000

DNS Structure

In most host name resolutions on Windows 2000 networks, the client resolves host name to IP address mapping by using a local host name lookup, the local host file, or more than likely, a DNS server. The Domain Name System that supports the operation of all DNS servers is a hierarchical naming system. The DNS hierarchy consists of the root-level domain, top-level domains, second-level domains, subdomains within the second-level domains, and resource records such as host names. Figure 4-2 displays the DNS naming hierarchical structure.

The root-level domain is the highest level in the DNS hierarchy. It is represented by a period, which is usually not shown on Fully Qualified Domain Names.

Top-level Domains

Top-level domains are the organizational domains created by the designers of the Internet to simplify the naming and logical structure of the DNS namespace. Figure 4-2 shows the .gov, .com, and .org top-level domains. Table 4-1 shows several of the top-level domains and the areas they represent.

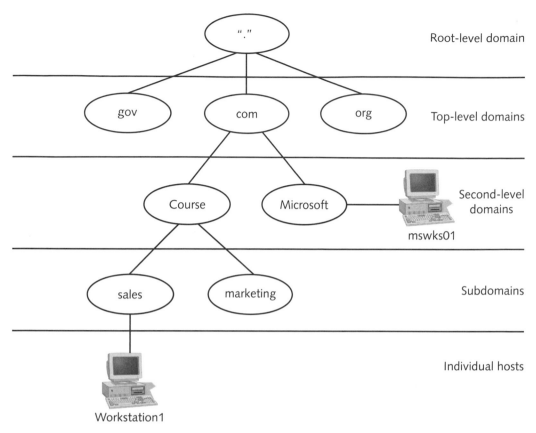

Figure 4-2   DNS hierarchical structure

Table 4-1   Top-level domains

Top-level Domain	Areas Represented
gov	U.S. government agencies (does not include most military services)
com	Commercial organizations
mil	U.S. military services
edu	Educational institutions
net	Internet Service Providers (ISPs)
org	Nonprofit organizations

The list in Table 4-1 is not complete. Top-level domains also exist for most countries, and new top-level domains will be introduced in the very near future.

Second-level Domains and Subdomains

Second-level domains are found beneath the top-level domains. It is at the second-level domains that most companies register their names with a **name registration company**, a company with the ability or authority to add second-level domains. In DNS, any company with **authority** over a particular portion of the DNS namespace can add domains to that space. Since name registration companies can add second-level domains, you must contact them to register a particular second-level domain name. For instance, Course Technology had to contact a name registration company to obtain the second-level domain name course.com. Once Course Technology registered and created course.com, it was said to have authority over that domain. Having authority allows Course Technology to create subdomains to divide the domain namespace further. DNS servers located within the Course Technology company have the course.com domain as their **zone of authority**, the portion of the DNS namespace for which a name server is responsible. The ability to be authoritative for the course.com domain allows the creation of subdomains such as sales.course.com and marketing.course.com.

Subdomains such as sales and marketing found in Figure 4-2 further divide second-level domains. Most companies use subdomains to create smaller administrative units in the DNS namespace.

On the lowest level of the DNS namespace are the actual resource records such as host names. In Figure 4-2, you can see that hosts (and therefore host names) reside at either the second-level domain or within subdomains. The host mswks01 in the Microsoft second-level domain is a computer in the microsoft.com domain. The host Workstation1 is a computer in the sales subdomain of the course.com second-level domain.

DNS Zones

Within DNS are the levels of domains depicted in Figure 4-2, along with a concept known as **DNS zones**. DNS zones are portions of the DNS namespace that can be administered as single units. Each zone has a **primary name server** that holds the **DNS zone file**. For each zone in which a primary DNS server holds the main DNS zone file, that server is considered authoritative for that portion of the namespace. Figure 4-3 shows the course.com domain and the authoritative server for each portion of the namespace.

In Figure 4-3, each server in the domain or subdomain is considered the primary name server for that portion of the DNS namespace. In each case, the DNS servers as primary name servers hold the read/write master copy of the DNS zone file for that domain or subdomain. **Primary name servers** hold a read/write copy of the zone file. In other words, changes to the DNS zone file only occur on primary name servers. **Secondary name servers** are DNS servers configured to hold a read-only copy of the primary name server's DNS zone file. Windows 2000 DNS primary servers replicate and send the information in the file to the secondary name servers at predefined intervals. Windows 2000 DNS also supports incremental zone transfers. When changes occur in the DNS database, Windows 2000 DNS primary servers send only the updates to configured secondary servers. Updates on Windows 2000 DNS servers are faster, thus reducing network traffic and consolidating network bandwidth. Previous versions of Windows DNS servers sent the entire DNS file when changes occurred.

4

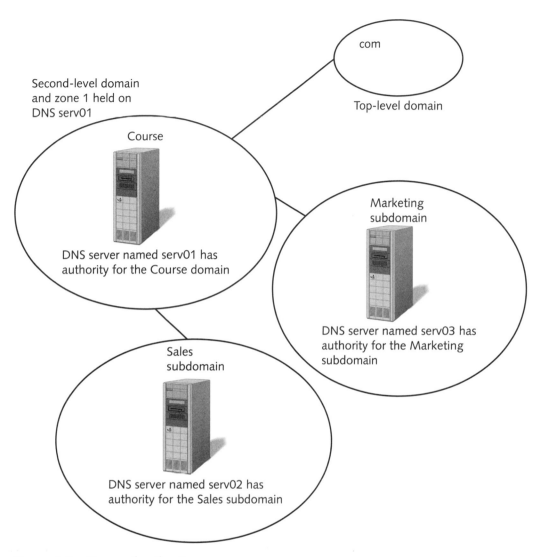

Figure 4-3   Zones of authority

All networks should minimally have a primary and a secondary DNS name server, or two DNS servers configured to use **Active Directory integrated zones**, which have DNS information stored and replicated using Active Directory. In addition, DNS servers can also be configured as caching-only servers. **Caching-only servers** hold no primary or secondary zone file for any particular portion of the DNS namespace. Instead, they build a cache of information from DNS resolutions they obtain from other primary or secondary name servers. Caching-only servers are good for areas that do not need a full secondary server or that do not have enough bandwidth to support **zones transfers**. Caching-only servers are ideal for remote offices connected to the central office via slow-speed WAN links such as ISDN.

DNS servers hold two types of DNS zones: forward lookup zones and reverse lookup zones. **Forward lookup zones** contain host name to IP address mappings. In other words, when a client has the host name of a destination computer and needs the IP address to complete communication, it receives that information from forward lookup zones. **Reverse lookup zones** contain IP address to host name mappings. A client that has the IP address of the destination computer and needs the host name uses reverse lookup zones to find an IP address to host name mapping. Reverse lookup zones are used many times to verify that an IP address is from a certain area or country. Using the IP address and a configured reverse lookup zone, DNS clients can determine in which DNS domain a computer resides.

To understand the DNS resolution process, you must first understand the two roles available to computers in the DNS system. In DNS, computers can be DNS servers that answer client requests or DNS resolvers, clients that initiate requests. Three types of requests or queries exist: recursive, iterative, and inverse. A DNS client sends a **recursive query** to a DNS server, which must directly answer the query. In a recursive query, the DNS server must respond with the best answer that its zone files currently have. To search higher up into the DNS namespace, DNS servers can use iterative queries. **Iterative queries** allow DNS servers to learn DNS information from other DNS servers. DNS servers use iterative queries to search for and find the DNS server with authority over the portion of the DNS namespace within which the requested host resides. This authoritative server responds to the iterative query with the host name to IP address mapping or a referral to another name server in the DNS domain that has authority. **Inverse queries**, the third type of query, find a host name from a known IP address. In other words, the client knows the IP address, but it needs to find the host name. Inverse queries use the reverse lookup zones, also known as **in-addr.arpa**.

Resource Records

Within the actual zone files, resource records are used to point to particular resources such as hosts, mail exchangers, and name servers. Table 4-2 lists many of the most common resource types. Later in this chapter you will learn how to create individual resource records.

Table 4-2   Common resource records

Resource Record	Use
SOA	All DNS zones begin with a Start of Authority (SOA) record that displays informational items such as the name of the authoritative server for that zone, the Time to Live (TTL) for zone records, and the e-mail address of the person responsible for the zone.
A	Provides host name to IP address mapping
NS	Name server (NS) record specifies the names of servers authoritative for a domain.
CNAME	Canonical Name (CNAME) allows an alias to be given to a machine that already has an A record entry. Canonical names allow machines to use common names such as *www.course.com* instead of *win2kweb.course.com*.

Table 4-2   Common resource records (continued)

Resource Record	Use
MX	Mail exchanger (MX) record specifies the mail servers considered authoritative for a particular domain.
SRV	Service (SRV) record is new to the Windows 2000 DNS service. Domain controllers add an SRV record to the DNS database automatically so clients can locate the domain controllers for services such as long on, resource permissions, and other network services. You can also add other service records to point to services running on particular servers.
PTR	Pointer (PTR) records are the IP address to host name mappings used to perform reverse lookups.

Windows 2000 DNS

The DNS server service that ships with Windows 2000 fully supports all parts of DNS mentioned in the overview section of this chapter. It also supports new features such as incremental zone transfers and dynamic DNS.

Unlike Windows NT DNS servers, Windows 2000 servers acting as primary DNS servers do not send the entire zone file to a secondary server. Windows 2000 sends just the changes in the DNS database. Sending only the changes instead of the entire database conserves network bandwidth.

The Windows 2000 DNS server also supports dynamic DNS as defined in RFC 2136. Dynamic DNS allows clients to register DNS information automatically with a DNS server. The implementation of DNS in Windows 2000 also supports dynamic registration of clients that do not support DDNS through the use of a service such as the Windows 2000 DHCP service.

The section, "DNS Client Configuration," later in this chapter presents the proper steps to configure a Windows 2000 client to register DNS information dynamically. You will also learn the dynamic registration process provided by the Windows 2000 DHCP service for non-DDNS Clients.

INSTALLING DNS SERVICE

Installing the DNS service requires that you configure certain items on the server before loading the service.

First, the server must have a static IP address, subnet mask, and default gateway (if your network has multiple networks or subnets). Microsoft also recommends that you set the domain name suffix on the server before installing the DNS service. This allows the service to create correct initial resource records when you install it. (For example, for the publishing.course.com domain, the suffix is course.com. Figure 4-4 displays the correct dialog box for configuring the DNS suffix. You access this dialog box via the Advanced TCP/IP Settings dialog box on the DNS tab.

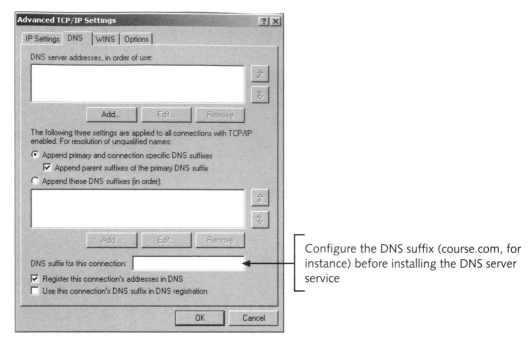

Figure 4-4   Domain name configuration

Once you meet these prerequisites, install the DNS server service with Optional Networking Components, accessible via the Advanced menu in Network and Dial-up Connections. Figure 4–5 shows the Windows Optional Networking Components Wizard dialog box.

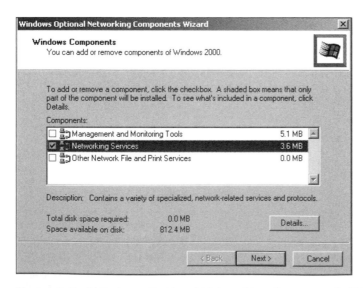

Figure 4-5   Windows Optional Networking Components Wizard

To install the DNS service, you must double-click Networking Services in the Windows Optional Networking Components Wizard and select the DNS service. Once you completely install the service, the DNS management console is added to the Administrative Tools folder under Start, Programs, Administrative Tools. Figure 4-6 shows the DNS management console.

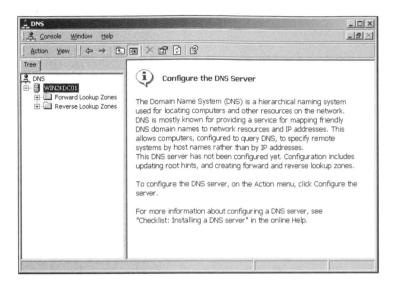

Figure 4-6   DNS management console

At this point you are ready to configure the DNS server service to act as a primary or secondary name server. If Active Directory is installed on your network, you have the option to create Active Directory integrated zones.

Another method of installing DNS is to install Active Directory first. If the DNS service is not installed, and you install Active Directory via the *dcpromo* command, you are prompted to install the DNS service or to configure it manually. Using the Active Directory install to configure DNS configures the DNS server with an Active Directory zone for use with AD.

CONFIGURING THE DNS SERVER SERVICE

Installing the DNS service may be easy, but configuration can become a very complicated task. In this section, you learn how to configure a root name server, primary zones, secondary zones, and caching-only servers. You also learn how to configure delegation for use with a subdomain. Finally, you learn how to configure the Windows 2000 DNS service to allow dynamic updates.

Configuring a Root Name Server

On networks not connected to the Internet or networks that cannot access the Internet's **root name servers** due to a firewall or proxy server, configuring a root name server for internal use may be necessary. If your DNS servers cannot connect to the DNS root servers, you must configure a root server on your machine for name resolution to occur correctly. Otherwise, your DNS servers may have trouble performing normal name resolutions.

To configure the root name server, open the DNS management console, right–click Forward Lookup Zones, and select New Zone. Figure 4-7 shows this process.

Figure 4-7   Configuring a new zone

The New Zone Wizard then starts and prompts you for a type of zone. Although you have options to create an Active Directory integrated zone (if AD is installed), primary zone, or secondary zone, you must choose a primary zone to configure a root zone server. You must also use a period as the zone name to create a root zone. Windows 2000 recognizes the period as a root zone and then configures the zone files correctly. Figure 4-8 shows the three zone type choices, while Figure 4-9 shows how to name a zone.

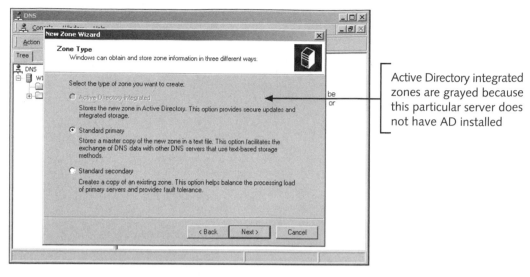

Figure 4-8   Types of zones

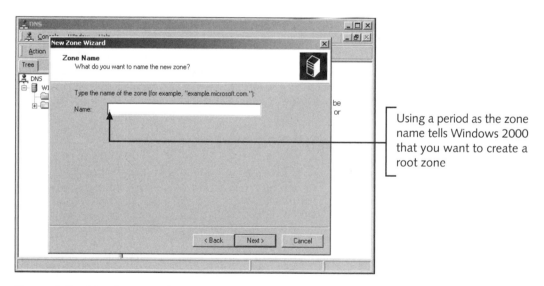

Figure 4-9   Naming a root zone

Figure 4-10 shows the zone files created by Windows 2000 when you name a zone file with a period.

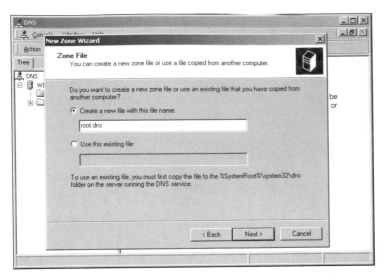

Figure 4-10   Root zone files created by Windows 2000

In Figure 4-10, the zone file name is root.dns, which signifies that Windows 2000 is creating a root zone for internal use.

 If you create a root zone when your organization is not connected to the Internet and then you later connect to the Internet, you must remove the root zone or DNS queries may not occur correctly.

Configuring Primary and Secondary Zones

On DNS servers using standard DNS zones, you must configure primary and secondary servers with the appropriate zone files. If you wish to create a primary name server, you must configure the DNS server to use a standard primary zone. Figure 4-8 shows the different types of zone files: Active Directory integrated, standard primary, and standard secondary. If you select a standard primary zone, the first item you must configure is a name for the zone. You must place the entire domain name in as the primary zone file name. For example, to create a primary zone file for Course Technology, you need to place the name course.com in the primary zone file name.

Figure 4-11 shows a standard primary zone with the name chap4.win2kbook.org.

Windows 2000 appends .dns to the name you provide to create the DNS zone files for the zone. Figure 4-12 shows this default naming for chap.4win2kbook.org.

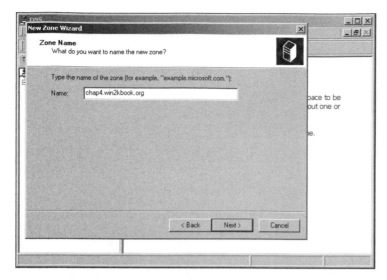

Figure 4-11   Naming a standard zone file

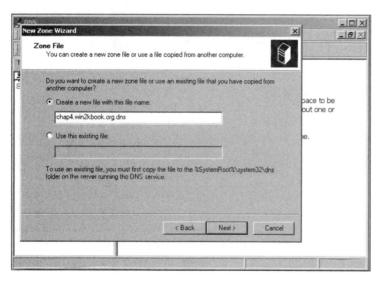

Figure 4-12   Default zone file naming

At this point, you configure a standard primary zone with the defaults and it's stored in the \winnt\system32\dns folder. A single DNS server can host as many standard primary zones as you want to configure. However, server resources limit the number of DNS zones.

Once you configure a primary zone, you may need to create a standard secondary zone on another DNS server in order to provide backup and faster responses to client DNS requests. Creating a standard secondary zone is very similar to configuring a standard primary zone. Right-click Forward Lookup Zones and select New Zone. Once you choose a standard secondary zone and provide a zone name, you must choose a Master DNS server or servers to provide zone information to the secondary name server. In effect, the Master DNS server setting refers the standard secondary zone to the correct primary name server for the zone. Figure 4-13 displays the portion of the New Zone Wizard where you specify the Master DNS server.

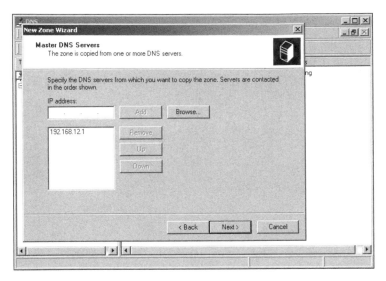

Figure 4-13 Configuring Master DNS servers

You can configure DNS servers to hold the primary zone file for one portion of the domain namespace and a secondary zone for another. Figure 4-14 shows a DNS server with a standard primary zone and a secondary zone configured. You should configure at least one primary and one secondary DNS zone for every standard DNS zone you create.

Active Directory integrated zones are stored in the Active Directory database and are automatically replicated when AD information is replicated. As a result, administrators do not have to configure zone replication for fault tolerance. Instead, the same services that replicate AD information handle replication of all DNS information within a zone. The problem with AD integrated zones comes from the problems of coexistence with UNIX-based DNS servers or other non-Windows 2000 servers.

If your network consists of Active Directory integrated zones only, you do not need to configure primary and secondary zones. Instead, all Active Directory DNS zones are replicated via the same mechanisms as the Active Directory itself.

Configuring Caching-only Servers

Many remote offices need to resolve host names via DNS. In very small offices, it may be possible to allow client DNS requests to pass over the WAN link to a DNS server located at the central office. Figure 4-15 shows a remote office where all DNS requests must pass over the WAN link.

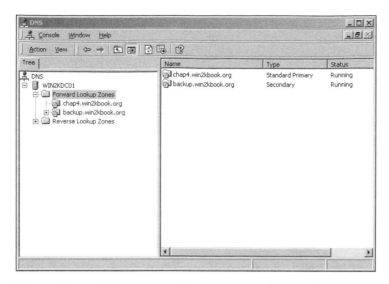

Figure 4-14   DNS server with a primary and secondary zone

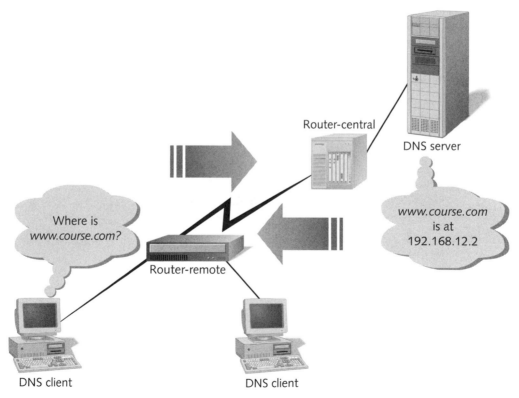

Figure 4-15   Remote office and DNS

With only a few clients at the remote office, the DNS traffic is normally not enough to affect the available bandwidth between the remote office and the central office. As the number of clients at the remote office increases, the traffic may overwhelm a slow WAN link. If the number of clients is high or the company expects rapid growth, you should place a caching-only server at the remote location. The caching-only server is not authoritative for any particular DNS zone, that is, it is not configured to hold a primary or secondary zone. However, as its name implies, it forwards DNS requests and then caches the DNS resolutions.

The process of creating a caching-only server consists of loading the DNS server service and then configuring forwarder addresses. Right-clicking the server in the DNS console, selecting Properties, and clicking the Forwarders tab allows you to configure the forwarder addresses. Figure 4-16 displays the Forwarders tab.

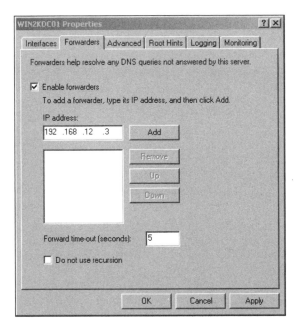

Figure 4-16   Configuring DNS forwarders

Implementing a Delegated Zone for DNS

Many networks use subdomains to break the DNS namespace into more manageable units. After creating subdomains, it is possible to delegate authority for a zone via the New Delegation Wizard. To access the New Delegation Wizard, right-click the zone or subdomain you wish to delegate, and select New Delegation. You are prompted for the name of the domain you want to delegate and the IP address or name of the DNS server to hold the delegation. Then select the person or group to whom you wish to delegate and assign the appropriate permissions.

Configuring Zones for Dynamic Updates

As mentioned earlier in this book and this chapter, Windows 2000 DNS supports dynamic registration of client A and PTR records. However, by default, standard zones on Windows 2000 DNS servers do not support dynamic registration. To configure a standard zone to accept dynamic updates, right-click the zone, select Properties, and then select Yes in response to "Allow dynamic updates?" Figure 4-17 displays the correct setting for dynamic updates.

4

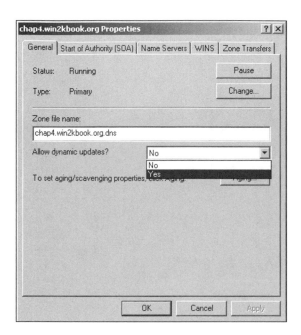

Figure 4-17   Configuring dynamic updates

Once the zone can accept dynamic updates, Windows 2000 clients automatically register A records and, if they are configured as DHCP clients, request that the DHCP server register PTR records. Non-Windows 2000 clients cannot automatically register either A records or PTR records with a DNS server configured for dynamic updates. To allow dynamic updates for these clients, you can configure the DHCP server to register DNS A and PTR records automatically for non-Windows 2000 clients. Figure 4-18 shows the DHCP console and the DNS dialog box for setting DHCP interaction with DNS.

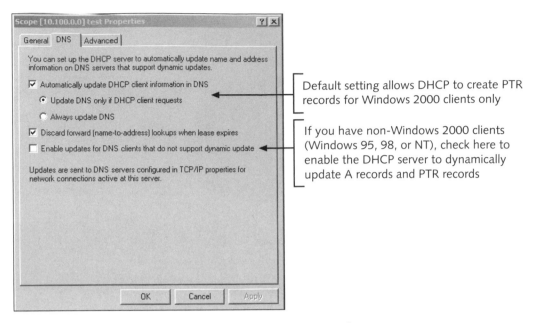

Figure 4-18   DHCP configuration for automatic DNS updates

CREATING RESOURCE RECORDS MANUALLY

Although Windows 2000 clients can automatically register A records, and A records and PTR records can automatically be registered through DHCP, it is still necessary to create many resource records manually.

To create a record manually you right-click the zone in which you wish to create a record and select one of the listed records or the Other New Records option. Figure 4–19 shows the options available.

Using the dialog box that opens, you can create resource records ranging from host or A records to service records. The number and type of manual records that you must create vary for each network, but at a minimum you must configure canonical names, or CNAMEs, for Web servers.

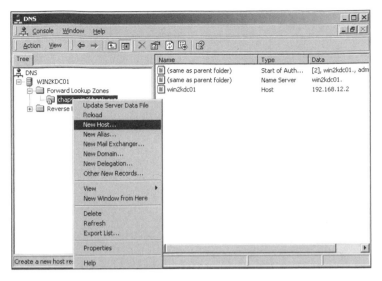

Figure 4-19   Manual resource record creation

DNS CLIENT CONFIGURATION

Once you correctly install and configure your DNS servers, you need to configure the clients on the network so they can use the DNS servers. How you configure the client depends on whether the client is configured with a static IP address or is a DHCP client.

For clients with static IP addresses, you must manually configure a Preferred DNS server and an Alternate DNS server in the TCP/IP properties DNS configuration tab for Windows 95 and 98 clients. Figure 4-20 shows the basic manual DNS configuration for Windows 2000 clients.

If you need to configure more than two DNS servers on a client, click the Advanced button at the bottom of the Internet Protocol (TCP/IP) Properties dialog box shown in Figure 4-20. Figure 4-21 displays the DNS tab in the Advanced TCP/IP Settings dialog box. Here you can add additional DNS servers and prioritize the order of use of DNS servers.

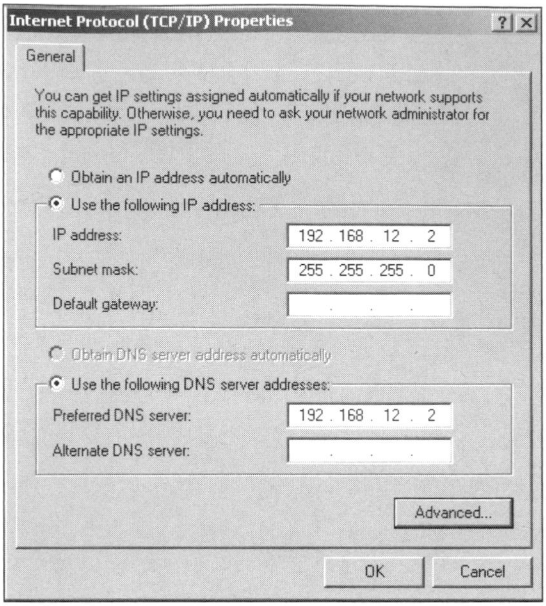

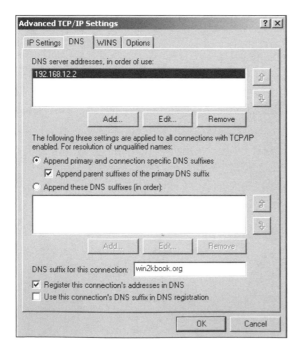

Figure 4-20   Configuring DNS settings manually

Figure 4-21   Advanced manual DNS configuration

If your clients use DHCP, configuring DNS for them is much easier. You need to configure the DNS options for the scope that the client will obtain an IP address from. Chapter 3 discusses how to perform this task.

MANAGING, MONITORING, AND TROUBLESHOOTING DNS

Overall, if installed and configured correctly, DNS servers and clients normally require very little administration. Still, problems can and do arise with all networking components. Therefore, you must know how to manage, monitor, and troubleshoot DNS.

Setting TTL Properties

All DNS servers maintain a cache of information that contains the resolutions they performed for clients. This cache speeds the DNS resolution process because the DNS server can pull information from this cache instead of performing an entire DNS query. Cache entries are maintained for a length of time determined by the time-to-live setting of the zones on a server. Figure 4-22 shows the Time To Live, or TTL, for a forward lookup zone. By default, the TTL is one day. You can open the dialog box shown in Figure 4-22 by right-clicking a zone in the DNS console and selecting Properties, and then selecting the Start of Authority (SOA) tab.

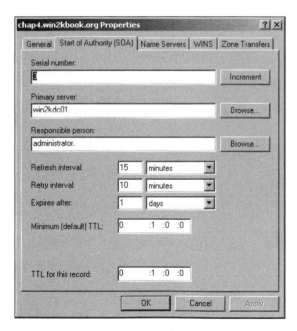

Figure 4-22   Setting TTL for a zone

The minimum (default) TTL setting specifies the amount of time a server can cache information in a zone. Other items of importance in Figure 4-22 are the Refresh interval, which determines how often secondary servers contact their primary server to update zone information; and the Retry interval, a wait period the secondary server uses if it cannot contact a zone's primary server. You may want to increase the TTL if your computer name to IP address mapping does not change often. In addition, the serial number in Figure 4-22 is the number used to determine if changes have occurred on the primary zone. The primary name server and secondary name servers compare this serial number to ensure that they are using the same zone files. If the primary name server has a newer version of the database (one with a higher serial number), the secondary servers know that they need to update their zone files.

Zone Transfer Settings

If you use standard primary and secondary name servers, you may also want to configure additional zone transfer settings to ensure optimal exchange of database information.

Figure 4-23 shows the Zone Transfers tab originally shown as the last tab in Figure 4-22. In this dialog box, you can configure how zone transfers occur (You must allow zone transfers to occur between primary and secondary servers.) Within this same tab, you can also configure exactly what servers can be involved in the zone transfer process. Specifying that only certain servers can participate in zone transfers increases the security of all DNS transactions.

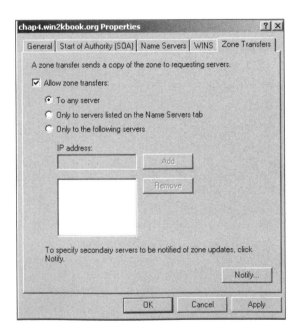

Figure 4-23   Zone transfer settings

Configuring the exact IP addresses or names of the servers that can participate in zone transfers ensures that all DNS information sharing is secure because only servers you specify can participate in zones transfers.

Monitoring and Testing Tools

Another administrative task is testing and logging DNS server activity. Windows 2000 provides two test utilities for this purpose: a simple graphical tool and the nslookup utility.

To access the simple graphical tool, right-click the server name in the DNS console and select Properties. Figure 4-24 displays the monitoring tool you can access via the Monitoring tab.

4

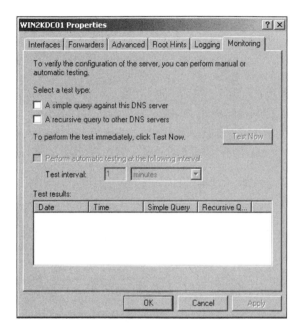

Figure 4-24   Monitoring a DNS server

Using the monitoring tool, you can perform a simple query that attempts a forward lookup query. The tool also allows you to perform a recursive query. Finally, you can perform the test immediately with the Test Now button, or you can have the tests occur automatically at a preset interval. With this tool, you can quickly determine the status of the DNS server. For more detailed logging and information, you can use the DNS log in Event Viewer. Also, as an administrator, you can configure the logging options on the Logging tab shown in Figure 4-24. Figure 4-25 shows the Logging options and the default path for the log file. Use with discretion: As with all logging, the more items you log, the more overhead you place on the DNS server.

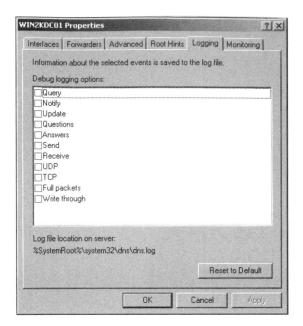

Figure 4-25   DNS logging

Additionally, you can use the nslookup utility to verify that a DNS server is available and that resource records have been created for the zone. You can use nslookup to perform a single lookup in non-interactive mode, or you can perform a series of lookups in interactive mode. To perform a single lookup, you must type the following after the command prompt:

nslookup [DNS name] [DNS server]

In the non-interactive syntax, you should replace the DNS variable with the DNS name you want to query the DNS server for. The DNS server is the server on which you wish to check the resource record. Also, instead of the DNS server name, you can use the IP address of the DNS server you want to query. The following shows a successful nslookup of the resource record for server win2dc01:

```
F:\>nslookup win2kdc01 192.168.12.2
Server:  win2kdc01.chap4.win2kbook.org
Address:  192.168.12.2

Name:    win2kdc01.chap4.win2kbook.org
Address:  192.168.12.2
```

From this nslookup, you can see that the DNS name and the DNS server being checked for resource records are the same machine.

You can also use Nslookup in interactive mode. Use this mode if you plan to enter multiple lookups. To enter interactive mode, type nslookup after the command prompt and press **Enter**. You can then use the ? to access help and information about the many different nslookup options available. The following shows how to enter interactive mode and the results of the help command:

```
F:\>nslookup
Default Server:  win2kdc01.chap4.win2kbook.org
Address:  192.168.12.2

> ?
Commands:    (identifiers are shown in uppercase, [] means
optional)
NAME            - print info about the host/domain NAME
using default server
NAME1 NAME2     - as above, but use NAME2 as server
help or ?       - print info on common commands
set OPTION      - set an option
all             - print options, current server and host
    [no]debug           - print debugging information
    [no]d2              - print exhaustive debugging
information
    [no]defname         - append domain name to each query
    [no]recurse         - ask for recursive answer to query
    [no]search          - use domain search list
    [no]vc              - always use a virtual circuit
    domain=NAME         - set default domain name to NAME
    srchlist=N1[/N2/.../N6] - set domain to N1 and search
list to N1,N2, etc.
    root=NAME           - set root server to NAME
    retry=X             - set number of retries to X
    timeout=X           - set initial time-out interval to X
seconds
    type=X              - set query type (ex. A,ANY,CNAME,MX,
NS,PTR,SOA,SRV)
    querytype=X         - same as type
    class=X             - set query class (ex. IN
(Internet), ANY)
    [no]msxfr           - use MS fast zone transfer
    ixfrver=X           - current version to use in IXFR
transfer request
server NAME     - set default server to NAME, using current
                  default server
lserver NAME    - set default server to NAME, using initial
                  server
finger [USER]   - finger the optional NAME at the current
                  default host
root            - set current default server to the root
ls [opt] DOMAIN [> FILE] - list addresses in DOMAIN
(optional: output to FILE)
    -a          -  list canonical names and aliases
    -d          -  list all records
```

```
        -t TYPE        -  list records of the given type (e.g. A,
                          CNAME,MX,NS,PTR etc.)
   view FILE           -  sort an 'ls' output file and view it
                          with pg
   exit                -  exit the program

   >
```

The > prompt signifies interactive mode. A very useful command in interactive mode is the ls command. Using this command, you can list all the A records with the –a switch, all records with the –d switch, and a particular type of record with the –t (type) switch. The following output show the results of each of these command-switch combinations being run in interactive mode:

```
F:\>nslookup
Default Server:  win2kdc01.chap4.win2kbook.org
Address:   192.168.12.2

> ls -a chap4.win2kbook.org
[win2kdc01.chap4.win2kbook.org]

> ls -d chap4.win2kbook.org
[win2kdc01.chap4.win2kbook.org]
  chap4.win2kbook.org.              SOA win2kdc01.chap4.win2kb
                                        ook.org administrator
                                        or. (9 900 600 86400 3600)
  chap4.win2kbook.org.              NS  win2kdc01.chap4.win2kb
                                        ook.org
  win2kdc01                         A   192.168.12.2
  win2kdc02                         A   192.168.12.3
  win2kdc02                         MX  10   win2kdc02.chap4.w
                                        in2kbook.org
  chap4.win2kbook.org.              SOA win2kdc01.chap4.win2kb
                                        ook.org administrator
  or. (9 900 600 86400 3600)

> ls -t mx chap4.win2kbook.org
[win2kdc01.chap4.win2kbook.org]
  win2kdc02                         MX  10   win2kdc02.chap4.win2k
                                        book.org
  >
```

Using this command and its switches, you can verify that the resource records do indeed exist in the DNS zone file.

CHAPTER SUMMARY

❑ Windows 2000 provides a full-featured DNS server that allows an administrator to create, maintain, and deploy a standards-based DNS infrastructure. Windows 2000 also supports the use of older methods of DNS name resolution, such as host files.

❑ DNS is a hierarchical system used to create a system that can resolve host name to IP address mapping. In Windows 2000, DNS is the primary name resolution method. The service is required on all Windows 2000 networks using Active Directory.

❑ You can easily start and configure the Windows 2000 server service to support standard and secondary zones with corresponding zone files stored on the server's hard drive. With primary and secondary zones, the DNS server is configured as a primary name server for a particular zone or as a secondary or back-up, name server for a zone. It is also possible for a DNS server to be the primary server for one zone and the secondary server for another.

❑ Additionally, Windows 2000 supports new Active Directory integrated zones that allow storage and replication of the DNS database within the AD database. Active Directory integrated zones ease the administrative tasks associated with manually setting up replication between primary and secondary name servers.

❑ All zones within Windows 2000, once configured to accept them, allow for dynamic DNS updates. Once configured to accept dynamic updates, all zones can allow Windows 2000 computers to create their own A records. Also, if your network uses DHCP, you can configure the DHCP servers to register PTR records for Windows 2000 clients and A and PTR records for non-Windows 2000 clients.

❑ You can manage, monitor, and troubleshoot DNS with the DNS console tool or the nslookup command-line tool. The DNS console allows an administrator to set most of the properties associated with the DNS server, including TTL, forwarders, and other configurations. The nslookup command allows an administrator to query DNS servers for information about resource records within the DNS database.

KEY TERMS

active directory integrated zones — DNS zones stored in the Active Directory database and replicated along with other Active Directory information.

authority — Ability to control what resource records, subdomains, and other attributes are associated with a particular DNS domain.

caching-only servers — DNS server configured without any zone files; a caching-only server contains IP addresses of DNS servers it can query to answer client requests and then store the information in a local cache.

DNS zone file — Text file, stored on a DNS server, that contains all information and resource records for a particular zone.

DNS zones — Portion of the DNS namespace that can be administered as a single unit.

Domain Name System (DNS) — Hierarchical naming system used to resolve host name to IP address mapping. It contains resource records.

forward lookup zones — DNS zone files that hold resource records that map host names to IP addresses. (They can also hold various other resource records.)

hostname — Command used after the command prompt to display the host name of the local machine.

host names — Common names given to network devices to allow users to interact with a name instead of an IP address.

host files — Text files that contain host name to IP address mapping; used to perform host name to IP address resolution. Precursor to the DNS system.

in-addr.arpa — Name given to the reverse lookup zone file.

Internet Service Providers (ISPs) — Companies that provide access to the Internet backbone.

inverse query — DNS query attempting to resolve a host name from a known IP address.

iterative query — DNS query to which the server responds with the best answer it can provide or by forwarding the request to another name server and then returning an answer.

LMHOSTS — Text file mapping NetBIOS names to IP addresses; precursor to WINS service.

name registration company — Company with the authority to register DNS domains within the DNS namespace.

primary name servers — DNS servers that hold a read/write copy of the zone file for a particular DNS zone; control replication with secondary name servers.

recursive query — DNS query which asks the server to respond either with the DNS information or an error message stating that it does not have the information; used between clients and DNS servers.

reverse lookup zone — Special DNS zone that holds PTR records, IP address to host name mapping.

root name servers — Servers that hold information about the overall Internet domain name servers.

secondary name servers — DNS servers that hold read-only copies of a zone file for a particular DNS zone; accept updates to the DNS zone file only from configured primary name servers.

Windows Internet Name Service (WINS) — Windows 2000 service that provides a dynamic database of NetBIOS name to IP address mapping.

zone of authority — Portion of the DNS namespace that an organization controls.

zones transfers — Copying zone file information from primary name servers to secondary name servers.

REVIEW QUESTIONS

1. Which one of the following holds a read/write version of DNS zone files?

   a. Domain Master Name server

   b. Primary name server

   c. Caching-only name server

   d. Secondary name server

2. A(n) _____ record maps a host name to an IP address.

3. Which one of the following occurs at the beginning of a DNS zone file and provides important information about what servers are authoritative and contact information?

   a. CNAME record

   b. NS record

   c. SOA record

   d. SRV record

4. Which one of the following lists the six steps in host name resolution in correct order?

   a. LMHOSTS file, local host name, HOSTS file, DNS server, WINS server, broadcast

   b. HOSTS file, local host name, DNS server, WINS server, broadcast, LMHOSTS file

   c. Local host name, HOSTS file, DNS server, WINS server, broadcast, LMHOSTS file

   d. DNS server, local host name, HOSTS file, WINS server, broadcast, LMHOSTS

5. If your company has the ability to create subdomains within your assigned domain from a name registration company, your company is considered _____ for that domain.

6. A query that must be answered with the best response a server has in its DNS files or with an error message stating that the query cannot be completed is considered:

   a. Recursive

   b. Iterative

   c. Authoritative

   d. Best-guess

7. To find a host name from a known IP address, you must perform a(n) _____ query.

8. Which one of the following resource records allows you to assign an alias or common name to a machine?

   a. A record

   b. MX record

   c. SRV record

   d. CNAME record

9. What types of DNS zones does Windows 2000 support? (Choose all that apply.)

    a. Standard primary zones

    b. Standard secondary zones

    c. Active Directory integrated zones

    d. All of the above

10. You must manually configure zone replication when using Active Directory integrated zones. True or false?

11. The portion of the namespace that a server is responsible for is called its _____.

12. Forward lookup zones contain:

    a. IP address to host name mapping

    b. No host name to IP address mapping

    c. MX records only

    d. Host name to IP address mapping

13. The new DNS record used by Windows 2000 to locate domain controllers is the _____ record.

14. Which of the following can automatically register A records and PTR records once a DNS zone has been configured for dynamic updates?

    a. Windows 2000 clients

    b. Windows 95 clients

    c. Windows 98 clients

    d. None of the above

15. Which of the following tools can you use to monitor DNS? (Choose all that apply.)

    a. DNS console

    b. Active Directory users and computers console

    c. Nslookup

    d. Hostname command

16. In order for non-Windows 2000 clients to use DDNS, the DHCP server service must be configured to register A and PTR records dynamically. True or false?

17. Which one of the following DNS servers is not authoritative for any particular zone and is used to reduce DNS resolution traffic to remote sites?

    a. Active Directory integrated server

    b. Caching-only server

    c. Secondary name server

    d. Primary name server

18. By default, all standard zones on Windows 2000 DNS servers automatically accept dynamic updates. True or false?

19. Nslookup can be run in either _____ mode or _____ mode.

20. The _____ is the amount of time that a DNS server caches information about a successful DNS query.

HANDS-ON PROJECTS

All Hands-on Projects in this chapter require two computers set up as described in the lab set-up section in the front of this book. For these exercises, you use the PCs named win2kdc01 and win2kdc02. To complete these exercises, you must have completed Hands-on Project 3-1 in Chapter 3. After completing the exercises in Chapter 3, win2kdc02 is already running DNS.

Project 4-1

To make win2kdc01 a member server in the win2kclass02.org domain:

1. Right-click **My Network Places** and click **Properties** to open the Network and Dial-up Connections dialog box.

2. Click **Advanced** and then click **Network Identification**.

3. Click the **Properties** button.

4. Select the **Domain** radio button, and then type **win2kclass02.org**. Click **OK**. If prompted for a username and password, enter the administrator name and password.

Under the TCP/IP properties for win2kdc01, you must configure the primary DNS as the IP address of win2kdc02 or the machine cannot join the domain.

5. Click **OK** to close the Welcome to win2kclass02.org domain dialog box.

6. Click **OK** to close the dialog box that states that you must restart your machine.

7. Click **OK** to close the Systems Properties dialog box.

8. Click **Yes** to restart your computer.

Project 4-2

To install the DNS server service on the server win2kdc01 and configure it as a caching-only server:

1. Log on to the **win2kclass02** domain as **Administrator** with the password **password**.

2. Right-click **My Network Places** and click **Properties** to open the Network and Dial-up Connections dialog box.

3. Click **Advanced** and then select **Optional Networking Components**.

4. Double-click **Networking Services** to display a list of available services.

5. Click in the box to the left of the **Domain Name System (DNS)** item, and then click **OK**.

6. Click **Next** to install the DNS server service. If prompted, provide a static **IP** address for the server.

   You may be prompted to insert your Windows 2000 server CD-ROM.

   You installed the DNS server service on win2kdc01. At this point, if you do not add any zone files to the server, and you verify that the root hints (available on the Root Hints tab when you right-click the server and select Properties) are configured, the server acts as a caching-only server.

Project 4-3

You must perform this exercise on win2kdc01.

To configure a root name server:

1. Click **Start**, **Programs**, **Administrative Tools**, **DNS** to start the DNS console.

2. Once the DNS console starts, expand the tree under win2kdc01 by clicking the **+** next to the server name.

3. Click to select **Forward Lookup Zones**.

4. Right-click **Forward Lookup Zones** and then select **New Zone**.

   This begins the New Zone Wizard.

5. Click **Next**.

6. Ensure that the **Standard Primary** radio button is selected, and then click **Next**.

7. Type a period in for the name of the zone. Click **Next**.

8. Accept the default zone file name of **root.dns**, and then click **Next**.

9. Click **Finish**.

   If you see a new zone represented by a folder with the name **.**, you successfully configured a root name server.

10. **Right-click** on the root zone (zone named .), and then click **Delete**. Click **OK** to confirm deletion.

This step is necessary to ensure that the following Hands-on Projects work correctly. You would not perform this step in a real-world configuration of a root name server.

Project 4-4

To configure a primary zone on the server win2kdc02:

1. Click **Start**, **Programs**, **Administrative Tools**, **DNS** to start the DNS console.
2. Once the DNS console starts, expand the tree under win2kdc02 by clicking the **+** next to the server name.
3. Click to select **Forward Lookup Zones**.
4. Right-click **Forward Lookup Zones**, and then select **New Zone**.

   This begins the New Zone Wizard.
5. Click **Next**.
6. Ensure that the **Standard Primary** radio button is selected, and then click **Next**.
7. For the zone name, use **project44**. Click **Next**.
8. Accept the default zone file name of **project44.dns**, and then click **Next**.
9. Click **Finish** and you see a new zone represented by a folder with the name **project44**.

Project 4-5

To add resource records manually to a DNS zone:

1. On the server win2kdc02, open the DNS console, expand the DNS zone information, and then click to select the **project44** zone file.
2. Right-click **project44** and then select **New Host**.
3. In the New Host dialog box, type **win2kdc01** for the host name and use **192.168.12.1** as the IP address.
4. Click **Add Host** to add the **A record** to the project44 zone file.
5. Repeat Steps 3 and 4 for **win2kdc02** using the IP address of **192.168.12.2**.

   You can add all other resource records using the same series of steps listed in this Hands-on Project.

Project 4-6

To configure a zone for dynamic updates:

1. On the server win2kdc02, open the DNS console, expand the DNS zone information, and then click to select the **project44** zone file.
2. Right-click **project44** and then select **Properties**.
3. In the **Allow Dynamic Updates** box, select **Yes**.

On an Active Directory integrated zone, you have three possible choices in the Allow Dynamic Updates box: only secure updates, yes, and no.

4. Click **OK**.

You configured the zone to accept dynamic updates.

Project 4-7

To test the DNS server service using the tools in the DNS console:

1. Open the DNS console on win2kdc01.

2. Right-click the server **win2kdc01** and select **Properties**.

3. Click the **Monitoring** tab and ensure that the check boxes for a simple query and a recursive query are selected.

4. Click **Test Now** to test the server.

You should see the results at the bottom of the dialog box in the area labeled "Test results".

You can also set up automatic testing at a certain time interval by clicking Perform automatic testing at the following interval: and selecting an interval.

CASE PROJECTS

Case 1

Your company consists of a central office of nearly 500 computers and 50 servers. You also have four remote sites connected to the central office via ISDN connections. Your boss asks you to design a DNS architecture for the company that meets the needs of the central office and the remote sites. Create a one-page document detailing your plans for the company's DNS servers.

Case 2

A company called Hogan Industries currently uses UNIX servers to host its DNS servers. The company is in the process of migrating to a full Windows 2000 network, but there are some concerns about replacing the UNIX DNS servers. You are asked to create two proposals: one for replacing the UNIX DNS servers completely with Windows 2000 DNS servers and another proposal for keeping the current UNIX DNS servers and integrating Windows 2000 DNS servers. Using the Microsoft Web site at *www.microsoft.com* and other resources, research the pros and cons of each proposal and then create a summary of each in a two- to three-page paper.

Case 3

As the senior engineer for Freytech Inc., one of your major tasks is providing training for new hires and existing junior engineers. For this month's training meeting, you are asked to discuss DDNS and its implementation in Windows 2000. Prepare a 15- to 30-minute training session on the Windows 2000 implementation of DDNS.

WINDOWS INTERNET NAME SERVICE

After reading this chapter and completing the exercises, you will be able to:

♦ Provide an overview of NetBIOS naming and NetBIOS name resolution

♦ Describe the features of the Windows Internet Name Service (WINS)

♦ Explain in detail the new features in the Windows 2000 implementation of WINS

♦ Install WINS

♦ Configure replication between WINS servers

♦ Configure a client to use WINS

♦ Manage, monitor, and troubleshoot WINS

Networks consisting only of Windows 2000 servers and clients use DNS exclusively for name resolution. However, most modern networks (those consisting of a mixed environment of Windows 2000, Windows NT, Windows 98, and Windows 95) must support NetBIOS name to IP address name resolution. The preferred method for NetBIOS name resolution is the Windows Internet Name Service (WINS). In this chapter, you learn how to install, configure, monitor, and troubleshoot WINS in a Windows 2000 environment.

NETBIOS NAMING

NetBIOS is a Session layer **Application Programming Interface (API)** used by applications to provide an upper-layer interface that is compatible with a multitude of lower-layer networking protocols. For the purpose of this chapter, you focus on the use of **NetBIOS over TCP/IP**, also known as **NetBT**.

Unlike the hierarchical DNS naming scheme, NetBIOS uses a flat namespace. In essence, this means that NetBIOS names can only be used once per machine on a network. Using a **NetBIOS scope** (an identifier added to the NetBIOS name) can overcome this limitation, but few modern networks make use of this parameter. Instead, most networks have a computer-naming scheme to ensure that no two machines have the same NetBIOS name.

Unique NetBIOS names are 16 bytes long and identify both the computer name and certain services running on a computer. An example of a unique NetBIOS name is a computer named win2kdc01. **Group NetBIOS names** identify multiple computers. An example of a group NetBIOS name is a domain named win2kbook. Regardless of the type of NetBIOS name, each consists of up to 15 characters for the computer or group name and a sixteenth character that identifies the particular service. Table 5-1 lists several of the most common unique and group NetBIOS name types.

Table 5-1   NetBIOS names, services, and examples

Type of NetBIOS Name	Specified Service	Example
Unique name	Server service	*computername*[20]
Unique name	Workstation service	*computername*[00]
Unique name	Messenger service	*computername*[03]
Group name	Domain controllers	*domain-name*[1C]
Group name	Domain name	*domain-name*[00]

You can view a list of all the services and their corresponding NetBIOS names by issuing the nbtstat –n command after the command prompt. The following is a typical response to this command:

```
C:\>nbtstat -n

    Local Area Connection:
    Node IpAddress: [192.168.12.2] Scope Id: []

            NetBIOS Local Name Table

        Name                Type         Status
    ---------------------------------------------------
        WIN2KDC02           <00>  UNIQUE      Registered
        WIN2KDC02           <20>  UNIQUE      Registered
        WIN2KCLASS02        <00>  GROUP       Registered
```

WIN2KCLASS02	<1C>	GROUP	Registered
WIN2KCLASS02	<1B>	UNIQUE	Registered
WIN2KDC02	<03>	UNIQUE	Registered
WIN2KCLASS02	<1E>	GROUP	Registered
INet~Services	<1C>	GROUP	Registered
IS~WIN2KDC02...	<00>	UNIQUE	Registered
WIN2KCLASS02	<1D>	UNIQUE	Registered
.._MSBROWSE_.	<01>	GROUP	Registered
ADMINISTRATOR	<03>	UNIQUE	Registered

Each name in the NetBIOS Local Name Table allows older clients such as Windows NT or Windows 95/98 to locate either services running on a particular machine or resources within a domain. For instance, suppose a Windows 95 machine running TCP/IP needs to connect to a shared file resource on a computer named win2kdc02 with the net use s: \\win2kdc02\sharename command. The Windows 95 machine attempts to connect with NetBIOS over TCP/IP to the win2kdc02[20] NetBIOS name, the computer name with the server service indicator. If the same machine needs to find the domain controllers on a domain named win2kclass02, it sends a request to the NetBIOS name win2kclass02[1C] in an attempt to find the domain controllers for that particular domain. In either of these cases, once found, the NetBIOS name and service must eventually be resolved to an IP address for network communication to occur.

NetBIOS Name Resolution

Windows 2000 supports six different methods for NetBIOS name to IP address resolution. Figure 5-1 shows each method in the order it is used.

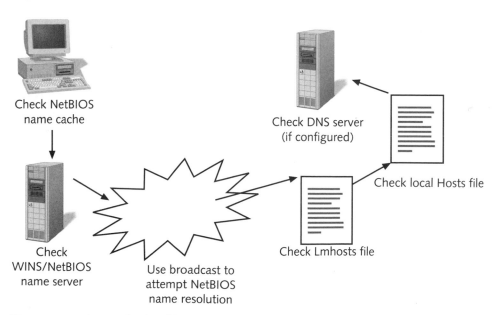

Figure 5-1   Six methods of NetBIOS name resolution in Windows 2000

Although Figure 5-1 shows the general order in which NetBIOS name resolution methods are attempted, clients can be configured with a node type that determines their exact method. Table 5-2 lists the major node types and briefly describes each.

Table 5-2   NetBIOS node types

Node Type	Description
b-node	Broadcast node uses broadcasts for all NetBIOS name resolutions; avoid b-node if possible
p-node	Point-to-point node configures a machine to use only a **NetBIOS Name Server (NBNS)**/WINS server for NetBIOS name resolution; works well, but can cause problems if your WINS servers go offline for some reason
m-node	Mixed node attempts broadcasts for NetBIOS name resolution first; if no response occurs, a client then uses a p-node request to a NBNS/WINS server; m-node suffers from its excessive use of broadcasts
h-node	Hybrid node is the node of choice; clients configured as h-nodes try to resolve NetBIOS names using directed communication with a NBNS/WINS server first and then switch to a b-node if they cannot locate the server

The easiest way to set the node type for a client is to assign it as a DHCP scope option. Figure 5-2 shows the 044 WINS/NBNS server and 046 WINS/NBT node type. You must set the 044 option to the IP addresses of the WINS servers that you want clients to use. The 046 or node type should always be set to 0x8, the value for h-node. Using h-node on your network ensures that clients first attempt to use directed communication with the WINS server and only use broadcast as a secondary method for name resolution.

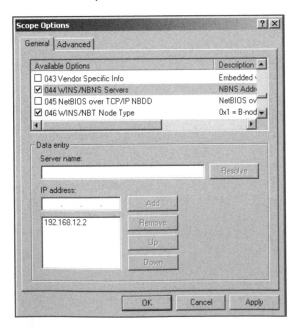

Figure 5-2   WINS scope options in DHCP

If a client is set to use a static IP address, you can also set the WINS servers IP addresses in the TCP/IP properties. This process is covered in detail later in this chapter. Two main methods for NetBIOS name resolution shown in Figure 5-1 are an Lmhosts file or a WINS server. By default, all Windows 2000 clients are configured to use the Lmhosts file if it is present and no other NetBIOS name resolution method can provide resolution. Figure 5-3 shows the dialog box where you enable the Lmhosts file. To open this dialog box, you must access the properties for the Local Area Connection and then double-click the Internet Protocol (TCP/IP) item. In the Internet Protocol (TCP/IP) Properties dialog box, you must click the Advanced button. Finally, click the WINS tab to open the dialog box show in Figure 5-3.

5

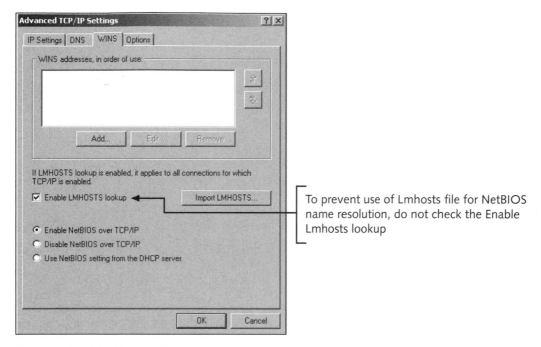

Figure 5-3   Disabling Lmhost lookup

The Lmhosts file is a static database of NetBIOS names to IP address mappings. Stored in the winnt\system32\drivers\etc folder, its name is Lmhosts with no extension. (The most common mistake made working with the Lmhosts file is accidentally assigning it an extension such as txt; it must have no extension in order for the system to use it for name resolution.) Windows 2000 contains a sample Lmhosts file. The file contains information concerning the correct syntax for entries. In general, the entries for an Lmhosts file are very simple. You simply type the IP address of the host and then type its NetBIOS name. Optional available parameters are mentioned in the following sample file:

```
# Copyright (c) 1993-1999 Microsoft Corp.
#
# This is a sample LMHOSTS file used by the Microsoft TCP/IP
#for Windows.
#
```

```
# This file contains the mappings of IP addresses to
# computernames
# (NetBIOS) names. Each entry should be kept on an individual
# line.
# The IP address should be placed in the first column
# followed by the
# corresponding computername. The address and the
# computername
# should be separated by at least one space or tab. The "#"
# character
# is generally used to denote the start of a comment (see the
# exceptions
# below).
#
# This file is compatible with Microsoft LAN Manager 2.x
# TCP/IP lmhosts
# files and offers the following extensions:
#
#    #PRE
#    #DOM:<domain>
#    #INCLUDE <filename>
#    #BEGIN_ALTERNATE
#    #END_ALTERNATE
#    \0xnn (non-printing character support)
#
# Following any entry in the file with the characters "#PRE"
# will cause
# the entry to be preloaded into the name cache. By default,
# entries are
# not preloaded, but are parsed only after dynamic name
# resolution fails.
#
# Following an entry with the "#DOM:<domain>" tag will
# associate the
# entry with the domain specified by <domain>. This affects
# how the
# browser and logon services behave in TCP/IP environments.
# To preload
# the host name associated with #DOM entry, it is necessary
# to also add a
# #PRE to the line. The <domain> is always preloaded although
# it will not
# be shown when the name cache is viewed.
#
# Specifying "#INCLUDE <filename>" will force the RFC NetBIOS
# (NBT)
# software to seek the specified <filename> and parse it as
# if it were
# local. <filename> is generally a UNC-based name, allowing a
# centralized lmhosts file to be maintained on a server.
```

```
# It is ALWAYS necessary to provide a mapping for the IP
# address of the
# server prior to the #INCLUDE. This mapping must use the
# PRE directive.
# In addition the share "public" in the example below must be
# in the
# LanManServer list of "NullSessionShares" in order for
# client machines to
# be able to read the lmhosts file successfully. This key is
# under
# \machine\system\currentcontrolset\services\lanmanserver\
# parameters\nullsessionshares
# in the registry. Simply add "public" to the list found
# there.
#
# The #BEGIN_ and #END_ALTERNATE keywords allow multiple
# INCLUDE
# statements to be grouped together. Any single successful
# include
# will cause the group to succeed.
#
# Finally, non-printing characters can be embedded in
# mappings by
# first surrounding the NetBIOS name in quotations, then
# using the
# \0xnn notation to specify a hex value for a non-printing
# character.
#
# The following example illustrates all of these extensions:
#
# 102.54.94.97    rhino      #PRE #DOM:networking #net group's
# DC
# 102.54.94.102   "appname \0x14"          #special app server
# 102.54.94.123   popular    #PRE        #source server
# 102.54.94.117   localsrv   #PRE        #needed for the
# include
#
# #BEGIN_ALTERNATE
# #INCLUDE \\localsrv\public\lmhosts
# #INCLUDE \\rhino\public\lmhosts
# #END_ALTERNATE
#
# In the above example, the "appname" server contains a
# special
# character in its name, the "popular" and "localsrv" server
# names are
# preloaded, and the "rhino" server name is specified so it
# can be used
# to later #INCLUDE a centrally maintained lmhosts file if
# the "localsrv"
```

```
# system is unavailable.
#
# Note that the whole file is parsed including comments on
# each lookup,
# so keeping the number of comments to a minimum will improve
# performance.
# Therefore it is not advisable to simply add lmhosts file
# entries onto the
# end of this file.
```

If you want to add an entry for a server with the NetBIOS name win2kdc02 (the identification name found under the Network Identification tab) with the IP address 192.168.12.2, you add the following to the above Lmhosts file:

```
192.168.12.2    win2kdc02 #PRE #DOM:win2kbook
```

The entry maps the IP address to the NetBIOS name and states that this entry should be preloaded into the NetBIOS name cache. Preloading entries into the name cache greatly increases name resolution speed because all clients first check their NetBIOS name cache for an entry for the machine they are trying to resolve. This entry also shows the use of the domain extension. Adding #DOM:*domainname* to the entry associates this particular server with browsing and logon capabilities for the domain specified. In other words, it marks this machine as a domain controller for the domain. Table 5-3 shows some of the more common extensions.

Table 5-3   Lmhosts extensions

Extension	Function
#PRE	Preloads the entry into the NetBIOS name cache
#DOM:*domainname*	Associates the machine in the entry with browsing and logon capabilities for the domain specified; place this on any machine that is a domain controller (The #DOM extension requires the #PRE extension; you must also place the #PRE in front of the #DOM entry in the Lmhosts syntax.)
#INCLUDE *filename*	The include statement normally uses a UNC path to a centrally stored Lmhosts file; if you use the #INCLUDE extension, you do not have to change Lmhosts files on every machine when a change occurs
#MH	Specifies that a server is **multi-homed** (containing more than one NIC) or configured with more than one IP address; this signifies that more than one IP address is assigned to the unique computer name

Lmhosts file entries should be in the format of IP address, followed by either a space or tab and then the NetBIOS name of the machine you are adding an entry for. You should add another tab after the NetBIOS names before placing any extensions you wish to use. Finally, you must complete the entire entry by pressing [Enter]. Also, unless the # sign precedes an extension mentioned either in the file above or in Table 5-3, the # sign normally designates a comment within the Lmhosts file.

The administrative overhead associated with maintaining Lmhosts files are their main draw-back. Since they are static databases, Lmhosts files require changes whenever new computers are added to the network or when IP addresses change. Using the #INCLUDE extension and a centralized Lmhosts file can alleviate some of this administration, but time-stressed administrators need a better method. To meet this need, Microsoft created and continues to provide the Windows Internet Name Service server.

WINS AND NETBIOS

5

WINS allows clients to register their NetBIOS name to IP address mappings in a dynamic database hosted on a WINS server. Each client, upon startup and at certain renewal intervals, contacts the WINS server through a directed communication to inform it of the client's current IP address and NetBIOS name. WINS servers are better than Lmhosts files because they provide a dynamic method to register NetBIOS names to IP addresses (definitely needed in any environment using DHCP for client IP assignment), and they allow clients to use directed communications to a WINS server instead of broadcasts. This second point is extremely impor-tant on routed networks, networks consisting of multiple IP subnets divided by routers. If clients on a routed network are configured to use only b-node for NetBIOS name resolution, they cannot resolve NetBIOS names for clients on the other side of a router because routers, by default, do not pass broadcasts. WINS queries, however, are directed communications, from the client IP address to the WINS server IP address. As a result, WINS clients can query WINS servers regardless of the server's location in relation to a router.

NetBIOS Name Registration

Figure 5-4 shows two clients, student1 and student2, as they register with the WINS server.

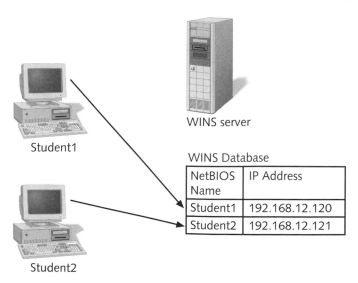

WINS server

WINS Database

NetBIOS Name	IP Address
Student1	192.168.12.120
Student2	192.168.12.121

Student1

Student2

Figure 5-4   Client registration with a WINS server

Clients send a **NetBIOS name registration** request to the configured WINS server stating their IP addresses and NetBIOS names. They request that the WINS server place the NetBIOS name to IP address mappings in the WINS database. If no other machines are currently using the requested NetBIOS names, the clients' requests to the name registration succeeds and they receive a Time to Live (TTL, the amount of time that the registration is valid). WINS clients must renew their name registrations at half the TTL value. This process is discussed in detail later.

 Clients actually register more than just the NetBIOS name to IP address mapping. As mentioned earlier, NetBIOS names can be used to distinguish between certain services on a particular machine. A server providing file and print sharing registers its NetBIOS name, plus entries for the server service, messenger service, and possibly many more.

If, during the name registration process for student1 and student2, the WINS server finds a mapping for the requested NetBIOS name already in the WINS database, it sends a challenge to the current owner of the name. If that owner successfully responds, the second client attempting to use that name cannot initialize NetBIOS and may not function correctly on the network. If the current owner does not respond to the challenge, the WINS server allows the second client attempting to use the name to create a new NetBIOS name to IP address entry, thereby taking over use of that NetBIOS name.

NetBIOS Name Renewal

The default TTL is expressed as the renewal interval in WINS properties. The renewal interval is six days by default. Therefore, at halfway through the renewal interval or every three days, the client attempts to renew its NetBIOS name registration with a **NetBIOS name renewal** request. If a client fails to renew its lease (for instance, because the machine cannot contact the primary or secondary WINS servers due to a network outage), the WINS servers eventually release the name registration and make the name available for use by any client that requests it.

NetBIOS Name Release

Clients can also request that a NetBIOS name be released from the WINS database with a **NetBIOS name release** request. This occurs when a WINS client shuts down. At shutdown, WINS clients request a name release from the WINS server. The server replies to each client with a successful release that gives the client a TTL of 0 for the name registration. In other words, the WINS server tells the client that it has released the name.

NetBIOS Name Query

Finally, WINS clients use the WINS server for NetBIOS name queries. In Figure 5-5, student2 wants to connect to a shared resource on student1. Before it can attach, it must resolve the NetBIOS name to an IP address.

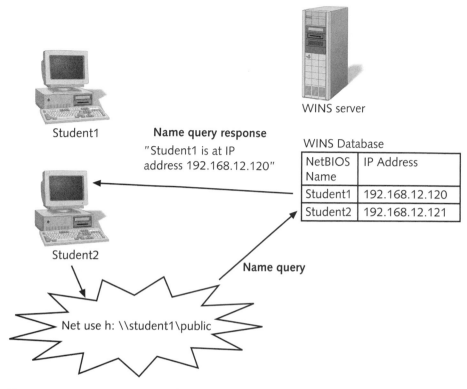

Figure 5-5 Name query and name query response

Student2 sends a **NetBIOS name query** to its configured primary WINS server, asking for a name resolution for student1. The WINS server checks its database and finds an entry for student1's server service. The WINS server then sends a **name query response** back to the client that contains the NetBIOS name to IP address mapping for student1. At this point, student2 can begin the connection process with student1 using TCP/IP.

In short, clients can access WINS servers to perform these four tasks:

- NetBIOS name registration
- NetBIOS name renewal
- NetBIOS name release
- NetBIOS name query

WINS servers can perform many tasks, but their primary interaction with clients involves either positive or negative name query responses. WINS in Windows 2000 functions almost exactly as it did under Windows NT 4.0. However, some improvements have been added. The next section details some of the new features in WINS under Windows 2000.

WINS IN WINDOWS 2000

Windows 2000 adds several new features to WINS. Most are attempts to make managing and using the WINS server easier. Others are designed to decrease the time used for **WINS replication**, the process of replicating WINS databases between multiple WINS servers. Three major new features are available in the Windows 2000 implementation of WINS:

- *Automatic Replication Partners*: If your network supports multicasting, you can configure Windows 2000 WINS servers to multicast to the IP address 224.0.1.24 to find other WINS servers that can act as WINS replication partners. Once other WINS servers are found, automatic replication is configured between servers. By default, this feature is not enabled, but you can turn it on in the WINS console using the Advanced tab in the Replication Partners Properties dialog box. Figure 5-6 shows this dialog box. If you use automatic replication partners, you must ensure that no unauthorized WINS servers exist on your network. Otherwise, WINS information may be replicated to unauthorized WINS servers.

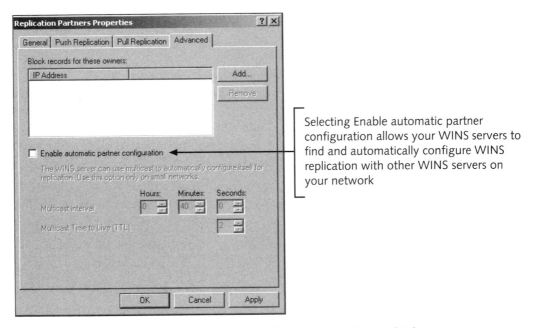

Figure 5-6 Replication Partners Properties dialog box—Advanced tab

- *Persistent connections*: You can now configure Windows 2000 WINS servers to keep a constant connection with replication partners. Keeping a constant connection reduces the overhead caused by opening and closing connections each time replication must occur.

- *Manual tombstoning*: Administrators now can mark an entry in the WINS database as **tombstoned**, or marked for deletion.

These three major changes along with other minor changes all serve to make WINS the preferred method for NetBIOS name resolution on networks running Windows 2000.

INSTALLING WINS

Installing the Windows Internet Name Service is essentially the same process as installing any optional networking component. Before you begin, however, you must ensure that your Windows 2000 server meets the following requirements:

- The server is configured with a static IP address, subnet mask, and default gateway.
- The WINS settings for the server point to its configured IP address. In other words, the WINS settings in the Internet Protocol Properties (TCP/IP) is configured to point to the server's own IP address.

Also, you need to determine exactly how many WINS servers your network needs. At a minimum, every network should have two WINS servers, one as primary and another as backup. These two servers perform replication (discussed later in this chapter) to ensure that their databases always contain the same information.

In general, a primary WINS server and a back-up WINS server should be able to support a network of 10,000 clients.

To begin installing WINS, you must right-click My Network Places and then click Properties. These steps open the Network and Dial-up Connections dialog box shown in Figure 5-7.

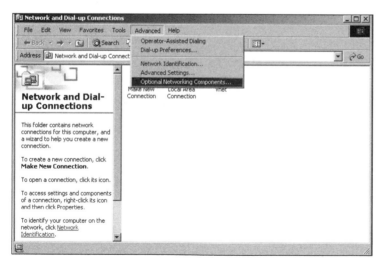

Figure 5-7   Optional Networking Components

Next you must click the Advanced menu item, and click the Optional Networking Components shown in Figure 5-7. The Windows Optional Networking Components Wizard and Networking Services dialog boxes open for use. Figure 5-8 shows both of these dialog boxes.

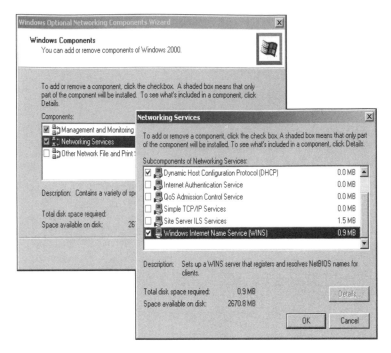

Figure 5-8   Windows Optional Networking Components Wizard and Networking Services
dialog boxes

You must click Windows Internet Name Service (WINS) and click OK to install the WINS
server. This installs the WINS server service and makes the WINS console available under
Administrative Tools. Figure 5–9 shows the WINS console.

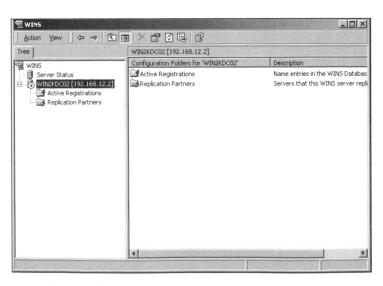

Figure 5-9   WINS console

In the WINS console in Figure 5-9, you can see the WINS server service loaded on the server WIN2KDC02 with the IP address 192.168.12.2. You can also see the Active Registrations and Replication Partners listed as configuration folders. If you click the Active Registrations folder, you see the text shown in Figure 5-10.

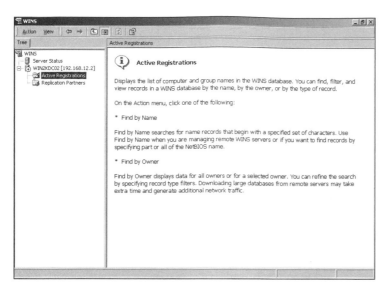

Figure 5-10   Finding active registrations

Administrators accustomed to WINS under Windows NT 4.0 may find it awkward that the entire WINS database does not appear. Instead, Windows 2000 WINS allows you to search by either name or owner. You must right-click on the Active Registrations folder and then click either Find by Name or Find by Owner. The results of your search appear in the right console pane. Figure 5-11 shows the results of a Find by Name search for all entries beginning with "w."

Now the WINS server is installed and running. Overall, the WINS server requires very little in the way of configuration. In fact, one Microsoft recommendation or best practice for WINS is to always use the default configuration. If you do this and configure your clients correctly, they automatically register their NetBIOS names and IP addresses with the WINS server. On occasion, you may want to add a static entry to the WINS database, usually to provide a WINS entry for a non-WINS client such as a UNIX box. To add a static mapping, you right-click Active Registrations and select New Static Mapping. The New Static Mapping dialog box shown in Figure 5-12 appears. You can use this box to add static mapping for the non-WINS client.

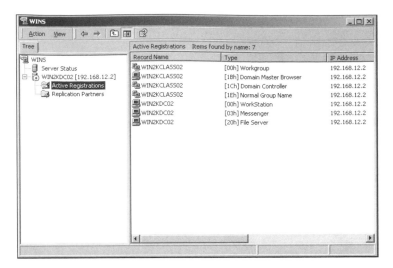

Figure 5-11   Search using Find by Name

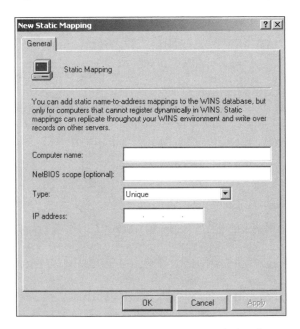

Figure 5-12   New Static Mapping dialog box

CONFIGURING WINS REPLICATION

In a network with more than one WINS server, you must configure the servers to replicate their databases. Otherwise, clients on the network may not be able to resolve certain NetBIOS names. Take, for instance, the network in Figure 5-13.

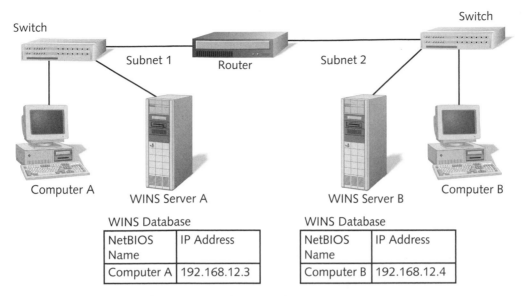

Figure 5-13   WINS replication: sample network

In this network, Computer A on subnet 1 is configured to use WINS Server A, and Computer B on subnet 2 is configured to use WINS Server B. This configuration works perfectly until Computer A attempts to contact Computer B via a NetBIOS name. Computer A performs a name query to WINS Server A for the NetBIOS name to IP address mapping for Computer B, only to get an error stating that the WINS Server A has no mapping for Computer B in its database. Computer A then broadcasts to find Computer B. Since a router separates the two computers, this, too, fails to resolve the NetBIOS name to an IP address. Failed communication between the two computers is the end result.

To fix this problem, you can configure replication between the two WINS servers. All WINS servers in your network should be configured to perform replication with one another. If you establish replication in the network shown in Figure 5-13, Server A learns the NetBIOS name mappings on Server B and vice versa. The end result is a successful name query response when Computer A queries Server A for information regarding Computer B.

You can set up replication partners automatically via multicast. This new feature of Windows 2000 is mentioned earlier in the chapter. In most cases, however, you need to configure replication manually to ensure that it meets the needs of your network. Two types of replication exist for WINS servers: pull and push.

Pull replication occurs at a predetermined interval. You should use it between WINS servers separated by slow links, such as slow WAN links. Using pull replication, you could set the WINS database replication to occur at off hours to conserve WAN bandwidth for data transfer.

Push replication occurs after a predetermined number of changes occur to the WINS database. Since you cannot control when that number of changes will be reached, you should configure push replication between servers that share a fast connection—servers on a LAN segment, for instance.

In most cases, WINS servers are configured as both push and pull replication partners. This ensures that the databases for each server remain consistent.

You configure replication through the WINS console. You must open the WINS console and then right-click the Replication Partners folder. If you select the New Replication Partner option, the dialog box shown in Figure 5-14 opens.

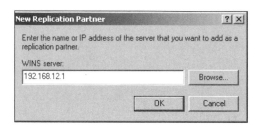

Figure 5-14   New Replication Partner dialog box

You then must type the IP address of the WINS server that you wish to configure as a replication partner, and click OK to continue. You must repeat this process on both servers that you wish to set up as replication partners. By default, the servers are set up as both push and pull replication partners. Figure 5-15 displays the replication partner WIN2KDC01 in the Replication Partners folder.

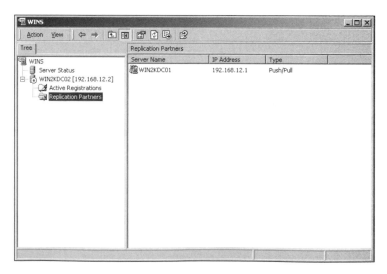

Figure 5-15   Configured replication partner

To configure the push/pull settings further, you can double-click the server in the Replication Partners folder and then select the Advanced tab shown in Figure 5-16. This opens the Advanced properties tab for a particular replication partner. In this tab you can set the interval for pull replication and the number of updates before push replication is triggered. You can also set whether the server uses a persistent connection with its replication partner.

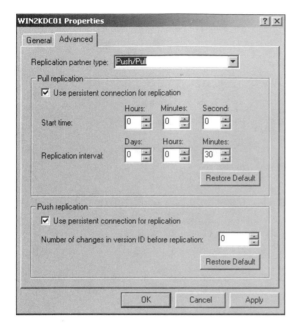

Figure 5-16   Advanced Properties tab for a replication partner

In addition to setting replication parameters and persistent connection settings, you can also use the Replication Partner Type box to configure the replication partners as just push or pull partners only. However, the Microsoft recommendation is that you leave the replication as both push and pull, and adjust the replication parameters to meet your company's needs.

Replication parameters depend on many factors. Some are the number of WINS users, the amount of bandwidth between servers, and the amount of change within your network. You must strike a balance between the least amount of possible WINS traffic and the amount of time you can afford for your databases to be inconsistent.

For example, if the computers in each subnet in the sample network shown in Figure 5-13 rarely need to talk to computers in the opposite subnet, it does not matter if the two WINS server databases are inconsistent for short periods of time. However, if the majority of your traffic occurs between subnets, you must configure your replication parameters to keep the databases as consistent as possible. Replication parameters are more of an art than a science. You probably need to experiment with the replication settings in your environment before deciding exactly what works for your network.

CONFIGURING CLIENTS FOR WINS

The easiest way to configure a client for WINS involves setting the DHCP 044 and 046 scope options mentioned earlier in the section, "NetBIOS Name Resolution," in this chapter. Using these options guarantees that all DHCP-enabled clients receive the IP address of WINS servers on your network and the correct node type for NetBIOS name resolution.

On clients with static IP addresses, you configure the WINS setting in the Advanced properties, WINS tab of the Advanced (TCP/IP) settings dialog box. Figure 5-17 displays the WINS tab.

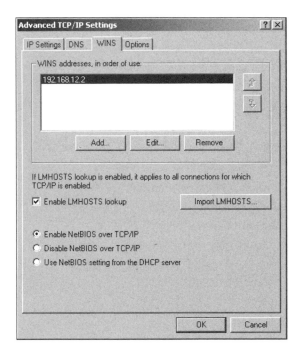

Figure 5-17   WINS tab in Advanced TCP/IP Settings dialog box

Using the various options on this tab you can configure a primary WINS server (the first server in the list) and a secondary WINS server. You can also enable or disable the use of the Lmhosts file. Finally this dialog box allows you to enable or disable NetBIOS over TCP/IP.

For all static clients, you must access the WINS tab and manually type WINS server information. Because this is an enormous administrative task in very large networks, most administrators use DHCP and the DHCP options whenever possible.

MANAGING, MONITORING, AND TROUBLESHOOTING WINS

Due to its dynamic nature, once configured, WINS normally requires very little interaction from the administrator. Still, you should always monitor all services on your network to ensure that they work correctly. The first place to discover WINS errors is the Event Viewer console found under Administrative Tools. The System Log displays any major errors or warnings that the WINS server encounters.

You can find further information about the WINS server service in the WINS console by right-clicking the server and clicking Display Server Statistics. Figure 5-18 shows the server statistics window.

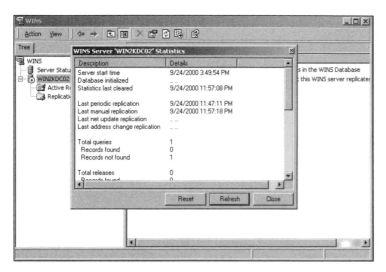

Figure 5-18   WINS Server Statistics window

In the server statistics window, you can see everything from the start time for the server to the last time replication occurred with configured replication partners. If you suspect that replication is not occurring correctly, you should view the WINS partner statistics at the very bottom of the server statistics window. It tells you the # of Replications and the # of Comm failures (communication failures between servers). If you see a high number of Comm failures, the first thing you should attempt is a ping between the two configured replication partners. Network problems may prevent the two servers from seeing each other.

Many other management, troubleshooting, and monitoring tools are also available by right-clicking the server item in the WINS console. Everything from verifying the database to initializing push/pull replication is available. Of particular interest is the Back Up Database item. You can use this to back up the database manually to a particular folder. You can set the default folder path on the General tab shown in Figure 5-19. You access this tab by right-clicking the WINS server and clicking Properties.

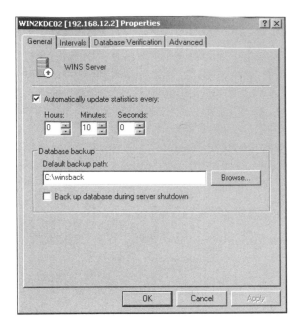

Figure 5-19   Server Properties dialog box

If you click the Backup Database at Server Shutdown shown in Figure 5-19, you guarantee that the WINS database is backed up each time the server shuts down.

To restore a WINS database using the information from a database backup, complete the following steps:

1. Stop the WINS service.

2. Then, navigate to the WINS database directory (%windir%\system32\wins, by default) and delete all files in this directory.

3. At this point, you must open the WINS console, right-click the WINS server, and select Restore Database.

4. Then point the Restore wizard to the directory that holds your backup of the WINS database, and you restore the database.

5. Restart the WINS service.

Most of WINS troubleshooting stems from incorrectly set WINS entries on the client or incorrect DHCP scope options on the DHCP servers. If you do have a client that cannot get NetBIOS name resolutions from a WINS server, first test to see if you can ping the WINS server. Then, verify that the correct WINS settings are in place on the client. Finally, if network connectivity is available and the client is configured correctly, check that WINS server service is running and correctly configured on the server using the tools discussed earlier.

One last management/configuration task may be necessary on a WINS server: compacting the WINS database. If the WINS database grows too large, it can slow name resolution responses. To compact the WINS database, you must use the following commands and syntax:

```
C:\>net stop wins
The Windows Internet Name Service (WINS) service is stopping.
The Windows Internet Name Service (WINS) service was stopped
successfully.


C:\>cd winnt\system32\wins

C:\WINNT\system32\wins>jetpack wins.mdb temp.mdb
Compacted database wins.mdb in 1.692 seconds.
moving temp.mdb => wins.mdb
jetpack completed successfully.

C:\WINNT\system32\wins>net start wins
The Windows Internet Name Service (WINS) service is
starting..
The Windows Internet Name Service (WINS) service was started
successfully.


C:\WINNT\system32\wins>
```

The net stop wins command stops the WINS server service. The cd command changes your current directory to the directory that contains the WINS database. The command jetpack wins.mdb temp.mdb performs actual compacting of the WINS database. The first .mdb database wins.mdb is the actual WINS database file. The second .mdb specified is just a temporary database used during the compaction process and then erased. The second .mdb can have any name, but the first must always be wins.mdb. Finally, the net start wins command restarts the WINS server service.

CHAPTER SUMMARY

❑ The Windows Internet Name Service provided with Windows 2000 provides a method for clients to obtain NetBIOS name to IP address resolution. NetBIOS names are 16-byte names that consist of a computer name of up to 15 characters and a sixteenth hexadecimal character that specifies exactly what service is on a computer. In routed LAN environments, WINS servers must be configured to allow clients to perform NetBIOS name resolution properly.

❑ Although Windows 2000 does support the use of the static Lmhosts file for NetBIOS name resolution, the preferred method is the dynamic database used with WINS. With the WINS server installed, clients can be configured to automatically register their NetBIOS names and IP addresses with Name Registration Requests. They can then use name queries to find NetBIOS name mappings on the WINS server.

❐ In an environment consisting of multiple WINS servers, it is necessary to configure replication properly to ensure that all WINS servers have a consistent database of NetBIOS names on the network. Replication partners can be configured to use pull replication, which replicates the database at a set interval; or push replication, which replicates the database after a predetermined numbers of changes occur. In most networks, replication partners are set up as both push and pull partners.

❐ Finally, once installed and configured, the WINS server must be monitored. Nearly all monitoring, from displaying the server statistics to backing up the WINS database, occurs within the WINS console. It is the single most important WINS management, configuration, and troubleshooting tool.

KEY TERMS

Application Programming Interface (API) — Standardized set of commands and programming parameters used to simplify the interaction between applications and lower-level networking components.

b-node — NetBIOS node type that uses broadcasts to resolve NetBIOS names to IP addresses.

group NetBIOS names — NetBIOS names used to register entire groups of computers; an example is domain controllers in a domain.

h-node — NetBIOS node type that first attempts directed communication to a WINS server to resolve NetBIOS names to IP addresses; if directed communication fails, clients with this node type then try a broadcast to resolve NetBIOS names to IP addresses.

m-node — NetBIOS node type that first attempts broadcasts to resolve NetBIOS names to IP addresses; if broadcasts fail, the client then tries directed communication with the WINS server.

multi-homed — Any computer configured either with multiple NICS or multiple IP addresses.

name query response — Response sent from a WINS server to the WINS client, either informing the client of the NetBIOS name to IP address resolution or of failure to achieve a resolution.

NetBIOS — Session-level API developed to provide high-level applications with easy access to lower-level networking protocols.

NetBIOS name registration — Sent by WINS clients to WINS servers to ask for registration of a particular NetBIOS name with an IP address.

NetBIOS name release — Sent by WINS clients to direct the WINS server to terminate the dynamic mapping of a NetBIOS name to an IP address.

NetBIOS name renewal — Sent by WINS clients to request that the WINs server extend NetBIOS name to IP address mapping; normally occurs halfway through the TTL.

NetBIOS name query — Used by WINS clients to query WINS servers for information about a particular NetBIOS name; in short, used to find NetBIOS name to IP address mappings.

NetBIOS Name Server (NBNS) — Server configured with the WINS server service.

NetBIOS over TCP/IP — NetBIOS using TCP/IP as its lower-level networking protocol stack.

NetBIOS scope — Optional parameter used to break NetBIOS domains into smaller sections; similar to subnets in TCP/IP.

NetBT — Common abbreviation for NetBIOS over TCP/IP.

p-node — NetBIOS node type that uses directed communication to a WINS server to resolve NetBIOS names to IP addresses.

pull replication — Replication of the WINS database that occurs at a preset time interval; used with slow WAN links.

push replication — Replication of the WINS database that occurs after a predetermined number of changes to the database occur; used with fast connections between replication partners.

Tombstoned — State of a WINS entry once it is marked for deletion.

unique NetBIOS names — NetBIOS names assigned to a single computer and its associated services.

WINS replication — Process of replicating the WINS databases between two WINS servers.

5

REVIEW QUESTIONS

1. Push replication occurs _____.

   a. After a certain number of changes occur

   b. Automatically without administrator intervention

   c. At a preset time interval

   d. Never

2. Which one of the following Lmhosts extensions indicates that a computer is multi-homed?

   a. #PRE

   b. #MH

   c. #DOM

   d. #INCLUDE

3. Which of the following use broadcast for part of their NetBIOS name resolution methods? (Choose all that apply.)

   a. B-node

   b. P-node

   c. H-node

   d. M-node

4. A computer name is considered a _____ NetBIOS name.

5. A group name is considered a _____ NetBIOS name.

6. Which one of the following commands can you use to see the current NetBIOS names on a machine?

   a. Nbtstat

   b. Hostname

   c. Winsconfig

   d. Set Wins=auto

7. What Lmhosts extension can you use to preload entries into the NetBIOS name cache?

   a. #DOM

   b. #INCLUDE

   c. #LOADNET

   d. #PRE

8. Clients attempt NetBIOS name renewal at _____ their TTL.

9. Pull replication occurs _____.

   a. After a certain number of changes occur

   b. Automatically without administrator intervention

   c. At a preset time interval

   d. Never

10. Which one of the following commands allows you to compact the WINS database?

    a. Net stop

    b. Jetpack

    c. Compact wins

    d. Set wins=compact

11. Which of the following must you have in order to install the WINS server service? (Choose all that apply.)

    a. A static IP address, subnet mask, and default gateway

    b. A Windows 2000 professional machine

    c. 650 MB free hard-drive space

    d. A Windows 2000 server machine

12. The preferred NetBIOS node type for all clients is _____.

13. Every network should have at least _____ primary WINS server(s) and _____ secondary WINS servers(s).

14. The 044 DHCP scope option lets you configure WINS/NBNS information that can be dynamically assigned to all DHCP clients. True or false?

15. Which one of the following do WINS clients use to find a NetBIOS name to IP address mapping on a WINS server?

   a. Name registration

   b. Name renewal

   c. Name release

   d. Name query

16. Which one of the new features in WINS under Windows 2000 reduces the amount of network traffic used for database replication?

   a. Push/pull replication

   b. Persistent connections

   c. Automatic replication partners

   d. None of the above

17. Which of the following are possible methods that clients can use for NetBIOS name resolution? (Choose all that apply.)

   a. Broadcasts

   b. NBNS/WINS servers

   c. DNS servers

   d. All of the above

18. A WINS entry with the syntax *computername*[20] specifies which service on the computer?

   a. Workstation

   b. Messenger

   c. Domain controller

   d. Server

19. You can configure the WINS server to back up the database automatically each time the WINS server shuts down. True or false?

20. WINS replication must be configured on both servers you wish to participate in replication. True or false?

HANDS-ON PROJECTS

All Hands-on Projects in this chapter require two computers set up as described in the lab set-up section in the front of this book. For these exercises, you use the PCs named win2kdc01 and win2kdc02.

Project 5-1

To install the WINS server service:

1. Log on to the **win2kclass02** domain at computer win2kdc01 as **Administrator** with the password **password**.

2. Right-click **My Network Places** and select **Properties** to open the Network and Dial-up Connections dialog box.

3. Click **Advanced** and then click **Optional Networking Components**.

4. Double-click **Networking Services** to display a list of available services.

5. Click in the box to the left of the **Windows Internet Name Service (WINS)** item, and then click **OK**.

6. Click **Next** to install the WINS server service. (You may be prompted to insert your Windows 2000 server CD-ROM.)

   You installed the WINS server service on win2kdc01.

7. Repeat this procedure on win2kdc02.

Project 5-2

To configure replication between two WINS servers:

1. On the server win2kdc01 click **Start**, **Programs**, **Administrative Tools**, **WINS**.

   This opens the WINS console.

2. Right-click the **Replication Partners** folder, and select **New Replication Partner**.

3. In the New Replication Partner dialog box, place the IP address of win2kdc02 (it should be 192.168.12.2) in the WINS server entry, and then click **OK**.

4. On the server win2kdc02 click **Start**, **Programs**, **Administrative Tools**, **WINS**.

   This opens the WINS console.

5. Right-click the **Replication Partners** folder, and select **New Replication Partner**.

6. In the New Replication Partner dialog box, place the IP address of win2kdc01 (it should be 192.168.12.1) in the WINS server entry, and then click **OK**.

At this point, you have configured servers win2kdc01 and win2kdc02 to replicated WINS database information.

Project 5-3

You can complete this Hands-on Project for either server.

To initiate a transfer of WINS database information between replication partners:

1. On the server click **Start**, **Programs**, **Administrative Tools**, **WINS**.

   This opens the WINS console.

2. Right-click **Replication Partners** and select **Replicate Now**.

3. Click **Yes** in the Are you sure you want to start replication now? dialog box.

4. Click **OK** in the next dialog box.

5. On the server click **Start**, **Programs**, **Administrative Tools**, **Event Viewer**.

   This opens the Event Viewer console.

Event Viewer should contain an entry stating that replication occurred. It may take some time for this entry to appear.

Project 5-4

You can complete this Hands-on Project for either server.

To display WINS server statistics:

1. On the server click **Start**, **Programs**, **Administrative Tools**, **WINS**.

   This opens the WINS console.

2. Right-click the **server name** in the WINS console, and then select **Display Server Statistics**.

3. Note the Server Start Time, Time of last replication, Total number of queries, and the WINS partner information (# of Replications and # of Comm Fails).

Project 5-5

To set up automatic WINS database backup on the WINS server:

1. Open Windows Explorer and create a folder named **winback** on the systemroot drive.

2. On the server click **Start**, **Programs**, **Administrative Tools**, **WINS**. This opens the WINS console.

3. Right-click the **server name** and then select **Properties**.

4. On the **General Tab** click **Browse**, select the **systemroot\winback** folder as the Default Backup path, then click **OK** to select the path.

5. Click the **Back up database during server shutdown** check box to ensure that the database is backed up when the server is shutdown.

Project 5-6

To initiate a manual backup of the WINS database:

1. On the server click **Start**, **Programs**, **Administrative Tools**, **WINS**.

   This opens the WINS console.

2. Right-click the **server name** and select **Back Up Database**. If you completed Hands-on Project 5-5, you are prompted to save the backup in systemroot\winback, the folder specified in Step 4 of that project.

3. Click **OK** to back up the WINS database.

CASE PROJECTS

Case 1

Your boss sends you an e-mail, upset that WINS is still running after he spent thousands of dollars to purchase and install Windows 2000 servers. Reply to his e-mail, explaining why you are still running WINS on your network, which consists of all Windows 2000 servers and Windows 2000 and Windows 98 clients.

Case 2

Your network consists of a central office and three remote sites connected by ISDN. The number of clients in the entire network totals 500. You need to prepare a short, one-page document describing the best way for your network to implement and use WINS. Be sure to include the number of WINS servers you need and how you plan to configure replication.

Case 3

As senior engineer for Freytech Inc., one of your major tasks is providing training for new hires and existing junior-level engineers. Once again, upper-level management has chosen you to provide the Friday afternoon training session. Prepare a 15-minute presentation describing NetBIOS names and NetBIOS name resolution methods. Be sure that you cover both Lmhosts files and WINS servers.

REMOTE ACCESS IN WINDOWS 2000

After reading this chapter and completing the exercises, you will be able to:

♦ Describe the use of Routing and Remote Access Service (RRAS)

♦ Install RRAS

♦ Configure Inbound RRAS Connections

♦ Create a remote access policy

♦ Configure a remote access profile

♦ Configure a Virtual Private Network

♦ Configure remote access security, including encryption and authentication protocols

♦ Configure multilink connections

♦ Configure routing and remote access for DHCP integration

♦ Manage, monitor, and troubleshoot remote access

Remote access in Windows 2000 comes in the form of a service named the **Routing and Remote Access Service**, or RRAS. Essentially, this service runs on a Windows 2000 server and enables other servers or client computers that are not connected to the network via a permanent cable to establish temporary connections over phone lines, Integrated Services Digital Network (ISDN) lines, or services such as X.25, a standard protocol suite in a packet-switched network. Once a computer establishes a connection with the RRAS server, that computer can access the resources on the RRAS server and possibly access the other computers on the same network as the server, depending on the server's configuration.

This chapter begins with an overview of remote access that includes a brief history of remote access in the Windows environment and an examination of the many features and components that make up RRAS. You then learn how to install, configure, secure, and manage an RRAS server.

REMOTE ACCESS OVERVIEW

Before you can understand the details of installing and configuring a remote access server, it is necessary to understand some of what goes on behind the scenes. Remote access uses many different protocols, including remote access protocols, networking protocols, and security protocols. This overview provides a look at the history, features, and concepts of remote access.

Brief History of Remote Access

The Remote Access Service, commonly called RAS, was first introduced with Windows NT 3.51 Service Pack 2 in an attempt to offer a simple and inexpensive way for remote users to dial in to a server and access network resources. This service was carried over almost fully intact to Windows NT 4.0.

Microsoft later introduced the Routing and Remote Access Service (RRAS), a substantial upgrade to RAS. Among other things, RRAS introduced the capability of multiprotocol routing to remote access. Previously, RAS supported only the NetBEUI networking protocol. For clients using other protocols, such as TCP/IP, RAS provided translation in the form of a NetBIOS gateway.

Windows 2000 includes significantly updated versions of RRAS. The Windows 2000 Server version now offers a number of new features:

- Internet Group Management Protocol (IGMP) support
- Network Address Translation (NAT), which allows computers on a LAN to share a single Internet connection
- Integrated AppleTalk routing
- Layer-Two Tunneling Protocol (L2TP) over IP Security (IPSec) support for router-to-router Virtual Private Networking (VPN) connections
- Improved support for Remote Authentication Dial-In User Support (RADIUS)

Routing and Remote Access Concepts

A Windows 2000 Server running the Routing and Remote Access Service can accept connections from users physically separated from the main network, but still needing to connect to the main network to access resources. Once connected, remote access clients use standard tools and applications to access these network resources. For example, once a user connects to a remote access server, that user can retrieve files with Windows Explorer, connect to a messaging server with a standard e-mail client, and open documents with applications like Microsoft Word. User's perceive themselves as directly connected to the network. In fact, at its heart, RRAS really is just another way to transmit standard networking protocols and commands already in use on the network. Instead of being put onto a network cable by a network interface card, the information is formatted (and possibly secured) by RRAS and transmitted across whatever type of link is configured.

Remote Access versus Remote Control

The concepts of remote access and remote control are often confused. Although both involve connecting to a remote computer, they are substantially different approaches.

In **remote access**, a client computer connects to a remote access server using a dial-up or other type of on-demand connection. Once connected to the network, the client can access network resources. All applications still run on the client computer.

In **remote control**, a client computer connects to a remote server and actually takes control over that server in a separate window on the client computer, as if the user were sitting at the server computer. All applications run on the server.

The Windows Routing and Remote Access Service does not support remote control. Remote control requires the use of Windows Terminal Service or third-party software like Symantec's pcAnywhere.

Remote Access Connection Types

Just like the RRAS service in Windows NT 4.0, Windows 2000 RRAS provides two distinct types of remote access connections to remote users:

- Dial-Up Networking
- Virtual Private Networking

Dial-Up Networking   With **Dial-Up Networking**, a client makes a temporary, dial-up connection to a physical port on the RRAS server. This connection uses the services of a public telecommunications provider, such as an analog phone line, an ISDN line, or X.25. A good example of dial-up networking is when both client and server have a standard modem. The client initiates the dial-up connection using the modem and makes the connection to the server modem over public phone lines. The server authenticates the user and provides the configured access.

Virtual Private Networking   **Virtual Private Networking (VPN)** provides a way of making a secured, private connection from the client to the server over a public network such as the Internet. Unlike dial-up networking, where client and server share a direct physical connection, a VPN connection is logical and not necessarily direct. Typically, a remote user connects to an Internet Service Provider (ISP) using a form of dial-up networking, though establishing a VPN connection over a standard cable-connected network is quite possible. The RRAS Server also connects to the Internet (probably via a persistent, or permanent, connection) and is configured to accept VPN connections. Once connected to the Internet, the client then establishes a VPN connection over that dial-up connection to the RRAS server.

VPN offers two significant advantages. First, remote users who are not in the same local calling area as the remote access server need not make long distance calls to connect to the network. Instead, they can make local calls to an ISP. Second, every standard dial-up connection requires that a physical device be present on the RRAS server and devoted to that connection. This limits the number of users that can connect remotely at a single time. Assuming a fairly high-bandwidth Internet connection from the RRAS server to the Internet, more remote users can connect at the same time using VPN than users with dial-up connections.

Protocols

A **networking protocol** is simply a defined and often standardized way of communicating between two devices on a network. You must be familiar with two general types of protocols to work with RRAS: remote access (or line) protocols and networking (or LAN) protocols.

Remote Access Protocols **Remote access protocols** govern how information is broken up and transmitted over wide area network (WAN) connections, of which a dial-up connection is one type. RRAS supports four remote access protocols:

- **Point-to-Point Protocol (PPP)**: an industry standard set of robust and flexible protocols, by far the most common remote access protocol used today. Most dial-in servers, including RRAS, support PPP, and it is generally considered the best choice for remote access situations. Windows 2000 RRAS supports PPP both for dial-out and dial-in connections.

- **Serial Line Interface Protocol (SLIP)**: an older protocol developed in UNIX and still widely used. Windows 2000 RRAS supports SLIP in dial-out configurations, but you cannot use a SLIP client to dial in to an RRAS server.

- RAS Protocol: a proprietary protocol, used only between Microsoft-based networks, that supports the NetBIOS naming convention. It is required to support NetBIOS naming and is installed by default when you install the RRAS server.

- NetBIOS Gateway: provides compatibility with older versions of RAS Server that do not support networking protocols such as TCP/IP and NWLink. The NetBIOS gateway translates data from the NetBEUI protocol to these other protocols.

Networking Protocols Networking protocols govern how information is transmitted between devices on a local area network (LAN). You can find detailed information on supporting networking protocols in Windows 2000 in Chapter 2, but a brief recap is in order here.

RRAS supports the use of three networking protocols:

- *NetBEUI*: a simple, efficient protocol primarily used on small networks that consist only of Microsoft clients. Although easy to configure and manage, NetBEUI does not support routing and is therefore not suitable for large, varied networks.

- *Transmission Control Protocol/Internet Protocol (TCP/IP)*: an extensive, robust protocol ideally suited for connecting different types of computers and operating systems. Thus, it is the standard choice of protocols for networks containing many different types of systems, such as Microsoft systems or those based on UNIX, and it is the standard protocol for the Internet.

- *Internetwork Packet eXchange (IPX)*: the protocol of choice for networks using Novell's NetWare. If your network uses NetWare and your remote clients need to access these resources, you must enable IPX.

You must choose at least one LAN protocol to use, but RRAS enables you to use all three simultaneously if necessary. Keep in mind that any remote client dialing in must support one of these protocols. RRAS also supports the Point-to-Point Tunneling Protocol (PPTP), an extension of PPP that you can use to establish a connection such as a Virtual Private Network.

Remote Access Clients

Just about any dial-up client software that supports PPP can connect to an RRAS server. Such clients include:

- Windows 2000
- Windows NT 4.0
- Windows NT 3.5
- Windows 95/98/ME
- Windows for Workgroups 3.1x
- MS-DOS
- Microsoft LAN Manager remote access clients
- UNIX and Apple Macintosh clients using third-party client software

Remote Access Features

Now that you are familiar with some of the concepts involved in remote access, it's time to look at some of the other features offered by RRAS in Windows 2000. The updated version provides new support for router discovery, network address translation, multicast routing, and powerful remote access policies.

Router Discovery

Windows 2000 supports a new feature called router discovery that provides a method for detecting default gateways. Manual gateway configuration or DHCP offers clients no way to adapt to changes in network configuration. Using router discovery, however, clients can dynamically determine the status of routers and switch to back-up routers, should a primary router fail. Chapter 7 covers this feature in more detail.

Network Address Translator

Network Address Translator (NAT) is a router standard that translates IP addresses on a private network into valid Internet IP addresses. This means that a single computer with Internet connectivity can share its Internet connection with other computers on the network through a single IP address. Windows 2000 Server features both a full-featured NAT named Connection Sharing and an easier to configure version named Shared Access. You learn about both later in this chapter.

Multicast Routing

Multicast routing, or multicasting, is a targeted form of network broadcasting that sends information to a select group of users instead of all users connected to a network. Standards are being developed to support multicasting over a TCP/IP network such as the Internet.

Windows 2000 Server supports multicast routing using what is known as a multicast proxy. You can use this proxy to extend multicast support to remote access users or to a single LAN network connected to the Internet. Windows 2000 Server behaves like a multicast client, communicating between local multicast clients on the LAN and multicast servers on the Internet.

Remote Access Policies

In earlier versions of Windows NT, remote access was granted to users based on a single option configurable in User Manager or the Remote Access Admin tool. With this option, named Grant Dial-In Permission To User, enabled for a user account, that user could dial in to the remote access server.

In Windows 2000, granting remote access privileges is more flexible and more complex. Each User object in the Users and Computers tool (or the Active Directory Users and Computers tool if a member of a domain) has certain dial-in properties.

In addition to the dial-in properties of a user, Remote Access Policies (RAPs) are used to configure conditions under which a user may connect using a specific remote access connection. Administrators may now include restrictions based on criteria such as time of day, type of connection, authentication, and even length of connection. You learn more about configuring RAPs later in this chapter.

Remote Access Security

Remote access has always been considered one of the weaker points of networking security. While it's always been fairly easy to secure a network from unauthorized physical access, the current popularity of Internet access and remote user access places larger security demands on the modern network. Fortunately, new security technologies and protocols have been developed to ease the problem of remote access security.

User Authentication

The primary method of securing a remote access connection involves authenticating the user trying to connect. To do this, the user (or the user's client computer) must present some sort of credentials that allow the RRAS server to verify that the user is indeed a valid user.

Windows 2000 supports five different user **authentication** protocols:

- Password Authentication Protocol (PAP)
- Shiva Password Authentication Protocol (SPAP)
- Challenge Handshake Authentication Protocol (CHAP)
- Microsoft CHAP (MS-CHAP)
- Extensible Authentication Protocol (EAP)

Password Authentication Protocol   Password Authentication Protocol is the most basic form of user authentication. A user's name and password are transmitted over the dial-up connection to the RRAS server. Transmitted in clear text with no encryption, this information is quite vulnerable to snooping. In addition, PAP provides no way for a client and server to authenticate one another. For the most part, better authentication protocols have rendered PAP obsolete. In fact, Microsoft recommends that you do not use it unless absolutely necessary.

Shiva Password Authentication Protocol   Windows 2000 Server includes Shiva Password Authentication Protocol mainly for compatibility with remote access hardware devices manufactured by Shiva, a private company now owned by Intel. SPAP isn't used much on most networks.

Challenge Handshake Authentication Protocol Considerably more secure than PAP or SPAP, Challenge Handshake Authentication is a form of authentication in which the server sends the client a key to encrypt the client's username and password. The client then sends the encrypted information across the dial-up connection to the server, which decrypts it and attempts to validate the user. The encrypted username and password are considerably less vulnerable to eavesdroppers. CHAP is also commonly called MD5-CHAP because it uses the RSA MD5 hash algorithm for encryption.

Microsoft CHAP A modified version of CHAP, Microsoft CHAP allows the use of Windows 2000 authentication information. Of the two versions of MS-CHAP, version 2 is most secure; all Microsoft operating systems support it. Other operating systems sometimes support version 1.

Extensible Authentication Protocol A general protocol for PPP authentication, Extensible Authentication Protocol supports multiple authentication mechanisms. Instead of selecting a single authentication method for a connection, EAP can negotiate an authentication method at connect time. The computer asking for the authentication method is called the authenticator and may require several different pieces of authentication information. This allows the use of almost any authentication method, including secure access tokens or one-time password systems.

Each authentication method supported in EAP is called an EAP type. Both the client and the server must support the same EAP type. Currently, Windows 2000 comes with the following two EAP types:

- *EAP MD5-CHAP*: virtually identical to the normal CHAP authentication, except that it packages and sends authentication information as EAP messages. This means that if you turn on EAP MD5-CHAP and disable regular CHAP on the server, regular CHAP clients cannot connect.

- *EAP Transport Level Security (TLS)*: lets you use public-key certificates for authentication. TLS is similar to Secure Sockets Layer (SSL) used in most Web browsers. With EAP TLS, both the client and the server send encrypted authentication messages. EAP TLS is one of the strongest authentication methods available but requires that your RRAS server belong to a Windows 2000 domain.

A third EAP authentication method is included with Windows 2000, although it is not technically an EAP type. EAP-RADIUS passes authentication information to a RADIUS server for authentication. A RADIUS server is usually devoted to running a large user account database against which it can identify remote users. In addition, RADIUS can authenticate users from a wide variety of accounts, including Windows domains, Novell Directory Services, SQL Server databases, and UNIX password files.

Connection Control

In addition to its ability to authenticate users in a variety of ways, Windows 2000 RRAS provides a number of methods for securing the actual connection from a client to a server. One such method, Callback Control Protocol, allows your RRAS servers or clients to negotiate a callback with the other end. For example, you may configure a server to hang up and call a user back at a specified number whenever that user tries to connect. This provides two advantages. First, a successful connection can only be made from a particular number—a good way of ensuring that only authorized users can make the connection. Second, for users dialing in from another calling area, the company can foot the bill for the long-distance call.

Another way to control connections is to configure an RRAS server to accept or reject calls based on Caller ID or Automatic Number Identification (ANI) information. For example, you could configure a server to accept calls only from a certain number or to reject calls from callers who may be trying to break into the system.

Access Control

RRAS supports a number of ways to control remote user access to the RRAS server. The primary access control method is enabling or disabling permission to dial in on individual user accounts. In addition to this basic method, RAPs allow you to extend control over whether users can dial in or not by setting a number of conditions on the access.

INSTALLING AND CONFIGURING ROUTING AND REMOTE ACCESS

Now that you have a basic grasp of the concepts behind the Routing and Remote Access Service, it is time to see how to actually implement and configure it. This is a fairly simple procedure, but unlike other software or Windows components, you cannot install RRAS using the Add/Remove Programs component of the Windows Control Panel. Instead, RRAS is automatically installed along with Windows 2000 Server but left in a disabled state. All you need to do is enable it. First, however, you must make sure that all dial-up equipment, interfaces, and protocols that you intend to use with the server are installed and configured correctly.

This section provides an overview of the set-up process and the choices you must make. Hands-on Project 6-1 at the end of this chapter walks you through the actual steps of setting up RRAS.

First, you log on to the server with Administrator privileges and open the Routing and Remote Access utility from the Administrative Tools program group on the Start menu. This utility (shown in Figure 6-1) is actually a snap-in for the Microsoft Management Console that controls most management features of Windows 2000.

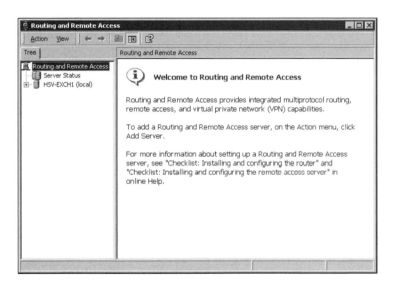

Figure 6-1   Routing and Remote Access snap-in

In the tree in the left pane, find and right-click the name of the server. From the shortcut menu that appears, choose the Configure and Enable Routing and Remote Access command to begin the Routing and Remote Access Server Setup Wizard. The wizard takes you through several configuration steps. The first, shown in Figure 6-2, asks you to select the type of configuration you want to install.

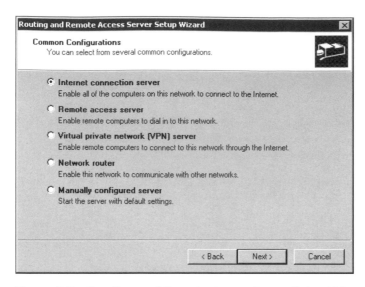

Figure 6-2   Routing and Remote Access Server Setup Wizard

Next, the RRAS Setup Wizard asks you to verify that the protocols you wish to use on the server are already installed and configured. If not, you must configure them before taking the next step.

Next, you configure some options for your network. These options include:

- Selecting the network adapter that you want to use on your internal network, as shown in Figure 6-3. This step is particularly important for a multi-homed server.

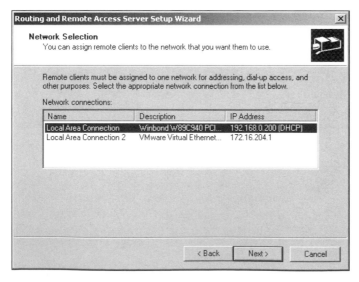

Figure 6-3   Selecting a network adapter

- Deciding whether to use DHCP or to define a static pool of IP addresses, as shown in Figure 6-4. If you have a DHCP server on the same subnet as the RRAS server, the DHCP option is usually best. You learn more about using RRAS and DHCP later in this chapter. If you choose to use a static pool of addresses, you are asked to configure the starting and ending IP addresses of the range you want to use.

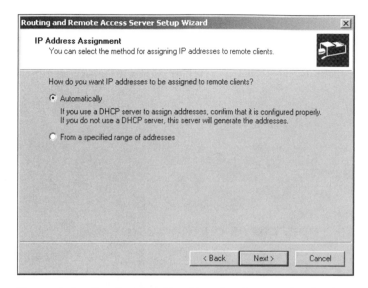

Figure 6-4   Configuring IP addressing for remote clients

- Deciding whether to use Windows authentication or RADIUS. Choosing RADIUS configures RRAS to be a RADIUS client using the EAP authentication protocol, as discussed previously in this chapter. You are also asked to configure settings for the RADIUS server.

And that's all there is to it. Once you enable RRAS, you can pause or stop the service by right-clicking the server in the Routing and Remote Access snap-in and choosing the appropriate action from the All Tasks menu on the shortcut menu.

The following section explains how to configure connections for the new server.

Configuring Remote Access

Once you enable RRAS on your server, you need to configure it to behave the way you want. This configuration occurs in three places:

- Most configuration of inbound connections happens at the server level using the Routing and Remote Access Service snap-in that you used to enable the service. In particular, you use the server object's property page to control whether the server allows connections at all, what protocols it supports and how, security options, and event logging. You also use RRAS to set policies and profiles and to monitor the status of a remote access server.

- A good bit of configuration also happens using the property pages for individual users in the Active Directory Users and Computers snap-in. Here you grant dial-in permissions for individual users, as well as set callback and other dial-in options.

- Once you configure the server and the user accounts for dial-in access, you also need to configure each client. Fortunately, all versions of Windows and most other operating systems come with some built-in form of dial-in capability that is relatively easy to configure. In Windows, this capability is named dial-up networking.

The following section discusses the first two types of configuration. Configuring clients is very similar in different versions of Windows, so we do not go into detail here. Hands-on Project 6-6 at the end of the chapter provides some practice configuring a dial-up connection in Windows 2000 Professional.

Configuring Inbound Connections on the Server

Like most objects in Windows 2000 management, RRAS servers are configured using the settings on a number of property pages. You can access these pages by right-clicking on the server and choosing the Properties command from the shortcut menu. This section explains the general use of each of these property pages.

General Properties

The first page you see when you open the properties for an RRAS Server is the General page, shown in Figure 6-5. The most important setting on this page is the **Remote access server** option, which allows the RRAS Service to operate as a remote access server. This means you can switch remote access on and off without actually stopping the RRAS service, an action that causes the service to erase its settings.

The other option on the General page, **Router**, lets you choose whether clients accessing the RRAS Server can also access the rest of the network that is connected to the server. With routing enabled, you can choose whether to allow routing access only to the LAN (computers that are directly connected to the computer) or to allow demand-dial routing as well. **Demand-dial routing** allows the RRAS server to make WAN connections to other remote networks.

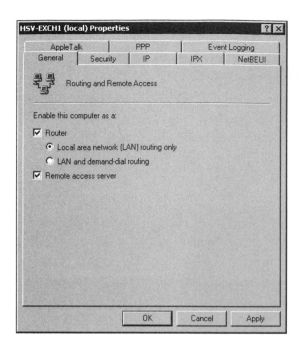

Figure 6-5   General property page for an RRAS server

Security Properties

You use the Security page, shown in Figure 6-6, to specify which authentication and accounting methods RRAS uses. You can choose one of two authentication providers from the list on this page:

- *Windows Authentication*: indicates the built-in authentication suite provided with Windows 2000. This suite includes several authentication protocols, including PAP, SPAP, CHAP, MS-CHAP, MS-CHAP v2, and EAP, all of which were discussed in detail earlier in the chapter. If you choose the Windows Authentication provider, you can click the Authentication Methods button to open a separate dialog box that lets you enable or disable individual authentication protocols.

- *RADIUS Authentication*: causes all authentication requests to be forwarded to a RADIUS server for approval. This authentication method is also discussed earlier in the chapter. If you choose the RADIUS Authentication method, you can click the Configure button to the right of the drop-down list to set up communications with the RADIUS server.

The **Accounting provider** list on the Security page allows you to configure whether connection request events are sent to the Windows Event Log (the Windows Accounting option) or to a RADIUS server (the RADIUS accounting option).

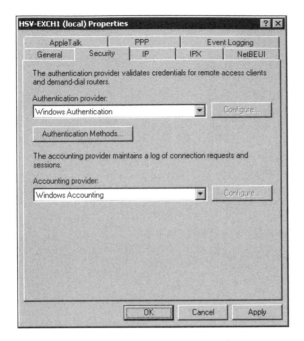

Figure 6-6   Security property page for an RRAS server

PPP Properties

Figure 6-7 shows the PPP property page used to control the PPP-layer options available to clients.

Options on this page include:

- *PPP **Multilink Protocol (MP)*** combines multiple physical links into a single logical link. For example, you could combine two 56-KB modem links into a 128-KB link. The multilink protocol is turned on by default, but if your clients are not using it (or your server does not support multiple physical connections), there is really no reason to leave it turned on. Hands-on Project 6-2 at the end of the chapter details steps for disabling the Multilink protocol.

- ***Bandwidth Allocation Protocol (BAP)*** *and **Bandwidth Allocation Control Protocol (BACP)***: allow a client to add and remove links dynamically during a multilink session to adjust for changes in bandwidth needs. This option is available only when you enable the Multilink option.

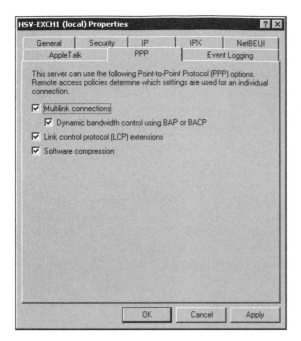

Figure 6-7 PPP property page for an RRAS server

- **Link control protocol (LCP)** extensions include a number of enhancements to the LCP protocol that establishes a PPP link and controls its settings. One of the primary enhancements included is the ability of the client and server to agree dynamically on protocols used on the connection. This option is turned on by default and, since Windows 9x, NT, and 2000 clients all support the extensions, you probably want to leave it that way.

- The Software compression option controls whether RRAS should allow clients to use the Compression Control Protocol (CCP) to compress PPP traffic. Again, this option is on by default, and leaving it that way is usually best.

IP Properties

The IP property page is one of four property pages that control the networking protocols supported by RRAS. Others include IPX, NetBEUI, and AppleTalk. These pages only show if the protocols were installed on the server before enabling RRAS. To install protocols after RRAS, you must disable and re-enable RRAS. Figure 6-8 shows the IP property page, which controls the following properties:

- *Enable IP Routing*: controls whether RRAS routes IP packets between the client and the rest of the network that the RRAS server is on. Enabled by default, this option gives all TCP/IP-based clients access to the network. When disabled, clients can only access resources located on the RRAS server itself. This option depends on the Router option that you enable on the General property page for the server. Since you can turn on routing for the server itself and turn off routing for the IP and other protocols individually, you can achieve pretty fine control over what clients can and cannot access on the network.

- *Allow IP-based remote access and demand-dial connections*: controls whether TCP/IP-based clients can connect to the RRAS server at all. Disabling this option makes the rest of the settings on this page moot (which may be a good choice if you want to allow access only to clients using other protocols).

- *IP address assignment*: controls how remote clients get their IP addresses when connecting to the RRAS server. The default setting is based on the answers you give when you work with the RRAS Setup Wizard. DHCP allows your RRAS server to refer clients to a DHCP server on your network to be assigned IP addresses dynamically. The section, "Configuring RAS for DHCP Integration," later in this chapter provides more information on DHCP. The Static address pool option lets you manually configure a pool of IP addresses that the RRAS server itself can assign to clients.

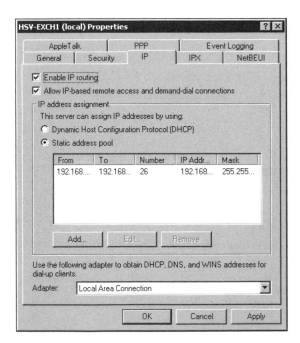

Figure 6-8   IP property page for an RRAS server

To practice configuring the protocols on an RRAS server, be sure to complete Hands-on Project 6-3 at the end of the chapter.

IPX Properties

IP and IPX are fairly similar protocols, even though some of their configuration details differ. On the IPX property page, shown in Figure 6-9, you can choose the following settings:

- *Allow IPX-based remote access and demand-dial connections*: specifies whether IPX-based clients can access the RRAS server at all.

- *Enable network access for remote clients and demand-dial connections*: works like the Enable IP Routing option on the IP page—it allows clients to access the network to which the RRAS server connects instead of just the RRAS server itself.

- *IPX Network Number Assignment*: controls the assignment of IPX addresses to remote clients. With the default option, the server takes care of this task automatically. This choice is probably the wisest, unless you have a specific reason for needing to assign addresses manually. You should also use the default setting, use the same network number for all IPX clients, so that clients can use all IPX resources. The Allow remote clients to request IPX node number option essentially lets remote clients configure their own addresses. Disabled by default, this option is often considered a security-risk: a client could misrepresent itself as another client.

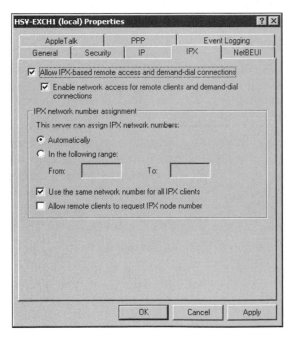

Figure 6-9   IPX property page for an RRAS server

Notice that both the IP and IPX property pages have an option that allows the client to access the rest of the network. However, also notice that the labels for these options are quite different for each protocol. You should be familiar with the wording of these labels for the exam.

NetBEUI and AppleTalk Pages

Both the NetBEUI and AppleTalk protocols are pretty simple, as exemplified by their property pages in RRAS. The NetBEUI protocol has an option for enabling the protocol and an option for whether clients can access only the server or the rest of the network as well. The AppleTalk page has only a setting for enabling the protocol.

Event Logging Page

The Event Logging property page lets you control the level at which events are logged either to the Windows Event Log or to a RADIUS server. The section, "Managing, Monitoring, and Troubleshooting RAS," discusses this page.

Configuring a User for Remote Access

Once you configure your RRAS server to support remote access, the next step is to configure what users can use that access and how. You will use three tools for doing this:

- *User profiles*: configuration settings associated with individual user accounts. Each user has exactly one profile, usually stored in the Active Directory. These profiles include options such as whether the user can connect remotely, whether callback for the user is enabled, and so on.

- *Remote access policies*: connection rules that apply to groups of users.

- *Remote access profiles*: associated with policies and containing settings that determine what happens during call setup and completion.

Configuring User Profiles

If your RRAS server is part of a Windows 2000 domain, the Active Directory, a central directory of resources and objects for the entire network, stores users' profiles. In this case, you use the Active Directory Users and Computers snap-in to manage these profiles. If your RRAS server is not part of a Windows 2000 domain, the local computer stores users' profiles and the Local Users and Groups snap-in controls them. Whichever tool you use, the configuration of the user profiles is the same. In this chapter, we assume that you are using Active Directory Users and Computers.

Each user profile has a host of settings scattered across a number of property pages. However, in relation to remote access, you should be most concerned with the Dial-in page shown in Figure 6-10.

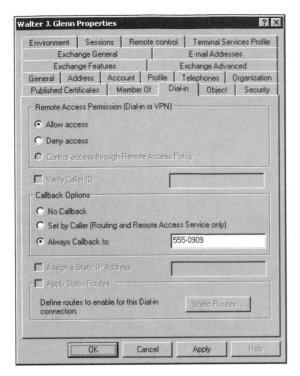

Figure 6-10   Dial-in property page of a user profile

6

A number of settings on this page control the user's remote access capability:

- *Remote Access Permission (Dial-in or VPN)*: enables remote access for the user. There are three options. The first two explicitly allow or deny access; these options override any policy settings that may apply to the user. The final option is to let a remote access policy control the user's access.

- *Verify Caller-ID Option*: lets you enter a phone number that is used to verify the remote caller using the Caller-ID information provided by the phone company. Calls from any other number are automatically rejected.

- *Callback Options*: provides two ways to use the callback feature of RRAS that lets the server automatically hang up on an incoming call and call the user back. The first option lets the caller set the number in the client software. This option does not add much security but can be a good way to let a company be billed for long-distance access instead of the caller. The second callback option sets a specific number that is always called for the user. This method adds some security, in that the user must call from a given number in order to access the network.

- *Assign a Static IP Address*: provides a user with the same IP address every time the user calls in. While it is generally a better idea to let RRAS work in conjunction with DHCP to assign dynamic IP addresses (covered later in the chapter), occasionally a client may need a static IP address for specific applications.

- *Apply Static Routes*: lets you define a set of routes always used to deliver information from the client to specified hosts on the network. If you do not enable this option, the client uses the default gateway assigned by DHCP or given manually. Once you enable this option, use the Static Routes button to add and remove routes.

Configuring Remote Access Policies

While user profiles define settings for an individual user, remote access policies define settings for a whole group of users. A policy is a set of rules that the system evaluates when it determines whether a user can access the network or not. User profiles and policies work together to provide dial-in capability. You can use a policy to define overall settings for a group of users, but individual settings in a user's profile override any policies in effect when that user logs on.

You manage remote access policies with the Routing and Remote Access Service snap-in through a container named Remote Access Policies, shown in Figure 6-11. As you can see, the only policy listed in the container by default is named Allow access if dial-in permission is enabled. This most basic of policies simply tells the RRAS service that if a user's profile grants dial-in access, it may grant that user remote access to the server.

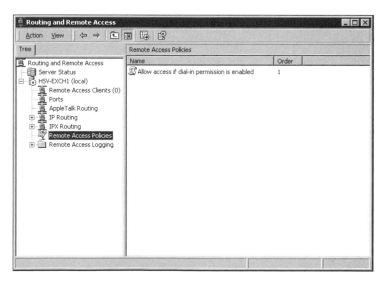

Figure 6-11   Remote Access Policies container

Creating a New Policy

To create a new policy using the RRAS snap-in, right-click the Remote Access Policies container and select the New Remote Access Policy command from the shortcut menu. This launches the Add Remote Access Policy Wizard.

You can practice using this wizard to create a policy in Hands-on Project 6-4. This section describes the general configuration of a new policy.

The first step the wizard takes you to is naming the policy. Once you do this, you see a page that lists the conditions for the new policy. Initially, this page is blank, but each new condition you add updates the list, as shown in Figure 6-12.

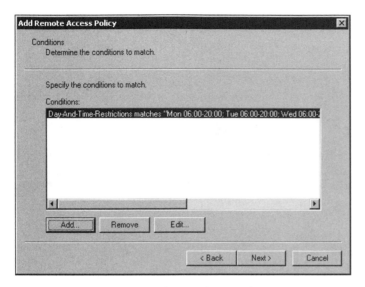

Figure 6-12   Setting conditions for a policy

To add a new condition, click the Add button. This opens the Select Attribute dialog box, which lists all available conditions. Table 6-1 details these conditions. Once you pick a condition from the list, a dialog box opens that lets you set configuration parameters that vary depending on the type of condition you choose. For example, choosing the Day-And-Time Restriction opens a dialog box that lets you restrict access by picking dates and times from a calendar.

Table 6-1   Remote access policy conditions

Attribute Name	What It Specifies
Called-Station-ID	Phone number dialed by user
Calling-Station-ID	Caller's phone number
Client-Friendly-Name	Name of the RADIUS server attempting to validate connection (IAS only)
Client-IP-Address	IP address of the RADIUS server attempting to validate connection (IAS only)
Client-Vendor	Manufacturer of RADIUS proxy or NAS (IAS only)

Table 6-1   Remote access policy conditions (continued)

Attribute Name	What It Specifies
Day-and-Time Restriction	Time periods and days during which connection attempts are accepted or rejected
Framed-Protocol	Remote access protocol (PPP, SLIP, and so on) used for framing incoming packets
NAS-Identifier	Name of the NAS that accepted the original connection (IAS only)
NAS-IP-Address	IP address of the NAS that accepted the original connection (IAS only)
NAS-Port-Type	Physical connection type (phone, ISDN, and so on) used by the caller
Service-Type	Type of service the user requested; types include framed for PPP or login for telnet
Tunnel-Type	Tunneling protocol that should be used (L2TP or PPTP)
Windows-Groups	Windows groups to which the user belongs

After choosing the conditions you want to apply in the new policy, the next step in creating a policy is to choose whether the policy is to allow users to connect or deny them connection. Each policy you create serves only one purpose.

The final step in the Add Remote Access Policy Wizard allows you to modify the remote access profile attached to the policy. You can do this when you establish the policy or come back to it later if you want. Configuring remote access profiles is discussed a bit later in the chapter. Once you finish the wizard, you have created the new remote access policy, you return to the RRAS snap-in, and the policy goes into effect.

Configuring Existing Policies   Policies are evaluated in the order that they appear in the Remote Access Policies container in the RRAS snap-in. You can rearrange this order by right-clicking any policy and using the Move Up and Move Down commands on the shortcut menu. Order is very important, as each condition of each policy is considered to determine whether a user can access the system. All conditions of all policies must be met before access is granted.

Aside from ordering the policies, you can open the properties for any particular policy by right-clicking it and selecting Properties from the shortcut menu. The policy object has only one property page, which is shown in Figure 6-13. On this page, you can change the name of the policy, add new conditions to the policy, switch between granting and denying access based on those conditions, and edit the remote access profile for a policy.

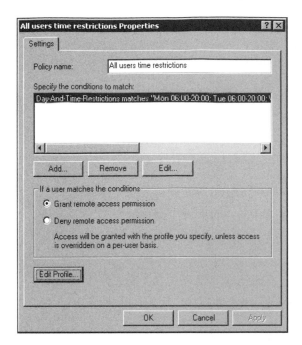

Figure 6-13   Editing properties for a condition

Configuring Remote Access Profiles

Remote access profiles are an important part of a good remote access policy strategy. The first thing, of course, is not to confuse remote access profiles with user profiles. User profiles, which we covered previously, are the collections of settings that pertain to an individual user and are stored in the Active Directory. Remote access profiles determine the remote access settings that apply to users when they meet the conditions in a policy and receive access. Each policy has one associated profile. You can open and edit the profile for a policy on the last page of the Add Remote Access Policy Wizard or later by using the property page for the policy. Either way, you click the Edit Profile button to begin making changes.

The remote access profile, sometimes referred to as a dial-in profile, has six tabs: Dial-In Constraints, IP, Multilink, Authentication, Encryption, and Advanced. The following sections explain these pages.

Dial-in Constraints Properties   The Dial-in Constraints page, shown in Figure 6-14, sports a number of general dial-in controls. These controls let you drop a user if a connection remains idle for a certain time, restrict the maximum session length, restrict access to specified days and times, restrict access to a particular number, and even restrict the dial-in media types (ADSL, ISDN, and so on) allowed.

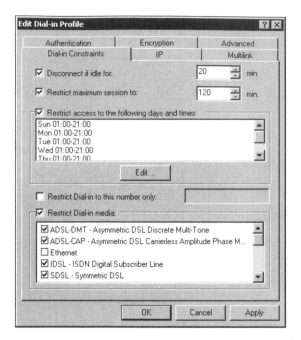

Figure 6-14   Dial-in Constraints page for a profile

IP Properties   The IP page, shown in Figure 6-15, lets you control the IP settings for incoming connections. You can make two settings on this page. The IP Address Assignment Policy section controls how the client is assigned an IP address when connecting. Remember that these settings apply to all users granted access based on the policy to which the profile is attached. Configurations made to individual users (such as a static IP address) override these settings. The IP Packet Filters section lets you add advanced filters to prevent the client or the server from sending certain types of IP packets.

Multilink Properties   Options on the Multilink page control how a client can connect using the Multilink Protocol and the Bandwidth Allocation Protocol. You can explicitly disable or allow multilink or you can set it to follow the default settings used for the server. The BAP settings allow you to specify the idle bandwidth threshold at which the number of lines in use is reduced.

Although the multilink properties suggest otherwise, any settings that you assign using a profile are not used at all unless the server settings match. For example, if you want to set the profile to allow multilink, then both multilink and BAP must be turned on at the server. Otherwise, the settings are ignored. This is true of other profile settings such as IP and authentication, as well.

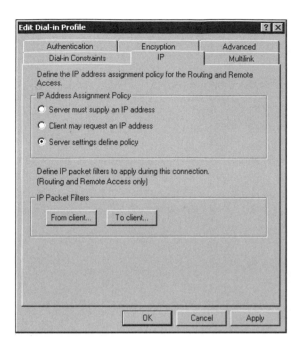

Figure 6-15   IP page for a profile

Authentication Properties   The Authentication page lets you specify the authentication methods used for the policy attached to the profile. Simply select any authentications that you want the profile to allow. Remember that any methods you select must also be enabled at the server.

Encryption Properties   The Encryption page, shown in Figure 6-16, lets you enable certain types of encryption for use on the connection. For some reason, though, Microsoft labeled these encryption methods as No Encryption, Basic, Strong, and Strongest instead of indicating the actual encryption algorithms used. Perhaps Microsoft wanted the ability to include any last minute changes without redoing the interface.

The following list defines the actual algorithms used:

- *No Encryption*: users can connect using no encryption at all. When this option is not checked, all connections must be encrypted or users are not allowed to connect. Obviously, leaving this option enabled is important unless you are sure you want to reject connections that use no encryption.

- *Basic*: allows connections using 40-bit connections, including forms of DES for IPSec or Microsoft Point-to-Point Encryption (MPPE) for PPTP.

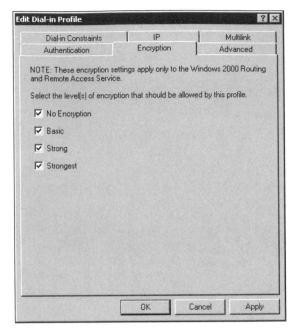

Figure 6-16   Encryption page for a profile

- *Strong*: allows connections using 56-bit encryption, also including forms of DES for IPSec or Microsoft Point-to-Point Encryption (MPPE) for PPTP.

- *Strongest*: allows connections using 128-bit encryption, including triple DES for IPSec and the 128-bit version of MMPE for PPTP.

At the end of the chapter, Hands-on Project 6-5 walks you through the step-by-step process of enabling encryption protocols.

Advanced Properties   You use the Advanced page mainly to configure the RRAS server to interact with a RADIUS server. The page lets you add specific attributes (some defined in the RADIUS standard and some for particular vendors) to incorporate into the profile.

 For the exam, it's not necessary that you know much detail on the attributes available through the Advanced page of the profile properties. It is enough to know the Advanced page is where you add additional attributes.

CONFIGURING A VIRTUAL PRIVATE NETWORKING CONNECTION

Virtual Private Networking (VPN) offers a way to create a logical connection between two computers over an existing IP routing infrastructure. This means that two computers connected by a public network like the Internet can create an additional private connection between them that runs TCP/IP or any other supported protocol and also supports authentication and encryption.

VPNs are typically used in one of two contexts:

- To connect a client to a VPN server. A common scenario is a remote user that first connects to the Internet via a local ISP and then establishes an additional, virtual connection over the Internet to a VPN server on the company network.

- To connect two VPN servers. A common scenario is a company with two locations (and therefore two LANs) that each have Internet access and an RRAS server configured for use with VPN. You can configure these servers to route messages between one another over the Internet using VPN.

In both of these contexts, the main reason you might use VPN instead of traditional dial-up access is simply cost. If you have remote users in a separate calling area from the main network or two networks separated by distance, connecting to the Internet locally instead of through long-distance calls means pretty good savings. Other features also make VPN attractive: it is often easier to configure and more secure than dial-up solutions.

VPN Components

Several components make up a complete VPN solution. These include:

- A VPN Server
- A VPN Client
- A connection between the client and server (VPN connection)
- VPN protocols

VPN Server

For the purposes of our discussion, a VPN server is a Windows 2000 server running the Routing and Remote Access Service configured to support VPN connections. In addition, the server typically has one connection to the Internet and a separate connection to the local network. When you enable RRAS on a server, it is automatically configured to support VPN ports. All you have to do is configure them. You can also specify a server to become a VPN server during the process of enabling RRAS.

VPN Client

A VPN client is any computer that can initiate a VPN connection to a VPN server. This client may be a remote user connecting to a main network or a router connecting to another router. Most operating systems have some sort of VPN client available, even if the operating systems themselves do not come with built-in support. Windows 98, Windows ME, Windows NT 4.0, and Windows 2000 all include built-in support for use as a VPN client.

VPN Connection

The routing infrastructure for a VPN connection must be some form of IP network, whether this network is the Internet or a private IP network. Often referred to as the **transit internetwork**, this network serves as the basis for the VPN connection. Once the client and server are both connected to the transit internetwork, the client can use TCP/IP or other networking protocols that it shares with the server to establish the VPN connection. For example, if the main company network uses IPX as its primary network protocol, the client probably wants to establish a VPN connection using IPX.

This capability of VPNs to use one networking protocol on top of another is often called tunneling; the virtual network tunnels through the actual network. Using a tunneling protocol supports the ability to tunnel; both sides of the connection use the protocol to create, monitor, and maintain the virtual network. Windows 2000 supports two tunneling protocols: Point-to-Point Tunneling Protocol (PPTP) and Layer 2 Tunneling Protocol (L2TP).

Point-to-Point Tunneling Protocol (PPTP) An extension of the PPP remote access protocol, **Point-to-Point Tunneling Protocol** uses a TCP connection for tunnel maintenance and allows IP, IPX, or NetBEUI traffic to be encrypted and then encapsulated within an IP header that can be sent across the IP internetwork.

Layer 2 Tunneling Protocol (L2TP) **Layer 2 Tunneling Protocol** combines PPTP and another protocol called Layer 2 Forwarding. Although the L2TP specifications support transit internetworks using IP, X.25, Frame Relay, or ATM, Windows 2000 only supports L2TP over IP. One distinct advantage that L2TP has over PPTP is that L2TP supports both authentication and encryption for a connection, while PPTP supports only encryption. In addition, L2TP is always used with IPSec, a more secure encryption mode than that used by PPTP, Microsoft Point-to-Point Encryption (MPPE).

Installing and Configuring a VPN Server

To act as a VPN server, a computer must have a permanent and dedicated link to the Internet or to whatever IP network you create the VPN on. Otherwise, the client cannot initiate a connection whenever it needs one. If you already installed RRAS on a server, then that server is already configured to use VPN; you may just not know about it. If you have not yet installed RRAS, you can enable it on your server and specify that it be used as a VPN server. This section discusses both methods.

Installing RRAS as a VPN Server

If you do not yet have RRAS enabled on your server, you need to enable it, activate it, and configure it for use with VPN. This procedure is relatively simple and, for the most part, the same as the procedure for enabling RRAS as an RRAS server. This chapter discussed this procedure in detail earlier, and there's really not much need to go over it again. The one difference is that when you come to the Common Configurations page of the wizard (refer to Figure 6-2 for a refresher), you should select the Virtual Private Network (VPN) Server option instead of the RRAS Server option. Once you complete the wizard's steps, your new VPN server is ready to accept connections.

Using VPN on an Existing RRAS Server

If you already enabled RRAS on your server and chose something besides the VPN option on the Common Configurations page, you can configure it as a VPN server without having to reinstall the service. All you have to do is open the property pages through the tabs for the server in the RRAS snap-in and make sure that the Remote Access Server option on the General page is enabled. Once you do this, your server can accept VPN connections.

Configuring VPN Ports

Just like enabling VPN on an RRAS server, configuring VPN is a pretty simple process. If you enabled VPN on the server using one of the two methods just discussed, then you have a pretty functional VPN server right off the bat. You can customize a few settings, however.

VPN is primarily managed through the Ports container in the RRAS snap-in. (It's under the server in the left pane.) When you select this container, shown in Figure 6-17, you see a number of objects in the right pane named WAN Miniport. Each represents a virtual port; each port supports either PPTP or L2TP. RRAS is configured by default to accept up to five connections of each type, and these default connections are numbered 0 through 4. Thus, the complete name of a port might be *WAN Miniport (L2TP)(VPN3-1)*.

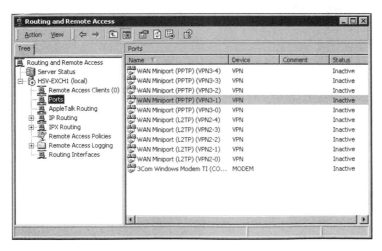

Figure 6-17   Ports container

Columns to the right of the device name list the type of port (in this case VPN) and the status of the port (active or inactive). You can also see a detailed status page for a port by right-clicking the port and choosing Status from the shortcut menu.

To configure settings for the ports on your system, right-click the Ports container itself and choose Properties from the shortcut menu. This opens the Ports Properties dialog box shown in Figure 6-18.

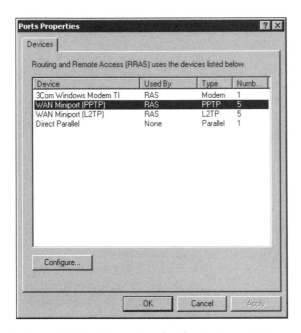

Figure 6-18   Properties for the Ports container

Notice that the dialog box lists both port types (PPTP and L2TP) and indicates the number of ports of each kind. To configure the properties for a port type, select it from the list and click the Configure button. This opens the Configure Device dialog box shown in Figure 6-19. Using this dialog box, you can specify whether the port type may accept incoming connections. Disabling this option essentially turns off the ports of that type. You can also specify whether the port type can be used for demand-dial connections. You need to disable this if you do not want your server to be able to connect to other servers using the port type. You can use the Phone Number field to enter the IP address of the public interface VPN clients use to connect. This would be necessary, for instance, if you had policies in place that granted or denied access based on the number dialed by the client. Finally, you can use this dialog to indicate the number of ports you want available for the port type. By default, you get five of each type, but you can set the number of ports to any number from 0 through 1000.

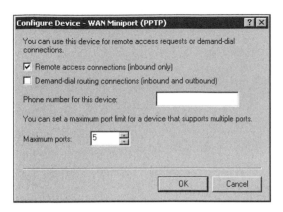

Figure 6-19   Configuring a device from the Ports property pages

Configuring a VPN Demand-dial Interface

A demand-dial interface enables your server to connect to another router or VPN server whenever it needs in order to route information. Creating a demand-dial interface is fairly straightforward, but you need to know a few things before you get started:

- The name and IP address of the router to which you will connect
- The tunneling protocol (PPTP or L2TP) supported by the other router
- A username and password so that the server can connect to the other router

You can practice setting up a demand-dial interface in Hands-on Project 6-7 at the end of the chapter.

CONFIGURING RAS FOR DHCP INTEGRATION

Dynamic Host Configuration Protocol (DHCP) automatically assigns IP addresses and other TCP/IP configuration parameters to clients on a network. This eliminates the administrative hassle of manually configuring every client with an IP address, a subnet mask, a default gateway, DNS and WINS information, and more—a time-consuming and often error-producing process. DHCP is designed to allow clients to broadcast requests for information received by DHCP servers on the same IP network. If clients and servers are on different IP networks, one device on the clients' network must act as a **DHCP Relay Agent** that receives client requests and forwards them to an appropriate DHCP server on another network. This means that a client must be on the same network with either a DHCP Server or a DHCP Relay Agent in order to use DHCP.

When deploying remote access, you must make some decisions about how to handle IP addressing for remote clients. Put simply, you have three choices:

- You can configure your clients with static IP addresses by going to the actual computer. This is usually only a good choice when you are configuring a relatively small number of clients.

- You can configure your RRAS Server as a DHCP Server. If your network is fairly small or if it is easy to deploy an additional DHCP Server, this choice is nice because it lets the RRAS Server assign IP addresses from its own address pool. For more information on configuring a Windows 2000 Server as a DHCP Server, see Chapter 3.

- You can configure your RRAS Server as a DHCP Relay Agent. This is a good option if your RRAS Server is on a separate network from your DHCP Server and your existing DHCP infrastructure makes it hard to simply configure the RRAS Server as a DHCP Server. This section focuses on this last option.

Installing the DHCP Relay Agent

The process of installing a DHCP Relay Agent on your RRAS server is done within the RRAS snap-in. You install it as a new protocol by right-clicking the IP Routing container on the appropriate RRAS server and selecting the New Routing Protocol from the shortcut menu. Hands-on Project 6-8 at the end of the chapter details this process.

Before you can install the DHCP Relay Agent, however, you need to be aware of two things:

- You cannot install a DHCP Relay Agent on a computer that already acts as a DHCP Server.

- You cannot install a DHCP Relay Agent on a computer that runs the Network Address Translation (NAT) protocol.

If you meet these requirements, however, you can install and begin configuring the DHCP Relay Agent.

Configuring the DHCP Relay Agent

Once you install the DHCP Relay Agent, you configure it from two different places. The first is the property pages of the DHCP Relay Agent itself. The second is on the actual interface to which the agent is attached.

Configuring DHCP Relay Agent Properties

Right-click DHCP Relay Agent inside the IP Routing container, and select Properties from the shortcut menu to open the General page for the agent, shown in Figure 6-20. You can configure only one setting for the agent, and that is to what specific DHCP servers the agent points. Just enter an appropriate IP address in the Server address field, and click Add. When you configure all of the DHCP Servers, click OK to finish.

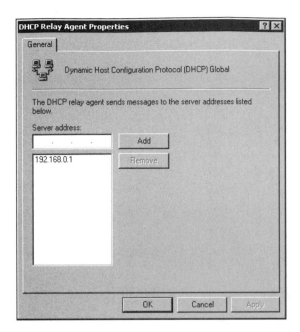

Figure 6-20   Property page for the DHCP Relay Agent

Configuring a Specific Interface

Once you configure the list of DHCP servers to which the agent can forward requests, you must attach the agent to the specific network interfaces that the agent will use. To attach an interface, right-click the DHCP Relay Agent object and select New Interface from the shortcut menu. A dialog box opens that lists all of the interfaces configured on the server. Choose the interface you want, and click OK to make the attachment.

Once you make the attachment, a property page for the interface, shown in Figure 6-21, opens automatically. You can also open these properties later by right-clicking the object for the interface (stored in the Routing Interfaces container for a server) and choosing Properties from the shortcut menu. Make sure the Relay DHCP packets option is enabled if you want the interface used for forwarding DHCP requests. The hop-count number controls the number of additional routers that a request is allowed to pass through, and the Boot threshold number controls how long the interface waits before forwarding any requests it receives.

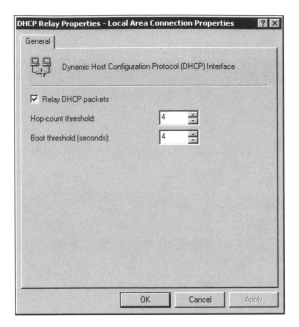

Figure 6-21   General property page for a new interface

MANAGING, MONITORING, AND TROUBLESHOOTING RAS

You manage and monitor an RRAS Server using several tools. You can monitor general server and port activity using the RRAS snap-in. You can also use the snap-in to configure logging for the RRAS Server. **Net Shell (netsh)** is a command-line tool used to configure and monitor Windows 2000 networking components, including RRAS. Finally, **Network Monitor** is a powerful application provided with Windows 2000 Server that allows you to capture and examine network packets going in and out of a server for troubleshooting purposes.

Monitoring Server Activity

Just above the list of servers in the RRAS snap-in is an object named Server Status. When you select this item, the details of all servers you are configured to administer show in the right pane. For each server, you receive information on the status of the server (started or stopped), the kind of server, the number of ports configured on it, the number of ports in use, and how long the server has been up. This window provides a snapshot of overall server activity.

Monitoring Ports

In addition to monitoring the status of servers, you can also view the status of each port on a server. To view the status of a port, right-click the port (you'll find it in the Ports container on a server) and select Properties from the shortcut menu. The dialog box that opens shows the line speed of the port, the amount of data transmitted and received over the port, and the network address for each protocol configured for use on the port. This tool provides a good way to determine whether or not a port is active and how much it is used.

Logging

If you recall, one of the property pages for an RRAS server is named Event Logging. Figure 6-22 shows this page on which you configure the level at which logging occurs for the RRAS server.

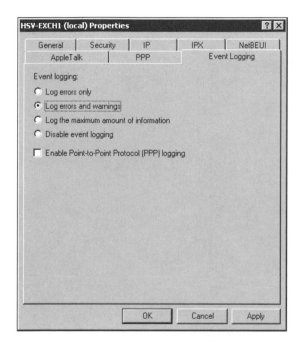

Figure 6-22   Event Logging property page for a server

The options on the Event Logging property page include:

- *Log errors only*: logs only the errors that occur on the RRAS server.

- *Log errors and warnings*: logs errors and warning messages. This is the default choice and usually also the best choice because logging errors and warnings give you good information about problems after they happen and often give fair warning of problems before they happen.

- *Log the maximum amount of information*: logs basically everything that happens on the server. This includes errors, warnings, and even information messages for successful events. This option causes the RRAS service to log a huge amount of messages and is usually only a good choice when you're troubleshooting a particular problem. Turn it on while troubleshooting, and be sure to turn it off when you finish.

- *Disable event logging*: is pretty self-explanatory.
- *Enable Point-to-Point Protocol (PPP) logging*: logs all messages regarding PPP connections to the server. This option is also useful for troubleshooting but can fill an event log pretty quickly if left on for an extended period.

Each RRAS server also has a container under it in the RRAS snap-in named Remote Access Logging. Within this folder are objects representing the actual log files stored for the server. Right-click any log file and choose Properties from the shortcut menu to further configure logging for that server. Figure 6-23 shows the Settings page with these properties. On this page, you can enable or disable the logging of accounting and authentication requests, as well as periodic status for the server.

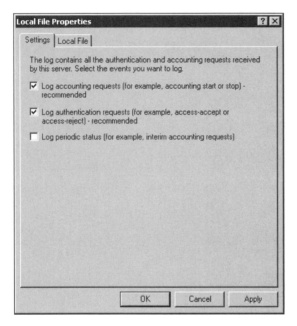

Figure 6-23   Settings property page for a log file

The Local File tab of the Local File property pages, shown in Figure 6-24, controls the physical aspects of how the file is written to disk. You can change the format of the log between the commonly used Internet Authentication Service (IAS) Format and a database compatible format, which makes it easy to import the log file into a database for processing. You can also change the period at which new log files are created and the directory for storing the file.

Using the Net Shell Tool

The Net Shell (usually called netsh) tool is a command-line and scripting tool that lets you configure and monitor Windows 2000 networking components. It is automatically installed with Windows 2000 in the \system32 subfolder of the Windows folder.

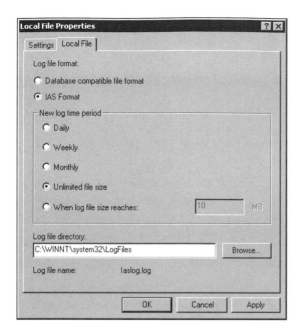

Figure 6-24   Local File property page for a log file

When you run netsh, you enter a shell that accepts special netsh commands. You can run this shell in one of two modes. In online mode, commands execute as soon as you type them into the shell. Offline mode saves commands as you type them and then executes them in batches when you use a special commit command.

With regard to RRAS, netsh provides the ability to access certain RRAS configuration settings, routing settings, and interface settings. You can learn more about the specifics of using the tool by typing netsh /? after the command prompt.

Using Network Monitor

Network Monitor is an application that comes with Windows 2000 and allows you to capture and view the actual packets of information being transmitted over a network interface. Once you capture a set period of traffic, you can filter your view of that traffic so that you can examine packets from, say, a specific protocol or time period. Using Network Monitor enables you to build a solid picture of network traffic patterns and to spot potential problems before they occur. You learn more about using Network Monitor in Chapter 7.

CHAPTER SUMMARY

- ❐ The RRAS Service runs on a Windows 2000 server and enables other servers or client computers that are not connected to the network via a permanent cable to establish temporary connections over phone lines, ISDN lines, or services such as X.25. Once a computer establishes a connection with the RRAS server, that computer can access the resources on the RRAS server and possibly access the other computers on the same network as the server, depending on the server's configuration.

❑ RRAS provides users with two types of remote access connections: dial-up networking connections, in which the user dials in to the RRAS Server using a phone or ISDN line, and Virtual Private Networking (VPN) connections, in which the user connects first to a transit internetwork such as the Internet and then establishes a virtual connection over that internetwork to the RRAS server.

❑ Two types of protocols govern the transmission of information between a client and an RRAS server. Remote access protocols control how a dial-up connection is actually established. (In the case of a VPN connection, tunneling protocols like PPTP and L2TP do the same thing.) The PPP protocol is the most common protocol in use today. Networking protocols determine how data is segmented and shaped for transmission over the connection once it is established. RRAS supports the IP, IPX, NetBEUI, and AppleTalk networking protocols.

❑ RRAS is installed by default along with Windows 2000 but not enabled. To enable it, you must use the Routing and Remote Access Server snap-in located on the Start menu. Once enabled, most RRAS configuration also happens within this snap-in. You use it to configure server properties, monitor servers and ports, create interfaces, and install new protocols. You also use it to create new remote access policies and profiles that determine what users may and may not access the system.

❑ The other primary tool for configuring RRAS is the Active Directory Users and Computers snap-in used for creating and managing user profiles. For each individual user, a Dial-in property page lets you configure whether the user can use remote access and several other settings that govern that access.

❑ Remote access security comes primarily in the form of authentication of a user's credentials. RRAS supports a number of authentication methods, including Password Authentication Protocol (PAP), Shiva Password Authentication Protocol (SPAP), Challenge Handshake Authentication Protocol (CHAP), Microsoft CHAP (MS-CHAP), and Extensible Authentication Protocol (EAP). In addition to authentication, RRAS also provides ways to control the connections made to the system and to control the access of individual users.

❑ Several tools are used in managing and monitoring an RRAS server. You can monitor general server and port activity using the RRAS snap-in. You can also use the snap-in to configure logging for the RRAS Server. Net Shell (netsh) is a command-line tool used to configure and monitor Windows 2000 networking components, including RRAS. Finally, Network Monitor is a powerful application provided with Windows 2000 Server that allows you to capture and examine network packets going in and out of a server for troubleshooting purposes.

KEY TERMS

Accounting provider — Server (typically a RADIUS server) that logs the activity and connection time for a remote user. This is often used to charge remote clients for online time, as in the case of an ISP providing Internet service.

Active Directory Users and Computers — Tool used to configure the objects in the Windows 2000 Active Directory. Among other things, you use this tool to configure the properties of user accounts. Dial-in properties for a user include whether the user may dial in to the RRAS server and whether a callback number should be used.

authentication — Process of verifying a user's credentials so that the user may log on to the system. Authentication is normally performed using a username and password. Authentication may be unencrypted (clear text) or use any of a number of **encryption** types.

Bandwidth Allocation Control Protocol (BACP) — *See* Bandwidth Allocation Protocol (BAP).

Bandwidth Allocation Protocol (BAP) — Together with the Bandwidth Allocation Control Protocol (BACP), allows a client to add and remove links dynamically during a multilink session to adjust for changes in bandwidth needs.

Challenge Handshake Authentication Protocol (CHAP) — Type of authentication in which the authentication agent sends the client program a key for encrypting the username and password.

demand-dial routing — Allows an RRAS server configured as a router to dial-up a remote router whenever it needs to send messages to that router.

DHCP Relay Agent — When they boot up, DHCP clients broadcast a message to their local IP subnet looking for a DHCP server to provide them with IP addressing information. These broadcast messages typically do not pass through routers. One way to avoid putting a full DHCP server on every subnet is to configure a computer as a DHCP Relay Agent. This computer intercepts the DHCP client requests and forwards them across the router to the DHCP server. RRAS has the capability to serve as a DHCP Relay Agent.

Dial-Up Networking — Name given to the process and interface that most versions of Microsoft Windows use to dial in to a remote server.

Dynamic Host Configuration Protocol (DHCP) — Protocol used to automatically assign IP addressing and other TCP/IP information to clients. DHCP is considered easier and more reliable than manual addressing.

Encryption — Process of translating information into an unreadable code that can only be translated back (decrypted) by using a secret key or password.

event logging — Most applications in Windows (and Windows itself) log events to a file. Events are bits of information and any errors generated by these applications. Once logged, you can view the events using the Event Viewer utility.

Extensible Authentication Protocol (EAP) — General protocol for PPP authentication that supports multiple authentication mechanisms. Instead of selecting a single authentication method for a connection, EAP can negotiate an authentication method at connect time.

Internet Group Management Protocol (IGMP) — Standard protocol for IP multicasting over the Internet. It is used to establish host memberships in particular multicast groups.

IP Security (IPSec) — Set of protocols that supports the secure exchange of data at the IP layer. In RRAS, IPSec is used in conjunction with L2TP in the formation of Virtual Private Networks.

IPX (Internetwork Packet eXchange) — Networking protocol developed by Novell for use primarily with their NetWare operating systems. Since NetWare is such a popular network operating system, most other operating systems, such as Microsoft Windows, provide an IPX-compatible networking protocol. In Windows 2000, this IPX-compatible protocol is named NWLink.

Layer-Two Tunneling Protocol (L2TP) — Extension of the PPP remote access protocol; one type of tunneling protocol used to form Virtual Private Networks.

Link control protocol (LCP) — LCP extensions include a number of enhancements to the LCP protocol used to establish a PPP link and control its settings. One of the primary enhancements included is the ability for the client and server to agree dynamically on protocols used on the connection.

Microsoft CHAP (MS-CHAP) — Modified version of CHAP that allows the use of Windows 2000 authentication information. There are two versions of MS-CHAP. Version 2 is the most secure, and all Microsoft operating systems support it. Other operating systems sometimes support version 1.

multicast routing — Targeted form of broadcasting that sends messages to a select group of users instead of all users on a subnet.

Multilink Protocol (MP) — Used to combine multiple physical links into a single logical link. For example, you could use MP to combine two 56-KB modem links into a 128-KB link.

NetBEUI — Enhanced version of the NetBIOS networking protocol primarily used on older versions of Microsoft and IBM operating systems.

Net Shell (netsh) — Command-line tool used to configure and monitor Windows 2000 networking components, including RRAS.

Network Address Translation (NAT) — Router standard that translates IP addresses on a private network into valid Internet IP addresses. NAT makes it possible for a single computer with Internet connectivity to share its Internet connection with other computers on the network through a single IP address.

Network Monitor — Tool that comes with Windows 2000 and allows you to capture and view data packets passing over the network.

networking protocols — Standard language used by two computers to communicate over a network. Networking protocols define how information is fragmented and shaped for passage over the network.

Password Authentication Protocol (PAP) — Authentication method that transmits a user's name and password over a network and compares them to a table of name-password pairs.

Point-to-Point Protocol (PPP) — Remote-access protocol used to establish a connection between two remote computers. RRAS supports PPP for dialing both in and out.

remote access — Broadly defines the ability of one computer to connect to another computer over a dial-up or other WAN connection and to access resources remotely.

remote access policy — Used to configure conditions under which users may connect using a specific remote access connection. You can include restrictions based on criteria such as time of day, type of connection, authentication, and even length of connection.

remote access profile — Associated with policies and containing settings that determine what happens during call set up and completion.

remote access protocols — Define the way in which one computer connects to another computer over a WAN link. PPP and SLIP are the two main remote access protocols in use today, though the newer and stronger PPP is much more common.

Remote Authentication Dial-In User Support (RADIUS) — Authentication and accounting system used by many ISPs to verify user credentials and log user activity while the user is connected to a remote system.

remote control — Process in which a client computer connects to a remote server and actually takes control over that server in a separate window on the client computer. Activities within this window seem to occur as if the user is actually sitting at the server computer. All applications run on the server. RRAS does not support remote control, only remote access.

router — Device used to connect different IP subnets and to route data between them.

Routing and Remote Access Service (RRAS) — Windows 2000 service that provides remote access and routing functionality to remote clients.

Serial Line Interface Protocol (SLIP) — Older protocol developed in UNIX and still in wide use today. Windows 2000 RRAS supports SLIP in dial-out configurations, but you cannot use a SLIP client to dial in to an RRAS server.

Shiva Password Authentication Protocol (SPAP) — Included mainly for compatibility with remote access hardware devices manufactured by Shiva, a private company now owned by Intel. SPAP isn't really used much on most networks.

transit internetwork — Basic IP infrastructure over which a Virtual Private Network is created. Typically, the transit internetwork is the Internet itself, though other IP networks may be the transit internetwork.

Transmission Control Protocol/Internet Protocol (TCP/IP) — Suite of networking protocols designed to transfer data between computers on the Internet. TCP/IP is becoming the most popular networking protocol used on private networks, as well.

user profile — Information associated with a user account. Profiles of users who are members of a Windows 2000 domain are stored in the Active Directory, and profiles of users who are not members of a domain are stored on the local computer.

Virtual Private Networking (VPN) — Secure, logical network constructed directly between a VPN client and a VPN server on top of a physical transit internetwork such as the Internet.

6

REVIEW QUESTIONS

1. Which of the following must be true in order to use remote access policies?

    a. The RRAS server must not be a domain controller.

    b. The RRAS server must be configured as a DHCP Server or DHCP Relay Agent.

    c. Active Directory must be running in native mode.

    d. RRAS must be running on Windows 2000 Advanced Server or Datacenter Server.

2. Which of the following are valid tunneling protocols for Virtual Private Networks?

    a. PPP

    b. PPTP

    c. L2TP

    d. IPSec

3. You need to configure callbacks for a group of remote users. Though you could do this by enabling callbacks for every individual user's profile, what is a better solution?

    a. Create a Remote Access Policy for the group.

    b. Create a remote access profile for the group.

    c. Enable callbacks for all users in the RRAS snap-in.

    d. Use DHCP to assign callback information.

4. The _____ protocol allows the sharing of a single Internet connection with other computers on a LAN.

5. The Windows 2000 implementation of L2TP supports access over IP, X.25, and ATM. True or false?

6. Which of the following remote access protocols can Windows 2000 use to accept incoming calls?

    a. PPP

    b. PPTP

    c. SLIP

    d. IP

7. An RRAS server can only support one networking protocol on a system. True or false?

8. You want your clients to be assigned IP addressing information automatically. Your network uses a DHCP system, but you configured your RRAS Server on a different IP network than the rest of your network. Which of the following solutions lets the existing DHCP servers assign addresses to the remote clients?

    a. Install a new demand-dial interface on the RRAS server.

    b. Configure the RRAS server as a DHCP server, and set it to forward requests.

    c. Install the DHCP Relay Agent protocol on the RRAS server.

    d. Install a WINS proxy agent on the RRAS server.

9. Which of the following statements is true?

   a. Settings made on a user's profile override settings made in a Remote Access Policy applied to that user.

   b. Settings made in a Remote Access Policy applied to a user override settings made on that user's profile.

   c. The Remote Access Profile determines conflicting settings in a user's profile and any remote access policy applied to that user.

   d. You can use a server's properties in the RRAS snap-in to specify whether user profiles override remote access policies or vice versa.

10. Conventional dial-up connections are much easier to configure and manage than VPN connections. True or false?

11. You can use the _____ tool to capture and view packets of information transferred over the network.

12. In the RRAS snap-in, what is the allowed number of incoming VPN connections configured through?

   a. Ports container

   b. Connections container

   c. Interfaces container

   d. VPN container

13. You want to ensure that all user authentication information passed between remote clients and an RRAS server is encrypted. Which of the following authentication methods should you disable?

   a. PAP

   b. CHAP

   c. SPAP

   d. EAP MD5-CHAP

14. What type of encryption does PPTP use?

   a. IPSec

   b. PAP

   c. MMPE

   d. DES

15. _____ is a targeted form of network broadcasting that sends information to a select group of users instead of all users connected to a network.

6

16. Which of the following is true of the DHCP Relay Agent protocol? (Choose all that apply.)

    a. It is used only on RRAS servers that use static addressing for clients.

    b. All RRAS servers require it.

    c. Servers running the DHCP service cannot use it.

    d. Servers running NAT cannot use it.

17. You want to assign a user the same IP address every time the user dials in to the RRAS server. How can you do this?

    a. Set up the DHCP Relay Agent on the server, and configure a reserved address for the user.

    b. Enter the IP address using the static IP option on the user's property pages in Active Directory Users and Computers.

    c. Configure a reserved address for the user with the property pages of the IP Routing container in the RRAS snap-in.

    d. You cannot do this.

18. You can create a remote access profile without association to a Remote Access Policy. True or false?

19. Your RRAS server currently lets log files grow to unlimited size. You want to configure it so that it creates new log files every week. Where can you do this?

    a. The Settings tab of the server's property pages

    b. The Event Logging tab of the server's property pages

    c. The Local File tab of the log file's property pages

    d. The IP tab of the log file's property pages

20. Stopping the RAS service causes the service to erase its settings. True or false?

HANDS-ON PROJECTS

All Hands-on Projects in this chapter require at least one server computer set-up as described in the lab setup section in the front of this book. To complete these exercises, you must have completed the projects in Chapters 2 and 3 on installing networking protocols and configuring DHCP.

Project 6-1

To install Routing and Remote Access Service:

1. Click **Start**, point to **Programs**, point to **Administrative Tools**, and then select **Routing and Remote Access**.

2. Right-click the computer name and select **Configure and Enable Routing and Remote Access** from the context menu.

3. On the Welcome screen for the Routing and Remote Access Server Setup Wizard, click **Next**.

4. On the Common Configurations screen, select the **Remote Access Server** option and then click **Next**.

5. On the Remote Client Protocols screen, under Protocols, make sure that TCP/IP is listed.

6. Verify that the **Yes, all the required protocols are on this list** option is selected, and click **Next**.

7. On the IP Address Assignment screen, make sure that the **From a specified range of addresses** option is selected, and then click **Next**.

8. In the Address Range Assignment window, click **New**.

9. In the Starting Address field, type **192.168.0.200**, and in the End Of IP Address field, type **192.168.0.225**.

10. Under Number of Addresses, verify that **26** is the number, click **OK** to close the Edit Address Range window, and then click **Next**.

11. On the Managing Multiple Remote Access Servers screen, verify that the **No, I don't want to set this server up to use RADIUS now** option is selected and then click **Next**.

12. Click **Finish**.

13. Click **OK** to respond to any warning messages that appear.

Project 6-2

To configure the multilink protocol for incoming connections:

1. Click **Start**, point to **Programs**, point to **Administrative Tools**, and then select **Routing and Remote Access**.

2. Right-click the server for which you want to configure multilink, and select the **Properties** command from the shortcut menu.

3. Click the **PPP** tab.

4. Remove the check mark next to the **Multilink connections** option.

5. Click **OK** to close the property pages.

Project 6-3

To configure the IP protocol to be the only protocol clients can use for remote access:

1. Click **Start**, point to **Programs**, point to **Administrative Tools**, and then select **Routing and Remote Access**.

2. Right-click the server you want to configure, and select **Properties** from the shortcut menu.

3. Click the **IP** tab.

4. Make sure that the **Enable IP Routing** and **Allow IP-based remote access and demand-dial connections** options are selected.

5. Click the **IPX** tab, if there is one.

6. Disable the **Allow IPX-based remote access and demand-dial connections** option.

7. Click the **NetBEUI** tab, if there is one.

8. Disable the **Allow NetBEUI-based remote access clients to access** option.

9. Click the **AppleTalk** tab, if there is one.

10. Disable the **Enable AppleTalk remote access** option.

11. Click **OK** to close the server's property pages.

Project 6-4

To create a new remote access policy:

1. Click **Start**, point to **Programs**, point to **Administrative Tools**, and then select **Routing and Remote Access**.

2. Right-click **Remote Access Policies** and select **New Remote Access Policy**.

3. Type **All users time restrictions** in the Policy friendly name field, and then click **Next**.

4. Click **Add** to add a condition.

5. Select **Day-and-Time Restrictions** and then click **Add**.

6. On the Time of day constraints dialog box that opens, select the times and days you want to allow or deny access to and then click OK.

7. Click **Add** to add another condition.

8. Select the **Windows Groups entry** and click **Add**.

9. On the Windows Groups dialog box that opens, click **Add**.

10. Select **Domain Users** and then click **Add**.

11. Click **OK** twice to close the window and click the **Groups** dialog box, then click **Next**.

12. Select the **Grant Remote Access** permission, and click **Next**.

13. Click **Finish**.

Project 6-5

To configure encryption protocols for a remote access server:

1. Click **Start**, point to **Programs**, point to **Administrative Tools**, and then select **Routing and Remote Access**.

2. In the left-hand pane, expand the server you want to configure and select the **Remote Access Policies** container.

3. Right-click the **Allow access if dial-in permission is enabled** policy, and choose **Properties** from the shortcut menu.

4. Click the **Edit Profile** button.

5. Click the **Encryption** tab.

6. Remove the check mark next to the **No Encryption** option.

7. Make sure that the other encryption policies are all enabled.

8. Click **OK** to exit the dialog box, and click **OK** again to return to the RRAS snap-in main window.

Project 6-6

6

To configure a Windows 2000 Professional client to access a remote server:

1. Click **Start**, point to **Settings**, and then select **Network and Dial-Up Connections**.

2. Double-click the **Make New Connection** icon.

3. On the Welcome page of the Network Connection Wizard, click **Next**.

4. On the Network Connection Type page, select **Dial-up to private network** and click **Next**.

5. On the next page, type the **phone number** to which you want to connect and if you want to use any established dialing rules, select that option and click **Next**. Then you need to decide whether to share this connection with other users who can log on to the computer. The default is to share the connection.

6. Click **Next**.

7. Type **a name** for the new dial-up connection, and click **Finish** to exit the wizard. The Connect dialog for the new connection opens automatically when you exit the wizard.

8. Enter **your username** and **password**, and then click **Dial** to connect to the remote network. Once connected, you should be prompted to log on to the remote network using your normal network credentials.

Project 6-7

To create a new VPN demand-dial interface:

1. Click **Start**, point to **Programs**, point to **Administrative Tools**, and then select **Routing and Remote Access**.

2. Right-click **Routing Interfaces**, select **New Demand-Dial Interface** from the shortcut menu, and click **Next**.

3. In the Interface Name field, type **a name** for the remote router to which you will connect and click **Next**.

4. On the VPN Type screen, select the **Automatic selection** option and then click **Next**.

5. Enter the **IP address** of the router to which you will connect, and then click **Next**.

6. On the Protocols and Security screen, select the **Route IP Packet On This Interface** option and then click **Next**.

7. Enter the **local router name** in the Dial-Out Credentials dialog box.

   This is the username the router will use when connecting to the remote router. This username will match the name of the demand-dial interface on the remote router.

8. Leave the Domain and Password fields blank, and click **Next**.

9. Click **Finish**.

Project 6-8

To configure a DHCP relay agent to work over Routing and Remote Access:

1. Click **Start**, point to **Programs**, point to **Administrative Tools**, and then select **Routing and Remote Access**.

2. Expand the container for the server on which you want to install the DHCP Relay Agent.

3. Right-click the **General** container under IP routing, and select the **New Routing Protocol** option from the shortcut menu.

4. Choose **DHCP Relay Agent** and then click **OK**.

5. In the IP Routing container, select the **DHCP Relay Agent** object and right-click **Properties** on the shortcut menu.

6. Use the dialog box that opens to configure the IP addresses of DHCP servers.

7. Click **OK** to close the DHCP Relay Agent Properties dialog box.

CASE PROJECTS

Case 1

Figure 6-25 shows the configuration of your company network. Your RRAS server sits on a separate IP subnet outside the perimeter of the rest of the company network. Until now, you had your RRAS server configured to assign IP addresses to remote clients from a pool of addresses you allocated to the server. Recently, many more users are accessing the network remotely and managing IP addresses is becoming harder. Given the layout of the network presented in Figure 6-25, what are your options?

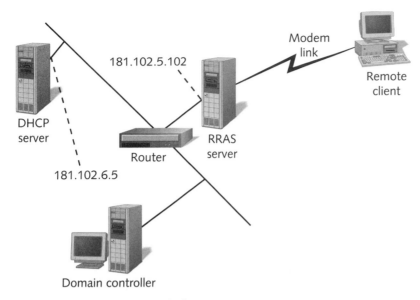

Figure 6-25   Case 1 network diagram

6

Case 2

The number of remote users in your company continues to grow and the number of users who connect to the company while traveling is also growing quite large. Quite frankly, your company does not want to pay the long-distance fees involved in allowing employees to connect from all over the country for extended periods of time. You mentioned to your manager that implementing a VPN solution using RRAS might be just the thing and she wants to know all the details. Sketch a diagram (using the diagram in Figure 6-25 as your basis, if you like) that shows the following details:

- The RRAS connection to the Internet
- The client at the other end of the Internet connection
- All protocols to be used, including the IP protocol for the Internet, the remote access protocol used by the client, the tunneling protocol used for the VPN connection, and the encryption protocol used by the chosen tunneling protocol
- How the VPN works and why it will be secure

Case 3

You want to create a series of policies that accept or reject users' dial-in attempts based on the following criteria:

- You use VPN as your only remote access method and want to accept only L2TP connections.
- Between 6:00 a.m. and 5:00 p.m., you want all users who have dial-in permissions to be able to dial in.

- Between 5:00 p.m. and 1:00 a.m., you want all users who are members of the Domain Admins, Executives, Engineers, and Marketing security groups to be able to dial in, but no one else.

- Between 1:00 a.m. and 6:00 a.m., you want only members of the Domain Admins group to be able to dial in.

- Using the conditions listed in Table 6-1 earlier in this chapter, outline the policies you need to create to meet these criteria and their proper order.

7

IP ROUTING IN WINDOWS 2000

After reading this chapter and completing the exercises, you will be able to:

♦ Describe the difference between interior and exterior routing protocols

♦ Describe the routing protocols supported by Windows 2000, including RIP and OSPF

♦ Configure static routing

♦ Configure demand-dial routing

♦ Manage and monitor border routing

♦ Manage and monitor interior routing

♦ Manage and monitor RIP and OSPF

♦ Manage, monitor, and troubleshoot network traffic

Internet Protocol (IP) routing is the method that the IP protocol uses to transfer data between computers on a network. In Windows 2000, the **Routing and Remote Access Service (RRAS)** supports IP routing. You learned about RRAS in Chapter 6, which mainly covered the remote access features it provides. This chapter looks at its routing features.

This chapter begins with an overview of IP routing. It examines different types of routing, routers, and routing protocols. It then covers the implementation of routing in Windows 2000, including the configuration of both static and demand-dial routing. Finally, the chapter examines techniques for managing, monitoring, and troubleshooting the various aspects of network routing.

ROUTING OVERVIEW

At its simplest, routing is the process of moving information along a path from a source to a destination on a network. On an IP network, the source and destinations are called hosts and the information is fragmented into small pieces called packets that are transferred between these hosts. When multiple IP networks are connected together, devices called routers help move information between these interconnected networks.

Direct Routing

Direct routing occurs when both the source and destination host are on the same network segment. Consider a small IP subnet with only three hosts (A, B, and C), all wired directly together, as shown in Figure 7-1.

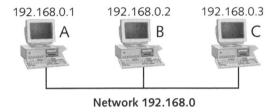

192.168.0.1   192.168.0.2   192.168.0.3

Network 192.168.0

Figure 7-1   Single subnet

Many examples in this chapter assume that you are familiar with IP addressing and subnetting, concepts Chapter 2 of this book covers.

In Figure 7-1, the network ID for the subnet is 192.168.0 and Hosts A, B, and C have assigned host IDs of 1, 2, and 3, respectively. Now, suppose that Host A needs to send some information to Host C.

IP on Host A compares its network ID with the network ID of Host C. Since the two network IDs match, IP knows that the hosts are on the same subnet and that it can route the information directly to Host C.

Remember that although IP communicates using IP addresses, network hardware actually uses **MAC addresses**—the physical addresses of network interfaces—to communicate. This means that IP must have a way of translating, or resolving, an IP address into a MAC address. This happens through a portion of IP known as ARP, or **Address Resolution Protocol**. **ARP** is a low-level protocol that resides within IP. It provides a way of resolving IP addresses to MAC addresses. When a TCP/IP-based application needs to send information from one host to another, it segments and encapsulates that information into packets and tags those packets with the IP address of the destination host. ARP is then consulted to match that IP address to an actual MAC address. When ARP determines the MAC address, it gives that information back to IP and IP sends the packet on its way

Indirect Routing

The procedure for direct routing works fine on a single network segment, but most large networks consist of smaller, connected networks and may also connect to the Internet. On these networks routing becomes a little more complex and is known as **indirect routing**.

Indirect routing takes place when the source and destination hosts are not on the same network segment and packets must pass through a router, a physical link between two or more networks. Routers are usually passive devices that do not pay attention to general network traffic. Packets destined for other networks must actually be sent directly to the router in order to be passed along, as Figure 7-2 shows.

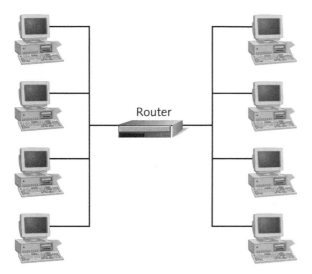

Figure 7-2 Sending packets across a router

You can actually think of a router as a computer with two or more network interface cards. Each card connects to a different network segment, and the computer can pass messages from one network to another.

Now, suppose that you take the single network segment just described and illustrated in Figure 7-1 and decide to connect another network to it, as shown in Figure 7-3.

The original network, shown on the left, has a network ID of 192.168.0. The second network, shown on the right, has a network ID of 192.168.1. The second network has three hosts, labeled L, M, and N. Hosts L, M, and N have host IDs of 1, 2, and 3, respectively.

A router labeled R1 joins these two networks. The router has two IP addresses, 192.168.0.25 and 192.168.1.25, because it has a separate interface on each network.

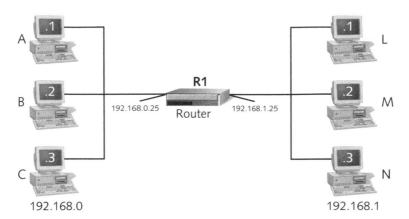

Figure 7-3   Two subnets connected by a router

Suppose now that Host A (192.168.0.1) needs to send a packet to Host N (192.68.1.3). The IP protocol on Host A examines the source and destination IP addresses and determines that the two hosts are on different network segments (because their network IDs do not match). IP now knows that this packet must be sent to a router.

IP determines the location of this router in one of two ways. IP first consults a locally maintained routing table. Figure 7-4 shows an example of this table, which is basically a list of networks that the system knows about and the IP addresses of routers that information must pass through to get to those networks. (The section entitled, "Static and Dynamic Routers," discusses routing tables in more detail.)

HSV-EXCH1 - IP Routing Table

Destination	Network mask	Gateway	Interface	Metric	Protocol
0.0.0.0	0.0.0.0	192.168.0.1	Local Area C...	1	Network ma...
127.0.0.0	255.0.0.0	127.0.0.1	Loopback	1	Local
127.0.0.1	255.255.255.255	127.0.0.1	Loopback	1	Local
172.16.204.0	255.255.255.0	172.16.204.1	Local Area C...	1	Local
172.16.204.1	255.255.255.255	127.0.0.1	Loopback	1	Local
172.16.255.255	255.255.255.255	172.16.204.1	Local Area C...	1	Local
192.168.0.0	255.255.255.0	192.168.0.200	Local Area C...	1	Local
192.168.0.200	255.255.255.255	127.0.0.1	Loopback	1	Local
192.168.5.0	255.255.255.0	192.168.0.200	Local Area C...	1	Static (non ...
192.168.8.0	255.255.255.0	192.168.0.200	Local Area C...	1	Static (non ...
224.0.0.0	240.0.0.0	192.168.0.200	Local Area C...	1	Local
224.0.0.0	240.0.0.0	172.16.204.1	Local Area C...	1	Local
255.255.255.255	255.255.255.255	192.168.0.200	Local Area C...	1	Local
255.255.255.255	255.255.255.255	172.16.204.1	Local Area C...	1	Local

Figure 7-4   Routing table, showing which gateway to use for each network address

If the network is not found in the static routing table, a default gateway is used. Defined on most TCP/IP hosts, the **default gateway** is simply a router where packets are sent if a destination network is not found in a routing table.

In this example, let's assume that Host A has its default gateway configured as 192.168.0.25, which is the network interface for Router R1. When IP determines that the packet destined for Host N needs to go to another network segment and it does not find the network in a routing table, it sends that packet to router R1.

Note ARP is still used in indirect routing but in a slightly different way. A packet destined for a remote network must be sent to a router. IP sends that packet using the router's IP address, but even the router's IP address must be resolved into a MAC address before the packet can be delivered. ARP resolves the router's IP address into a MAC address and the packet is sent. That router then determines whether to put the packet on another local subnet it connects to or to direct the packet to another router. Either way, its own IP must use ARP to establish the MAC address of the host to receive the packet.

In Figure 7-4, Router R1 directly connected to Network 192.168.1 and could forward the packet directly to Host N. It is possible, however, to create even more complicated networks where routers must send packets to other routers, as shown in Figure 7-5.

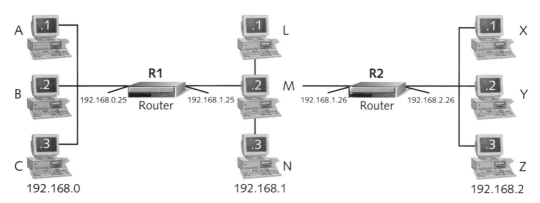

Figure 7-5   Three subnets connected by two routers

Figure 7-5 shows a third network added using Router R2. Suppose here that Host A (192.168.0.1) needs to send a packet to Host Z (192.168.2.3). As before, Host A determines that it must send the packet to another network segment and forwards the packet to Router R1 (its default gateway). This time, however, Router R1 does not directly connect to the destination network. Router R1 must forward the packet to another router, R2, whose address is again determined through a routing table or by using a default gateway. Router R2 directly connects to the destination network and can forward the packet straight to Host Z.

As you can see, routing can quickly become quite complex. The Internet itself is just a series of networks of varying complexity, each connected to one another using routers.

Static and Dynamic Routers

A router is a physical device used to connect a number of network segments together. Routers can be dedicated pieces of hardware whose sole purpose is being a router, or they can be computers that have more than one network adapter card, each connected to a different network segment. Computers configured this way are called **multihomed**. Most routers can have an interface on many different networks at the same time.

As mentioned in the previous section, when a router receives a packet from a sending host, it does one of two things. If the router is directly connected to the destination network, it can send the packet straight to the destination host. If the router is not directly connected to the destination network, it forwards that packet to another router, which then makes a similar decision.

Routers can do this because they maintain local routing tables that IP can consult for routing information. A **routing table** is basically a list of networks on the internetwork and the adjacent routers used to get to those networks. All routers have routing tables, but routers handle entries in these tables in a couple of ways. For the purposes of this discussion, routers are of two basic types: static and dynamic.

Static Routers

On a **static router**, you must enter routing tables manually. A static router only knows about networks that directly connect to it or networks that you tell it about. Consider the illustration in Figure 7-6.

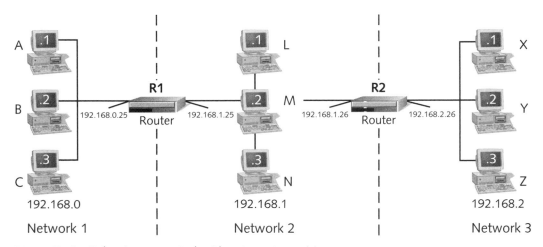

Figure 7-6   Subnets connected without routing tables

Here three small networks connect to one another using two static routers, R1 and R2. Router R1 only connects directly to Networks 192.168.0 and 192.168.1. Router R2 only connects directly to Networks 192.168.1 and 192.168.2. This means that, by default, Network 1 and Network 2 can communicate and Network 2 and Network 3 can communicate. However, Network 1 and Network 3 cannot.

In order to allow a static router to communicate with networks to which it is not directly attached, you can use one of two methods:

- Provide an entry in the routing table for every network on the internetwork.

- Configure each router with a default gateway (which will be the address of an adjacent router).

You must configure static routing tables manually and must include all known networks on the internetwork in order for the tables to work efficiently. Consider the configuration shown in Figure 7-7.

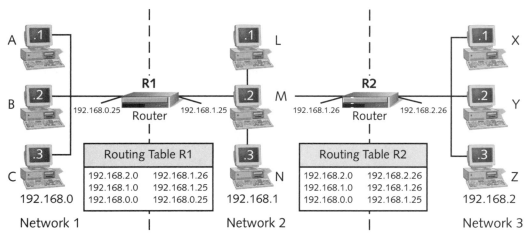

Figure 7-7 Subnets connected with routing tables

This example shows routing tables added to each of the routers. In the table for router R1, notice the first entry. The left column describes the network ID (192.168.2.0) for Network 3. The right column defines the IP address (192.168.1.26) to which router R1 forwards packets destined for that network. Through this one simple entry, Network 1 can now communicate with Network 3. The third entry in the table for router R2 allows Network 3 to communicate with Network 1.

All static routing table entries include the following information:

- *Network address*: network ID or network name of the network where packets might be sent

- *NetMask*: subnet mask for the corresponding network

- *Gateway address*: IP address where packets destined for the corresponding network should be forwarded

Dynamic Routers

As you can see, managing static routers on a complex network could require considerable time. Fortunately, larger networks use some form of **dynamic router**. Dynamic routers are simply routers having some automatic method of sharing their routing information with other routers on the network. If routing or network information changes, a router automatically updates its routing tables and forwards that information to other dynamic routers that it knows about.

When all routers on an internetwork have the correct routing information in their tables, the network has **converged**. When a link or router fails, all routers on the network must reconfigure themselves with the proper information. The time needed to do this is called the **convergence time** of a network.

Several protocols provide dynamic routing, the two most popular being Routing Information Protocol (RIP) and Open Shortest Path First (OSPF). The next section examines these and other types of routing protocols.

Routing Protocols

A routing protocol is a standard language that lets routers exchange routing information, freeing the administrator from the hassle of maintaining static routing tables. The following sections describe and provide examples of the two basic types of routing protocols: interior and exterior.

Before learning about interior and exterior protocols, though, you need to be familiar with another concept: the **autonomous system**. Loosely defined, an autonomous system is one with a set of networks and routers all under the same administration. For example, a corporate LAN that was segmented into many different subnets with routers is an autonomous system because it is administered separately from any other networks (such as the Internet) that it may connect to.

Interior Routing Protocols

A routing protocol used to connect two routers in the same autonomous system is called an interior routing protocol. Windows 2000 supports two interior routing protocols: **Routing Information Protocol (RIP)** and **Open Shortest Path First (OSPF)**.

Routing Information Protocol By far the most common interior routing protocol in use today is Routing Information Protocol (RIP). RIP is a distance vector routing program, meaning that it not only supplies information about the networks a router can reach, but information about the distances to these networks as well. This distance simply reflects the number of routers a packet must cross, or **hop**, in order to reach a particular network. This distance is referred to as a hop count, or sometimes as a metric. The maximum hop count allowed in RIP is 15. Any network with a hop count of 16 or greater is always considered unreachable. Routers use hop counts to determine the best route to use for a given packet at a given time.

The way RIP works is fairly simple. At a given interval (30 seconds is the default on a Windows NT router), a RIP-enabled router broadcasts (or multicasts, depending on the version of RIP) its routing table to the network. RIP-enabled routers receiving this broadcast add the routing information to their own tables, increasing the hop counts to each network by one in order to account for crossing the router that sent the broadcast. If the receiving router already has a route to any particular network, it compares routes and keeps only the one with the smallest hop count.

As of this writing, Windows 2000 supports both versions of RIP (RIPv1 and RIPv2). **RIPv1** is simple to use and well-supported, but requires a few considerations:

- Since each router maintains a list of all networks up to 15 hop counts away, routing table sizes can grow quite large on a complicated network. This means that routers need to be more powerful to handle the large table sizes.

- Every RIPv1-enabled router makes a MAC-level broadcast every 30 seconds. On internetworks with many routers, broadcast traffic volume can actually grow quite high.

- RIPv1-enabled routers give entries received from other routers a three-minute life span or time to live (TTL). If it does not receive a new broadcast from that other router within three minutes, the RIPv1-enabled router removes the entries from that router. When a router goes down, therefore, propagating accurate changes throughout the network can take some time.

- Because RIPv1 does not include the subnet mask along with its routing announcements, routers must try to determine the network ID using limited information. As a result, routers often incorrectly assume the default subnet mask.

RIPv2, the latest version of the protocol, addresses many of these shortcomings. While still limited to 15 hops, RIPv2 does provide a multicast option in addition to broadcasts for routing announcements and includes the subnet mask. In addition, RIPv2 now supports the authentication of incoming announcements from other routers.

Open Shortest Path First A link-state routing protocol, Open Shortest Path First (OSPF) enables routers to exchange routing information. It is called a link-state protocol because it actually creates a map (a routing table) of the network that calculates the best possible path to each network segment by maintaining information on the state of links (whether they are up or down).

To help keep this routing table from growing too large, OSPF divides the internetwork into collections of contiguous networks called **areas**, as shown in Figure 7-8. Each router only keeps a link state database for those areas connected to the router. Areas are connected to one another via a special type of area called a **backbone area**. Any router inside a backbone area is called a **backbone router**. Routers with interfaces on more than one area are called **area border routers**.

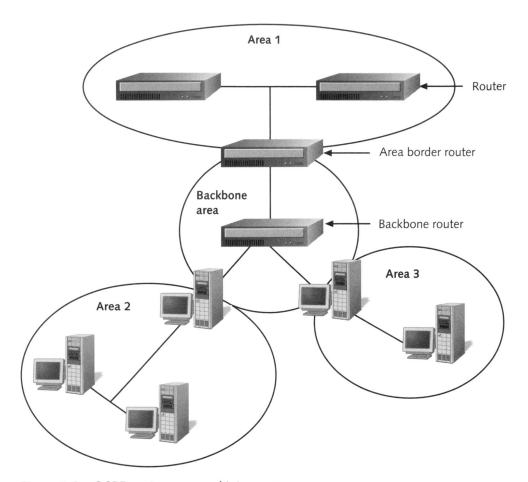

Figure 7-8   OSPF routers grouped into areas

One of OSPF's biggest advantages over either version of RIP is a lower convergence time, since it was designed specifically to maintain link-state tables. OSPF's primary disadvantage is that it is usually much more difficult to plan and configure than RIP.

Exterior Routing Protocols

Exterior routing protocols are used to exchange routing information between networks that are not autonomous (that is, do not share a common administration). The first exterior routing protocol developed was the **Exterior Gateway Protocol (EGP)**. Since then, a newer and more powerful exterior routing protocol has been developed named the **Border Gateway Protocol (BGP)**. Now in its fourth version, this protocol is often called BGP4. Windows 2000 RRAS does not support any external routing protocols, so this book does not provide any configuration information. It is important, however, to be aware that these protocols exist and their purpose.

Actually, you can use BGP as either an internal or exterior routing protocol, so you may often see it called internal BGP (IBGP) and external BGP (EBGP). Since Windows 2000 does not support exterior routing protocols, a full discussion of the BGP protocol is beyond the scope of this book.

INSTALLING AND CONFIGURING RRAS

Now that you understand the concepts behind routing, it's time to see how it actually works on a Windows 2000 system. The first step in configuring a Windows 2000 server as a router is to install the Routing and Remote Access Service (RRAS) on the server. Actually, as you may remember from Chapter 6, RRAS is automatically installed along with Windows 2000 Server, but left disabled. All you need to do is enable it.

This section provides an overview of the set-up process and the choices you make. Hands-on Project 7-1 at the end of this chapter walks you through the actual steps of setting up RRAS as a network router.

First, you must log on to the server with Administrator privileges and open the Routing and Remote Access utility from the Administrative Tools program group on the Start menu. Shown in Figure 7-9, this utility is actually a snap-in for the Microsoft Management Console used to control most of Windows 2000 management features.

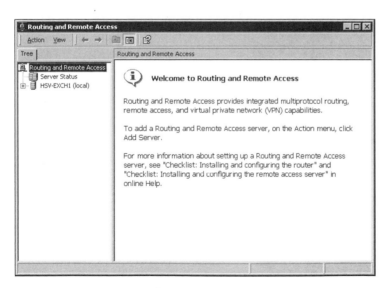

Figure 7-9   Routing and Remote Access snap-in

In the list in the left pane, find the name of the server and right-click it. From the shortcut menu that appears, choose the Configure and Enable Routing and Remote Access command to begin the Routing and Remote Access Server Setup Wizard. The wizard takes you through several configuration steps. The first, shown in Figure 7-10, asks you to select the type of configuration you want to install. Choose the Network Router option. For details on what some of the other options mean, see Chapter 6.

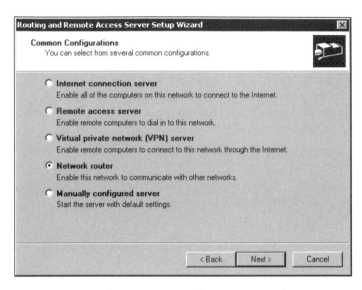

Figure 7-10   Selecting a type of router to configure

Next, the RRAS Setup Wizard asks you to verify that the protocols you wish to use on the server are already installed and configured. If not, you must configure them before taking the next steps with the wizard.

The next page that you see asks you whether you want to configure the server to use demand-dial connections or not. If you elect not to allow them, you see a summary page for the wizard where you can just click Finish. If you choose to allow demand-dial connections, you must complete one more step before you finish: deciding whether to use DHCP or to define a static pool of IP addresses for remote clients. You see, when you enable demand-dial routing, you are essentially configuring a remote access server. Even if you do not plan to allow remote users to dial in to the server, other routers must have the option of connecting to it as needed. If you have a DHCP server on the same subnet as the RRAS server, the DHCP option is usually the best option. You learn more about configuring demand-dial connections later in this chapter, and you can find information on integrating DHCP with RRAS in Chapter 6.

And that's all there is to it. When the summary screen of the wizard appears, it reminds you that you still need to do a few things to create a working router:

- You must add **demand-dial interfaces** that can dial a remote router whenever a connection needs to be made and supports demand-dial routing.
- You must install and configure any routing protocols (RIP or OSPF) if you want your new router to function as a dynamic router. If you do not, you can configure static routing instead. You do not need to install any routing protocols in order for your RRAS server to be a functional router.

- You must give each routable interface on the server (network adapter card or demand-dial) a network address for each protocol you allow to be used over the interface. (This chapter discusses IP only.)

Once you exit the wizard, your RRAS server is set up and ready to start routing. Figure 7-11 shows the basic Routing and Remote Access snap-in window.

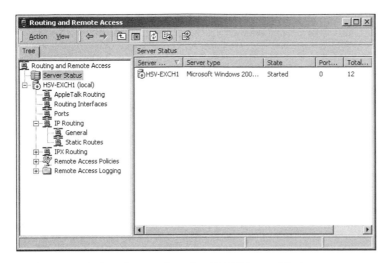

Figure 7-11   RRAS snap-in after RRAS is enabled

Chapter 6 covered most of the topics related to the management of the RRAS server, so we won't rehash it here. Instead, the following presents a brief management recap:

- Click the Server Status container to view the status of the server in the right pane. Status information includes the name of the server, whether it's running or not, the number of ports configured on it, and so on.

- Directly below the Server Status container is a container for a server, identified by the server's NetBIOS name. If more than one RRAS server is configured on the network, you see a list of server containers to choose from. Right-click the Server container (HSV-EXCH1 in Figure 7-11), and choose Properties from the shortcut menu to access a number of configuration parameters for the server. Chapter 6 details all these, but the important one to note here is the Router option on the General page. Use this option to turn the router on and off.

- Inside the server container, you see a number of containers named IP Routing, IPX Routing, and AppleTalk Routing. These containers hold different configuration objects, depending on the protocol. This chapter discusses the IP Routing container later.

- The Routing Interfaces container displays information on all routing interfaces configured on the server.

CONFIGURING STATIC ROUTING

When you enable RRAS on a server, routing turns on by default for each protocol configured on the server. This means that the server begins passing data packets immediately if clients are configured to use one of its interfaces as a default gateway. If the RRAS server is the only server on your network, or if you just don't want to set it up as a dynamic router, you do not need to install any routing protocols. Your RRAS server can function perfectly well as a static router. Of course, you have to update the routing tables yourself.

You can update static routing tables on an RRAS server in two ways: using the ROUTE command and using the RRAS snap-in.

Managing Static Routes with the Route Command

You use the **ROUTE command** to manipulate static entries in a routing table. The format for the route command is as follows:

```
Route [-f] [-p] [command [destination] [netmask] [gateway]
[metric]]
```

Table 7-1 defines the options you may use with the ROUTE command.

Table 7-1   Switches for the ROUTE command

Switch	Action
-f	Flushes all entries from the routing table
-p	Used with the ADD command to make a route persistent; used with the PRINT command to display all persistent routes
Command	Add, Delete, or Change (see the next three table entries)
Add	Adds a route to the routing table
Delete	Deletes a route from the routing table
Change	Changes a gateway address for a route that already exists
Destination	Network ID to which packets might be sent
Netmask	Subnet mask that tells IP how to calculate the network ID
Gateway	IP address where packets for the network being entered are sent; if the router is attached to this network, the address is one of the router's own interfaces; otherwise, it is the IP address of another router.
Metric	Hop count used in determining the route a packet takes

For example, entering ROUTE PRINT on the command line displays the contents of the current routing table. This should look something like Figure 7-12.

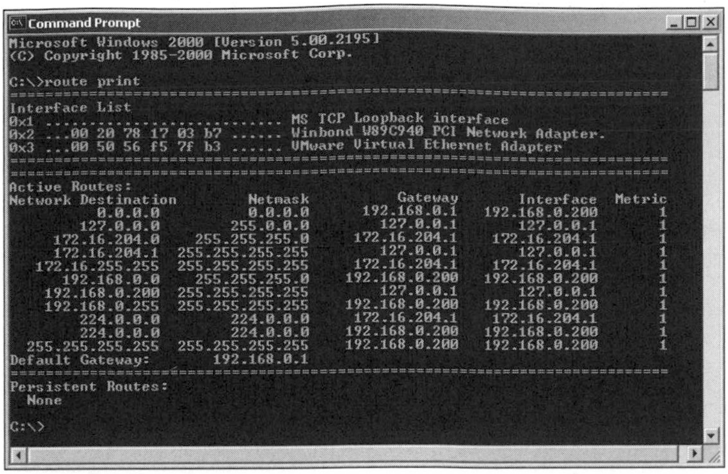

Figure 7-12   ROUTE PRINT command

Note the several entries in the table shown in Figure 7-12. Windows 2000 routing tables maintain the following default values:

- *Default route (0.0.0.0)*: route used for any network not specified in the routing table

- *Subnet Broadcast (255.255.255.255)*: address used for broadcasting to all nodes on the local subnet

- *Network Broadcast*: address used for broadcasting to all nodes on the internetwork

- *Local Loopback (127.0.0.0)*: address used for testing IP configurations and connections

- *Local Network*: address used to direct packets to nodes on the local network

- *Local Host:* address of local computer

Managing Static Routes with RRAS

While the ROUTE command is the traditional way of managing static routing tables (and useful to understand), the RRAS snap-in provides a much easier and less error-prone way. Hands-on Project 7-2 at the end of the chapter outlines the steps for adding and removing a static route from the routing table with RRAS. This section provides a brief overview of the process.

To view the routing table, first navigate to and highlight the Static Routes container inside the IP Routing container. The right pane shows any static routes that you added manually. (See Figure 7-13.) This pane shows none of the default routes configured by Windows 2000; however, don't be surprised if you find it empty the first time you look.

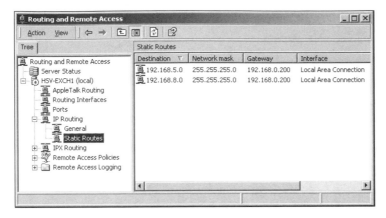

Figure 7-13   Viewing manually added static routes in RRAS

You can right-click any route in the right pane and select Delete from the shortcut menu to remove it from the routing table. Another way to view the routing table is to right-click the Static Routes container and choose the Show IP Routing Table command from its shortcut menu. This opens a dialog box similar to the one in Figure 7-14 that shows all routes in the table, including the default routes. You cannot manage routes from this dialog box, however. It's only there for looking.

HSV-EXCH1 - IP Routing Table

Destination	Network mask	Gateway	Interface	Metric	Protocol
0.0.0.0	0.0.0.0	192.168.0.1	Local Area C...	1	Network ma...
127.0.0.0	255.0.0.0	127.0.0.1	Loopback	1	Local
127.0.0.1	255.255.255.255	127.0.0.1	Loopback	1	Local
172.16.204.0	255.255.255.0	172.16.204.1	Local Area C...	1	Local
172.16.204.1	255.255.255.255	127.0.0.1	Loopback	1	Local
172.16.255.255	255.255.255.255	172.16.204.1	Local Area C...	1	Local
192.168.0.0	255.255.255.0	192.168.0.200	Local Area C...	1	Local
192.168.0.200	255.255.255.255	127.0.0.1	Loopback	1	Local
192.168.5.0	255.255.255.0	192.168.0.200	Local Area C...	1	Static (non ...
192.168.8.0	255.255.255.0	192.168.0.200	Local Area C...	1	Static (non ...
224.0.0.0	240.0.0.0	192.168.0.200	Local Area C...	1	Local
224.0.0.0	240.0.0.0	172.16.204.1	Local Area C...	1	Local
255.255.255.255	255.255.255.255	192.168.0.200	Local Area C...	1	Local
255.255.255.255	255.255.255.255	172.16.204.1	Local Area C...	1	Local

Figure 7-14   Viewing the full static route table in RRAS

To add a route to the table, right-click the Static Routes container and select the New Static Route command from the shortcut menu. This opens a dialog box like the one in Figure 7-15. Select the interface for which you want to create the route, specify a destination network and subnet mask, enter a gateway, and configure the number of metric hops allowed to reach the destination.

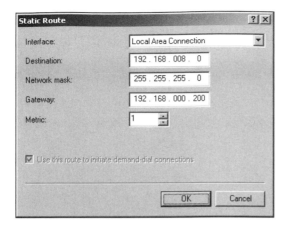

Figure 7-15   Adding a static route in RRAS

7

Using Dynamic Routing Protocols

If you find managing static routing tables not to your liking, or if you must manage large number of routers, you'll be glad to know that dynamic routing protocols are actually pretty easy to set up and configure. Once you decide between using RIP and OSPF (or both) and install the actual protocol, the protocol engine itself takes care of exchange routes with other routers it can find. In fact, you cannot even edit the contents of a dynamic routing table.

Whichever protocol you decide to use, the procedure for installing it is the same. Hands-on Project 7-3 at the end of the chapter provides a step-by-step look at the installation, but here's a brief rundown. First, find the IP Routing container inside the server for which you want to install the protocol. Inside that container, right-click the General container and select the New Routing Protocol command from the shortcut menu. Select the protocol you want and click OK. This installs the protocol and adds the new container for the protocol inside the IP Routing container. All you need to do is configure it.

Configuring RIP

There is really not much to configure for the RIP protocol. Once you install the protocol, RIP pretty much takes care of itself by looking for other RIP routers on the network and exchanging information with them. To configure what is available, right-click the new RIP container and choose Properties from the shortcut menu. There are two property pages available for configuration: General and Security.

General Properties

The General property page for the RIP protocol, shown in Figure 7-16, makes two properties available for configuration. The first is the maximum delay (in seconds) for how long a router waits to send an update notification to its peers. The second property is the level of event logging that the RIP protocol should perform.

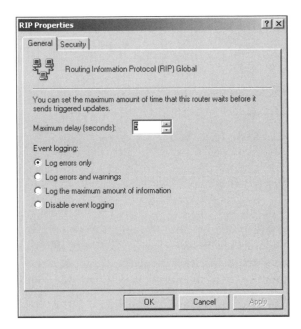

Figure 7-16   General property page for the RIP protocol

Security Properties

The Security page for RIP, shown in Figure 7-17, lets you select properties that control what router announcements your router accepts from other routers. By default, the router accepts all announcements, but you have the option of creating a list of routers whose announcements your router accepts or rejects.

Configuring OSPF

In the same way that you set RIP properties, you can also set many OSPF properties by opening the property pages for the OSPF container. Table 7-2 lists the available property pages and describes their general use.

While it may seem that this chapter glosses over the OSPF properties you can set, much of this information is too detailed to be presented here and not prominently featured on the exam. It's important to know some of the features available and generally where to configure them, but you do not need to get mired in the specifics of the OSPF protocol.

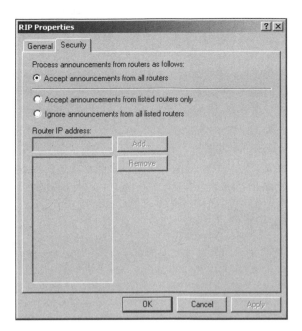

Figure 7-17   Security page for the RIP protocol

Table 7-2   Property pages for the OSPF protocol

Property page	Properties
General	Lets you configure the level of logging that the OSPF protocol performs, plus two other parameters: a Router Identification lets you enter an IP address that your router uses to identify itself; Enable Autonomous System Boundary controls whether your OSPF router advertises routers it finds outside your system
Areas	Lists the OSPF areas that your router knows about; you can add, edit, or remove areas from the list on this page; areas were discussed earlier in this chapter
Virtual Interfaces	OSPF divides routers into areas, some backbone areas and other regular areas; virtual links are used to configure non-backbone routers to exchange information with backbone routers
External Routing	Quite possibly your OSPF router can acquire routes from a number of sources besides other OSPF routers, including RIP routers and static routes; the External Routing page lets you control which external sources can add routes to the OSPF router

WORKING WITH INTERFACES

Once you install and configure dynamic routing protocols, the next step is to add the interfaces (network adapters, demand-dial interfaces, and so forth) you want to use with those protocols. You must add at least two interfaces to each protocol. After all, the router is there to accept traffic on one interface and send it out over another. That's what routing is. You can add as many interfaces as you have to a protocol, but adding all available interfaces is not necessary.

Actually, you are not really adding a new interface. You are taking an existing interface on the RRAS server and binding it to the protocol. However, Microsoft calls this adding an interface, so who are we to argue?

Managing LAN Interfaces

Before you start adding interfaces to protocols, it may be helpful to look at the properties you can configure for the LAN interfaces themselves. First, expand the IP Routing container and highlight the General container. This displays a list of LAN interfaces in the right pane, as shown in Figure 7-18.

You can also see a list of LAN interfaces in the Routing Interfaces container directly under the server container, but you cannot open the properties of the interfaces there. You must go to the General container to do this. Go figure.

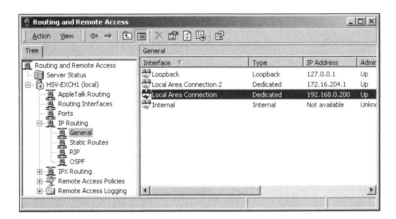

Figure 7-18   Viewing LAN interfaces in RRAS

Right-click any LAN interface and click Properties to open the property pages for that interface. There are four property pages presented: General, Configuration, Multicast Boundaries, and Multicast Heartbeat. The two that involve multicasting are beyond the scope of this book and the exam, and are not covered here. The next sections discuss the other two pages.

General Properties

The General page shown in Figure 7-19, lets you set properties for the entire interface. These include the following:

- *Enable IP router manager*: controls whether this interface allows IP routing. When disabled, the interface does not route packets and other routers cannot exchange information with it.

- *Enable Router Discovery Advertisements*: controls whether the router broadcasts router discovery messages. These are the messages used to find neighboring routers automatically. With this option enabled, you can also configure how long advertisements are valid, the preference level assigned to those advertisements (clients use routers with higher preferences first), and the minimum and maximum intervals for sending advertisements.

- *Input Filters and Output Filters*: let you selectively accept or reject packets on the interface. For example, you could create a filter that rejects all packets from a specified network address.

- *Enable fragmentation checking*: lets your router reject fragmented packets. With this option disabled, the router must accept and try to process fragmented packets. Sending fragmented packets is a popular form of denial-of-service attack on routers.

7

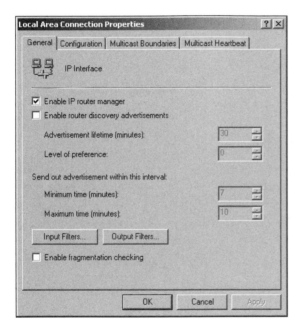

Figure 7-19   General page of a LAN interface

Configuration Properties

You use the Configuration page shown in Figure 7-20, to specify whether the interface should have static IP addressing information or receive it automatically from a DHCP server.

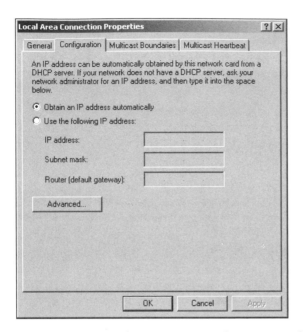

Figure 7-20   Configuration page of a LAN interface

Demand-dial Routing Interfaces

When you install RRAS, it automatically configures all the LAN connections that it can find. However, you must configure any demand-dial interfaces on your own. To start creating a demand-dial interface, right-click the Routing Interfaces container in RRAS and choose New Demand-Dial Interface from the shortcut menu. Hands-on Project 7-4 at the end of the chapter provides step-by-step instructions for creating a new demand-dial interface.

Here is a list of the basic steps involved in creating the interface:

1. Name the interface.

   If possible, choose a name that represents both the source and destination of the connection.

2. Choose a connection type.

   You can choose either a physical connection (modem, ISDN, and so forth) or a Virtual Private Networking connection. The choices for the rest of the wizard differ slightly depending on the choice you make here. Chapter 6 details the creation of a VPN connection, so we just focus on the physical connection here.

3. Choose the actual physical device for the interface.

   Since you cannot add a device from within this wizard, you need to set up any devices beforehand.

4. Enter a phone number for the connection.

   This is the number of the remote router.

5. Set routing and security options.

   Figure 7-21 shows this dialog. You can enable or disable the IP and IPX protocols for the connection, as well as establish some security guidelines. These guidelines include whether to add a user account so a remote user can dial in (selecting this adds another page to the wizard where you can fill in user information); allowing plain text passwords if you cannot use a more secure authentication, and using a script to complete the connection with the remote router (some routers require this).

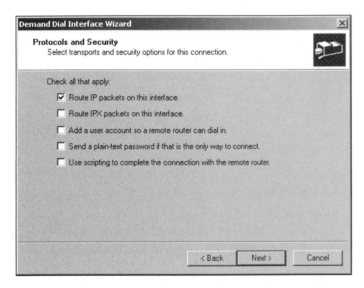

Figure 7-21   Routing and security options for a new demand-dial interface

6. Establish dial-out credentials.

   This includes any user information that your router needs to connect to and authenticate itself with the remote router.

Adding a LAN Interface to a Protocol

To add a LAN interface to a protocol, simply right-click the protocol container (for example, the RIP container) and choose the New Interface command from the shortcut menu. A dialog box opens that lists the available interfaces. Choose one and click OK to create the new interface. As soon as you create the new interface, you immediately see the property page for the interface. You can also configure these properties later by right-clicking the interface inside the protocol container and choosing Properties from the shortcut menu. The property pages for the RIP and OSPF protocols differ a bit, and the following sections discuss each.

RIP Interface Properties

Four pages with dialog boxes are available on interfaces attached to the RIP protocol: General, Security, Neighbors, and Advanced.

General Properties   The General page for the RIP interface, shown in Figure 7-22, let you control several properties:

- *Operation mode*: defines how the router updates its neighbors. By default, demand-dial interfaces are set to auto-static update, and LAN interfaces are set to periodic updates.

- *Outgoing packet protocol*: determines how packets are sent. If you have all RIPv2 routers on your network, the RIP version 2 multicast option is the most efficient. Other options exist for networks that use RIPv1 or a mix of RIPv1 and RIPv2. A final option, Silent RIP, lets your router listen for and accept updates from other routers without sending its own updates.

- *Incoming packet protocol*: specifies what kinds of RIP packets your router accepts from other routers.

- *Added cost for routers*: lets you control how much this router increases the hop count added to other router's routing tables. The higher you set the cost, the less likely your router will be used.

- *Tag for announced routes*: lets you supply a tag to be included in RIP updates. RRAS does not use this feature, but other routers may.

- *Activate authentication* and *password*: provide some security for your router. Once you turn on authentication, other routers must be configured with the same password in order to exchange information.

Security Properties   The Security page for the RIP interface, shown in Figure 7-23, lets you add restrictive properties to your router. First, select an action from the drop-down menu to specify whether the restrictions apply to incoming or outgoing packets. Next, select whether to accept all routes (or announce all routes for outgoing packets), accept only those in the specified ranges, or reject those in the specified ranges. Finally, specify the ranges to which the option applies.

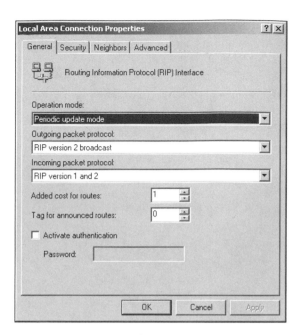

Figure 7-22   General page of the RIP interface

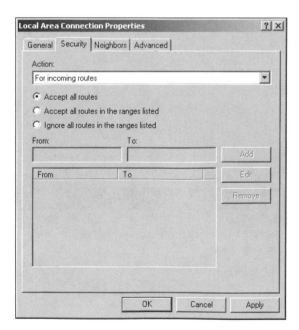

Figure 7-23   Security page for the RIP interface

Neighbors Properties The Neighbors page for the RIP interface, shown in Figure 7-24, lets you choose properties that control how the router interacts with its neighboring routers. By selecting a list of trusted neighbors (by entering IP addresses), you can choose to use those neighbors' routes in addition to, or instead of, broadcast and multicast RIP announcements.

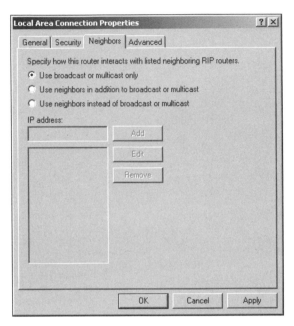

Figure 7-24   Neighbors page of the RIP interface

Advanced Properties The Advanced page lets you set a number of properties that you may never need to worry about, but will need to know for the exam. Table 7-3 lists and describes these properties.

Table 7-3   Advanced properties for a RIP interface

Available pages	Use
Periodic announcement interval	Controls the interval at which periodic router announcements are made; works in conjunction with the Operation mode set in the General page
Time before routes expire	Controls how long the route may stay in the routing table before it expires; routes destined to expire can be refreshed if another router sends the route again
Time before route is removed	Controls how much time may pass between the time a route expires and its removal from the table

Table 7-3   Advanced properties for a RIP interface (continued)

Available pages	Use
Enable split-horizon processing	Enables the router to not rebroadcast routes learned from a specific network back onto that network; this helps prevent loops from occurring
Enable poison-reverse split horizon	Modifies the way split-horizon processing works; with poison-reverse enabled, routes learned from a network are rebroadcast back to that network with a hop count of 16, a special value that tells other routers that the route is unreachable; also helps prevent looping while keeping routing tables up-to-date
Enable triggered updates	Controls whether you want routing table changes to be sent immediately when they are noticed
Send clean-up-updates when stopping	Controls whether RRAS sends announcements that mark the routes it was handling as unavailable when the service stops
Turn on host routes in received announcements	By default, RRAS ignores any host routes it sees in RIP announcements; with this property RRAS sees those routes instead
Include host routes in sent announcements	Directs RRAS to send host route information as part of its RIP announcements; off by default
Process default routes in received announcements and Include default routes in sent announcements	Properties that work the same way as the host routes properties defined above
Disable subnet summarization	When off, RIP doesn't advertise subnets to routers on other subnets; only available with RIPv2

7

OSPF Interface Properties

The following property pages are available: General, NBMA Neighbors, and Advanced.

General Properties   The General page for the OPSF interface, shown in Figure 7-25, has a number of properties. These include:

- *Enable OSPF for this address*: along with the address drop-down list, controls whether OSPF is active at the selected address. Since a single interface can have multiple IP addresses, you can use this drop-down list to specify which addresses are and are not OSPF-capable.

- *Area ID*: drop-down list lets you select to which OSPF area this interface belongs. Each IP address assigned to the interface can be in a separate area.

- *Router priority*: controls the priority of the interface relative to other routers in the area. The router with the highest priority in an area is the preferred router for the area.

- *Cost*: controls the hop count cost associated with the interface.

- *Password*: works just like it does for RIP. Any routers configured with the same password can communicate.

- *Network type*: controls how the router interacts with other routers. A broadcast router can communicate with any number of other routers. A point-to-point router communicates with only one other router. A **non-broadcast multiple access (NBMA) router** communicates with multiple other routers without using a broadcast. If you set up your router as an NBMA router, you can set additional properties using the NBMA Neighbors page.

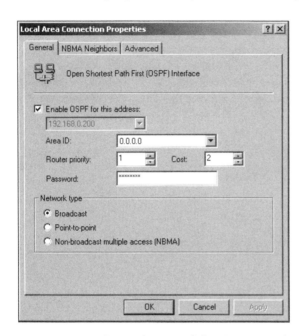

Figure 7-25   General page of the OPSF interface

NBMA Neighbors Properties The NBMA Neighbors page shown in Figure 7–26, lets you choose the neighboring routers with which you want your router to communicate if it is set up as an NBMA router. Just use the IP address drop-down menu to select the IP address for which you want to configure neighbors. (Remember that an interface can have more than one IP address.) For each IP address, enter the IP addresses of the routers you want to configure as neighbors. For each neighbor, you can also set a router priority relative to other neighbor routers.

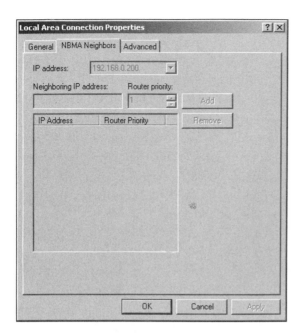

Figure 7-26   NBMA Neighbors page of the OPSF interface

Advanced Properties The Advanced page for the OSPF interface holds six miscellaneous properties. At the top of the page, you can choose the IP address for which you want to configure properties. You can apply different properties to different IP addresses, including:

- *Transit delay*: controls how long it should take for a link-state update to propagate from the router. This information helps other routers determine how fresh information is.

- *Retransmit interval*: controls the estimated round-trip delay when two routers communicate. If the round trip takes longer than this interval, communications are retransmitted.

- *Hello interval*: controls how often routers send packets to discover other routers on the network. You must set the same value for all routers on the network.

- *Dead interval*: controls how long peers wait before they mark a non-responding router as dead. Microsoft recommends using an integral multiple of the Hello interval for this setting. For example, if you set the Hello interval to 10 seconds, you should set the Dead interval to 20, 30, 40, and so on.

- *Poll interval*: controls how long an NBMA router waits before attempting to contact an apparently dead router to see if it is really dead. Microsoft recommends setting this to at least twice the Dead interval.

- *Maximum transmission unit (MTU) size*: specifies how big an OSPF packet can be.

MONITORING IP ROUTING

The RRAS snap-in has a number of displays for monitoring the status of various components. You already saw a few of these displays in this chapter, including:

- *Server Status*: displays the state and type of each RRAS server, as well as the number of ports configured and the number of users connected.

- *General container inside the IP Routing container*: displays all interfaces configured on the server. These include both LAN and demand-dial interfaces. Also displays the state of the interface (up or down) and the IP address associated with the interface.

- *Static Routes container*: displays all static routes added manually to the routing table. Right-clicking the Static Routes container and choosing the Show IP Routing Table command opens a dialog with a more complete version of the routing table that includes the default routes created by Windows 2000.

- *Dynamic routing protocol containers (RIP and OSPF)*: displays the interfaces associated with the protocols and various statistics about each interface's use.

In addition, you may find a few other displays helpful in monitoring and troubleshooting your IP routing implementation. These include:

- *IP Routing Statistics*: include the number of routes in the routing table, the number of IP and UDP datagrams forwarded and received, and the number of connection attempts. To display routing statistics, right-click the General container and choose the Show TCP/IP Information command.

- *Router Status*: displays how many bad packets and bad routers each router tried to send to your RRAS server. To view existing RIP neighbors, right-click the RIP container and select the Show Neighbors command.

- *Defined Areas*: lists the state of the area (up or down) and the number of shortest-path computations performed. To see the list of all defined areas, right-click the OSPF container and select the Show Areas command.

- *Link-State Database*: displays the entire contents of the link-state database. To view the contents, right-click the OSPF container and select the Show Link-State Database command.

- *List of Neighbors*: displays each neighbor's type (broadcast, point-to-point, or NBMA) and state. Right-click the OSPF container and select the Show Neighbors command to see a list of neighbors.

Hands-on Project 7-5 at the end of the chapter details steps for monitoring router status.

CHAPTER SUMMARY

- IP Routing is the method that the IP protocol uses to transfer data between computers on a network. In Windows 2000, the Routing and Remote Access Service (RRAS) supports IP routing. Direct routing occurs when both the source and destination hosts are on the same network segment. Indirect routing occurs when the source and destination hosts are not on the same network segment and packets must pass through a router.

- A router is a physical device used to connect a number of network segments. Routers can be dedicated pieces of hardware, or they can be computers with more than one network adapter card, each connected to a different network segment.

- On a static router, you must enter routing tables manually. A static router only knows about networks directly connected to it or networks that you tell it about. Dynamic routers are routers that have some automatic method of sharing their routing information with other routers on the network. If routing or network information changes, a router automatically updates its routing tables and forwards that information to other dynamic routers that it knows about.

- A dynamic routing protocol used to connect two routers in the same autonomous system is called an interior routing protocol. Windows 2000 supports two interior dynamic routing protocols: Routing Information Protocol (RIP) versions 1 and 2 and Open Shortest Path First (OSPF). RIP is a distance vector routing program, meaning that it not only supplies information about the networks a router can reach, but supplies information about the distances to these networks as well. This distance simply reflects the number of routers a packet must cross, or hop, to reach a particular network.

- OSPF is a link-state routing protocol that enables routers to exchange routing information. It is called a link-state protocol because it actually creates a map (a routing table) of the network that calculates the best possible path to each network segment by maintaining information on the state of links (whether they are up or down).

- Exterior routing protocols are used to exchange routing information between networks that are not autonomous (that is, do not share a common administration). The first exterior routing protocol developed was the Exterior Gateway Protocol (EGP). Since then, a newer and more powerful exterior routing protocol has been developed: the Border Gateway Protocol (BGP).

- Enabling routing on a Windows 2000 server is a three-step process. First, you must enable the RRAS service. Next, you must install and configure any routing protocols (RIP or OSPF) if you want your new router to function as a dynamic router. If you do not, you can configure static routing instead. Finally, you must give each routable interface on the server (network adapter card or demand-dial) a network address for each protocol you allow to be used over the interface. If you want to use demand-dial routing, you must also configure a demand-dial interface.

7

KEY TERMS

Address Resolution Protocol (ARP) — Low-level protocol that resides within the IP protocol. It is used as a way of resolving IP addresses to MAC addresses.

area border routers — OSPF router that has an interface in more than one OSPF area.

areas — OSPF division of the internetwork into collections of contiguous networks that help keep routing tables from growing too large. Each router only keeps a link-state database for those areas connected to the router.

autonomous system — One in which a set of networks and routers are all under the same administration.

backbone area — OSPF areas connected by a special type of area called a backbone area.

backbone router — Any router configured in an OSPF backbone area.

Border Gateway Protocol (BGP) — Newer and more powerful exterior routing protocol that has largely replaced the older Exterior Gateway Protocol.

converged — Status of an internetwork when all its routers have the correct routing information in their tables.

Convergence time — When a link or router fails, the time taken for all routers on the network to reconfigure themselves with the proper information.

default gateway — Defined on most TCP/IP hosts and simply a router where a packet is sent if its destination network is not found in a routing table.

demand-dial interfaces — Interface configured in RRAS that can dial a remote router whenever a connection needs to be made.

dynamic router — Routers that automatically share their routing information with other routers on the network using a router protocol such as RIP or OSPF.

Exterior Gateway Protocol (EGP) — Exterior routing protocol used to connect different autonomous systems.

hop — Each router that a packet of information must pass between its source and destination hosts. The number of hops is also referred to as metric count or metric cost.

indirect routing — Occurs when a packet of information must pass over a router at some point between its source and destination.

IP (Internet Protocol) — Network layer protocol of the TCP/IP protocol suite that is responsible for routing packets between hosts.

MAC address — Physical address of a network interface. The Address Resolution Protocol is responsible for translating between MAC and IP addresses.

multihomed — Describes a computer with an interface on more than one network.

non-broadcast multiple access (NBMA) router — Router that can communicate with other routers without broadcasting.

Open Shortest Path First (OSPF) — Link-state routing protocol that enables routers to exchange routing information. Called a link-state protocol because it actually creates a map (a routing table) of the network that calculates the best possible path to each network segment by maintaining information on the state of links (whether they are up or down).

RIPv1 — Simple-to-use and well-supported interior routing protocol. RIP is a distance vector routing program, meaning that it not only supplies information about the networks a router can reach, but supplies information about the distances to those networks as well.

RIPv2 — Protocol developed to address several shortcomings in RIPv1, for example, by providing a multicast option in addition to broadcasts for routing announcements and by including the subnet mask in announcements.

ROUTE command — Command-line utility used to manipulate static entries in a routing table.

routing table — List of networks that the system knows about and the IP addresses of routers that packets must pass through to get to those networks.

static router — Router to which routes must be added manually using either the ROUTE command or the RRAS snap-in.

7

REVIEW QUESTIONS

1. Which of the following can you use for a demand-dial interface? (Choose all that apply.)

   a. Modem

   b. Parallel port

   c. VPN port

   d. Ethernet adapter

2. You have three network adapters in your RRAS server, each with a separate IP address. You plan to use two different routing protocols. How many default gateways must you define on the server?

   a. 1

   b. 2

   c. 3

   d. 6

3. Routing table entries usually contain which of the following? (Choose all that apply.)

   a. Destination address for a remote network

   b. Metric for the router

   c. Date and time of the route's creation

   d. Forwarding address for remote traffic

4. A _____ is a connection that brings up a link when it's needed to pass packets.

5. ARP is an example of an exterior routing protocol. True or false?

6. How do you configure router discovery messages?

   a. Through the General page of the LAN interface properties

   b. Through the Discovery page of an OSPF or RIP interface properties

   c. Through the General page of an OSPF or RIP interface properties

   d. By adding an input filter that rejects them

7. An RRAS server can only support one networking protocol on a system. True or false?

8. You use OSPF on a router on your local area network. How should you configure the router?

   a. As a point-to-point router

   b. As an NBMA router

   c. As a broadcast router

   d. As a multicast router

9. Which of the following statements is true of a border router?

   a. It acts as a gateway between routing areas.

   b. It routes traffic internal to an area.

   c. It cannot be used with RRAS.

   d. None of the above.

10. You can manually update a dynamic router's routing table. True or false?

11. _____ refers to the amount of time all routers on the network take to reconfigure themselves after a link or router fails.

12. Which of the following protocols are forms of interior routing protocols? (Choose all that apply.)

   a. RIP

   b. EGP

   c. OSPF

   d. VPN

13. _____ is an example of a vector-based routing protocol.

14. Which of the following refers to an OSPF router that has an interface on more than one network?

   a. Backbone router

   b. Dynamic router

   c. Area border router

   d. Area router

15. _____ is the primary advantage of OSPF over RIP.

16. Which of the following switches do you use with the ROUTE command to remove all entries from a static routing table?

    a. –f

    b. –r

    c. –d

    d. –remove

17. _____ is the local loopback IP address used for testing IP configurations.

18. You can configure a password for both RIP and OSPF routers. True or false?

19. You want to configure your OSPF router *not* to advertise routers it finds outside your system. Where would you do this?

    a. The General page of the IP Routing container's properties

    b. The General page of the OSPF container's properties

    c. The General page of an OSPF interface's properties

    d. The General page of the Static Routes container's properties

20. Windows 2000 supports both the EGP and BGP exterior routing protocols. True or false?

HANDS-ON PROJECTS

All Hands-on Projects in this chapter require at least one server computer set up as described in the lab set-up section in the front of this book. To complete these exercises, you must have completed the projects in Chapters 2 and 3 on installing networking protocols and configuring DHCP.

Project 7-1

To install the Routing and Remote Access Service, follow these steps:

1. Click **Start**, point to **Programs**, point to **Administrative Tools**, and then select **Routing and Remote Access**.

2. Right-click the computer name and select **Configure and Enable Routing and Remote Access** from the context menu.

3. On the Welcome screen for the Routing and Remote Access Server Setup Wizard, click **Next**.

4. On the Common Configuration screen, select the **Network Router** option and then click **Next**.

5. On the Remote Client Protocols screen, under Protocols, make sure that TCP/IP is listed.

6. Verify that **Yes, all the required protocols are on this list** option is selected, and click **Next**.

7. On the Demand-Dial Connections page, choose the **Yes** option.

8. On the IP Address Assignment screen, make sure that the **Automatically** option is selected and then click **Next**.

9. Click **Finish**.

Project 7-2

To add and remove static routes with the RRAS snap-in, follow these steps:

1. Click **Start**, point to **Programs**, point to **Administrative Tools**, and then select **Routing and Remote Access**.

2. Find the server you want to configure in the left pane, and expand it.

3. Find the **IP Routing** container under that server, and expand it.

4. Right-click the **Static Routes** container, and choose the **New Static Route** command from the shortcut menu.

5. Select the interface you want to use from the Interface drop-down list.

6. Enter a **destination address** for the network you want to route to and a **subnet mask**.

7. In the Gateway field, enter the **IP address** of your RRAS server.

8. Click **OK** to close the Static Route dialog box.

9. Right-click the **Static Routes** container, and select the **Show IP Routing Table** command from the shortcut menu.

10. In the dialog box that opens, verify that the new route you just added is in the table.

11. Click the **Close** button to close the dialog.

12. Highlight the **Static Routes** container.

    Notice the routing table in the right pane.

13. Right-click the **static route** you just created, and select **Delete** from the shortcut menu to remove it from the table.

Project 7-3

To install a dynamic routing protocol, follow these steps:

1. Click **Start**, point to **Programs**, point to **Administrative Tools**, and then select **Routing and Remote Access**.

2. Find the server you want to configure in the left pane, and expand it.

3. Find the **IP Routing** container under that server, and expand it.

4. Right-click the **General** container and select **New Routing Protocol** from the shortcut menu.

5. Select the **RIP Version 2 protocol** from the list, and click **OK**.

6. Right-click the **General** container again, and select **New Routing Protocol** from the shortcut menu.

7. Select the **Open Shortest Path First (OSPF)** protocol from the list, and click **OK**.

   The RRAS display should update to show the two new protocols inside the IP Routing container.

Project 7-4

To create a new demand-dial interface, follow these steps:

1. Click **Start**, point to **Programs**, point to **Administrative Tools**, and then select **Routing and Remote Access**.

2. Right-click **Routing Interfaces**, select **New Demand-Dial Interface** from the shortcut menu, and click **Next**.

3. In the Interface Name field, type a **name** for the remote router to which you will connect, and click **Next**.

4. Select **Connect using a modem, ISDN adapter**, or **other physical device**, and click **Next**.

5. If your system contains more than one network adapter, select the **physical device** that the interface will use, and click **Next**.

6. If you choose to connect using the modem in Step 4, you are now shown a Phone number page. Enter the number of the router to which you want to connect.

7. On the Protocols and Security page, make sure that only the **Route IP Packets** option is selected and click **Next**.

8. On the Dial-Out Credentials page, enter the **user information** needed to connect to the remote router and click **Next**.

9. Click **Finish**.

Project 7-5

To monitor the status of IP routing, follow these steps:

1. Click **Start**, point to **Programs**, point to **Administrative Tools**, and then select **Routing and Remote Access**.

2. Expand the server whose status you want to monitor in the left pane.

3. Select the **Routing Interfaces** container.

   Note that the right pane now lists all the interfaces available on the server along with their connection state.

4. Select the **General** container beneath the IP Routing container.

   The right pane displays the IP routing interfaces and their status.

5. Right-click the **General** container and choose the **Show TCP/IP information** command.

   Check the number of IP routes shown.

6. Right-click the **Static Routes** container, and select the **Show IP Routing Table** command.

   This displays all routes available in the routing table.

CASE PROJECTS

Case 1

Your company network consists of four subnets configured with the following network IDs:

❒ 192.168.0.0

❒ 192.168.1.0

❒ 192.168.2.0

❒ 192.168.3.0

You plan to configure a single RRAS server with four network adapters as the single router on this network. Sketch a network diagram showing how you will configure the network. Include an IP address for each of the four interfaces on the RRAS server.

Case 2

Your network has grown steadily, and you decided to implement several more network segments. You propose moving to a dynamic routing system, and your supervisor seems interested. In response to her request, prepare a list showing the advantages and disadvantages of using RIPv1, RIPv2, and OSPF.

8

IP SECURITY

After reading this chapter and completing the exercises, you will be able to:

♦ Describe the features and benefits of the IP Security protocol

♦ Describe the two modes of operation for IP Security: transport and tunnel

♦ Describe the IP Security authentication and architecture

♦ Configure IP Security for transport mode on a Windows 2000 server

♦ Configure IP Security for tunnel mode on a Windows 2000 server

♦ Customize IP Security policies and rules

♦ Manage and monitor IP Security

Security has always been an important issue in computer networking, and the wealth of security options the modern administrator can choose from proves this. The many different forms of networking security include the authentication of users when they log on to the network; the restriction of physical access to computers and networking equipment; the authentication of computers as they pass data to other computers; and the protection of the actual data being sent across the networks. IP Security (IPSec) falls into this last category. IPSec is an extension of the IP protocol that provides point-to-point encryption of data being sent between two computers on an IP-based network.

This chapter begins with an overview of the benefits, features, and operations of IPSec. From there, it moves on to cover the actual implementation, configuration, and management of this promising security protocol.

IPSec Overview

IPSec is an extension to the familiar **Internet Protocol (IP)** that is responsible for routing data packets on a TCP/IP-based network. Actually, IPSec is not a single protocol, but a suite of protocols designed to work together to secure data being sent between two computers on a network. Like IP, IPSec works at the Network layer. This means that higher-level protocols and applications in the TCP/IP protocol suite, like FTP, can ignore the encryption process. They carry out their functions normally, passing data down the protocol layers, unaware of whether that data is eventually encrypted or not.

Any Windows 2000 computer may act as an **IPSec client** or an **IPSec server**. The IPSec client is the computer that initiates the IPSec connection, and the IPSec server is the one that receives it. Nothing special about IPSec configuration makes a computer an IPSec client or server; it just depends on which computer makes the initial connection attempt.

This overview examines what functions the IPSec protocol actually performs and the benefits that it provides. IT also looks at the individual protocol components that make up IPSec and how they all work together to send encrypted data from one computer to another.

What IPSec Does

IPSec is a framework of open standards developed by the IPSec working group of the Internet Engineering Task Force (IETF). The framework provides a way to ensure transfer of encrypted data over IP-based networks. The Microsoft Windows 2000 implementation of IPSec is based on those standards.

IPSec provides two basic services. The first is a way for two computers to determine whether they trust one another. This is referred to as **authentication**. The second service is to provide a reasonable way to **encrypt** data on one end of the connection and **decrypt** it on the other end. IPSec is often called an end-to-end security measure, meaning that only the sending and receiving computers must know about IPSec. The medium over which the data travels is assumed to be insecure, and the IPSec process requires no other computers on the network to be involved. Also, routers that forward packets of data between networks also do not need to know anything about IPSec.

Features of IPSec

Since it is enabled at the Networking level, the greatest benefit of IPSec is that it is completely transparent to users, applications, and protocols above and below the Networking layer. The following list describes some of the additional features offered by the Windows 2000 implementation of IPSec:

- IPSec uses the Windows 2000 domain as a trust model. By default, **IPSec policies** use the default Windows authentication method (**Kerberos V5**) to validate communicating computers. IPSec policies can also be configured to use **public key certificates** or **pre-shared keys** for authentication.

- **IPSec policies**, sets of rules assigned to clients that define how those clients use IPSec, are assigned centrally through the **Active Directory Group Policy** feature. This chapter covers IPSec policies in detail later.

- All packets are encrypted using time-specific information so that they cannot be captured and played back later in an attempt to crack the encryption code.

- Long key lengths and dynamic changes of keying are used during ongoing communications for added security. (You can learn more about the basics of encryption in Chapter 10.)

- Private network users can connect using secure end-to-end links with any trusted domain in the enterprise.

- Remote users and private network users can connect using secure end-to-end links based on IP addresses.

Modes of Operation

IPSec can operate in two different modes, depending on the scope of the communication. These two modes of operation are transport mode and tunnel mode.

Transport Mode

When used to secure communication between two specific clients, such as two computers on the same LAN, IPSec operates in **transport mode**. The two endpoints of communication are the two computers, and both must have IPSec configured. For this mode to work, both computers must use the TCP/IP protocol.

Tunnel Mode

IPSec can also be used to secure communication that passes through a transit network such as the Internet. In this case, called **tunnel mode**, the two communicating computers do not use IPSec themselves. Instead, the gateways connecting each client's LAN to the transit network create a virtual tunnel that uses the IPSec protocol to secure all communication that passes through it. Communication from the clients themselves is encapsulated in the tunnel protocol headers, encrypted, and passed through the tunnel. The gateway at the other end decrypts the packet, removes the tunnel protocol header, and sends the packet to the destination computer.

Tunnels can be created using only the IPSec protocol or by combining IPSec with the Layer 2 Tunneling Protocol (L2TP) to establish a Virtual Private Network (VPN) connection. In this case, L2TP, rather than IPSec, actually creates the tunnel. For more information on L2TP and VPNs, see Chapter 6.

In tunnel mode the actual clients are not involved in IPSec communication. This frees the clients to use other networking protocols such as IPX/SPX and AppleTalk; they are not restricted to TCP/IP.

IPSec Authentication

As mentioned previously, IPSec supports three different types of authentication:

- **Kerberos** is the default authentication system used by Windows 2000. An open standard, it is thus widely supported by other operating systems, as well.

- **Certificates** are provided by a certificate authority. Each end of the IPSec connection uses the other end's public certificate for authentication. This model provides good security but also requires that a certificate server be accessible for the distribution of certificates. Chapter 10 covers this topic in detail.

- **Pre-shared keys** are simply passwords entered into each computer. As long as both computers are configured with the same pre-shared key, they trust one another. While the pre-shared key itself is never transmitted between the clients, it is stored in the Active Directory in an unencrypted format. For this reason, pre-shared keys are considered less secure than the other available forms of authentication.

IPSec Architecture

Once the two communicating clients authenticate one another, they are ready to begin encrypting and sharing data. This section first introduces the various components that are a part of this process and then describes the process itself.

IPSec Components

IPSec is implemented using a number of different components. The following sections introduce these.

IPSec Policy Agent Service The **IPSec policy agent service** resides on each Windows 2000 computer that is configured with IPSec. It starts automatically when the computer starts and performs several tasks at specified intervals. The policy agent is responsible for retrieving the computer's assigned IPSec policy from the Active Directory. If it cannot connect to the Active Directory, or if it finds no policy there, it tries to retrieve the policy from the computer's registry. If it finds no policy, IPSec cannot continue. If it does find a policy, the policy agent sends the information in the policy to the ISAKMP/Oakley Service.

ISAKMP/Oakley Service A key management service, the **ISAKMP/Oakley Service** also resides on each Windows 2000 computer involved in IPSec communication. Before two computers attempting a connection can send any data, they must first establish a security association. This **security association** defines the common security mechanisms, such as keys, that the two computers use to create the IPSec connection. The ISAKMP/Oakley Service is also responsible for generating the keys used to encrypt and decrypt the data sent over the IPSec connection.

IPSec Driver The **IPSec driver** also resides on each Windows 2000 computer involved in IPSec communication. The IPSec driver starts when the policy agent starts. It watches all IP datagrams for a match with a filter list configured in the computer's security policy. Filters are used to define what computers can and cannot establish connections with other computers. If it finds a filter match, the IPSec driver uses the keys created by the ISAKMP/Oakley Service to encrypt the data and send it over the IPSec connection. The IPSec driver on the receiving computer decrypts the data.

To force the IPSec driver to restart, you can restart the IPSec Policy Agent using the Services console in the Administrative Tools program group.

The IPSec Process

Now that you've been introduced to the major components involved in IPSec communication, here's how they all work together:

1. An application on one computer (call it Host 1) sends data to another computer (call it Host 2).

2. The data passes down through the networking layers of Host 1, where it is fragmented and shaped into packets to be sent over the network.

3. When the data reaches the networking level and is ready for routing by the Internet Protocol, the IPSec driver for Host 1 notifies the ISAKMP/Oakley Service that an IPSec connection is needed.

4. The ISAKMP/Oakley Services on both computers establish a security association and generate a shared key.

5. The ISAKMP/Oakley Services on both computers transfer the shared key to the IPSec drivers on those hosts. Now, the IPSec drivers on both computers have the same shared key.

6. The IPSec driver on Host 1 uses the key to encrypt the data and then sends the data to Host 2.

7. The IPSec driver on Host 2 receives the data and uses the shared key to decrypt it.

8. The IPSec driver passes the data up to the next networking layer.

9. When the data works its way up to the top layer, the application on Host 2 receives the data and never knows it was encrypted.

INSTALLING IPSEC

All IPSec components are installed by default when you install Windows 2000. All you really need to do to enable IPSec is to create a custom console using the Microsoft Management Console that includes the IP Security Policy Management snap-in (called the IPSec snap-in from now on) and then use the snap-in to assign policies and filters. Hands-on Project 8-1 at the end of the chapter outlines the actual steps for creating a console and assigning a policy.

During the creation of the snap-in console, there is really only one option to which you have to give some thought. You must choose whether you want the snap-in to manage local IPSec policy, the default policy for your computer's domain, the default policy for another domain, or the local policy on another computer. See Figure 8-1.

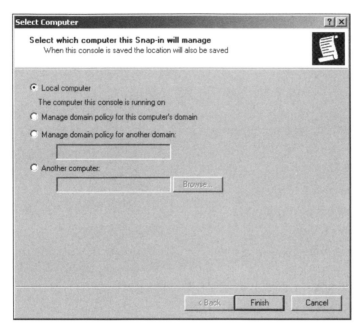

Figure 8-1   Enabling IPSec

While the real power of IPSec lies in configuring group policies in the Active Directory, a discussion of group policy management is really outside the scope of this book and, for the most part, the scope of the certification exam, as well. Instead, this chapter focuses on customizing and controlling the IPSec settings themselves. While you can manage policies at a variety of levels, you always use the IPSec snap-in to manage them. Furthermore, the management of policies at the local level and at the Active Directory level uses essentially the same techniques.

CONFIGURING IPSEC

You can modify the existing IPSec policies to suit your needs, create policies of your own, or both. You create policies using a wizard that steps you through the process of configuring the policy. You manage the policies you create using property pages, just like you manage objects in other snap-ins you work with. For each policy, property pages allow you to configure general settings and a set of rules under which the policy operates. The Rules page lets you tie general filters you create to filter actions taken when that filter is in effect. This section covers all of this creation and configuration. First, though, it may be helpful to get our bearings straight with regard to the IPSec snap-in, shown in Figure 8-2.

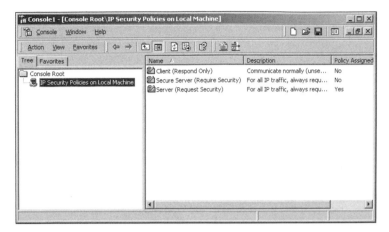

Figure 8-2   IPSec snap-in

Selecting the IP Security Policies on Local Machine object displays a list of available policies in the right pane. The list describes each policy and also tells whether the policy is assigned, or functional. You can right-click any existing policy and choose the Properties command from the shortcut menu to configure the policy. The same shortcut menu also contains commands for assigning or unassigning the policy, depending on its current state.

As shown in Figure 8-3, right-clicking the IP Security Policies on Local Machine object reveals that there are no properties to configure for that object, but that you can perform a number of tasks at this level.

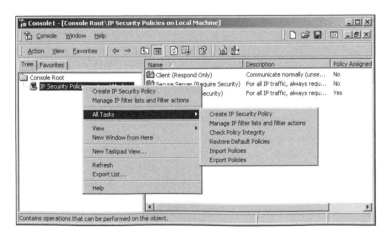

Figure 8-3   IPSec tasks for a local machine

Your main tasks are creating a new policy and managing the list of filters and filter actions available for use in the rules you create for policies. Other tasks include checking policy integrity, restoring default policies, and importing/exporting polices for use in other IPSec snap-ins. The following sections cover all these tasks.

Creating a New Policy

Creating a new policy is a wizard-based process that you start by right-clicking the IP Security Policies on Local Machine object and choosing New IP Security Policy from the shortcut menu. The first couple of the wizard's pages simply inform you of the actions the wizard performs and ask you to name the new policy—simple enough. The next page, shown in Figure 8-4, asks whether you want to enable the default response rule for the policy.

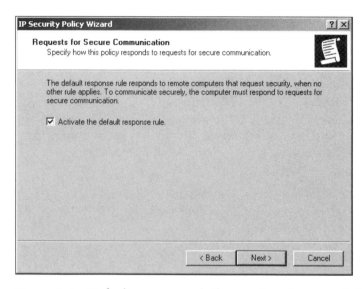

Figure 8-4   Default response rule for a policy gives permission to accept a connection

This default rule basically permits the local computer to accept an IPSec connection from anyone requesting one. Unless you customize the default rule (something discussed a bit later in the chapter), it's probably a good idea not to enable it. It's better to set policies that allow only known hosts to connect. If you choose not to use the default rule, the wizard finishes right then and creates the new policy.

If you do enable the default rule, the wizard next asks you to configure an authentication method for the rule, as shown in Figure 8-5. You can choose any of the three authentication methods (Kerberos, certificates, and pre-shared keys) discussed earlier in the chapter.

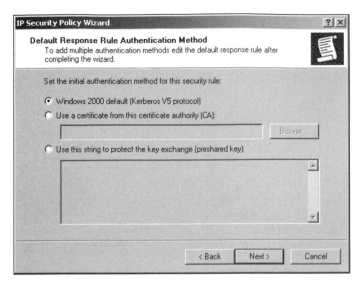

Figure 8-5 Choosing an authentication method for a new rule

Configuring a Policy

Once you create a policy, you can configure it by right-clicking the policy and choosing Properties from the shortcut menu. A policy holds only two property pages, General and Rules, which the following sections discuss. Hands-on Project 8-2 at the end of the chapter gives you a chance to practice configuring a policy.

General Properties

The General page for a policy, shown in Figure 8-6, lets you change the name of the policy and the description. Even though these items only appear in the IPSec snap-in, it's a good idea to create descriptive names that help you identify the policies. The Check for policy changes every x minutes field lets you change the interval at which clients that use this policy check to see if the policy has been updated.

The Advanced button opens the Key Exchange Settings dialog box shown in Figure 8-7. This dialog box lets you control how often the policy requires the communicating computers to regenerate new keys. The default is after about 480 minutes (eight hours), but you can change this to any value you like or configure it to require new keys after a set number of sessions. While the default setting usually works fine, regenerating new keys more often is more secure. You must strike a balance between your need for security and the time consumed generating new keys.

The Methods button displays a list of security methods used to exchange the keys. The Master key Perfect Forward Secrecy option lets you prohibit the reuse of keying material or keys. If you select this option, you may only set the regeneration of keys to occur at timed intervals. The sessions field becomes unavailable.

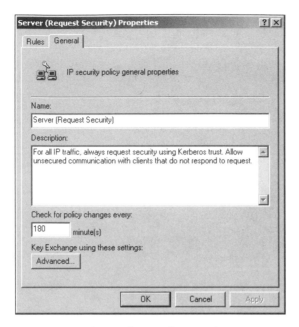

Figure 8-6   General page for a policy

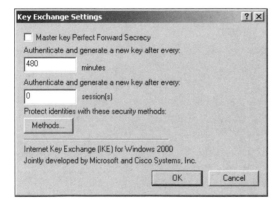

Figure 8-7   Key Exchange Setting dialog box

Rules Properties

You use the Rules page of a policy, shown in Figure 8-8, to define the rules included with that policy. Each rule listed includes the following entries:

- check box to the left of the rule, which specifies whether the rule is actually turned on or off

- Filter List, a list of filters that defines the connections to which a particular rule applies

- Filter Action, determines what happens when a connection meets the criteria set by a filter list

- Authentication Method that the rule uses

- Tunnel Setting, covered later in this chapter

- Connection Type, defines the type of connection to which the rule applies

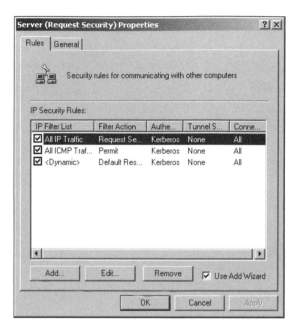

Figure 8-8   Rules page of a policy

You can use the Add button to create a new rule, the Edit button to open the property pages for a rule so that you can configure it, and the Remove button to delete a rule. When you add a new rule, one of two things happens:

- If the Use Add Wizard option is not enabled, the property pages for the new rule open and you can configure it directly.

- If the Use Add Wizard option is enabled, a wizard steps you through the configuration of the rule. Since the wizard really just asks you questions and then fills in the parameters on the property pages for you, we're just going to cover the property pages themselves rather than the wizard. Once you understand the property pages, the wizard will be easy to use. The following sections describe each of the property pages available for a rule.

IP Filter List Properties   The IP Filter page, shown in Figure 8-9, shows all of the filter lists associated with the policy. The list includes all filter lists available on the server, and you simply select one to associate with the rule. You can create new filter lists here using the Add button, this is a topic discussed later in the section, "Managing Filter Lists and Actions." The reason we do not recommend constructing filter lists at the individual policy level is that filter lists apply to all policies and are better managed at that level.

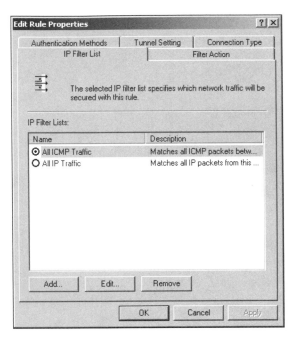

Figure 8-9   IP Filter page of a rule

Filter Action Properties The Filter Action page, shown in Figure 8-10, shows all of the filter actions associated with the policy. This list shows all filter actions available on the server, and you can select any one of them to associate with the rule. As with the Filter Lists page, you can create new filter actions from this page, but we find it more appropriate to create them at the level of the policy instead.

Authentication Methods Properties The Authentication Methods page, shown in Figure 8-11, lets you define one or more authentication methods to use with the rule. If you select more than one, IPSec attempts to use them in the order that they appear on the list. Earlier sections of this chapter discuss the three authentication methods, Kerberos, certificates, and pre-shared keys.

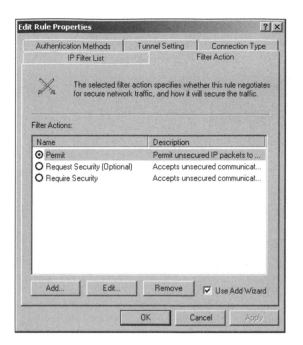

Figure 8-10   Filter Action page of a rule

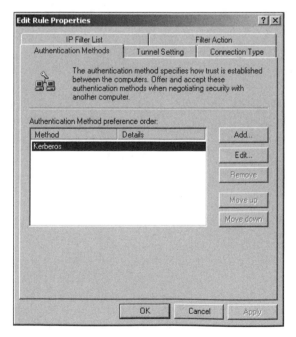

Figure 8-11   Authentication Methods page of a rule

Tunnel Setting Properties You use the Tunnel Setting page, shown in Figure 8-12, to specify whether or not a connection is tunneled. This means that you specify whether connections are tunneled on a per-rule basis. To enable tunneling, select the tunnel option and enter an IP address to serve as the tunnel endpoint.

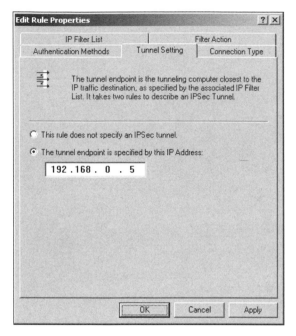

Figure 8-12 Tunnel Setting page of a rule

Of course, setting up a tunnel requires some additional steps. To properly construct a tunnel, you need two tunnel rules on both ends of the tunnel (one for inbound traffic and one for outbound traffic) with the appropriate filter lists and filter actions in place. You need to configure each end as follows:

- Configure an outgoing rule with a filter list that specifies the other end of the tunnel as the tunnel endpoint.

- Configure an incoming rule with a filter for incoming traffic from any subnet from the remote end of the tunnel.

Hands-on Project 8-4 outlines the steps involved in setting up one end of a tunnel.

Connection Type Properties The Connection Type page, shown in Figure 8-13, lets you specify the kind of connections to which the rule applies. Your choices are to have the connection apply to LANs only, remote access connections only, or all network connections (both LAN and remote access).

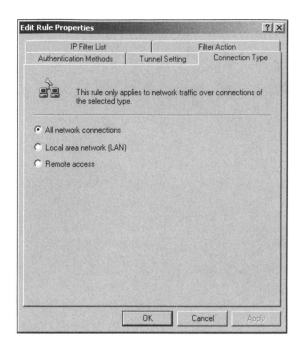

Figure 8-13   Connection Type page of a rule

Managing Filter Lists and Actions

The previous section explained how you can configure filter lists and actions from the Edit Rule Properties dialog box. However, since filter lists and actions are available to all policies creating and managing them at a higher level makes more sense. To do this, right-click the IP Security Policies on Local Machine object and choose the Manage IP Filter Lists and Filter Actions command from the shortcut menu. This opens a dialog box with two pages, Manage IP Filter Lists and Manage Filter Actions, which show you exactly what this dialog box is used for. The following sections discuss each of these pages.

Managing IP Filter Lists

You use the Managing IP Filter Lists page, shown in Figure 8-14, to manage filter lists available to all policies. This list simply shows the filters available for your policies and has nothing to do with the application of those filter lists.

To edit an existing filter list, select the list and click the Edit button. This opens a dialog box similar to the one shown in Figure 8-15. You can also click the Add button to open a blank version of the same dialog box and add a new filter. This dialog box shows a name and description for the filter list, as well as the actual filters in that list.

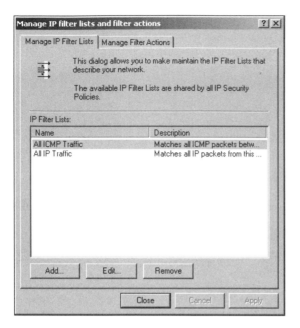

Figure 8-14   Managing IP Filter Lists

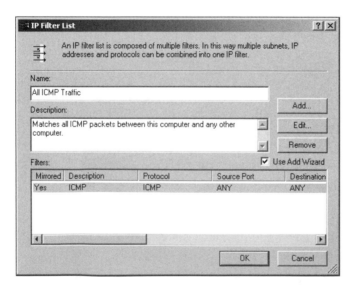

Figure 8-15   Editing filters on a filter list

The same kind of logic applies to creating and configuring individual filters that applies to creating rules. As you learned earlier, selecting a filter and clicking Edit opens the filter's property pages. Clicking Add either opens property pages for a new filter or starts a wizard, if you enabled the Use Add Wizard option. Since the wizard simply fills in the properties for you, the next sections jump right in to the property pages. The Description page has only a single field for entering a free-form description of the filter. The following sections cover the other two pages, Addressing and Protocol.

Addressing Properties   You use the Addressing page, shown in Figure 8-16, to specify the source and destination addresses you want the filter to match. The figure shows a specific IP Subnet selected for the Source address, but you have the following options:

- My IP Address is the address of the IPSec server.

- Any IP Address means that any IP address passes the filter.

- A Specific IP Address displays fields on the page for entering an IP address and subnet mask to use in the filter.

- A Specific IP Subnet also displays fields on the page, but you should only enter a subnet mask for use in the filter.

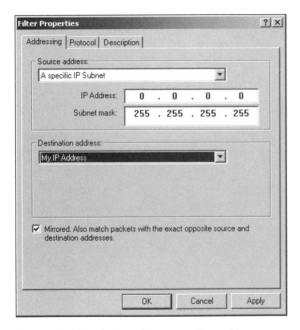

Figure 8-16   Addressing page for a filter

The Destination address presents all of the same options plus an option for specifying a particular DNS name. You use the source and destination addresses in combination in the filter. For example, you might want to create a filter that only matches hosts using the subnet 255.255.255.0 to connect to a specific IPSec server.

The Mirrored option, featured at the bottom of the Addressing page, makes a filter reciprocal. For example, choosing this option for the example in the previous paragraph creates a filter that matches a specific IPSec server connecting to hosts on the subnet 255.255.255.0. This is useful for creating both inbound and outbound filters simultaneously.

Protocol Properties   The Protocols page, shown in Figure 8-17, lets you match traffic being sent or received on a particular port or protocol. For example, you might want to match all ICMP traffic or all TCP traffic coming in over port 80.

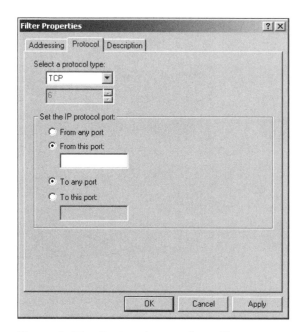

Figure 8-17   Protocols page for a filter

Managing Filter Actions

You use a filter list to match a connection and a filter action to define what happens when a match is made. As you saw when creating rules previously, a filter list and a filter action always work together to produce a desired result. The Manage Filter Actions page, shown in Figure 8-18, defines actions available to policies. By default, you get three actions: permit the connection, request security before allowing the connection, and require security before allowing the connection.

You can use the Edit button to edit properties for a selected action and the Add button either to open blank property dialog boxes or launch a wizard. The General page has only two parameters: they allow you to name and describe the action. The Security Methods page, shown in Figure 8-19, is where all the action happens.

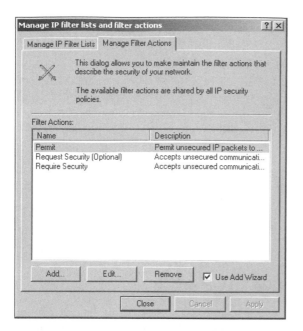

Figure 8-18   Managing Filter Actions

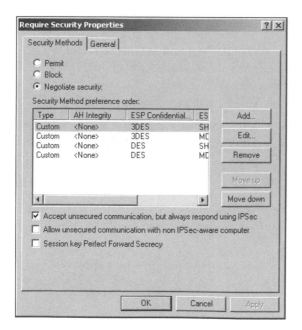

Figure 8-19   Security Methods of an action

This page presents three basic options that the action can perform when a connection matches a filter list: permit the connection with no further intervention, block the connection altogether, or negotiate security for the connection. All of the remaining controls on the page relate to the Negotiate Security option and are unavailable when you select Permit or Block. These controls include:

- *Security Method preference order list*: shows which security methods the connection is allowed to use. You can add new methods or edit existing methods. Methods are attempted starting at the top of the list and working down, so you also have the option of moving methods up and down the list.

- *Accept unsecured communication, but always respond using IPSec* option: sets it up so that incoming requests are always answered by an attempt at an IPSec negotiation. If no IPSec connection can be made, the connection is allowed to proceed anyway.

- *Allow unsecured communication with non IPSec-aware computer*: lets computers not configured with IPSec make the connection anyway.

- *Session key Perfect Forward Secrecy*: prohibits the reuse of keying material.

Applying Policies to the Active Directory

Most of this chapter focuses on applying policies to a local computer, but knowing how to apply policies to the Active Directory is also valuable. First, you must configure the IPSec snap-in to configure default policies for a domain: either the local domain or a remote trusted domain. See Figure 8-1 for a refresher.

For the most part, policy management is exactly the same. You define policies, rules, authentications, filter lists, and filter actions. The difference comes when it is time to attach the policy to a domain or organizational unit within Active Directory. For this, you use the Group Policies snap-in, which you can add to a console in the same way you added the IPSec snap-in. Hands-on Project 8-3 at the end of the chapter outlines the steps for doing this.

IPSec policies must follow the same rules that apply to other objects assigned by group policy. Even though this chapter does not go into detail on Group Policy management, it presents four pretty simple rules to keep in mind:

- A policy applied at the domain level always overrides a policy applied at the local computer level.

- A policy applied to an organizational unit overrides policies applied at the domain level.

- If you have configured a hierarchy of organizational units, policies applied at lower levels in the hierarchy override policies applied at higher levels in the hierarchy.

- If you assign an IPSec policy and then delete the Group Policy object that created the policy, the policy remains in effect. The IPSec policy agent simply figures that the Group Policy object is unavailable and uses a cached version of the policy from the local computer. You must actually unassign the policy before removing the Group Policy object.

MANAGING AND MONITORING IPSEC

Once created and configured, policies have several management options related to them. You already learned how to assign and unassign a policy using the policy shortcut menu. In addition, you can use the shortcut menu to perform the following actions:

- *Check Policy Integrity command*: verifies that any changes you made to policy settings have been properly propagated by Group Policy to the computer accounts in the Group Policy Object (GPO). When you select the command, the IPSec snap-in just returns a dialog stating whether integrity is good or bad.

- *Restore Default Policies command*: restores all predefined default policies to their original state. This does not affect any new policies you create.

- *Import and Export Policies commands*: move policies between consoles so that you may copy policies to different local computers or domains once you create them.

The final tool for monitoring IPSec discussed in this chapter is actually named the IPSec Monitor. This very simple tool allows you to view the active security associations on local and remote computers. To activate the tool, use the Run command on the Start menu and issue the command ipsecmon.exe. If you want to manage a remote computer, you can add the computer's name after the command. Figure 8-20 shows a sample screen from IP Security Monitor.

8

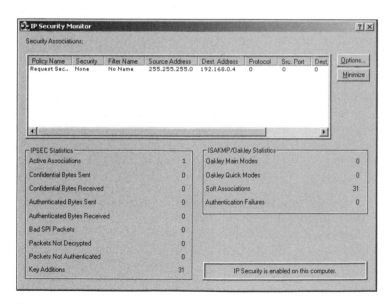

Figure 8-20   IPSec Monitor

There's really not much to configure for this tool. The only commands you can issue within it are to minimize the screen and open an options dialog box that lets you set the interval at which the monitor refreshes itself. The default refresh rate is every 15 seconds. As you can see, the monitor provides a good bit of information about each active security association, including the policy name, security level, filter name, and the source and destination addresses. In addition, the monitor shows you a number of statistics related to IPSec itself and to the IASKMP/Oakley Service.

CHAPTER SUMMARY

- ❏ IP Security (IPSec), an extension of the IP protocol, provides point-to-point authentication and encryption of data being sent between two computers on an IP-based network. Like IP, IPSec works at the Network layer. This means that higher-level protocols and applications in the TCP/IP protocol suite, like FTP, have nothing to do with the encryption process. They carry out their functions normally, passing data down the protocol layers, unaware of whether their data is eventually encrypted or not. Three forms of authentication (Kerberos, certificates, and pre-shared keys) are available to use with IPSec by default.

- ❏ IPSec can operate in two different modes, depending on the scope of the communication. These two modes of operation are transport mode and tunnel mode. In transport mode, two computers configured to use IPSec create a security association between themselves and carry out secure communication. In tunnel mode, an IPSec connection is created between two routers that connect two networks over a transit internetwork. Computers on one network can communicate with computers on the other network without having IPSec configured on the communicating computers.

- ❏ IPSec is actually installed by default on any Windows 2000 computer. All you do to enable it is to create an MMC console using the IP Security Management snap-in and then assign policies to be used. You can also use the snap-in to create and edit new policies. A policy is essentially a set of rules that governs a connection. Each rule is defined with a filter list, which is a list of filters a connection must pass to be considered a match; and a filter action, which is the action taken for any connection that makes the match.

- ❏ Once you create and assign policies, IPSec is ready to go. You can monitor it on a local or remote computer using the IPSec Monitor tool, which displays configured and active connections and a number of IPSec statistics.

KEY TERMS

authentication — A method for validating the identity of a user or a computer. IPSec supports three modes of encryption: Kerberos, certificates, and pre-shared keys.

decrypt — Process of decoding encrypted data.

encrypt — Process of sealing data using a special coding algorithm so that only intended recipients can decrypt and read it.

filter action — Actions assigned to a connection whose properties match an associated list of filters. Typical actions are to accept and block connections or to negotiate security for the connection.

filter list — List of filters assigned to a rule. Connections whose properties match the list of filters have an associated filter action applied to them.

Internet Protocol (IP) — Protocol in the TCP/IP protocol suite responsible for routing data over a network.

IP Security (IPSec) — Extension to the Internet Protocol (IP) used to secure data being sent between two computers on a network.

IPSec client — Computer that initiates the IPSec connection.

IPSec driver — IPSec component that actually encrypts and decrypts data using keys prepared by the ISAKMP/Oakley Service, and sends the data between computers.

IPSec policies — Sets of rules assigned to clients that define how those clients use IPSec.

IPSec policy agent service — IPSec component responsible for retrieving the computer's assigned IPSec policy from the Active Directory.

IPSec server — Computer that responds to an IPSec connection.

ISAKMP/Oakley Service — IPSec component that creates the security association between communicating computers and is also responsible for generating the keys used to encrypt and decrypt the data sent over the IPSec connection.

Kerberos V5 — Default authentication system used by Windows 2000. It is an open standard widely-supported by other operating systems, as well.

pre-shared keys — Passwords entered into each computer communicating with IPSec. As long as both computers are configured with the same pre-shared key, they trust one another.

public key certificates — Provided by a certificate authority. Each end of the IPSec connection uses the other end's public certificate for authentication.

security association — Defines the common security mechanisms, such as keys, that two computers use to create the IPSec connection.

transport mode — Mode in which the two endpoints of IPSec communication are two computers that have IPSec configured. For this mode to work, both computers must use the TCP/IP protocol.

tunnel mode — Mode in which two communicating computers do not use IPSec themselves. Instead, the gateways connecting each client's LAN to the transit network create a virtual tunnel that uses the IPSec protocol to secure all communication that passes through it.

REVIEW QUESTIONS

1. At what level of the OSI networking model does IPSec work?

   a. Application layer

   b. Transport layer

   c. Network layer

   d. Physical layer

2. Which of the following is a responsibility of the IPSec policy agent?

   a. Retrieves policy information from the Active Directory

   b. Generates keys based on defined policies

   c. Oversees the creation of a security association

   d. Encrypts and decrypts data based on security keys

3. Which of the following is *not* an available form of IPSec authentication.

   a. Kerberos

   b. Pre-shared keys

   c. Windows Integrated

   d. Clear Text

   e. Certificates

4. The _____ is the IPSec component responsible for creating the keys used to encrypt and decrypt data.

5. The ISAKMP/Oakley Service is responsible for creating a security association. True or false?

6. Which of the following networking protocols may be used by two computers that communicate between networks configured to use IPSec in tunnel mode?

   a. TCP/IP

   b. IPX/SPX

   c. AppleTalk

   d. All of the above

7. Restarting the IPSec driver is the best way to restart the IPSec Policy Agent. True or false?

8. What must you do to enable IPSec on a local computer?

   a. Install IPSec using the Add/Remove Software Control Panel applet.

   b. Create an IPSec policy using the IPSec snap-in.

   c. Assign an IPSec policy using the IPSec snap-in.

   d. Install the IPSec Policy Agent.

9. Which of the following can you use to verify that IPSec is running on a local computer?

    a. The ipconfig tool

    b. The ipsecmon tool

    c. The tracert tool

    d. All of the above

10. When defining a rule, you must associate a filter list with a filter action. True or false?

11. The _____ protocol is used in conjunction with IPSec to create a Virtual Private Network.

12. You are configuring IPSec in tunnel mode between two remote networks. How many total rules do you need to configure?

    a. 1

    b. 2

    c. 4

    d. 8

13. You use the Perfect Forward Secrecy options available for sessions and rules to make sure that _____.

14. Which of the following filter actions are available by default? (Choose three.)

    a. Permit a connection.

    b. Block a connection.

    c. Request security before allowing the connection.

    d. Require security before allowing the connection.

15. A _____ is a set of rules governing how a client uses IPSec when making a connection.

16. In what order are IPSec policies applied?

    a. Local, domain, then organizational unit

    b. Organizational unit, domain, then local

    c. Domain, local, then organizational unit

    d. Domain, organizational unit, then local

17. In one form of IPSec authentication, _____, identical passwords are entered into each computer communicating with IPSec.

18. Restoring default IPSec policies in the IPSec snap-in deletes any custom policies and restores the original policies to their default configuration. True or false?

8

19. Which of the following is true of IPSec authentication?

   a. It only lets you enable one mode of authentication per rule.

   b. It allows multiple authentications, but always uses Kerberos as the default method.

   c. It allows multiple authentications, but always uses pre-shared keys as the default method.

   d. It prevents you from using Kerberos and certificates together but lets you combine either of these with pre-shared keys.

20. When configuring IPSec in tunnel mode, only DNS names can specify tunnel endpoints. True or false?

HANDS-ON PROJECTS

All Hands-on Projects in this chapter require at least one server computer set up as described in the lab set-up section in the front of this book.

Project 8-1

To enable IPSec on a local computer:

1. Click **Start** and then click **Run**.

2. In the **Run** field, type **mmc** and click **OK**.

3. From the **Console** menu of the Microsoft Management Console, select the **Add/Remove snap-in** command.

4. Click the **Add** button.

5. From the **Available Standalone Snap-Ins** list, select the **IP Security Policy Management** entry and click **Add**.

6. Make sure that the **Local Computer** option is selected, and click **Finish**.

7. Click **Close** to close the **Add Standalone Snap-In** dialog box.

8. Click **OK** to close the **Add/Remove Snap-In** dialog box.

9. In the left pane of the MMC main window, select the **IP Security Policies on Local Machine** object.

10. In the policies list in the right pane, right-click the **Server (Request Security)** policy and select the **Assign** command.

11. Verify that the entry in the Policy Assigned column for that policy changed to **Yes**.

Project 8-2

This project assumes that the MMC console that you created in Hands-on Project 8-1 is still open. If not, you must open or recreate it to proceed.

To configure the properties for a policy:

1. In the left pane of the MMC main window, select the **IP Security Policies on Local Machine** object.

2. In the policies list in the right pane, right-click the **Server (Request Security)** policy and select the **Properties** command.

3. Select the **All IP Traffic** rule, and then click the **Edit** button.

   Note that this rule matches all IP packets from the local computer to any other computer.

4. Click the **Filter Action** tab.

5. Change the default setting **(Request Security)** to **Require Security**.

6. Click the **Edit** button.

7. Disable the **Accept unsecured communication, but always respond using IPSec** option.

8. Click **OK** to return to the **Edit Rule Properties** dialog box.

9. Click the **Authentication Methods** tab.

10. Click the **Add** button.

11. Select the **Use this string to protect the key exchange** option.

12. In the field below the option, type **a password**.

13. Click **OK** to return to the **Edit Rule Properties** dialog box.

14. Click **Close** to return to the Policy property pages.

15. Click **Close** to return to the IPSec snap-in.

Project 8-3

To enable IPSec for an entire domain:

1. Click **Start** and then click **Run**.

2. In the **Run** field, type **mmc.exe**, and click **OK**.

3. From the **Console** menu of the Microsoft Management Console, select the **Add/Remove snap-in** command.

4. Click the **Add** button.

5. From the **Available Standalone Snap-Ins** list, select the **Group Policy** entry and click **Add**. The **Select Group Policy Object** dialog box opens.

6. Click the **Browse** button to open a dialog box that lets you specify a group policy object.

7. Select the **Default Domain Policy** entry, and click **OK**.

8. Click **Finish** to return to the **Add Standalone Snap-In** dialog box.

9. Click the **Close** button to return to the **Add/Remove Snap-In** dialog box.

10. Click the **OK** button to return to the console.

11. Expand the **Default Domain Policy** object in the left pane of the console until you can find and then select the **IP Security Policies on Active Directory** object. The right pane shows available policies in the Active Directory.

12. Right-click the **Server (Request Security)** policy, and select **Assign** from the shortcut menu.

Project 8-4

To create the local end of an IPSec tunnel:

1. Right-click the **IP Security Policies on Local Machine** object, and select the **Create IP Security Policy** command to open the New Policy Wizard.

2. Click **Next** to skip the Welcome window.

3. Enter **a name** for the new policy, and click the **Next** button to continue.

4. On the **Requests For Secure Communications** page, disable the **Activate Default Response Rule** option and click **Next**.

5. On the **Summary** page, make sure the **Edit Properties** button is selected and click **Finish**.

   The property pages for the new policy open.

6. On the **Rules** tab, make sure the **Use Add Wizard** button is enabled and click the **Add** button.

7. Click **Next** to skip the wizard's Welcome window.

8. On the **Tunnel Endpoint** page, select the **Tunnel Endpoint is specified by this IP address** option, enter the **IP address** for the remote tunnel interface on the transit network, and click **Next** to continue.

9. On the **Network Type** page, select the **Local Area Network (LAN)** option and then click **Next**.

10. On the **Authentication Method** page, select the **Windows 2000 Default (Kerberos V5)** option and then click **Next**.

11. On the **IP Filter List** page, select the **All IP Traffic** list and click **Next**.

12. On the **Filter Action** page, select the **Request Security (Optional)** action and click **Next**.

13. Click **Finish** to return to the policy properties dialog box.

14. Click **Close** to return to the IPSec snap-in.

CASE PROJECTS

Case 1

You are the network administrator for a large company based in San Francisco. Your company has just acquired a smaller company in Boston and you have been given the task of joining the two networks. You plan to connect the networks to one another using the Internet. The network in San Francisco is TCP/IP-based and the one in Boston is IPX/SPX-based. Each is connected to the Internet via a router to an Internet Service Provider. You would like to establish a Virtual Private Network between the two networks and secure it using IPSec. Write out a plan for this. Include what mode you would use IPSec in and whether any additional protocols would be needed on the networks.

Case 2

You have now finished planning the IPSec configuration from Case 1 and have enabled IPSec on one server from each network. These servers will be governing the IPSec communications over the routers. Describe the rules you would need to put in place on each end of the connection so that the IPSec configuration is complete.

8

NETWORK ADDRESS TRANSLATION IN WINDOWS 2000

> **After reading this chapter and completing the exercises, you will be able to:**
> - ◆ Explain the differences between Internet Connection Sharing (ICS) and Network Address Translation (NAT)
> - ◆ Describe the address translation process
> - ◆ Install and configure ICS on Windows 2000 Server or Professional
> - ◆ Install and configure NAT on Windows 2000 Server
> - ◆ Monitor and manage NAT

Network Address Translation (NAT) is a protocol that provides a way for multiple computers on a network to share a single connection to the Internet via an Internet Service Provider. In Windows 2000, two different services provide access to this protocol and you choose a particular service based on your networking needs. In typical Microsoft style, the names of these services often generate a bit of confusion.

Internet Connection Sharing (ICS), a service that is easy to configure and manage, offers most of the features of the Network Address Translation protocol. However, you cannot control many ICS features. It's more of a "turn it on and watch it run" service. ICS is available in a number of Microsoft operating systems, including Windows 98 Second Edition, Windows Millennium Edition, Windows 2000 Professional, and Windows 2000 Server (or Advanced Server).

NAT runs only on the Windows 2000 Server family and is implemented as a routing protocol within the Routing and Remote Access Service that you learned about in earlier chapters. While it provides many of the same services as ICS, NAT is much more configurable and offers some added features discussed later in this chapter.

Confusion often arises because one of the implementations of the Network Address Translation protocol is named NAT. This chapter uses the full name "Network Address Translation," to refer to the protocol itself. The abbreviation "NAT" refers to the implementation of the protocol within RRAS. Keep in mind, however, that other literature and the certification exam may refer to the protocol and the service in either way.

This chapter begins with an overview of address translation and the differences between ICS and NAT. From there, the chapter moves on to the actual configuration and management of both these services.

Overview

Until recently, most operating systems did not include a way for more than one computer to use a single connection to the Internet. In a typical setup, a computer was configured to use a dial-up connection (like a modem or ISDN adapter) or a persistent connection (like a DSL line or cable modem) to connect to an Internet Service Provider. If you had more than one computer, say on a small home or office network, you were forced to configure a separate connection for each system or purchase a third-party proxy program to allow those computers to share access.

SOHO is an acronym for Small Office/Home Office. Microsoft regards SOHO networks as the main beneficiaries of ICS and NAT. Though SOHO networks configuration varies a great deal, Microsoft normally considers a SOHO network to have one network segment, use peer-to-peer networking, and support TCP/IP. For larger networks, Microsoft generally recommends a separate product, such as Microsoft Proxy Server, to provide address translation services. In the real world, these definitions really don't mean too much. NAT is often used on large networks quite effectively. However, for the certification exam, you should be aware of the distinctions that Microsoft draws.

With the advent of Windows 98 Second Edition, Microsoft began incorporating a simplified version of the Network Address Translation protocol into the operating system so that no third-party software was required to share Internet connections. They named the service Internet Connection Sharing. Windows Millennium Edition, Windows 2000 Professional, and Windows 2000 Server also come with ICS. In addition, Windows 2000 Server supports the full version of NAT, which offers a good deal more flexibility than ICS.

This overview discusses the Network Address Translation protocol and address sharing in a conceptual fashion. The end of the overview presents the actual differences between these two implementations of the Network Address Translation protocol.

Benefits of Address Sharing

So, why share addresses in the first place? Address sharing really provides three benefits:

- Using address translation instead of routing provides an inherent security benefit. Hosts on the Internet only see the public IP address of the external interface on the computer that provides address translation—not the private IP addresses on the internal network.

- Cost is another big reason to share addresses. It's obviously cheaper to configure one computer with a high-speed Internet connection than to provide one for every computer on your network.

- Simplicity is the third reason to share addresses. Setting up one Internet connection (especially with some of the more complicated connection options out there today) and then sharing that connection is easier than configuring a connection for every computer.

Public and Private Addressing

In Chapter 2, you learned all the gory details of IP addressing, including the different classes of addresses available on the Internet. You also learned that, although you can subnet and supernet your networks in many ways to maximize the efficiency of IP address assignments, only a finite number of IP addresses are available. In addition, the amazing growth of the Internet has greatly strained the capacity of current IP addressing.

In an early attempt to work around this problem, the Internet Network Information Center (InterNIC) and the Internet Assigned Numbers Authority (IANA) designated three network IDs as private networks:

- 10.0.0.0 with a subnet mask of 255.0.0.0. This provides a range of **private addresses** from 10.0.0.1 through 10.255.255.254.

- 172.16.0.0 with a subnet mask of 255.240.0.0. This provides a range of private addresses from 172.16.0.1 through 172.31.255.254.

- 192.168.0.0 with a subnet mask of 255.255.0.0. This provides a range of private addresses from 192.168.0.1 through 192.168.255.254.

No host with any of the addresses in these ranges is ever allowed to transfer information directly to a host on the Internet that has a **public address**. The original intent behind assigning these private address ranges was that they would be used on networks that would not connect to the Internet. You could address your local network, and even subnet it, any way you liked as long as your addresses stayed within the private ranges and did not try to connect to any public hosts.

With NAT, private networks now have a way of transferring information to the Internet, even though they use private addresses. Your ISP only need assign you one public IP address (though NAT can handle multiple public addresses), and NAT translates between the private IP addresses on your network and that public IP address. To the Internet, it looks like you have one host (the NAT server), even though your private network may have dozens of computers hiding behind that host.

How NAT Works

A NAT server is basically an IP router that translates the IP addresses and TCP/UDP port numbers of packets as those packets are forwarded between the public and private interfaces of the NAT server. This section examines the actual NAT process in more detail.

Static and Dynamic Address Mapping

When NAT receives a packet from a private IP address and translates that packet to look as though it comes from the NAT server's public IP address, this process is called "mapping." Two forms of mapping are available in NAT:

- **Dynamic mappings** are created when users on the private network initiate traffic with a public Internet location. The NAT service automatically translates the IP address and source ports, and adds these mappings to its mapping table. The NAT server refreshes these mappings each time they are used. Dynamic mappings that are not refreshed are removed from the NAT mapping table after a certain amount of time. For TCP connections, the default time is 24 hours. For UDP connections, the default time is one minute.

- **Static mappings** define in advance the mapping of certain addresses and ports instead of letting mapping happen automatically. Although you can create static mappings for outbound traffic, the most common reason to use static mapping is if you want to host some form of Internet service (that is, Web server, FTP server, and so forth.) on a private computer. For hosts on the Internet to reach that server, a static mapping must be defined so that the NAT server knows where to route the incoming requests. You cannot host any Internet services on your private network using dynamic mapping.

NAT Editors

For NAT to translate packets directly between a private and public network, two things must be true:

- The packets must have an IP address in the IP header.
- The packets must have either a TCP or UDP port number in the IP header.

While this works fine for the majority of protocols and applications that send IP traffic (since many of them use TCP or UDP), some do not fulfill these requirements. For example, neither FTP nor PPTP uses TCP or UDP, so NAT could not translate them without a little help.

This help comes in the form of a **NAT editor**, an installable component that modifies packets so that NAT can translate them. Windows 2000 includes built-in NAT editors for the following protocols:

- FTP

- Internet Message Control Protocol (ICMP)

- Point-to-Point Tunneling Protocol (PPTP)

- NetBIOS over TCP/IP (NetBT)

In addition to the built-in NAT editors, the NAT protocol in Windows 2000 includes proxy software for the following protocols:

- H.323, a protocol voice and data transmission

- Direct Play, a protocol used in multiplayer gaming

- LDAP-based Internet Locator Service (ILS) registration, a protocol used by NetMeeting

- Remote Procedure Call (RPC)

It is important to note that the NAT protocol does not at this point support either the Kerberos authentication method used in Windows or the IPSec protocol. Chapter 8 discusses both of these protocols.

DHCP Allocator

Both forms of NAT offered by Windows 2000 (ICS and NAT) can automatically assign IP addresses to computers on the private network using a **DHCP Allocator**, a simplified version of a DHCP server. This works well on small networks, as most clients are set up to receive IP addresses automatically by default.

 You can learn more about using DHCP in Chapter 3 and more about configuring it to work with NAT later in this chapter.

When a client starts, it broadcasts a message looking for DHCP allocation; the NAT server assigns it an IP address and subnet mask on the same subnet using a private addressing range. In addition, the NAT server configures the default gateway and DNS server for clients to be the IP address of the NAT server. Note that there is no WINS server allocation.

As you learn later in the chapter, the DHCP Allocator in ICS is enabled by default and cannot be disabled. Although you can assign static addresses to the other computers on the network if you want, the ICS server always responds to DHCP requests. When using NAT on a Windows 2000 Server, you can disable the DHCP Allocator and either assign static addresses from the NAT server or let another DHCP Server on the network handle requests.

Host Name Resolution

When using the DHCP Allocator, clients are configured to use the NAT server as their primary DNS server. This allows both local and remote host names to be resolved. **DNS proxying** is used to resolve remote host names on the Internet. In this process, a client submits a name resolution request to the NAT server. The NAT server then queries the DNS server specified in its own configuration for the resolution. When it receives a response, it forwards that response to the originating client.

Differences Between NAT and ICS

Since both ICS and NAT use the same protocol to translate addresses, this overview features a combined discussion of their similar features. Table 9-1 shows how each service implements the NAT protocol differently.

Table 9-1   Differences between ICS and NAT

ICS	NAT
Available on Windows 98 Second Edition, Windows Millennium Edition, Windows 2000 Professional, and the Windows 2000 Server family	Available only on the Windows 2000 Server family
Configured in Windows 2000 by checking a single option on the Sharing page of a network adapter	Requires you to use the Routing and Remote Access snap-in for installation and management; provides a lot more configuration options
Allows only one public IP address	Can expose any number of public addresses
Links only one private network to a public network	Can link many private networks
Does not allow you to disable the DHCP Allocator or the DNS Proxy	Allows you to disable the DHCP Allocator or the DNS Proxy, so ICS cannot be used on a network already using a DHCP Server or DHCP Relay Agent

INSTALLING AND CONFIGURING INTERNET CONNECTION SHARING

Installing and configuring ICS is actually one of the simplest things you do in Windows. As you learned previously, though, this ease comes at the price of a good deal of flexibility. ICS is primarily for users with a small home or office network on a single network segment and a single Internet connection to share. In addition, unless you run Windows 2000 Server on the computer with the Internet connection, ICS is your only choice.

This chapter focuses on using ICS in Windows 2000. Though ICS is available in Windows 98 Second Edition and Windows Millennium Edition, the configuration differs a good deal from the configuration in Windows 2000 and gives you even less control than Windows 2000. Also, the certification exam includes only the Windows 2000 version.

Installing the ICS service

You must meet only a couple of requirements before enabling ICS. First, you must make sure that the computer on which you plan to enable it (called the ICS computer from now on) actually has a functioning Internet connection, whether that connection is a 56 KB modem, cable modem, or some other type. Second, you must make sure that you have a network adapter installed in the ICS computer, that the adapter is configured and functioning properly, and that it connects properly to the other computers on the network.

When you meet these requirements, you are ready to install ICS. Hands-on Project 9-1 at the end of the chapter outlines the steps for installing ICS, but all you really need to do is open the properties dialog box for the Internet connection. (You can find it in the Network and Dial-up Connections container in the Control Panel.) Click the Sharing page, shown in Figure 9-1, and select the Enable Internet Connection Sharing for this connection option. If you want the connection to start automatically whenever other computers need to connect to the Internet (and you probably do), also select the Enable on-demand dialing option.

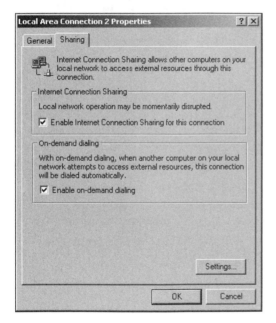

Figure 9-1   Sharing a connection with ICS

When you install ICS, several changes take place. These include:

- The network adapter in the ICS computer is assigned the IP address 192.168.0.1 and the subnet mask 255.255.255.0. If you recall from earlier in the chapter, this is the first address in one of the private addressing ranges.

- The ICS service starts and is configured to start automatically each time the computer starts. You can change this behavior, as well as stop and start the service manually, using the Services Control Panel.

- The DHCP Allocator service starts and is configured to start automatically with Windows. The allocator dynamically assigns IP addresses to other clients on the network using the IP address range 192.168.0.2 through 192.168.0.254 and the subnet mask 255.255.255.0.

Once the ICS computer is configured, you only need to ensure that all other computers on the network are configured to obtain IP addresses automatically and everything should work just fine.

Configuring ICS

With ICS enabled, configuring also takes place from the Sharing page of the adapter's properties dialog box, shown in Figure 9-1. The Settings button becomes available, and clicking it opens a dialog box that lets you configure two groups of settings that determine what entries are preloaded in the NAT mappings table on the ICS computer. Two property pages, Applications and Services, represent these groups of settings, which the next two sections discuss.

Applications Properties

The Applications page, shown in Figure 9-2, controls static outbound mappings. You use these mappings to create predefined routings for Internet services that you want users to be able to access. Normally, you do not need to worry about configuring these routings but might need to if a user's application must use a specific port number or make additional associated connections.

To add a mapping, just click the Add button to open the Internet Connection Sharing Application dialog box shown in Figure 9-3. In this dialog box, fill in the Name of application (name it anything you like), the Remote server port number and type (TCP or UDP), and the Incoming response ports that servers use to send information back to the client.

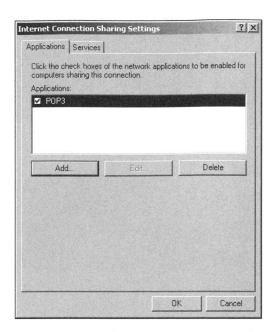

Figure 9-2   Applications property page for ICS setting

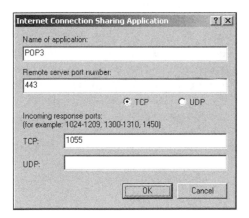

Figure 9-3   Adding an application mapping in ICS

Services Properties

The Services page, shown in Figure 9-4, lets you control static inbound mappings. You use this feature to allow hosts on the Internet to access certain resources on the private network. Six of the most common service types are listed (but not enabled) on the page: FTP, IMAP3, IMAP4, SMTP, POP3, and TELNET.

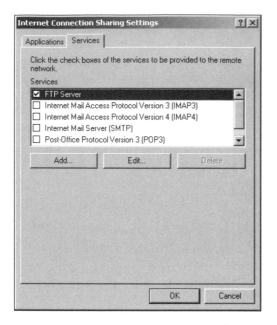

Figure 9-4   Services property page for ICS settings

To enable a service for inbound connections, first turn it on by checking the box next to the service. Then, click the Edit button to open the Internet Connection Sharing Service dialog box shown in Figure 9-5. Note that most options are dimmed, including the Name of service, the Service port number, and the type of port. This is because these services must use the ports commonly associated with the protocols, so that outside applications can access the service without special configuration. The one setting you need to change is the name or the address of the server on the private network that hosts the service. For example, you might have a specific server dedicated to handling POP3 mail.

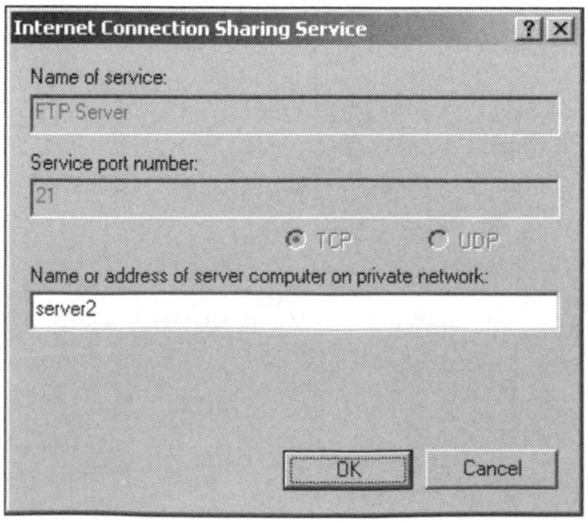

Figure 9-5   Enabling a service for an inbound connection

Adding a new service (using the Add button shown in Figure 9-4) uses the same dialog as editing a predefined service (Figure 9-5), but you need to enter a name and port settings in addition to a server name.

INSTALLING AND CONFIGURING NETWORK ADDRESS TRANSLATION

The NAT protocol offers much more potential for configuration than you just saw in its ICS implementation. If you run Windows 2000 Server or Advanced Server, you can implement NAT in its full glory by installing it as a routing protocol in the Routing and Remote Access snap-in. This, of course, requires that the Routing and Remote Access Server service is enabled on the server.

As with ICS, you must meet some preliminary requirements before installing NAT. First, you need to make sure that your Internet connection (or connections, since NAT supports multiple public interfaces) works. Next, you need to make sure that any adapters connected to internal networks are configured properly.

Installing the NAT Service

Once you take care of the preliminary requirements, it's time to install NAT. If you have not already configured RRAS for remote access or routing (Chapters 6 and 7 focus on these procedures), a simple wizard can guide you through the process of setting up RRAS with NAT enabled and configured for Internet sharing. Alternately, you can disable RRAS and re-enable it to remove all current settings and launch the wizard again.

If you already set up and configured RRAS and now want to add support for NAT, you do so by first ensuring that your server supports routing and then installing NAT as a routing protocol in the RRAS snap-in. Once you do this, you then add the NAT protocol to the interfaces you want to use and configure the protocol and interfaces for use. This section discusses both of these procedures.

Installing NAT Along with RRAS

If you recall from Chapters 6 and 7, RRAS is actually installed by default along with Windows 2000 Server but left disabled. You just have to enable it. This section provides an overview of the set-up process and the choices you make.

First, you must log on to the server with Administrator privileges and open the Routing and Remote Access utility from the Administrative Tools program group on the Start menu. Figure 9-6 shows this utility, which is actually a snap-in for the Microsoft Management Console used to control most management features of Windows 2000.

9

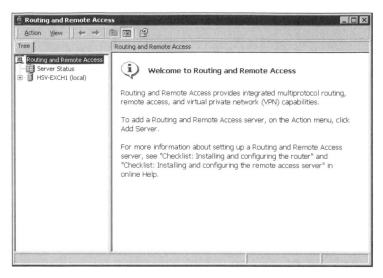

Figure 9-6   RRAS snap-in

In the tree in the left pane, find and right-click the name of the server. From the shortcut menu that appears, choose the Configure and Enable Routing and Remote Access command to begin the Routing and Remote Access Server Setup Wizard. The setup wizard takes you through several configuration steps. The first asks you to select the type of configuration you want to install. Figure 9-7 shows this screen. Choose the Internet connection server option. For details on some of the other options, see Chapter 6.

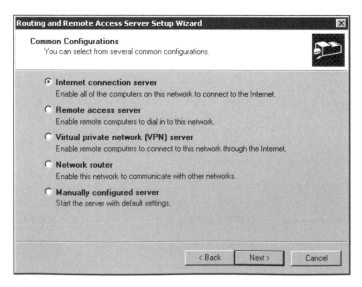

Figure 9-7   Installing RRAS as an Internet connection server

Next, the wizard asks whether you want to set up ICS or NAT. If you select ICS, a dialog box opens, telling you to use the Network and Dial-Up Connections folder to configure ICS. You do this following the procedures outlined earlier in this chapter. To set up a NAT server, of course, you must choose the NAT option.

In the next step, the wizard asks you to choose the Internet connection that you want to share, as shown in Figure 9-8. You can choose a connection from the list (you can always set up additional connections later), or you can create a new demand-dial connection. If you choose an existing connection, just pick one from the list and click Next. If you choose to create a demand-dial connection, the Demand Dial Interface Wizard opens and allows you to configure the interface before proceeding. Chapter 7 details how to set up a demand-dial interface with this wizard.

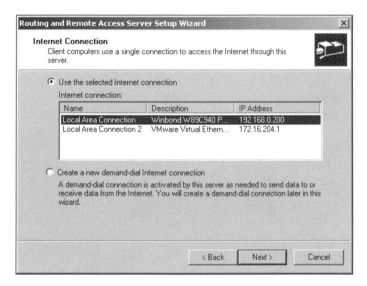

Figure 9-8   Choosing a connection to share in the RRAS Setup Wizard

Once you finish this screen, the wizard closes and the NAT server is set up. You are ready to configure the protocol or set up any additional interfaces using the RRAS snap-in. This chapter covers these procedures a bit later.

Installing NAT on an Existing RRAS Server

If you already enabled RRAS to provide remote access or routing functions, installing the NAT protocol is simple. Hands-on Project 9-2 at the end of the chapter outlines the actual steps involved. Once you install the protocol, you are ready to set up interfaces and configure other NAT properties.

Configuring NAT Interfaces

In earlier chapters you learned that, when working with RRAS, you must actually install and configure an interface in the RRAS snap-in before RRAS can utilize the actual network interface that the RRAS interface represents. NAT is no different. Before you can use NAT on your network, you must make sure that a **NAT interface** exists both for any interfaces on your local network and any interfaces on the public network. Following one simple rule when setting up your interfaces is best: create the interfaces for the local network first and the public network second.

Adding a NAT Interface

Adding an interface is a straightforward procedure that simply involves right-clicking the Network Address Translation container in RRAS, choosing a New Interface command, and then selecting the appropriate network adapter for which to create the interface. Hands-on Project 9-3 at the end of the chapter outlines the actual steps involved in creating a public interface. Creating a private interface follows the same procedure. Right after you create the interface, a set of property pages for the interface opens so that you can provide further configuration information. You can also open these pages later by right-clicking the interface object (shown in Figure 9-9) and choosing Properties from the shortcut menu.

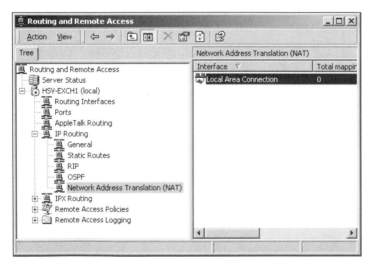

Figure 9-9   NAT Interface object in RRAS

Configuring NAT Interface Properties

Each NAT interface has its own set of property pages that is individually configurable. The three property pages for a public NAT interface are General, Address Pool, and Special Ports. The next few sections discuss each of these. The only available page for a private NAT interface is General, which is identical to the General page for the public interface.

General Properties The General page, shown in Figure 9-10, lets you choose the type of interface. You have two choices. The first is to create an interface connected to the private network. The second choice is to create an interface connected to the public network. The Translate TCP/UDP headers option controls whether the built-in NAT editors (discussed earlier in the chapter) are functional. You should always turn this on if you want computers on the private network to communicate with the outside world.

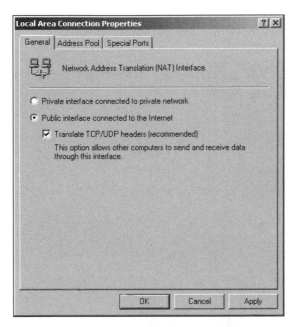

Figure 9-10   General property page of a NAT public interface

Address Pool Properties You use the Address Pool page, shown in Figure 9-11, to control the public IP addresses associated with the interface. The window lists any ranges of addresses you specified. To create a new range, click the Add button and supply the starting and ending IP addresses and the subnet mask for the range. To specify a single IP address, just enter it as the starting address and leave out the ending address.

The Reservations button lets you reserve individual IP addresses from the public range and add static mappings in the NAT table that point to particular hosts on your private network. In other words, this gives you a way to let a specific computer on your private network have a static IP address exposed to the public interface. This allows you, for example, to create a Web server and register a domain name for that Web server using the public IP address.

Special Ports Properties The Special Ports page, shown in Figure 9-12, provides another way to edit the NAT mapping table; it allows you to specify to which ports inbound traffic should map. For example, you could set it up to route all incoming traffic on port 110 (the POP3 common port) to a specific port number on a specific host on the private network—a POP3 server, most likely.

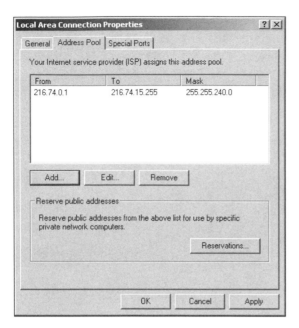

Figure 9-11   Address Pool property page of a NAT public interface

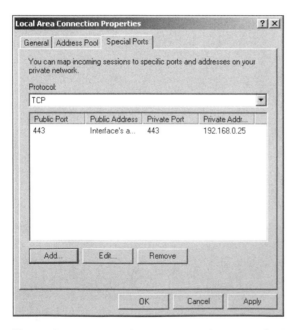

Figure 9-12   Special Ports property page of a NAT public interface

For each protocol listed in the Protocol drop-down menu, you can specify any number of public port numbers that you want channeled to special private hosts. Just select the protocol and then use the Add button to open the Edit Special Port dialog box shown in Figure 9-13.

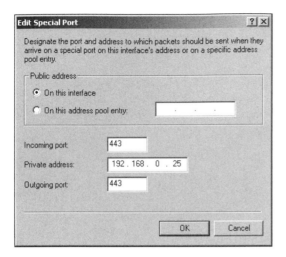

Figure 9-13   Editing a special port

This dialog box sports four controls:

- *Public Address*: controls what public address can receive traffic for the port. Choose the On this interface option (the default choice) to accept traffic on the specified port for all public IP addresses in the address pool. Choose the On this address pool entry option to specify only a specific IP address.

- *Incoming port*: specifies the port number that public hosts use to contact the service.

- *Private address*: specifies the server to which the incoming traffic should be routed.

- *Outgoing port*: specifies the port used for outbound traffic generated by hosts on the private network.

Configuring NAT Properties

In addition to setting up and configuring the individual NAT interfaces, you can set a number of global parameters for the NAT protocol itself. You can access these parameters by right-clicking the Network Address Translation container in the RRAS snap-in, shown in Figure 9-9, and choosing Properties from the shortcut menu. The four property pages for the NAT protocol are General, Translation, Address Assignment, and Name Resolution. The following sections cover each of these.

General Properties

You use the General page, shown in Figure 9-14, only to configure the level of event logging that the NAT protocol sends to the Windows 2000 system event log. The default is to log only errors, but higher levels of logging may be useful in troubleshooting problems with the protocol. You can learn more about the specific levels of logging in Chapter 6.

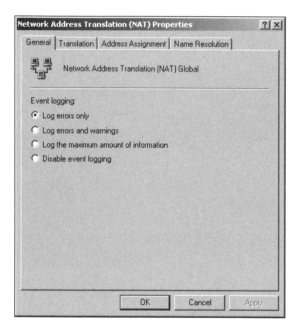

Figure 9-14   General property page of NAT Properties

Translation Properties

The Translation page, shown in Figure 9-15, lets you set the lifetime for both TCP and UDP mappings in the NAT table. The defaults are to keep TCP entries for 24 hours and to keep UDP entries for one minute; for most applications, these defaults work just fine. The Applications button opens a separate dialog box that lets you add, remove, and edit application mappings. This dialog works the same as the Applications page described for editing ICS properties earlier in the chapter and illustrated in Figure 9-2.

Address Assignment Properties

The Address Assignment page, shown in Figure 9-16, controls whether the DHCP Allocator is used or not. With this option enabled, you can specify the range of addresses the allocator can assign by entering a starting IP address and a subnet mask. By default, the same range used by ICS is used: 192.168.0.1 through 192.168.0.254. Use the Exclude button to specify IP addresses within the range that the allocator should not assign.

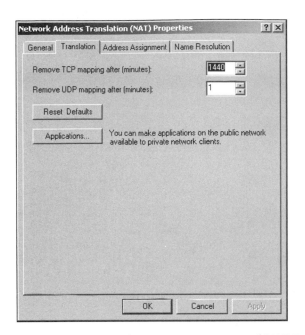

Figure 9-15   Translation property page of NAT Properties

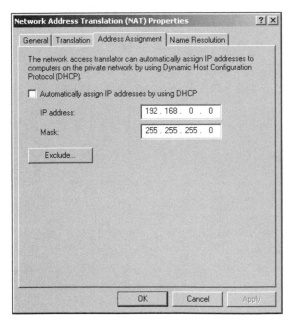

Figure 9-16   Address Assignment property page of NAT Properties

If you have no other form of DHCP service on your network and you do not check the option on the Address Assignment page for the NAT protocol, NAT does not work. This is something to look out for on the certification exam and in the real world.

Name Resolution Properties

The Name Resolution page, shown in Figure 9-17, controls whether the NAT server should resolve DNS names to IP addresses for connecting clients. Enabling the Clients using Domain Name System (DNS) option activates the name resolution component of NAT and specifies the NAT server as the default DNS server for clients on the private network via the DHCP Allocator. With the option disabled, another DNS solution must be present on the network. The other option on this page, Connect to the public network when a name needs to be resolved, specifies whether a demand-dial interface is invoked just to resolve a DNS name.

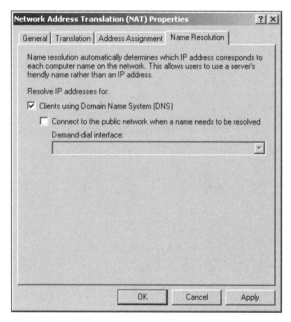

Figure 9-17 Name Resolution property page of NAT Properties

CHAPTER SUMMARY

- ❏ The Network Address Translation protocol provides a way for multiple computers on a network to share a single connection to the Internet via an Internet Service Provider. In Windows 2000, this protocol comes in two flavors: ICS, a simplified version of the Network Address Translation protocol that is easy to configure and manage; and NAT, a full version of the protocol that is more flexible but also more difficult to set up and only available on Windows 2000 Server.

❒ A NAT server is basically an IP router that maps the IP addresses and TCP/UDP port numbers of packets as those packets are forwarded between the public and private interfaces of the NAT server. Two forms of mapping are available in NAT. Dynamic mappings are created when users on the private network initiate traffic with a public Internet location. Static mappings define in advance the mapping of certain addresses and ports instead of letting it happen automatically. Static mappings are required for hosting any services on the private network that will be available to the Internet.

❒ You install ICS using a single check box on the Sharing property page of an Internet connection's properties. You can configure whether demand-dialing should be used and specify some limited application and port mapping for ICS, but that's about it for configuration. NAT is installed (on Windows 2000 Server only) as a routing protocol within the RRAS snap-in. After you install the protocol, you must create and configure any public and private interfaces you want the NAT protocol to use. You can also configure a number of properties for the protocol itself. Aside from being a good bit more configurable than ICS, NAT offers other advantages over ICS as well. These include the ability to control the DHCP Allocator and DNS Proxy (they are always on in ICS) and the fact that NAT can maintain multiple public IP addresses while ICS can only maintain one.

9

KEY TERMS

DHCP Allocator — Simplified version of a DHCP server used by NAT to assign IP addressing information automatically to clients on the private network.

DNS proxying — Method of relaying DNS name resolution requests from clients on a private network through the NAT server to a DNS server on the Internet.

dynamic mappings — Created when users on the private network initiate traffic with a public Internet location. The NAT service automatically translates the IP address and source ports and adds these mappings to its mapping table.

Internet Connection Sharing (ICS) — Simplified version of the NAT protocol that is easy to configure and manage and is available in Windows 98, Windows Millennium Edition, Windows 2000 Server, and Windows 2000 Professional. ICS is not as configurable as NAT.

NAT editor — Installable component that modifies packets so NAT can translate them. Windows 2000 includes built-in NAT editors for protocols, including FTP, ICMP, PPTP, and NetBT.

NAT interface — Virtual interface in the RRAS snap-in that represents an actual private or public network interface on the NAT server.

Network Address Translation (NAT) — Protocol that provides a way for multiple computers on a network to share a single connection to the Internet via an Internet Service Provider. NAT also refers to the full implementation of the protocol within the Routing and Remote Access Service in Windows 2000 Server.

private address — Any address belonging to one of the three ranges of IP addresses designated as private by Internet authorities. A host with a private address may only communicate with hosts on the Internet through a service such as NAT.

public address — Any address not belonging to one of the three ranges of IP addresses designated as private by Internet authorities.

SOHO — Acronym that stands for Small Office/Home Office. SOHO networks are considered the main beneficiaries of ICS and NAT. Though they vary a great deal in configuration, a SOHO network, as defined by Microsoft, has one network segment, uses peer-to-peer networking, and supports TCP/IP.

static mappings — Define in advance how to map certain addresses and ports instead of letting mapping happen automatically. Although you can create static mappings for outbound traffic, the most common reason to use a static mapping is to host some form of Internet service (that is, Web server, FTP server, and so forth.) on a private computer.

REVIEW QUESTIONS

1. On which of the following operating systems can the NAT protocol run?

   a. Windows 98 Second Edition

   b. Windows Millennium Edition

   c. Windows 2000 Professional

   d. Windows 2000 Server

2. Which of the following does *not* happen when you install ICS?

   a. local network adapter's IP address is reconfigured.

   b. DHCP Allocator is enabled.

   c. Internet connection is configured automatically.

   d. ICS service is configured to start automatically when Windows starts.

3. NAT must maintain mapping tables that link which of the following?

   a. Source port and address with the destination port and address

   b. Source port and address with the destination port and address of the NAT server

   c. Source port and NAT server address with the destination port and address

   d. Source port and address with the destination address and NAT server port

4. The _____ is the NAT component responsible for assigning IP addresses to local clients on the private network.

5. The ICS service assigns IP addresses ranging from 192.168.0.1 through 192.168.0.254 by default, but you can change this range if you want. True or false?

6. Which of the following protocols does not work over a NAT connection?

   a. TCP/IP

   b. IPSec

   c. FTP

   d. PPTP

7. You cannot disable the DNS proxy in NAT. True or false?

8. Which of the following must you specify when defining a NAT special port? Choose all that apply.

   a. Public address to receive traffic for the port

   b. Port numbers used for inbound and outbound traffic

   c. Private IP address that receives traffic on the special port

   d. Subnet mask used for the port

9. If you are using a modem rather than a dedicated link to the Internet, which option must you enable?

   a. ICS automatic dialing

   b. On-demand dialing

   c. Automatic dialing

   d. Dynamic linking

10. RRAS can act as a NAT server and a remote access server simultaneously. True or false?

11. A _____ is used to support the translation of traffic generated by protocols or applications that do not use TCP or UDP.

12. For what is the Translation property page of the NAT protocol used?

   a. To create application-specific port mappings

   b. To specify which NAT editor to use

   c. To create port mappings for individual hosts

   d. To specify which port filters to apply

13. To allow a host on your private network to act as a Web server accessible from the Internet, you must configure a _____.

14. You must decide whether to use NAT or ICS on your small office network. You want to choose the simplest service to set up and manage, but you do need to run an FTP server inside your private network and make it accessible to users on the Internet. Which service would you choose?

15. A _____ is an automatic translation of IP addresses and source ports performed by the NAT protocol when users on the private network initiate traffic with a public Internet location.

16. You have a small network with two network segments and want to keep different subnet addresses for them. How do you do this?

   a. Add NAT interfaces for both networks.

   b. Disable the DHCP Allocator.

   c. Define two static address pools with the subnets you want to use.

   d. Manually assign IP addresses to the server's internal interfaces.

17. You use the _____ property page of the NAT interface to choose whether it is a public or private interface.

18. You can use ICS only with demand-dial connections. To use a dedicated Internet connection, you must configure NAT. True or false?

19. Which of the following IP addresses are private addresses?

    a. 10.35.202.1

    b. 172.16.18.2

    c. 172.101.201.44

    d. 192.168.201.1

20. Remote Procedure Calls can be used over NAT. True or false?

HANDS-ON PROJECTS

All Hands-on Projects in this chapter require at least one server computer set up as described in the lab set-up section in the front of this book.

Project 9-1

To install Internet Connection Sharing, you must log on to the local computer under an account with Administrator privileges.

To install ICS on a local computer:

1. Click **Start**, point to **Settings**, and then click **Network and Dial-up Connections**.

2. Right-click the icon for the adapter that represents your Internet connection, and select the **Properties** command.

3. Click the **Sharing** tab to switch to that page.

4. Select the **Enable Internet Connection Sharing For This Computer** option.

5. Select the **Enable On-Demand Dialing** option.

6. Click the **OK** button.

7. A dialog box appears, warning you that the IP address of the adapter will change if you continue. Click **Yes** to finish the installation.

Project 9-2

To install NAT on an existing RRAS Server:

1. Click **Start**, point to **Programs**, point to **Administrative Tools**, and then select **Routing and Remote Access**.

2. Find the server you want to configure in the left pane, and expand it.

3. Inside the **IP Routing** container for the server, right-click the **General** container and select the **New Routing Protocol** command from the shortcut menu.

4. In the **New Routing Protocol** dialog box that opens, select the **Network Address Translation** item from the list of routing protocols and click **OK**. The **IP Routing** container should now contain a new object named **Network Address Translation**.

Project 9-3

To add and configure a public NAT interface:

1. Click **Start**, point to **Programs**, point to **Administrative Tools**, and then select **Routing and Remote Access**.

2. Find the server you want to configure in the left pane, and expand it.

3. Inside the **IP Routing** container for the server, right-click the **Network Address Translation** container and select the **New Interface** command from the shortcut menu.

4. In the **New Interface for Network Address Translation** dialog box, select the adapter you want to use for the interface from the list and click **OK**.

5. The **Network Address Translation Properties** dialog box appears. On the **General** page, select the **Public interface connected to the Internet** option and click **OK**.

9

CASE PROJECTS

Case 1

Your small network consists of two subnets. You configured one subnet with the network ID 192.168.0.0 and the other with the network ID 192.168.1.0. A computer running Windows 2000 Server and configured with RRAS serves as a router between the two networks. All computers on both network segments are configured with static IP addressing. You just installed a DSL line and successfully established an Internet connection from the Windows 2000 Server. Describe the steps you must take in order to share that Internet connection with both network segments.

Case 2

You provide consulting services for a small company with a single network segment and 12 computers, all running Windows 2000 Professional. You just helped the company install a cable modem, and the owner wants all computers on the network to have access to the connection. The owner has read about NAT and is convinced that he needs to install a Windows 2000 Server computer and configure it with RRAS. His main reason: he and a few employees want to connect to the network from home using Virtual Private Networking. Write an explanation detailing why ICS would meet his needs and why it would be preferable over NAT.

CHAPTER 10

CONFIGURING CERTIFICATE SERVICES

After reading this chapter and completing the exercises, you will be able to:

♦ Describe the components of a public key infrastructure
♦ Explain the public/private key encryption process
♦ Explain the use of certificates
♦ Install and configure Microsoft Certificate Server
♦ Issue, manage, and revoke certificates
♦ Remove EFS recovery keys

Windows 2000 incorporates many industry-standard methods of securing data and other network resources. You read about many of these methods, such as IP Security and remote access authentication, throughout this book. Windows 2000 also incorporates a component named **Microsoft Certificate Server (MCS)** as part of a system to help ensure the accuracy and privacy of data as it is transferred over the network.

This chapter begins with an overview of concepts such as keys and certificates and looks at how Windows 2000 implements those concepts. Following the overview, the chapter turns to the actual installation of Microsoft Certificate Server and the management of digital certificates.

CERTIFICATE SERVICES OVERVIEW

Traditionally, security on company networks has been largely a matter of restricting access to the network to authorized users, ensuring the proper assignment of permissions to users of network resources, and if the company network connected to a public network like the Internet, making sure that a good firewall kept out all the bad guys.

Certificates and public key encryption were originally designed for use on the Internet. Encryption keys were handed out between Web servers and from Web servers to clients using certificates or cookies. These keys were used primarily to give the client some assurance that the server was a trusted source for data. However, the trends toward requiring increasing levels of security while at the same time requiring greater scalability and exposure to the Internet led to the incorporation of certificate services on many private networks.

To meet these needs, Windows 2000 implements security using a technology called **public key infrastructure (PKI)**. While its name makes it sound complicated, a PKI is really just a system of components working together to verify the identity of users who transfer data on a system and to encrypt that data if needed. In fact, PKI is still an emerging standard, so you'll likely find that many systems incorporate a rather loose version of it. You learn about the components of PKI throughout this overview and then put them to work later in the chapter.

Certificate-based security is a complicated subject, and we do our best to explain it in the most straightforward manner in this chapter. It's helpful to keep in mind that no matter how complicated the system becomes, security is basically about two things: authentication and privacy. Authentication provides a way to let users know that the information they receive is really from the person or service that they think it is from and a way to ensure that the information has not been altered in some way since it left its source. Privacy is a means of securing the data through encryption while it is en route from source to destination. This ensures that, even if the data is intercepted, those who intercept it cannot read it.

Security Keys

In its early days (and in some systems today), encryption used a single key both to encrypt and decrypt data. Sometimes this key was a server-generated numerical sequence, but it was often a simple password shared with both the encrypting and decrypting parties beforehand. In fact, this type of key is referred to as a **pre-shared key**.

While this method did work, it was wrought with security and administration problems. It required a secure method of distributing keys and a way to keep them safe. Changing the keys frequently was also necessary to ensure security, and many applications did not lend themselves easily to this endeavor.

A method of encryption called **public key encryption** addressed the shortcomings of the pre-shared key method. This method employs two separate keys—a **public key** available to everyone on a system and a **private key** kept secret and available only to the person who holds the key. PKI uses a number of public key encryption algorithms, the most common of which is the **Rivest–Shamir–Adleman (RSA) algorithm**.

The public-key system provides two capabilities:

- Users can sign data digitally so that the recipient of the data can verify the authenticity of both the sender and the data. During this process, the sender uses her own private signing key to sign the data. The signing process does not encrypt the data in any way. The recipient uses the sender's public signing key to verify the digital signature. The message is valid if the public and private signing keys correspond to one another.

- Users can also encrypt data for secure transfer. During this process, the sender uses the recipient's public key to encrypt the data, and the recipient uses her own private key to decrypt the data.

Certificates

While the public-key encryption method is highly secure, a piece is still missing. How do you know that the public key is valid? The answer to this question comes in the form of a certificate. You can think of a **certificate** as a message of authenticity associated with a public key and coming from a trusted source. It's like getting a public key notarized. Certificates allow verification of the claim that a given public key actually belongs to a given individual. This helps prevent an impersonator from using a phony key.

In Recommendation X.509, the International Telecommunications Union (ITU) defines the most widely used format for certificates. An **X.509 certificate** contains not only the public key, but also information identifying the user and the organization that issued the certificate. This information includes the certificate's serial number, validity period, issuer name, and issuer signature.

10

Certificate Authorities

The issuer of a certificate is called a **Certificate Authority (CA)**. The CA is any trusted source willing to verify the identities of the people to whom it issues certificates and to associate those people with certain public and private keys. Because anyone can become a CA, certificates are only as trustworthy as the CA that issues them.

A CA issues certificates in response to a request to do so and based on the CA's policy for issuance. CAs can issue certificates to end users and computers and to other CAs. A CA accepts a certificate request, verifies the requester's information according to the policy for the CA, and then uses its own private key to sign the certificate digitally. The CA then issues the certificate to the subject (end user or other CA) of the certificate.

A third party, like VeriSign, can provide a CA, or you can set up your own CA for use in your organization. Windows 2000 provides the Microsoft Certificate Server (MCS) component for setting up a CA.

There are two different classes of CAs, and each type can operate in a number of different roles. The following sections discuss the types and roles of CAs.

Classes of CAs

MCS includes two policy modules that permit two different classes of CAs: Enterprise CAs and Stand-alone CAs. The policy modules define what actions a CA can take when it receives a certificate request.

The Enterprise CA   The **Enterprise CA** acts as a CA for an enterprise, so it should come as no surprise that this type of CA requires access to the Active Directory. The Active Directory does not, however, need to be installed on the same server functioning as the CA. Enterprise CAs have a number of special features:

- All users and computers in the same domain always trust the Enterprise CA.

- Users and computers can use certificates issued by an Enterprise CA to log on to Windows 2000 domains using smartcards.

- Enterprise CAs publish certificates and **Certificate Revocation Lists (CRL)** in the Active Directory so that the information is available throughout the enterprise.

- Enterprise CAs use certificate types and templates stored in the Active Directory (and discussed a bit later in the chapter) to construct new certificates.

- Enterprise CAs always approve or reject a certificate request immediately and never mark a request as pending. The CA makes the decision based on the security permissions on the security template and on permissions and group memberships in the Active Directory.

The Stand-Alone CA   The **Stand-alone CA** issues certificates to users outside the enterprise and does not require Active Directory access. For example, you might use a stand-alone CA to issue certificates to Internet users who access your company's Web site. Unlike Enterprise CAs, Stand-alone CAs typically mark incoming certificate requests as pending, because the CA is not presumed to have access to the Active Directory to validate the request. Also, Stand-alone CAs generate but do not publish certificates if no Active Directory access is present—they must be distributed manually. Finally, certificates generated by Stand-alone CAs cannot be used for smartcard logons.

Roles of CAs

Each CA class, Enterprise or Stand-alone, can operate as either a root CA or a subordinate CA. A **root CA** is at the top of a CA hierarchy, and a client trusts it unconditionally. Figure 10-1 shows how all certificate chains terminate at a root CA. The root CA must sign its own certificate because no higher authority exists in the certification hierarchy. Enterprise root CAs can issue certificates to end users but are more often used to issue certificates to subordinate CAs, which in turn issue certificates to end users.

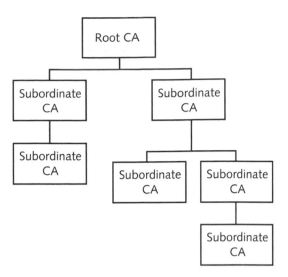

Figure 10-1   Certificate Authority hierarchy

A subordinate CA is found beneath the root CA in the CA hierarchy and maybe even under other subordinate CAs. Subordinate CAs are typically used to issue certificates to users and computers in the organization.

An organization does not need its own root CA. For example, you may establish a subordinate CA that receives certificates from another CA that belongs to a third-party company like Verisign. That way, you can let a trusted third-party take care of the security policy and use a subordinate CA mainly for convenience within your own network.

Table 10-1 lists the requirements for installing each type of CA on a Windows 2000 network.

Table 10-1   Requirements for different CA roles

Role	Requirements
Enterprise root CA	• Windows 2000 DNS Service installed • Windows 2000 Active Directory installed • Enterprise Administrator privileges on the DNS, Active Directory, and CA servers
Enterprise subordinate CA	• A parent CA, which could be an Enterprise root CA, an external commercial CA, or a Stand-alone CA • Windows 2000 DNS Service installed • Windows 2000 Active Directory installed • Enterprise Administrator privileges on the DNS, Active Directory, and CA servers
Stand-alone root CA	• Administrator privileges on the local server
Stand-alone subordinate CA	• A parent CA, which can be a Stand-alone root CA or an external CA • Administrator privileges on the local server

10

The Certificate Store

The **Certificate Store** is a database created during the installation of a CA. Installing certificate services on an Enterprise root CA creates the store in the Active Directory. Installing certificate services on a Stand-alone root CA creates the store on the local server. The store is a repository of certificates issued by the CA, and each store can support up to 250,000 certificates.

The Certificate Trust List

The **Certificate Trust List (CTL)** for a domain holds the set of root CAs whose certificates can be trusted. You can designate CTLs for groups, users, or an entire domain. If a CA's certificate is not on the CTL, a client responds to the untrusted certificate depending on the client's configuration. For example, you might configure a client to prompt the user for instruction on whether to allow the certificate or you might configure it to disallow the certificate automatically. Trust in root CAs can be set by policy or by managing the CTL directly. In addition to establishing a root CA as trusted, you can also set usage properties associated with the CA. If specified, these restrict the purposes for which the CA-issued certificates are valid. The Group Policy snap-in, which is beyond the scope of this book, performs all these actions.

INSTALLING THE CERTIFICATE AUTHORITY

Setting up a server as a Certificate authority is actually a pretty simple installation. As you learned from the preceding overview, planning the CAs in your network is what can get complicated. You undertake two activities to set up a CA. First, you install the MCS component on the Windows 2000 Server that will act as a CA. Second, you create an MMC console with two snap-ins, Certificates and Certificate Authority, that manage certificates. The following sections discuss both of these activities.

Installing Microsoft Certificate Server

Hands-on Project 10-1 at the end of the chapter outlines the actual steps taken to install MCS. This section provides an overview of the process. Before you actually install the MCS component, however, you need three pieces of information:

- You need to know the type of CA server you want to install: Enterprise or Stand-alone.

- You need to know the role the CA server will play in the organization: root or subordinate.

- You need to decide whether to allow users to request certificates using the optional Web interface included with MCS. This interface makes requesting certificates easier.

When you are ready to install MCS, start the Add/Remove Programs Control Panel applet and click the Add/Remove Windows Components button. You see a list of components similar to that shown in Figure 10-2.

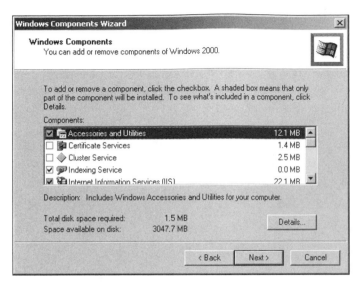

Figure 10-2   Adding Windows Components

Select the Certificate Services entry. You immediately receive a warning that after installing the component you cannot change the computer name or your current domain membership. To select specific subcomponents of the Certificate Services component to install, click the Details button to see a list of choices.

Once you select the components and click Next, the Certification Authority Type Selection page of the Window Components Wizard appears, as shown in Figure 10-3. On this page you specify your CA server's role in your organization.

If you select the Advanced option shown in Figure 10-3, you see the Public and Private Key Pair selection page shown in Figure 10-4. If you do not select the Advanced option, you skip this step altogether.

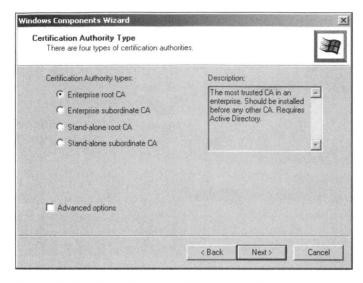

Figure 10-3   Selecting a Certification Authority type

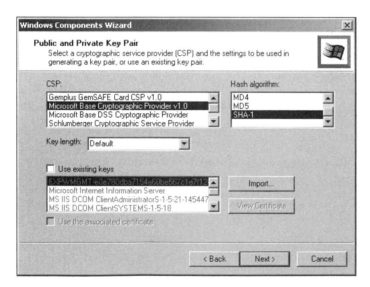

Figure 10-4   Selecting public and private key pairs

The key pair selection page lets you specify the cryptographic service providers (CSPs) you want to use. The Microsoft Base Cryptographic Provider is the standard CSP (and the only one provided with Windows 2000), but you can choose others if you have other cryptographic software or hardware installed on your network. Other options on this page include:

- *Hash Algorithm*: lists the available algorithms for computing digital signatures. SHA-1 is the default choice and the strongest algorithm available.

- *Key length*: lets you select a key length if you are generating a key pair. The default value is 1024 bits, but you can choose a value up to 4096 bits if your CSP supports it.

- *Use Existing Keys*: lets you reuse an existing key pair for the CA's key, as long as it was generated with algorithms compatible with your CSP.

- *Import button*: lets you import certificates from a PFX/PKCS#12 file (a way of distributing certificates manually).

- *View Certificate button*: shows you properties of the selected certificate.

- *Use the associated certificate*: lets you use an existing certificate if one is associated with the key pair you select and if it is compatible with your CSP.

The next step you take in the MCS setup wizard is the CA Identifying Information page, shown in Figure 10-5. This information identifies your CA to subjects requesting certificates. You must enter a CA name and an e-mail address. The rest of the information is optional but helpful. Once you enter this information and create the CA, you cannot change any of the information.

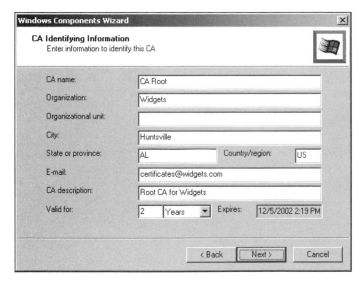

Figure 10-5 Identifying CA information

The final step in the MCS setup wizard takes you to the Data Storage Location page shown in Figure 10-6. The database configured on this page holds the certificates that the CA received from other CAs, not the certificates that the CA itself issues—those are published in the Active Directory or in another specified location. The Store configuration information in a shared folder option lets you specify a folder where the CA stores the certificates it issues. This is useful if the CA will not use Active Directory. You can use the shared folder to distribute certificates. Finally, the Preserve existing certificate database option lets you install the CA on top of an existing CA. This is the only way you can change set-up parameters for the CA without erasing old certificates.

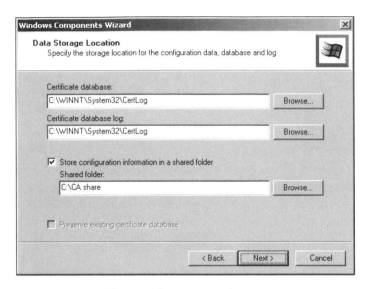

Figure 10-6   Selecting data storage locations

Installing the Certificates and Certificate Authority Snap-ins

You use two different snap-ins to manage certificates for your server. The first, named Certification Authority, manages aspects of the CA, such as policy settings, issued and revoked certificates, and pending requests. You can find this snap-in already installed in the Administrative Tools folder on your Start menu. The second snap-in, named Certificates, manages the certificates that the CA receives from other CAs. This snap-in is not installed by default; you must create a console and add the snap-in yourself. While you're creating a console for the Certificates snap-in, why not go ahead and install the Certification Authority snap-in in that console as well? That way, you can manage everything from one interface. Hands-on Project 10-2 at the end of the chapter outlines the steps for creating a new console and adding these two snap-ins to it.

MANAGING THE CERTIFICATE AUTHORITY AND CERTIFICATES

Once you install MCS and create the console with the Certification Authority and Certificates snap-ins, you are ready to start managing Certificate Services. This section covers the management tasks you undertake using the CA snap-in, shown in Figure 10-7.

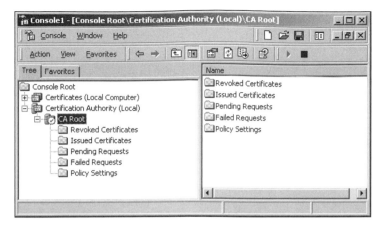

Figure 10-7   Certification Authority snap-in

Each CA node (Figure 10-7 shows only one named CA Root) holds five subfolders:

- The Revoked Certificates folder holds all certificates that the CA has ever revoked.

- The Issued Certificates folder displays the certificates the CA issued since its installation. Right-clicking a certificate allows you to revoke that certificate or open its property pages.

- The Pending Requests folder shows any requests for certificates queued on the server. An Enterprise server never has any requests queued. A Stand-alone server may. To work with pending requests, simply right-click the request and deny or approve the request right from the shortcut menu.

- The Failed Requests folder shows all failed or rejected requests.

- The Policy Settings folder shows the certificate templates available on the server. You may change the available templates by right-clicking the Policy Settings folder and using the New Certificate to issue command or the Delete command. Opening a template's property pages shows some basic information about the template, but you cannot directly edit a template.

Working with the CA

A number of commands are available for working directly with the CA. To start, you can right-click the Certification Authority container itself and use the Retarget Certification Authority command to point the snap-in at a different CA on the network. You can also access a number of commands by right-clicking the CA container itself. These include

10

commands for stopping and starting the CA service, backing up and restoring the service, and renewing certificates. The following sections discuss these commands.

Controlling the CA Service

By default, the CA service is configured to start each time Windows starts. You can stop and restart the service manually by right-clicking the CA container and choosing the appropriate commands. You can also stop and start the service, as well as configure whether the service starts with Windows, by using the Services item in the Computer Management snap-in. Many administrators choose not to have the service load automatically; they start the service manually during periods when they want the CA server to be able to issue certificates.

Backing Up and Restoring the CA

Right-clicking the CA container also makes commands available for backing up and restoring the CA data. The following sections discuss these commands.

Backing Up the CA   Choosing the Backup CA command from the CA container's shortcut menu opens the Certification Authority Backup Wizard, which guides you through the steps for backing up the CA data. After the introductory page, you see the page shown in Figure 10-8, which lets you choose configuration settings.

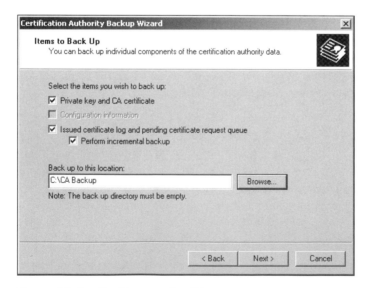

Figure 10-8   Backing up the CA

The following settings are available on this page:

- *Private key and CA certificate*: specifies that you want to back up the CA's private key and certificate. If you choose this option, the wizard asks you for a password it will use to encrypt the data.

- *Configuration information*: controls whether the configuration data for the CA is also backed up. This box is not available for Enterprise CAs, because the Active Directory stores their configuration information.

- *Issued certificate log and pending request queue*: controls whether the CAs log files for issued certificates and any pending requests are backed up. Select the Perform incremental backup option if you want to back up only those requests that changed since the last backup. Otherwise, all requests are backed up.

- *Back up to this location*: specifies the location for the backup file created. You must specify an empty directory here. You cannot store multiple backups in the same folder. The wizard creates a file named using the CA's name and the .p12 filename extension. It also creates a directory named database in the same folder.

Once you configure these settings, you are asked for the password to back up private key information if you chose that option. Then the wizard finishes and backs up the CA data.

Once the backup process is complete, you have a backup of the CA data on your hard disk. It is important, however, to include this backup in the routine backup of your server.

Restoring the CA   Restoring the CA follows basically an identical, but reversed, procedure to that of backing up the CA. When you select the Restore CA command, you start a wizard that first asks you whether it can stop the CA service. You must allow it to stop the service for the restore to continue. Once the service stops, the main page of the wizard, which looks strikingly similar to the backup page shown in Figure 10-8, lets you select the items you want to restore.

10

Renewing a Certificate

Occasionally, you may need to renew a certificate granted to your CA. You do this by right-clicking the CA container and choosing the Renew CA Certificate command. If your CA is a subordinate CA, it requests a new certificate from its parent CA. If your CA is a root CA, it grants its own renewal request. It does this in one of two ways:

- The CA takes its existing keys and binds them to a new certificate. This is a common choice because it allows you to keep reusing existing keys for signature verification and signing. However, repeatedly using existing keys can cause the CA's Certificate Revocation List to grow quite large.

- The CA can also generate a new key pair and use it to create a new certificate. This choice is useful to keep the CRL from growing large and when you think the security of your old certificate may be compromised.

Figure 10-9 shows the dialog box that offers both these options.

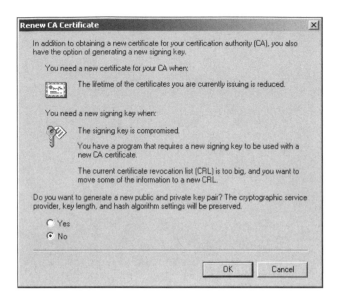

Figure 10-9   Renewing a certificate

Configuring Properties for the CA Object

In addition to using the CA container to use the commands just discussed, you can also open the property pages for the CA container to configure parameters governing the CA's behavior. The next few sections discuss each of these pages.

General Properties

The General page, shown in Figure 10-10, really only provides some information not related to configuration, such as the name and description of the CA and the current security settings. You can also use the View Certificate button to see the details of the CA's certificate.

Policy Module Properties

The Policy Module page, shown in Figure 10-11, displays the policy module currently active for the CA. Usually, this module is the default Enterprise and Stand-alone Policy Module supplied with Windows 2000. You can use the Select button if you want to use a new policy instead.

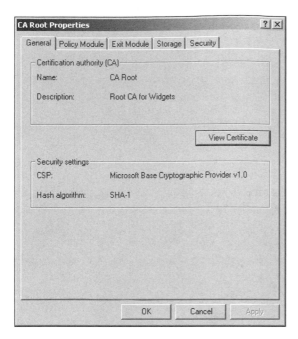

Figure 10-10   General page of CA object

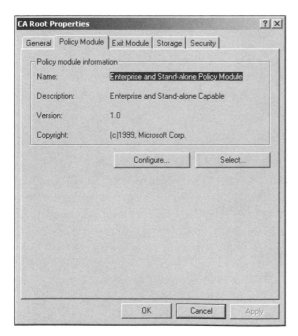

Figure 10-11   Policy Module page of CA object

The Configure button opens a separate dialog box with options for controlling the installed policy module. This dialog box has two pages:

- The Default Action page provides control over the processing of incoming requests. You can configure the CA to always issue a certificate when it receives a request or to mark the request as pending so that you can approve it manually.

- The X.509 Extensions page lets you edit a list of locations where CRLs are published and a list that specifies locations where users can retrieve the CA's certificate.

Exit Module Properties

The Exit Module page, shown in Figure 10-12, displays any exit modules configured for the CA. Exit modules define what happens after a certificate is issued. Only the default exit module, Enterprise and Stand-alone Exit Module, is available in Windows 2000. You can configure additional exit modules if you have them. The Configure button opens a separate dialog box that lets you control whether certificates are published in the Active Directory and in a local file system location.

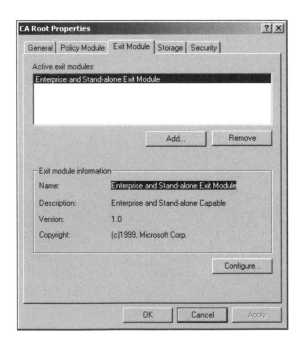

Figure 10-12   Exit Module page of the CA object

Storage Properties

The Storage page, shown in Figure 10-13, displays the paths where the CA keeps its configuration information and certificate database files. You cannot change these values once you install the CA, however. The Active Directory option lets you move the information on a Stand-alone CA with Active Directory access into the directory.

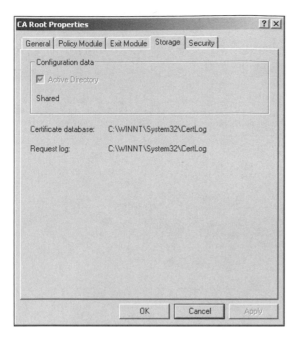

Figure 10-13   Storage page of CA object

Security Properties

The Security page looks like most other Security pages you see on objects in the Active Directory and allows you to assign access permissions on the CA object. Table 10-2 shows the permissions available for the CA object.

Table 10-2   Permissions available on the CA object

Permission	Description
Manage	Lets users change anything on the CA; granting this permission also grants all other permissions
Enroll	Lets users request new certificates for users or computers
Read	Lets users read certificates from the database
Write configuration	Lets users save CA configuration changes
Read configuration	Lets users read CA configuration data
Read control	Lets users read control information for the CA
Delete	Lets users remove objects from the CA database
Modify permissions	Lets users modify permissions on the CA object
Modify owner	Lets users modify ownership of CA objects
Revoke certificate	Lets users revoke certificates
Approve certificate	Lets users approve certificates marked as pending
Read database	Lets users read certificate information from the database

Certificate Enrollment

When a client obtains a certificate from a CA, this is called **certificate enrollment**. Windows 2000 provides two ways for a client to obtain a certificate.

Requesting a Certificate Using the Certificates Snap-in

The first way for a user to request a certificate is to use the Certificates snap-in shown in Figure 10-14.

Figure 10-14   Using the Certificates snap-in

Just right-click the Personal folder and choose the Request New Certificate command from the All Tasks submenu. This starts a Certificate Request wizard that guides you through the process. Hands-on Project 10-3 at the end of the chapter outlines the steps for requesting a new certificate. The basic steps you follow are selecting a template for the certificate, selecting a particular CSP and CA if you want, and entering a friendly name for the certificate to help you remember its purpose.

Web Enrollment

If you chose to install the Web enrollment component of the CA during its initial setup, your CA also supports Web-based certificate requests from clients. By default, users can access the Web enrollment page using the URL http://*ca-name*/certsrv. On that page, users have three options:

- *Retrieve the CA Certificate or Certificate Revocation List button*: opens a set of pages for examining the certificate of the CA itself, the CRL, or the whole certification chain all the way to the root CA.

- *Request a certificate button*: leads you through a set of Web pages that simulate the wizard used to request a new certificate in the Certificates snap-in. For the most part, the settings are all the same. One difference is that the Web interface allows you to supply the CA with a certificate request generated by another program in PKCS#10 format.

- *Check on a pending certification button*: looks up any pending requests and tells you whether they have been approved or not.

Managing Revocation

Generally, certificates are fairly long-lived. In fact, the default life of a new certificate issued by MCS is two years. When a certificate becomes untrustworthy prior to its expiration (such as through a security compromise or change in the subject's situation), you can revoke the certificate. Do not take this action lightly, however; revocation is a permanent action.

You can revoke any certificates issued by the CA you are managing by right-clicking the certificate in the Certification Authority snap-in and selecting the Revoke Certificate command from the All Tasks submenu. A dialog box opens that lets you mark a reason for the revocation—the default reason is "unspecified." Hands-on Project 10-4 at the end of the chapter outlines the steps for revoking a certificate.

As soon as you revoke a certificate, it is added to a Certificate Revocation List (CRL) for the server. The Revoked Certificates folder of the Certification Authority snap-in displays the certificates on this list. CAs publish CRLs containing revoked certificates for downloading or online viewing by client applications so that users can determine the status of certificates.

10

Removing Encrypting File System (EFS) Recovery Keys

Windows 2000 used the **Encrypting File System (EFS)** protocol to encrypt data on a computer by combining the data in those files with the public key certificate of the user logged on to the computer. Once encrypted, only that user's private key can be used to decrypt the files. In fact, the whole process is invisible to the user. From the user's perspective, encrypted folders appear normal and all the documents in them can be used normally. Access is denied to any other user attempting to view the contents of the folder. If access is somehow obtained, only encrypted information is presented.

Consult your Windows 2000 Professional or Windows 2000 Server documentation for details on how to encrypt and decrypt data.

For encrypted data, Windows 2000 creates a private encryption key for the file that it uses to encode the data. Then it creates a public encryption key to encrypt the private key. This is commonly referred to as lock-box security. In addition, the process generates a spare private encryption key called the **EFS Recovery Key** that can decrypt the data and then map that key to a trusted account called a **Recovery Agent**. By default, the administrator of a computer is designated the Recovery Agent. Removing this spare key provides an extra level of security, in that only the person with access to the original private key can decrypt the data. Hands-on Project 10-5 at the end of the chapter outlines the steps for removing the EFS Recovery Key.

CHAPTER SUMMARY

❏ Windows 2000 incorporates a component named Microsoft Certificate Server (MCS) as part of a system to help ensure the accuracy and privacy of data as it is transferred over the network. MCS issues and manages certificates in an organization. Certificates provide two basic services to an organization: privacy, in the form of encrypting data; and authentication.

❏ MCS works using public key encryption, in which two separate keys—a public key and a private key—form a key pair to encrypt and decrypt data. Certificates are also used to allow verification of the claim that a given public key actually belongs to a given individual. The issuer of a certificate is called a Certificate Authority (CA).

❏ MCS acts as a CA for Windows 2000. MCS includes two policy modules that permit two different classes of CAs: Enterprise CAs and Stand-alone CAs. Within each class, Enterprise and Stand-alone, a CA can operate as either a root CA or a subordinate CA.

❏ Once installed in Windows 2000, the MCS component is managed using two snap-ins: the Certification Authority snap-in and the Certificates snap-in. Primary management tasks include certificate enrollment, renewal, and revocation.

KEY TERMS

Certificate Authority (CA) — Any trusted source willing to verify the identities of people to whom it issues certificates and to associate those people with certain public and private keys.

certificate enrollment — Process whereby a client obtains a certificate from a certificate authority.

Certificate Revocation Lists (CRL) — List of revoked certificates and the codes defining the reasons for revocation.

certificates — Allow verification of the claim that a given public key actually belongs to a given individual. This helps prevent an impersonator from using a phony key.

Certificate Store — Database created during the installation of a CA. Installing certificate services on an Enterprise root CA, creates the store in the Active Directory. Installing services on a Stand-alone root CA creates the store on the local server.

Certificate Trust List (CTL) — Holds the set of all root CAs whose certificates users and computers can trust.

EFS Recovery Key — Spare private encryption key capable of decrypting the data. The key maps to a trusted account called a Recovery Agent.

Encrypting File System (EFS) — Protocol Windows 2000 uses to encrypt data on a computer by combining the data in those files with the public key certificate of the user logged on to the computer.

Enterprise CA — Acts as a CA for an enterprise and requires access to the Active Directory.

Microsoft Certificate Server (MCS) — Windows 2000 component that acts as an authority for issuing and managing certificates.

pre-shared key — Single key used both to encrypt and decrypt data. This key is often a simple password shared beforehand by both the encrypting and decrypting parties.

private key — Part of a public/private key pair kept secret; the private key is only available to the person who holds the key.

public key — Part of a public/private key pair made publicly available.

public key encryption — Encryption method in which a recipient's public key encrypts data and then that same recipient's key decrypts the data.

public key infrastructure (PKI) — System of components working together to verify the identity of users who transfer data on a system and to encrypt that data if needed.

Recovery Agent — User designated as able to access the EFS Recovery Keys on a computer. By default, this is the administrator.

Rivest-Shamir-Adleman (RSA) algorithm — Most common public key encryption algorithm in use today, and the MCS default.

root CA — CA at the top of a CA hierarchy and trusted unconditionally by a client.

subordinate CA — CA beneath the root CA in the CA hierarchy and perhaps even under other subordinate CAs. Subordinate CAs typically issue certificates to users and computers in the organization.

Stand-alone CA — Used to issue certificates to users outside the enterprise and does not require access to the Active Directory.

X.509 certificate — Most widely used format for certificates, as defined by the International Telecommunications Union (ITU) in Recommendation X.509.

10

REVIEW QUESTIONS

1. Which of the following keys form a key pair used to encrypt and decrypt data? (Choose two.)

   a. Private key

   b. Secret key

   c. Public key

   d. Shared key

2. What is the default encryption algorithm used by Windows 2000?

   a. Kerberos

   b. DEC

   c. RSA

   d. MD-5

3. Which of the following constructs verifies the identity of a person associated with a public key?

   a. Certificates

   b. Private Key

   c. Trust

   d. Certificate authority

4. A _____ is at the top of the CA hierarchy, and all clients in an organization can trust it.

5. A Stand-alone CA requires Active Directory access. True or false?

6. Which of the following are requirements for installing an Enterprise Root CA? (Choose all that apply.)

   a. Windows 2000 DNS Service

   b. Windows 2000 Active Directory Service

   c. Windows 2000 WINS Service

   d. Windows 2000 Routing and Remote Access Service

7. A Stand-alone subordinate CA requires a parent CA that is in the same domain. True or false?

8. Which of the following is the default hash algorithm used for computing digital signatures?

   a. MD-4

   b. MD-5

   c. SHA-1

   d. RSA

9. Which of the following permissions would you assign to a user on the CA object to allow that user to handle pending certificate requests?

   a. Modify certificate

   b. Approve certificate

   c. Write configuration

   d. Enroll

10. You cannot store multiple backups of a CA in the same folder using the CA Backup Wizard. True or false?

11. A _____ is the database used to hold certificates issued by a CA.

12. Which of the following actions does the Web enrollment feature of MCS allow you to do? (Choose all that apply.)

   a. View a certificate revocation list.

   b. Request a certificate.

   c. Renew a certificate.

   d. Remove a pending request that you generated, as long as it has not already been approved or denied.

13. _____ is a protocol used by Windows 2000 to encrypt data by combining the data in those files with the public key certificate of the user logged on to the computer.

14. What is the primary concern when renewing a CA's certificate by binding a new certificate to existing keys?

15. Assigning a user the _____ permission on a CA object automatically assigns the user all other permissions as well.

16. Which of the following standards is most commonly used for formatting certificates?

    a. X.25

    b. X.500

    c. X.506

    d. X.509

17. The _____ property page of the CA object is used to control which actions are performed after a certificate is issued.

18. A CA can store no more than 150,000 certificates in its database. True or false?

19. By default, which of the following users is designated the Recovery Agent and given a spare copy of the EFS Recovery Key used to encrypt a particular folder?

    a. The folder's owner

    b. The user who encrypted the folder

    c. The administrator

    d. Any user in the local Administrators group

20. A root CA must always renew its own certificates. True or false?

HANDS-ON PROJECTS

All Hands-on Projects in this chapter require at least one server computer set up as described in the lab set-up section in the front of this book.

Project 10-1

In this procedure, you install Microsoft Certificate Server as an Enterprise Root CA. To do this, your computer must have access to Active Directory and DNS services, and you must have enterprise Administrator privileges on the DNS and Active Directory. You must also have Administrator privileges on the local server.

To install Microsoft Certificate Server on a local computer:

1. Click **Start**, point to **Settings**, and then click **Control Panel.**

2. Double-click the **Add/Remove Programs** icon.

3. In the dialog box that opens, click the **Add/Remove Windows Components** button.

4. When the Windows Components Wizard starts, select **Certificate Services** from the list of components.

   You should see a warning that once you install the services, you cannot rename the computer, nor can it join or leave a domain.

5. Click **Yes** to continue.

6. Click the **Next** button.

7. Make sure that the **Enterprise root CA** option is selected, and click **Next** to continue.

8. On the **CA Identifying Information** page, enter the information appropriate to your CA, then click the **Next** button.

9. Note the locations of the database and database logs, and click the **Next** button.

10. If Internet Information Services is running on the computer, the wizard needs to stop the services. Click **OK** to allow the wizard to proceed.

11. The wizard begins copying necessary files. It may prompt you for the location of the Windows 2000 set-up files and any files for service packs that have been installed. When the wizard finishes, click **Finish** to exit.

Project 10-2

To create a new MMC console and add the Certification Authority and Certificates snap-ins:

1. Click **Start** and then click **Run**.

2. In the Run field, type **mmc** and then click the **OK** button.

3. From the Console menu, select the **Add/Remove snap-in** command.

4. In the Add/Remove snap-in dialog box, click the **Add** button.

5. From the list of available snap-ins, select the Certification Authority snap-in and click the **Add** button.

6. In the Certification Authority dialog box that opens, make sure **Local computer** is selected and click **Finish**. If you want to manage another computer (say you want to manage the CA server from your workstation), select the Another computer option and enter the computername. Then return to the Add Stand-Alone Snap-In dialog box.

7. Select the **Certificates snap-in** from the list, and click the **Add** button.

8. In the Certificates Snap-In dialog box, choose **Computer Account** and then click **Next**.

9. Make sure the Local option is selected and click **Finish**.

10. Click **OK** to return to the new console.

11. The new console should now show both snap-ins. Make sure to save the console so that you do not have to re-create it later.

Project 10-3

To request a new certificate:

1. In the Certificates snap-in, right-click the **Personal** folder and choose the **Request New Certificate** command from the All Tasks submenu.

2. On the introductory page of the wizard, click **Next** to go on.

3. The next page of the wizard lists all available templates that you can access. The list's content depends on the permissions set up for templates in your domain. Make sure the default is selected, and click **Next**. If you select the **Advanced** option, the wizard presents two additional steps covered in Steps 4 and 5.

4. If you selected the **Advanced** option in Step 3, the next page you see lets you choose a Cryptographic Service Provider, if one in addition to the default Windows 2000 option is available. Click **Next**.

5. If you selected the **Advanced** option, you also see a wizard page where you can choose the specific CA and computer to which your request is sent. Click **Next**.

6. The next page you see (whether or not you chose to view advanced options) lets you enter a friendly name and description for the certificate. Type a **name** and **description** that helps you remember the certificate's purpose, and click **Next**.

7. The final page summarizes your choices. Click **Finish** to complete your request. Depending on the CA's setup, you may get an immediate response or have to wait for an administrator's approval.

10

Project 10-4

To revoke a certificate:

1. In the Certification Authority snap-in, expand the Certificate Authority that issued the certificate you want to revoke.

2. Select the **Issued Certificates** folder in the left pane.

3. In the right pane, right-click the certificate you want to revoke and choose the **Revoke Certificate** command from the **All Tasks** submenu.

4. Select a **reason code** for the revocation, and click **Yes**.

Project 10-5

To remove an EFS Recovery Key:

1. Click **Start**, point to **Programs**, point to **Administrative Tools**, and then click **Local Security Policy**.

2. Expand the **Public Key Policies** container, and select the **Encrypted Data Recovery Agents** container inside.

3. Right-click **an agent** in the right pane, and select **Delete Policy** from the shortcut menu.

4. A warning dialog appears asking you to confirm the deletion. Click **Yes** to continue.

If you want, you can right-click the agent and select the Export command to copy the recovery key to a floppy disk before removing it from the Local Security Policy. Since you can fit many such keys on a single floppy disk, this provides a way to create a master key disk of sorts.

CASE PROJECTS

Case 1

You are the administrator of a large network and need to set up secure access to information on your extranet for your customers as well as for the internal users on your network. You decide to purchase services from VeriSign, an external CA, so that you do not have to validate your customers' identities yourself. You have also decided to set up Certificate Services within your own organization to help ease the burden of certification traffic from your internal users. Outline the steps you will take to set up these services.

Case 2

Your security needs change and you decide to reconfigure the PKI on your network to not use any external CA. Your organization consists of a single Active Directory Forest and one domain tree that contains six domains. You want to set up a CA in each domain, but configure one central CA to be the most trusted in the organization. Sketch the CA hierarchy you will use and indicate the class and role of each CA in that hierarchy.

EXAM OBJECTIVES FOR MCSE CERTIFICATION EXAM #70-216:
IMPLEMENTING AND ADMINISTERING A MICROSOFT WINDOWS 2000 NETWORK INFRASTRUCTURE

INSTALLING, CONFIGURING, MANAGING, MONITORING, AND TROUBLESHOOTING DNS IN A WINDOWS 2000 NETWORK INFRASTRUCTURE

Objective	Chapter: Section	Hands-on Project(s)
Install the DNS Server service	Chapter 4: Installing DNS Service	Project 4-2
Configure a root name server	Chapter 4: Configuring a Root Name Server	Project 4-3
Configure zones	Chapter 4: Configuring Primary and Secondary Zones	Project 4-4
Configure a caching-only server	Chapter 4: Configuring Caching-only Servers	Project 4-2
Configure a DNS client	Chapter 2: TCP/IP configuration section Chapter 4: DNS Client Configuration	Process described in Chapter 2 and Chapter 4 text. (Screen shots and text guide students through the process.)
Configure zones for dynamic updates	Chapter 4: Configuring Zones for Dynamic Updates	Project 4-6
Test the DNS Server service	Chapter 4: Managing, Monitoring, and Troubleshooting DNS	Project 4-7
Implement a delegated zone for DNS	Chapter 4: Implementing a Delegated Zone for DNS	Process described in text (Screen shots and text guide students through the process.)
Create DNS resource records manually	Chapter 4: Creating Resource Records Manually	Project 4-5
Manage and monitor DNS	Chapter 4: Managing, Monitoring, and Troubleshooting DNS	Project 4-7

INSTALLING, CONFIGURING, MANAGING, MONITORING, AND TROUBLESHOOTING DHCP IN A WINDOWS 2000 NETWORK INFRASTRUCTURE

Objective	Chapter: Section	Hands-on Project(s)
Install the DHCP Server service	Chapter 3: Installing the DHCP Server Service	Project 3-2
Create and manage scopes, superscopes, and multicast scopes	Chapter 3: Configuring Scopes	Project 3-4
Configure DHCP for DNS Integration	Chapter 3: Integrating DHCP and DNS	Project 3-6
Authorize a DHCP Server in Active Directory	Chapter 3: DHCP and Active Directory	Project 3-3
Manage and monitor DHCP	Chapter 3: Managing, Monitoring, and Troubleshooting DHCP	Project 3-7 Project 3-8 Project 3-9

INSTALLING, CONFIGURING, MANAGING, MONITORING, AND TROUBLESHOOTING NETWORK PROTOCOLS IN A WINDOWS 2000 NETWORK INFRASTRUCTURE

Objective	Chapter: Section	Hands-on Project(s)
Install and configure TCP/IP	Chapter 2: Static and Dynamic TCP/IP Addresses	Project 2-1 Project 2-2 Project 2-4
Install the NWLink protocol	Chapter 2: Internetwork Packet eXchange/Sequenced Packet Exchange Chapter 2: Installing and Configuring NWLink IPX/SPX	Project 2-5
Configure network bindings	Chapter 2: Network Protocol Bindings	Project 2-8
Configure TCP/IP packet filters	Chapter 2: TCP/IP Packet Filtering	Project 2-7
Configure and troubleshoot network protocol security	Chapter 2: TCP/IP Packet Filtering Chapter 8: Configuring IPSec Chapter 8: Managing and Monitoring IPSec	Project 2-7 Project 8-1
Manage and monitor network traffic	Chapter 2: Troubleshooting TCP/IP	Project 2-2 Project 2-3

Objective	Chapter: Section	Hands-on Project(s)
Configure and troubleshoot IPSec	Chapter 8: Configuring IPSec Managing and Monitoring IPSec	
Enable IPSec	Chapter 8: Configuring IPSec	Project 8-1 Project 8-3
Configure IPSec for transport mode	Chapter 8: Configuring IPSec Configuring a Policy	Project 8-1 Project 8-2
Configure IPSec for tunnel mode	Chapter 8: Tunnel Setting Properties	Project 8-4
Customize IPSec policies and rules	Chapter 8: Creating a New Policy Configuring a Policy Managing Filter Lists and Actions Applying Policies to the Active Directory	Project 8-2
Manage and monitor IPSec	Chapter 8: Managing and Monitoring IPSec	

INSTALLING, CONFIGURING, MANAGING, MONITORING, AND TROUBLESHOOTING WINS IN A WINDOWS 2000 NETWORK INFRASTRUCTURE

Objective	Chapter: Section	Hands-on Project(s)
Install, configure, and troubleshoot WINS	Chapter 5: WINS and NetBIOS WINS in Windows 2000 Installing WINS	Project 5-1
Configure WINS replication	Chapter 5: Configuring WINS Replication	Project 5-2 Project 5-3
Configure NetBIOS name resolution	Chapter 5: NetBIOS Naming NetBIOS Name Resolution Configuring Clients for WINS	Shown in text screen shots and in Chapter 5 projects
Manage and monitor WINS	Chapter 5: Managing, Monitoring, and Troubleshooting WINS	Project 5-4 Project 5-5 Project 5-6

Configuring, Managing, Monitoring, and Troubleshooting Remote Access in a Windows 2000 Network Infrastructure

Objective	Chapter: Section	Hands-on Project(s)
Configure inbound connections	Chapter 6: Configuring Inbound Connections on the Server	Project 6-1 Project 6-2 Project 6-3
Create a remote access policy	Chapter 6: Configuring Remote Access Policies	Project 6-4
Configure a remote access profile	Chapter 6: Configuring Remote Access Profiles	Project 6-4
Configure a virtual private network (VPN)	Chapter 6: Configuring a Virtual Private Networking Connection	Project 6-7
Configure multilink connections	Chapter 6: Multilink Properties	Project 6-2
Configure Routing and Remote Access for DHCP Integration	Chapter 6: Configuring RRAS or DHCP Integration	Project 6-8
Manage and monitor remote access	Chapter 6: Managing, Monitoring, and Troubleshooting RAS	
Configure authentication protocols	Chapter 6: User Authentication Security Properties	
Configure encryption protocols	Chapter 6: Encryption Properties	Project 6-5
Create a remote access policy	Chapter 6: Configuring Remote Access Policies	Project 6-4

Configuring, Managing, Monitoring, and Troubleshooting IP Routing in a Windows 2000 Network Infrastructure

Objective	Chapter: Section	Hands-on Project(s)
Install, configure, and troubleshoot IP routing protocols	Chapter 7: Routing Protocols Using Dynamic Routing Protocols	Project 7-3
Update a Windows 2000-based routing table by means of static routes	Chapter 7: Configuring Static Routing	Project 7-2
Implement Demand-dial Routing	Chapter 7: Demand-dial Routing Interfaces	Project 7-4
Manage and monitor IP routing	Chapter 7: Installing and Configuring RRAS Monitoring IP Routing	Project 7-1 Project 7-5

Objective	Chapter: Section	Hands-on Project(s)
Manage and monitor border routing	Chapter 7: Using Dynamic Routing Protocols Monitoring IP Routing	Project 7-5
Manage and monitor internal routing	Chapter 7: Using Dynamic Routing Protocols Monitoring IP Routing	Project 7-5
Manage and monitor IP routing protocols	Chapter 7: Using Dynamic Routing Protocols Monitoring IP Routing	Project 7-5

INSTALLING, CONFIGURING, AND TROUBLESHOOTING NETWORK ADDRESS TRANSLATION (NAT)

Objective	Chapter: Section	Hands-on Project(s)
Install Internet Connection Sharing	Chapter 9: Installing and Configuring Internet Connection Sharing	Project 9-1
Install NAT	Chapter 9: Installing the NAT Service	Project 9-2
Configure NAT Properties	Chapter 9: Configuring NAT Properties	Project 9-2
Configure NAT Interfaces	Chapter 9: Configuring NAT Interfaces	Project 9-3

INSTALLING, CONFIGURING, MANAGING, MONITORING, AND TROUBLESHOOTING CERTIFICATE SERVICES

Objective	Chapter: Section	Hands-on Project(s)
Install and configure Certificate Authority (CA)	Chapter 10: Installing the Certificate Authority Managing the Certificate Authority and Certificates	Project 10-1 Project 10-2
Issue and revoke certificates	Chapter 10: Certificate Enrollment Managing Revocation	Project 10-3 Project 10-4
Remove the Encrypting File System (EFS) recovery keys	Chapter 10: Removing Encrypting File System (EFS) Recovery Keys	Project 10-5

Glossary

A records — Host name to IP address mappings in the DNS database that are used in host name resolution.

Accounting provider — Server (typically a RADIUS server) that logs the activity and connection time for a remote user. This is often used to charge remote clients for online time, as in the case of an ISP providing Internet service.

active directory integrated zones — DNS zones stored in the Active Directory database and replicated along with other Active Directory information.

Active Directory (AD) services — Enterprise-level directory service designed to combine domain structures into a manageable, extensible, network structure.

Active Directory Users and Computers — Tool used to configure the objects in the Windows 2000 Active Directory. Among other things, you use this tool to configure the properties of user accounts. Dial-in properties for a user include whether the user may dial in to the RRAS server and whether a callback number should be used.

Address Resolution Protocol (ARP) — Low-level protocol that resides within the IP protocol. It is used as a way of resolving IP addresses to MAC addresses.

Advanced Research Projects Agency Network (ARPANet) — Original name for the Internet; ARPA was the government agency responsible for sponsoring the research that lead to the TCP/IP protocol stack and the modern-day Internet.

ANDing — Logically combining binary numbers; the results are similar to multiplying binary numbers; ANDing a 1 and a 1 gives a 1. All other combinations (1 and 0, and 0 and 0) result in 0.

Application Programming Interface (API) — Standardized set of commands and programming parameters used to simplify the interaction between applications and lower-level networking components.

areas — OSPF division of the internetwork into collections of contiguous networks that help keep routing tables from growing too large. Each router only keeps a link-state database for those areas connected to the router.

area border routers — OSPF router that has an interface in more than one OSPF area.

Asynchronous Transfer Mode (ATM) — Cell-based LAN/WAN networking technology that can handle voice, video, and data traffic; Windows 2000 provides native ATM support.

attributes — Specific values associated with an object; an example is the attribute of First or Last name for the User object.

authentication — Process of verifying a user's credentials so that the user may log on to the system. Authentication is normally performed using a username and password. Authentication may be unencrypted (clear text) or use any of a number of **encryption** types.

authority — Ability to control what resource records, subdomains, and other attributes are associated with a particular DNS domain.

Automatic Private IP Addressing (APIPA) — New feature in Windows 98 and Windows 2000 that allows DHCP clients to select an IP address from the private range 169.254.0.0/16 whenever they cannot find a DHCP server on the local segment.

autonomous system — One in which a set of networks and routers are all under the same administration.

b-node — NetBIOS node type that uses broadcasts to resolve NetBIOS names to IP addresses.

backbone area — OSPF areas connected by a special type of area called a backbone area.

backbone router — Any router configured in an OSPF backbone area.

Bandwidth Allocation Control Protocol (BACP) — *See* Bandwidth Allocation Protocol (BAP).

Bandwidth Allocation Protocol (BAP) — Together with the Bandwidth Allocation Control Protocol (BACP), allows a client to add and remove links dynamically during a multilink session to adjust for changes in bandwidth needs.

binary format — IP address displayed as four sets of eight binary numbers separated by periods.

binding — Associating or connecting a network layer protocol (or even a network service) to a specific network interface card.

BootP — Older alternative to DHCP that diskless workstations used to obtain IP addresses.

Border Gateway Protocol (BGP) — Newer and more powerful exterior routing protocol that has largely replaced the older Exterior Gateway Protocol.

boundary layers — Layers in the Windows 2000 networking architecture that act as intermediaries between upper layers, the network protocols, and lower layers of the model.

broadcast domain — That portion of a network where broadcasts are propagated; normally broadcast domains are created by router placement in a network.

caching-only servers — DNS server configured without any zone files; a caching-only server contains IP addresses of DNS servers it can query to answer client requests and then store the information in a local cache.

certificates — Allows verification of the claim that a given public key actually belongs to a given individual. This helps prevent an impersonator from using a phony key.

Certificate Authority (CA) — Any trusted source willing to verify the identities of people to whom it issues certificates and to associate those people with certain public and private keys.

certificate enrollment — Process whereby a client obtains a certificate from a certificate authority.

Certificate Revocation Lists (CRL) — List of revoked certificates and the codes defining the reasons for revocation.

certificate services — Networking service in Windows 2000 that creates and manages a public key infrastructure within an organization.

Certificate Store — Database created during the installation of a CA. Installed certificate services on an Enterprise root CA, creates the store in the Active Directory. If installing services on a Stand-alone root CA creates the store on the local server.

Certificate Trust List (CTL) — Holds the set of all root CAs whose certificates users and computers can trust.

Challenge Handshake Authentication Protocol (CHAP) — Type of authentication in which the authentication agent sends the client program a key for encrypting the username and password.

clustering support — Ability of an operating system to connect multiple servers in a fault-tolerant group. If one server in the cluster fails, all processing continues on another server. Clusters ensure high availability and reliable performance.

converged — Status of an internetwork when all its routers have the correct routing information in their tables.

Convergence time — When a link or router fails, the time taken for all routers on the network to reconfigure themselves with the proper information.

Data Link Control (DLC) — Nonroutable protocol used mainly to connect to Hewlett-Packard printers using Jet Direct network cards.

dead gateway detection — Feature of Windows 2000 that allows a machine to detect when a default gateway is unreachable and then switch to a configured back-up default gateway.

decrypt — Process of decoding encrypted data.

default gateway — IP address of the router port to networks outside the local network.

demand-dial interfaces — Interface configured in RRAS that can dial a remote router whenever a connection needs to be made.

demand-dial routing — Allows an RRAS server configured as a router to dial-up a remote router whenever it needs to send messages to that router.

DHCP Allocator — Simplified version of a DHCP server used by NAT to assign IP addressing information automatically to clients on the private network.

DHCP relay agent — Software component loaded via Routing and Remote Access Service to a Windows 2000 machine; allows a machine to act as a proxy for DHCP clients on a segment.

DHCPAcknowledgment — Packet broadcast by a DHCP server to a DHCP client that grants the client a lease for a particular IP address; fourth step of four-step DHCP lease process.

DHCPDiscover — Packet broadcast by DHCP clients to find DHCP servers on the local segment; first step of four-step DHCP lease process.

DHCPNack — Negative acknowledgment that a DHCP server broadcasts if it must decline a client's request for a particular IP address.

DHCPOffer — Packet broadcast by a DHCP server to a DHCP client that contains a possible IP address for lease; second step of four-step DHCP lease process.

DHCPRequest — Packet broadcast by a DHCP client requesting the IP address offered in a DHCPOffer packet; third step of four-step DHCP lease process.

Dial-Up Networking — Name given to the process and interface that most versions of Microsoft Windows use to dial in to a remote server.

DNS proxying — Method of relaying DNS name resolution requests from clients on a private

network through the NAT server to a DNS server on the Internet.

DNS zone file — Text file, stored on a DNS server, that contains all information and resource records for a particular zone.

DNS zones — Portion of the DNS namespace that can be administered as a single unit.

Domain Name System (DNS) — Hierarchical naming system used to resolve host name to IP address mapping. It contains resource records.

dotted decimal — IP addresses displayed as a series of four decimal numbers separated by periods, for example, 192.168.12.2.

dynamic assignment — Configuring a host to obtain an IP address automatically using DHCP.

Dynamic Domain Name System (DDNS) — Extension to the DNS systems that allows dynamic updates to the DNS database. The Windows 2000 DHCP server service can integrate with DDNS to allow dynamic DNS registration for clients that receive dynamic IP addresses.

Dynamic Host Configuration Protocol (DHCP) — Protocol used to automatically assign IP addressing and other TCP/IP information to clients. DHCP is considered easier and more reliable than manual addressing.

dynamic mappings — Created when users on the private network initiate traffic with a public Internet location. The NAT service automatically translates the IP address and source ports and adds these mappings to its mapping table.

dynamic router — Routers that automatically share their routing information with other routers on the network using a router protocol such as RIP or OSPF.

EFS Recovery Key — Spare private encryption key capable of decrypting the data. The key maps to a trusted account called a Recovery Agent.

Encrypting File System (EFS) — Protocol Windows 2000 to uses encrypt data on a computer by combining the data in those files with the public key certificate of the user logged on to the computer.

Encryption — Process of translating information into an unreadable code that can only be translated back (decrypted) by using a secret key or password.

enhanced security — Increased security measures available in Windows 2000 via the inclusion of Kerberos version 5 security and IP security.

Ethernet — Most widely used networking architecture; contention-based architecture that uses carrier sense multiple access/collision detection as its access method.

Enterprise CA — Acts as a CA for an enterprise and requires access to the Active Directory.

event logging — Most applications in Windows (and Windows itself) log events to a file. Events are bits of information and any errors generated by these applications. Once logged, you can view the events using the Event Viewer utility.

Extensible Authentication Protocol (EAP) — General protocol for PPP authentication that supports multiple authentication mechanisms. Instead of selecting a single authentication method for a connection, EAP can negotiate an authentication method at connect time.

Exterior Gateway Protocol (EGP) — Exterior routing protocol used to connect different autonomous systems.

Fat allocation table (FAT) 32 support — Ability of an operating system to read, write, and otherwise fully support the new version of the file allocation table file system introduced in the Win9x product family.

File Transfer Protocol (FTP) — Provides for file transfer between two TCP/IP hosts; uses TCP as its transport protocol.

filter action — Actions assigned to a connection whose properties match an associated list of filters. Typical actions are to accept and block connections or to negotiate security for the connection.

filter list — List of filters assigned to a rule. Connections whose properties match the list of filters have an associated filter action applied to them.

forward lookup zones — DNS zone files that hold resource records that map host names to IP addresses. (They can also hold various other resource records.)

Fully Qualified Domain Name (FQDN) — Entire name of a host that includes the host name and the domain name; for example, host1.win2k.org signifies the computer host1 in the win2k.org DNS domain.

global options — Options that apply to all clients in all scopes configured on a DHCP server.

group NetBIOS names — NetBIOS names used to register entire groups of computers; an example is domain controllers in a domain.

h-node — NetBIOS node type that first attempts directed communication to a WINS server to resolve NetBIOS names to IP addresses; if directed communication fails, clients with this node type then try a broadcast to resolve NetBIOS names to IP addresses.

hop — Each router that a packet of information must pass between its source and destination hosts. The number of hops is also referred to as metric count or metric cost.

host ID — Portion of an IP address that represents the bits used for host identification.

host files — Text files that contain host name to IP address mapping; used to perform host name to IP address resolution. Precursor to the DNS system.

host names — Common names given to network devices to allow users to interact with a name instead of an IP address.

hostname — Command used after the command prompt to display the host name of the local machine.

in-addr.arpa — Name given to the reverse lookup zone file.

indirect routing — Occurs when a packet of information must pass over a router at some point between its source and destination.

Internet Assigned Numbers Authority (IANA) — Group responsible for controlling allocation of IP addresses to the Internet community.

Internet Connection Sharing (ICS) — Simplified version of the NAT protocol that is easy to configure and manage and is available in Windows 98, Windows Millennium Edition, Windows 2000 Server, and Windows 2000 Professional. ICS is not as configurable as NAT.

Internet Control Message Protocol (ICMP) — Handles the communication of errors and status messages within the TCP/IP protocol stack.

Internet Group Management Protocol (IGMP) — Standard protocol for IP multicasting over the Internet. It is used to establish host memberships in particular multicast groups.

Internet Protocol (IP) — Connectionless, best-effort delivery protocol in the TCP/IP protocol stack that handles routing of data and logical addressing with IP addresses.

Internet Protocol version 6 (IPv6) — Advanced version of the Internet Protocol that uses 128-bit addresses in hexadecimal format.

Internet Service Providers (ISPs) — Companies that provide access to the Internet backbone.

Internetwork Packet eXchange (IPX) — Connectionless, layer three protocol that provides routing function for the IPX/SPX protocol stack.

Internetwork Packet eXchange/Sequenced Packet eXchange (IPX/SPX) — Routable protocol stack designed by Novell to provide networking services for the Netware network operating system.

inverse query — DNS query attempting to resolve a host name from a known IP address.

IP (Internet Protocol) — Network layer protocol of the TCP/IP protocol suite that is responsible for routing packets between hosts.

IP address — 32-bit logical addresses that must be assigned to every host on a TCP/IP network.

IP Security (IPSec) — Set of protocols that supports the secure exchange of data at the IP layer. In RRAS, IPSec is used in conjunction with L2TP in the formation of Virtual Private Networks.

ipconfig — Command-line tool used to verify IP settings; can also be used to renew or release dynamically assigned IP addresses and DNS information.

IPSec client — Computer that initiates the IPSec connection.

IPSec driver — IPSec component that actually encrypts and decrypts data using keys prepared by the ISAKMP/Oakley Service, and sends the data between computers.

IPSec policies — Sets of rules assigned to clients that define how those clients use IPSec.

IPSec policy agent service — IPSec component responsible for retrieving the computer's assigned IPSec policy from the Active Directory.

IPSec server — Computer that responds to an IPSec connection.

IPX (Internetwork Packet eXchange) — Networking protocol developed by Novell for use primarily with their NetWare operating systems. Since NetWare is such a popular network operating system, most other operating systems, such as Microsoft Windows, provide an IPX-compatible networking protocol. In Windows 2000, this IPX-compatible protocol is named NWLink.

ISAKMP/Oakley Service — IPSec component that creates the security association between communicating computers and is also responsible for generating the keys used to encrypt and decrypt the data sent over the IPSec connection.

iterative query — DNS query to which the server responds with the best answer it can provide or by forwarding the request to another name server and then returning an answer.

Kerberos version 5 — Shared secret key encryption mechanism used to provide security for authentication sessions in a Windows 2000 network.

Layer-Two Tunneling Protocol (L2TP) — Extension of the PPP remote access protocol; one type of tunneling protocol used to form Virtual Private Networks.

Link control protocol (LCP) — LCP extensions include a number of enhancements to the LCP protocol used to establish a PPP link and control its settings. One of the primary enhancements included is the ability for the client and server to agree dynamically on protocols used on the connection.

LMHOSTS — Text file mapping NetBIOS names to IP addresses; precursor to WINS service.

local area network (LAN) — Network confined within a small area such as a single building or a small campus.

m-node — NetBIOS node type that first attempts broadcasts to resolve NetBIOS names to IP addresses; if broadcasts fail, the client then tries directed communication with the WINS server.

Media Access Control (MAC) address — Physical address burned in the EPROM on a network card when it is manufactured.

member scopes — Scopes joined together in superscopes.

Microsoft Certificate Server (MCS) — Windows 2000 component that acts as an authority for issuing and managing certificates.

Microsoft CHAP (MS-CHAP) — Modified version of CHAP that allows the use of Windows 2000 authentication information. There are two versions of MS-CHAP. Version 2 is the most secure, and all Microsoft operating systems support it. Other operating systems sometimes support version 1.

Microsoft Management Console (MMC) — Extensible framework within which Windows 2000 management snap-ins such as the DHCP snap-in reside.

mixed mode — Mode that Windows 2000 domain controllers use when the network consists of Windows 2000 servers and Windows NT servers (or machines not Active Directory-aware). All Windows 2000 servers run in mixed mode by default. You must manually change them to native mode.

multicast routing — Targeted form of broadcasting that sends messages to a select group of users instead of all users on a subnet.

multicast scopes — Ranges of multicast addresses configured to be dynamically assigned to host via DHCP.

multicasting — Broadcasting packets to only certain hosts on a TCP/IP network.

multi-homed — Any computer configured either with multiple NICS or multiple IP addresses.

Multilink Protocol (MP) — Used to combine multiple physical links into a single logical link. For example, you could use MP to combine two 56-KB modem links into a 128-KB link.

name query response — Response sent from a WINS server to the WINS client, either informing the client of the NetBIOS name to IP address resolution or of failure to achieve a resolution.

name registration company — Company with the authority to register DNS domains within the DNS namespace.

NAT editor — Installable component that modifies packets so NAT can translate them. Windows 2000 includes built-in NAT editors for protocols, including FTP, ICMP, PPTP, and NetBT.

NAT interface — Virtual interface in the RRAS snap-in that represents an actual private or public network interface on the NAT server.

native mode — Mode used by Windows 2000 domain controllers when the entire network consists of only Windows 2000 servers and Active Directory-aware clients.

nbtstat — Command-line tool that displays NetBIOS over TCP/IP information.

Net Shell (netsh) — Command-line tool used to configure and monitor Windows 2000 networking components, including RRAS.

NetBIOS — Session-level API developed to provide high-level applications with easy access to lower-level networking protocols.

NetBIOS Enhanced User Interface (NetBEUI) — Small, fast, efficient, nonroutable protocol stack used in small networks only.

NetBIOS name query — Used by WINS clients to query WINS servers for information about a particular NetBIOS name; in short, used to find NetBIOS name to IP address mappings.

NetBIOS name registration — Sent by WINS clients to WINS servers to ask for registration of a particular NetBIOS name with an IP address.

NetBIOS name release — Sent by WINS clients to direct the WINS server to terminate the dynamic mapping of a NetBIOS name to an IP address.

NetBIOS name renewal — Sent by WINS clients to request that the WINs server extend NetBIOS name to IP address mapping; normally occurs halfway through the TTL.

NetBIOS Name Server (NBNS) — Server configured with the WINS server service.

NetBIOS over TCP/IP — NetBIOS using TCP/IP as its lower-level networking protocol stack.

NetBIOS scope — Optional parameter used to break NetBIOS domains into smaller sections; similar to subnets in TCP/IP

NetBT — Common abbreviation for NetBIOS over TCP/IP

netdiag — New command-line tool in Windows 2000 that tests a large portion of the networking components on a machine. Provides much of the same information as other command-line tools such as netstat, nbtstat, and ipconfig.

netstat — Command-line tool that provides information about current TCP/IP connections.

Netware Core Protocol (NCP) — Primary upper-layer protocol in IPX/SPX that facilitates client/server interaction.

Netware Link State Protocol (NLSP) — More advanced link state routing protocol in the IPX/SPX protocol stack Designed to replace the RIP protocol.

Network Address Translation (NAT) — Network service used to "translate" between public TCP/IP addresses and private internal addresses specified in Request for Comments 1918.

network driver interface specification (NDIS) — Boundary layer in the Windows 2000 networking architecture that serves as an intermediary between the networking protocols and the Data Link layer drivers and network interface cards.

Network ID — Portion of an IP address that represents the bits reserved for the network number.

Network Monitor — Tool that comes with Windows 2000 and allows you to capture and view data packets passing over the network.

network operating system (NOS) — Computer software designed to provide network services to clients.

networking protocols — Standard language used by two computers to communicate over a network. Networking protocols define how information is fragmented and shaped for passage over the network.

non-broadcast multiple access (NBMA) router — Router that can communicate with other routers without broadcasting.

objects — Components found within the Active Directory structure; an object represents each network resource in the Active Directory structure

Open Shortest Path First (OSPF) — Link-state routing protocol that enables routers to exchange routing information. Called a link-state protocol because it actually creates a map (a routing table) of the network that calculates the best possible path to each network segment by maintaining information on the state of links (whether they are up or down).

Open System Interconnection model (OSI model) — Seven-layer conceptual model designed to help standardize and simplify learning, implementing, and creating network communication between two network hosts.

Options — Extra IP configuration parameters that can be given to DHCP clients when they lease an IP address.

p-node — NetBIOS node type that uses directed communication to a WINS server to resolve NetBIOS names to IP addresses.

Packet Internet Groper (ping) — Command-line tool used to test connectivity between two IP hosts.

Password Authentication Protocol (PAP) — Authentication method that transmits a user's name and password over a network and compares them to a table of name-password pairs.

pathping — Command-line tool that combines ping and tracert functions with new statistics reporting functions.

plug and play support — Ability of an operating system to automatically detect and install drivers for devices that conform to plug and play standards; simplifies hardware device management and installation.

Point-to-Point Protocol (PPP) — Remote-access protocol used to establish a connection between two remote computers. RRAS supports PPP for dialing both in and out.

pointer (PTR) resource records — Map an IP address to a fully qualified domain name (FQDN). *See also* reverse lookup records.

pre-shared keys — Passwords entered into each computer communicating with IPSec. As long as both computers are configured with the same pre-shared key, they trust one another.

pre-shared key — Single key used both to encrypt and decrypt data. This key is often a simple password shared beforehand by both the encrypting and decrypting parties.

primary name servers — DNS servers that hold a read/write copy of the zone file for a particular DNS zone; control replication with secondary name servers.

private address — Any address belonging to one of the three ranges of IP addresses designated as private by Internet authorities. A host with a private address may only communicate with hosts on the Internet through a service such as NAT.

private key — Part of a public/private key pair kept secret, the private key is only available to the person who holds the key.

protocol stack — Group of protocols working together to complete the network communication process.

Public address — Any address not belonging to one of the three ranges of IP addresses designated as private by Internet authorities.

public key — Part of a public/private key pair made publicly available.

public key certificates — Provided by a certificate authority. Each end of the IPSec connection uses the other end's public certificate for authentication.

public key encryption — Encryption method in which a recipient's public key encrypts data and then that same recipient's key decrypts the data.

public key infrastructure (PKI) — System of components working together to verify the identity of users who transfer data on a system and to encrypt that data if needed.

pull replication — Replication of the WINS database that occurs at a preset time interval; used with slow WAN links.

push replication — Replication of the WINS database that occurs after a predetermined number of changes to the database occur; used with fast connections between replication partners.

Recovery Agent — User designated as able to access the EFS Recovery Keys on a computer. By default, this is the administrator.

recursive query — DNS query which asks the server to respond either with the DNS information or an error message stating that it does not have the information; used between clients and DNS servers.

remote access — Broadly defines the ability of one computer to connect to another computer over a dial-up or other WAN connection and to access resources remotely.

remote access profile — Associated with policies and containing settings that determine what happens during call set up and completion.

remote access policy — Used to configure conditions under which users may connect using a specific remote access connection. You can include restrictions based on criteria such as time of day, type of connection, authentication, and even length of connection.

remote access protocols — Define the way in which one computer connects to another computer over a WAN link. PPP and SLIP are the two main remote access protocols in use today, though the newer and stronger PPP is much more common.

Remote Authentication Dial-In User Support (RADIUS) — Authentication and accounting system used by many ISPs to verify user credentials and log user activity while the user is connected to a remote system.

remote control — Process in which a client computer connects to a remote server and actually takes control over that server in a separate window on the client computer. Activities within this window seem to occur as if the user is actually sitting at the server computer. All applications run on the server. RRAS does not support remote control, only remote access.

Request for Comments (RFC) — Proposals presented to the Internet community describing everything from possible TCP/IP standards to simple informative tracts.

reservations — Using the MAC address of the client to ensure that a particular IP address is always leased to that client.

Reserved client options — Scope options created for a single client that has been given a DHCP reservation.

reverse lookup records — Another name for PTR records. These records resolve a host name from a known IP address.

reverse lookup zones — Special DNS zones that holds PTR records, IP address to host name mapping.

RIPv1 — Simple-to-use and well-supported interior routing protocol. RIP is a distance vector routing program, meaning that it not only supplies information about the networks a router can reach, but supplies information about the distances to those networks as well.

RIPv2 — Protocol developed to address several shortcomings in RIPv1, for example, by providing a multicast option in addition to broadcasts for routing announcements and by including the subnet mask in announcements.

Rivest-Shamir-Adleman (RSA) algorithm — Most common public key encryption algorithm in use today, and the MCS default.

root CA — CA at the top of a CA hierarchy and trusted unconditionally by a client.

root name servers — Servers that hold information about the overall Internet domain name servers.

ROUTE command — Command-line utility used to manipulate static entries in a routing table.

router — Device used to connect different IP subnets and to route data between them.

Routing Information Protocol (RIP) — Routing protocol provided with the IPX/SPX protocol stack.

Routing and Remote Access Service (RRAS) — Windows 2000 service that provides remote access and routing functionality to remote clients.

routing table — List of networks that the system knows about and the IP addresses of routers that packets must pass through to get to those networks.

Scopes — Ranges of IP addresses configured for lease to clients via DHCP.

scope options — Options that apply to all clients in one scope only.

secondary name servers — DNS servers that hold read-only copies of a zone file for a particular DNS zone; accept updates to the DNS zone file only from configured primary name servers.

security association — Defines the common security mechanisms, such as keys, that two computers use to create the IPSec connection.

Sequenced Packet eXchange (SPX) — Layer four protocol that provides guaranteed delivery; similar in function to TCP.

Serial Line Interface Protocol (SLIP) — Older protocol developed in UNIX and still in wide use today. Windows 2000 RRAS supports SLIP in dial-out configurations, but you cannot use a SLIP client to dial in to an RRAS server.

serial links — Generally slow-speed connections used for wide area network connectivity.

server options — Options that apply to all clients in all scopes configured on a DHCP server.

Service Advertisement Protocol (SAP) — Protocol used on IPX/SPX networks by clients to find network services and by servers to advertise network services.

Shiva Password Authentication Protocol (SPAP) — Included mainly for compatibility with remote access hardware devices manufactured by Shiva, a private company now owned by Intel. SPAP isn't really used much on most networks.

Simple Mail Transfer Protocol (SMTP) — Application layer TCP/IP protocol that provides mail delivery services.

SOHO — Acronym that stands for Small Office/Home Office. SOHO networks are considered the main beneficiaries of ICS and NAT. Though they vary a great deal in configuration, a SOHO network, as defined by Microsoft, has one network segment, uses peer-to-peer networking, and supports TCP/IP.

Stand-alone CA — Used to issue certificates to users outside the enterprise and does not require access to the Active Directory.

static assignment — Manually assigning an IP address to a host.

static mappings — Define in advance how to map certain addresses and ports instead of letting mapping happen automatically. Although you can create static mappings for outbound traffic, the most common reason to use a static mapping is to host some form of Internet service (that is, Web server, FTP server, and so on) on a private computer.

static router — Router to which routes must be added manually using either the ROUTE command or the RRAS snap-in.

subnet mask — 32-bit number used to determine the portion of an IP address that represents the network ID and the host ID.

subnetting — The process of borrowing host bits to increase the number of network bits.

subordinate CA — CA beneath the root CA in the CA hierarchy and perhaps even under other subordinate CAs. Subordinate CAs typically issue certificates to users and computers in the organization

superscopes — Multiple scopes grouped together to allow centralized management; also allow for more than one range of IP addresses on a single physical subnet.

telnet — Application layer protocol in TCP/IP that allows a user to log on to a remote host and execute programs remotely.

terminal services — Services that allow a server to host applications for clients; with terminal services, clients no longer used to run applications can act as dumb terminals for applications on a terminal server.

Tombstoned — State of a WINS entry once it is marked for deletion.

tracert — Trace route command-line tool that allows testing of the entire path between two hosts.

transit internetwork — Basic IP infrastructure over which a Virtual Private Network is created. Typically, the transit internetwork is the Internet itself, though other IP networks may be the transit internetwork.

Transmission Control Protocol (TCP) — Transport layer protocol in the TCP/IP protocol stack that is connection-oriented and reliable; provides guaranteed delivery.

Transmission Control Protocol/Internet Protocol (TCP/IP) — Suite of networking protocols designed to transfer data between computers on the Internet. TCP/IP is becoming the most popular networking protocol used on private networks, as well.

transport device interface (TDI) — Boundary layer in the Windows 2000 networking architecture between networking protocols and the upper-layer services.

transport mode — Mode in which the two endpoints of IPSec communication are two computers that have IPSec configured. For this mode to work, both computers must use the TCP/IP protocol.

Trivial File Transfer Protocol (TFTP) — Like FTP, provides file transfer between two TCP/IP hosts; TFTP uses UDP as its transport protocol and is faster, but more unreliable than FTP.

tunnel mode — Mode in which two communicating computers do not use IPSec themselves. Instead, the gateways connecting each client's LAN to the transit network create a virtual tunnel that uses the IPSec protocol to secure all communication that passes through it.

unique NetBIOS names — NetBIOS names assigned to a single computer and its associated services.

Universal Serial Bus (USB) — Hardware specification that allows for hot insertion and removal of hardware devices.

User Datagram Protocol (UDP) — Connectionless, best-effort delivery transport layer protocol in the TCP/IP stack.

user-defined option classes — Allow expansion of DHCP options to include parameters determined by the network administrator for a particular client.

user profile — Information associated with a user account. Profiles of users who are members of a Windows 2000 domain are stored in the Active Directory, and profiles of users who are not members of a domain are stored on the local computer.

vendor-defined option classes — Expanded DHCP options created for one particular vendor's computers or network hardware.

Virtual Private Networking (VPN) — Secure, logical network constructed directly between a VPN client and a VPN server on top of a physical transit internetwork such as the Internet.

wide area network (WAN) — Network or collection of networks spread across a large geographical area.

Windows 2000 Advanced Server — Enterprise or large department version of Windows 2000; supports clustering and eight-way multiprocessor systems with up to 8 GB of RAM.

Windows 2000 DataCenter Server — Data warehouse or extremely large-scale version of Windows 2000; designed for processor intensive simulations or massive processing tasks; supports up to 32 processors with 64 GB of RAM in special original equipment manufacturer versions.

Windows 2000 Professional — Client version of the Windows 2000 product family; designed to provide a stable, reliable, and fast platform for end users to run their applications.

Windows 2000 Server — Small department or workgroup version of Windows 2000; supports four-way multiprocessor systems with up to 4 GB of RAM.

Windows Internet Name Service (WINS) — Windows 2000 service that provides a dynamic database of NetBIOS name to IP address mapping.

Windows Internet Naming Service (WINS) — Network service that provides NetBIOS name to TCP/IP address resolution.

WINS replication — Process of replicating the WINS databases between two WINS servers.

X.509 certificate — Most widely used format for certificates, as defined by the International Telecommunications Union (ITU) in Recommendation X.509.

zone of authority — Portion of the DNS namespace that an organization controls.

zones transfers — Copying zone file information from primary name servers to secondary name servers.

Index